CHALLENGE AND CHANGE IN THE TEACHING OF ENGLISH

Edited by

ARTHUR DAIGON
RONALD T. LACONTE
Both, The University of Connecticut

Allyn and Bacon, Inc., Boston

CONTENTS

INTRODUCTION

To fathom what prompted this collection of articles about English education, consider our original (and still preferred) title—*Zapping the English Curriculum*. It somehow expressed our purpose as we sought out statements and materials that would be helpful to new and experienced teachers looking for ways out of the morass of traditional English instruction.

In our minds "zapping" was due a whole range of institutional commitments to materials, teaching methods, and convictions about just *why* arrangements are made in American secondary schools for all students and many teachers to meet in classes specifically designated "English." Traditional English instruction, with its trappings of venerated literary white elephants, with its old and new linguistic litanies, with its classic configuration of performing teachers and passive students—all protected by intricate systems of multiple-choice barricades and pitfalls—still makes its daily claim on the intellects and sensibilities of the large majority of young people who attend those classes.

Challenge and Change in the Teaching of English attempts to explore some alternatives to such instruction. Several developments in educational thinking and practice have made such alternatives possible and available for teachers ready to try new directions.

The first is a reawakened interest in the humanities as an occasion for forays into issues and concerns of interest to learners. As we make those issues the focus of instruction, we provide opportunities for a whole spectrum of communicative activities to be performed, scrutinized, modified, and learned. They are learned because the student finds that these activities are logical means of inquiry into worthwhile subjects. At the same time, we demonstrate the validity of English—of English*ing*—as a way of comprehending increasingly complex personal, social, and intellectual dilemmas otherwise ignored by those who decide *what* is important to learn. This interest in issue-centered learning we owe to a resurgent Deweyism and to the pleas (and demands) of those who are to be taught.

The second development, a messianically delivered dividend of a burgeoning electronic technology, is a new interest in other-than-print possibilities for stimulating students and providing other-than-writing possibilities for their responses. New means of "input" (showing and telling) have become part of English instruction. Films, slides, overhead and opaque projections show, and tapes and records tell, either separately or exquisitely synchronized by computerized teaching machines. And all feed stimuli—information, metaphor, suggestion, judgments—emotionally and affectively loaded, into students.

New "outputs" (ways of responding to the provocations of books, films, records, and teachers) have more recently found adherents disappointed with the traditional writing response. Students *make* films, *make* film strips to be shown with musical accompaniment, *make* taped sound collages, *provide* appropriate sound effects to readings of poems as their means of coherent, disciplined response. And as they perform these nonverbal communicative activities, they are drawn into the process of inquiry, learning both substance and skill.

How much more are these activities in the liberal arts tradition than ritualistically parroting linguistic formulas and definitions, than memorizing the literary-critical ideas of "authorities," than going through the two-chapters-for-homework-and-a-quiz-tomorrow master plottings of the limited literary canon of secondary school English?

The third development is a renewed interest in language (standard and dialect forms) as a system of meaning with social consequences, rather than as an occasion for classification, rearrangement, and correction of lexical and syntactic elements. This we owe to a second generation of semanticists, to heightened interest in social and regional dialects, and to a general idea-centered climate which rejects the mastery of formal systems in favor of more humane language activities.

Another development is an increased interest in how students learn and less emphasis on how teachers teach, accompanied by a concern for a better balance between the development disciplines of students and the disciplines of subjects.

The virtuoso teaching performance that excludes all spurs to learning but the text and the voice of the teacher, which discourages all modes of response but the exercise, the paper, and the test, no longer commands the respect of those who evaluate what happens in English classrooms. They look for what students do and say rather than for what teachers do and say. The dais and lectern are disappearing as the teacher's role shifts from fount of wisdom and dispenser of knowledge to poser of significant questions, problem-presenter, and resource. This emphasis on learning by students rather than teaching by teachers we owe to a revived interest in Dewey and to the profound influence of British educators.

Challenge and Change in the Teaching of English explores each of these developments as they bear upon the total English curriculum and on the literature, language, composition, and media phases of such a curriculum.

It must be stressed that division of this book into sections specifically addressed to each of these phases (literature, language, writing, and other media) should not be taken as evidence of the editor's conviction that they should be so separated in the classroom. These activities should overlap and intertwine with a complexity related to what is being done in class and who is doing it. How to organize such a collection of varied articles is the vexation of editors who are committed to the premise that no hard boundaries can be drawn separating the various communication activities in classrooms, but who feel that such divisions *can* be made in a book. The editors finally decided to use the conventional pattern of organization because important things are said in articles specifically taken up with each of these phases, and these sections follow one called "The English Curriculum," which stresses the ecological balance among all phases of inquiry useful to teachers and students working in issue-centered English classrooms.

Readers will note the absence of articles specifically devoted to programs for "reluctant learners." (Shrag's "Growing Up On Mechanic Street" is a description of a group trapped in an educational —or anti-educational system totally unresponsive to its needs.) The articles we considered, and rejected, failed to go beyond the usual platitudes calling for relevance, involvement, variety, concrete applications—all of those elements appropriate to the education of any group. Indeed, it is our conviction that *all* of the articles in *Challenge and Change in the Teaching of English* are addressed to the teaching of the reluctant, the slow, the disadvantaged, and the disaffected, as well as to the teaching of the bright—from Rosenblatt's emphasis on literary experience rather than literary knowledge, to Murray's call to help the writer find his own subject, from the articles advocating other-than-print communications, to those calling attention to dialects, idea-centered curriculum, electives, and independent study.

Finally, while we regret giving up *Zapping the English Curriculum* for a more moderate title, we hope that the teaching activity generated by those who read this book retains the vigor and intent of the original.

ARTHUR DAIGON
RONALD T. LACONTE

THE ENGLISH CURRICULUM

Should English be about what matters to students or what matters to teachers? To what extent and under what circumstances can what matters to teachers be made to matter to students? Can teachers use what matters to students to enlarge their charges' view of what matters? And what matters most—values, skills, insights, or knowledge? All of these matters, the basic questions that must be considered by curriculum planners, are the concerns of the contributors to this section on the English curriculum.

Pointing to the decline in communication between teacher and student and the increased distance between what is happening in the world and what happens in classrooms, Charles Greiner demands a more relevant curriculum. "If we're going to move him [the student] at all, we must, as the saying goes, 'grab him where he lives!'" The grabbing, he says, can only happen through use of contemporary media—film, paperbacks, records, all addressed, initially at least, to what students want to know.

Arthur Daigon, answering the question "What is English?" suggests that it is *anything* that requires disciplined employment of the language by speaker, or writer, or listener, or reader, and sketches an issue-centered curriculum that is elective, partially nongraded, and open to independent study. Major sections of his article argue against old and new formal grammars and literature programs based on obsessions of academicians for the "disciplines of literature" and the transmission of literary traditions.

Ray Scofield's "Why not?" is a lyrical excursion into what really matters and provides a poetic obbligato to Peter Schrag's account of how schools defeat those "who will not go to college, who will not become affluent, who will not march the streets, who will do no more, no less, than relive the lives of their parents." Doomed by a system geared to college admissions, they soon accept "the low esteem in which school, society, and often their parents regard them . . ."

1

For such students (and others) adrift in the intellectual doldrums of rote learning and perfunctory coverage of materials and ideas unrelated to their realities, Kirschenbaum and Simon suggest value-centered learning activities. They make the case for using verbal artifacts, such as quotations, poems, and articles, to involve students in making personal applications and value judgments.

Ed Cohen and Robert F. Hogan take up the knotty issue of behavioral objectives and how they apply to instructional activities aimed at heightening sensibilities, developing values, and stimulating whole areas of presently unmeasurable affect. Hogan deplores the drive to focus English teaching effects on kinds of learning that can be anticipated by statements of behavioral objectives and verified by the daily quiz or the standardized test. Ed Cohen, however, insists that the important question is "What can the learner do as a result of instruction that he couldn't do before?" He suggests that the "systems" approach, with its predetermined behavioral expectations and testing procedures can accommodate creativity, and problem-value-centered instruction.

David W. Berg supplies at least a partial antidote for depressed minds and spirits of those exposed to the teacher-telling, student-recording and regurgitation model of traditional English instruction. Independent study, imaginatively handled, could lead to an increase in productivity and enthusiasm by students and a consequent increase in much-needed gratification for teachers.

Eugene Smith, a college professor responsible for the preparation of English teachers, becomes a high school teacher and documents the massive indifference to English "of students dulled by traditional materials and instruction."

A profile of a composite curriculum based on the imperatives presented in these articles would be one that (1) is centered on ideas and issues that address themselves directly and unequivocally to students, (2) is concerned with values and their implications to students, (3) provides for a variety of communication activities in which students can participate, (4) utilizes not only a variety of media to feed information into students, but permits them a wide range of responses through visual and sound, as well as print, media.

HOOK-UP, PLUG IN, CONNECT: RELEVANCY IS ALL

Charles F. Greiner

Have you ever gone for a drive with a five-year-old in the back of the car? Even a ride to the corner grocery is a trip, is a trip, is a trip. If you are attentive, and patient, and "think happy thoughts," he'll lead you down the yellow brick road to Never-Never Land. His sugar cube is made up of equal parts of curiosity and imagination. If you let him take you by the hand, his how's, what's, when's, where's, and why's gradually cause you to see the world in a different way— in the bright new way that the hippies keep murmuring about. In the way that Eppie shows the world to Silas, in the way that Holden sees it through the eyes of Phoebe, in the way of Whitman the child who, "went forth every day,/ And the first object he looked upon, that object he became."

The child whose head is filled with impossible dreams and innumerable questions has little difficulty making connections, relating, absorbing. His bag is the world. Then we send him to school for the cure. By the time he is fifteen we've succeeded; not many dreams are left; very few questions are asked. We've schooled him into complete withdrawal. We've taken from him the ability to abandon himself to illusion. He goes to see *Peter Pan* and looks for the wires. If he has any questions, he's learned to keep them to himself. We've smothered his imagination and strangled his curiosity. In spite of all our protestations to the contrary, one wonders how far removed we are from the Gradgrinds and the McChookumchilds. How much telling and asking do *we* do? How often is the youngster given the chance to do some telling and asking of his own? In a given week, how many sincere questions do we get other than, "May I be excused?" or "Is that stuff gonna be on the test?"

From the *English Journal* (January, 1969), pp. 23–29. Reprinted with the permission of the National Council of Teachers of English and Charles F. Greiner.

Charles F. Greiner teaches English in Patchogue High School, Patchogue, New York.

After the eighth grade, students just don't ask many questions. If they do, only certain kids ask only certain questions—the *right* questions, the expected questions, the questions designed to con the teacher into believing that the student has really flipped over dangling modifiers or the identity of the third murderer. Brownie-point questions. We know it. They know it. The other kids know it. Yet we play the game. It's the only one we both understand. Ultimately, of course, brownie-points are redeemed for A's and B's. It's only the ambitious ones, the climbers, who ask the questions. These poor slobs were programmed into the "brownie track" from the start. Daddy made junior's first "Harvard Fund" deposit before the obstetrician's bill was paid. These are the students who have been trained to look upon schooling as the shortest and safest route to the $35,000 a year job. They see education as a kind of super highway down which they must race. It's a straight, quick shot to the end of the rainbow, but highly competitive. They speed along, tired and tense, with no stops and nothing to see but the taillights of the cars ahead. The winners rush off to Smith or Yale, and even the losers qualify for the time trials at Morpheus State Teachers. Different tracks, perhaps, but the same old scenery. Some trip! No wonder 100,000 college students threatened suicide last year.

A growing number of bright youngsters don't ask any questions at all. The ride for the big money doesn't interest them. They'd rather wander down the side roads or look closely at their own backyards. They are the ones who long ago discovered that school was not the place to ask the real questions. These are the youngsters who have a tendency to "tune in, turn on, and drop out." They are discovering that there is more than one way to take a trip!

This tuned-in group is partially responsible for a new trend that seems to be developing in the dropout picture. Those who used to quit—the nonacademic, the culturally deprived, the disadvantaged, the "dum-dums"—are staying. We've provided them with elaborate print shops and beauty culture courses and conned them with a five-million-dollar advertising campaign, "Your high school diploma is worth $150,000." They learn how to set type and get their kicks dyeing each other's hair, and, so, they stick it out. Space, equipment, and small classes are expensive. In most schools the cost of educating a vocational student is about twice that of an academic student. We may soon have quite a surplus of hairdressers and typesetters, but

at least the youngsters are off the streets. The one who is interested
in finding out who he is and where he fits in, the one who wants to
know, "what's it all about, Alfie," is the one who's quitting these
days. In a recent article, Nat Hentoff[1] describes this student
problem:

> The independent youngster with strong interests in particular areas that
> are not currently regarded as having a high degree of social usefulness
> gets in the way—particularly if he has questions for which answers are
> not to be found in the textbooks or the teachers at hand. He takes too
> much time and must either be cut to fit or leave school.

Such a student is a dropout or because of parental insistence he
hangs on until he graduates. Scribbled all over such a student's
permanent record cards are comments like "does not relate," "is not
a group person," "underachiever," "bright but lazy," "fails to realize
potential." Ask *him* about his high school experience, "A freak out,
man. A real drag. Nothing happened."

In the same article Hentoff quotes a girl who had tried several
secondary schools in an attempt to find herself:

> They're all geared to examination statistics. Like, they have set
> curriculums. The records at each stage of your "advancement" through
> school must show that you have taken so many units in math, science, in
> languages. Without the right assortment of credits, you're going to have
> trouble getting into college. And so we're not allowed to learn what *we*
> want to learn. . . . We're all locked in, locked into the same set of building
> blocks from elementary school on.

The *real* questions never get asked.

As for the "slow" students—their expressed curiosity never moves
very far beyond, "Can I go to the nurse?" and "What time is this
period over?" Who can blame them when we're still subjecting them
in the twelfth grade to the same things that have been unsuccessful
since the third grade—drills and skills, skills and drills. "What are
the objective case pronouns?" "I before E, certainly you've heard
that before." "Now your WPM score has gone up ten points, but
word recognition is down thirty. We've got to bear down on that
word rec.!" To hell with word rec.! No wonder it takes fifty-ton letter

[1] Nat Hentoff, "Youth—The Oppressed Majority," *Playboy* (September 1967).

presses and gleaming rows of pink and white hair dryers to hold them.

Who decided that everyone should read at at least the tenth-grade level? Isn't is possible that some people don't want to read, never have wanted to read, and never will want to read? Maybe they'd rather go to the movies. Each of our students will have watched about 15,000 hours of TV by the time he graduates from high school. Maybe we ought to spend less time scrutinizing verbal images and more time talking with this picture-oriented generation about visual images. The *Playboy* stories are fine, but which page gets turned to first? Right. And after that the cartoons are next in line. Why must everyone learn to write clearly and correctly? There's always the telephone. I don't mean to disparage reading and writing, but perhaps the slow student has to find out some things about himself first. Maybe he has to learn to ask questions again—all kinds of questions, even very, very stupid ones. Maybe we ought to get him talking about the world he lives in, about *his* life. Nothing that we try to teach him, no experience that we try to lead him toward has meaning until it connects and the youngster sees the connection, until he sees its relevancy to his own life, to his particular time and place, to his own personal and unique "bag." Where is he? Not where is he on the reading ladder, or the verbal scale, but where is he *really*? Find out and start there. If we're going to move him at all we must, as the saying goes, "grab him where he lives!"

Close observers of the education scene agree that the communication gap between teacher and student is rapidly widening. On the surface we seem to be getting through to the potential Ivy Leaguer, our buddy with all the brownie-points. If we accept his idea of what education means, we are, indeed, connecting. He equates it not with a "leading out" but with a "leading up." Up to the caddy, the house in Scarsdale, the countryclub membership. Feed the right information in down here and the right answers come out up there, along with all the other goodies that comprise the good life.

The potential hippie, however, seems to have a different idea about what education should be. That's why he rejects the computerized synthetic we offer him. He hasn't forgotten "the child who went forth every day"; he doesn't look for the wires holding up Peter Pan; he's still inclined to wonder about things like where the Central Park ducks go in the winter time. His attitudes and actions suggest that he has a feeling education must begin with an understanding of who he is, of what it means to be alive in the world. But he's "cabin'd, cribb'd, confined, bound in" by the "learn to earn" value system and the egg-crate structure of our public schools. He either tunes out or chooses to dance to a different piper.

That teachers of the academic subjects and the potential manicurist inhabit different planets is readily acknowledged by both. The teacher concentrates on word recognition drills and vocabulary skills with "free reading in the *Reader's Digest* on Fridays." The students become quite accomplished at pretending to *try* or decide to drop off, usually to sleep. So, in too many classrooms, too much of the time nothing happens that is relevant.

How do we narrow the gap, how do we move toward what's relevant, toward making connections? There are many ways. First, we must realize that the place to start is home, the youngster's home, the "place he hasn't to deserve," whether it's a palace or a poolhall, a duplex or a drag-strip. Relevance is all. In writing about the communication gap, the Reverend John Culkin[2] has this to say:

You can't communicate with kids unless you know what they're really like. This doesn't at all mean that you have to accept their values. It has nothing to do with becoming their pal, with over-identifying with their group mores. That's no help at all. Your job is to lead them, or better, to help them lead themselves along certain worthwhile patterns of behavior. But wherever you want to take them, there is only one starting place— *where they are*. It's not what you say that counts. It's what they hear.

Father Culkin suggests the films as a way to meet the students where they live. He doesn't have in mind films like *How To Finish Furniture* or *Career Opportunities in the U.S. Air Force* but rather films that generate excitement, films that make the scene, films that get right down to the old nitty-gritty. And you needn't interfere with the chem lab, the lunch program, or the bus schedule to show exciting movies. There are hundreds of fine short films available. Order a few like *Lonely Boy, Occurrence at Owl Creek Bridge, Glass, Clay*, and *Phoebe*. Show them. Talk about them. Don't play "teacher." Most important, don't test—absolutely NO tests! See what happens.

[2] The Rev. John M. Culkin, "Film Study in the High School," (Fordham, New York: Fordham Film Study Center).

Certainly paperbacks have opened up many ways for the teacher to connect with his students that were impossible with the expensive but safe anthologies. Holden is aging, but he's still a grabber. So are the *Nine Short Stories*. How about *Up the Down Staircase* for the slow kids and *Zorba* for the fast ones, or a collection of Bergman film scripts? With younger groups try *Rascal* or *Karen* or even *The Sword and the Stone*.

What about recordings? I don't mean John W. Nesbitt reading John G. Whittier. Listen to some of the folk-rock lyrics; the step from Bob Dylan to Dylan Thomas isn't as great as you might suspect. Forget James Whitcomb Riley and try Janis Ian. Have you ever really listened to "Society's Child"? Next time you're in the record store put back Bach and Brubeck. Instead, pick up the Beatles' "Sgt. Pepper's Lonely Hearts Club Band." It connects. Take it to class and play it. Examine the lyrics. If you don't know what they're all about, ask your students. You'll connect, too. If you think this sounds like a "media is the message" commercial, you're right. It is. If what youngsters hear is what matters, we've got to hook-up and plug into what they listen to.

There are other ways to get at what's relevant though. I'd like to describe one that has worked for me. I've tried it at all grade levels seven through twelve and with all kinds of groups: slow learners, regulars, and the academically talented (the labels are through the courtesy of the establishment).

I began to suspect all was not right with the world some years ago when the five-year-old youngster in the back seat of my Ford asked more questions in six minutes than the one hundred and fifty students in my tenth-grade classes asked in six hours. Oedipus-like, I began to search for the slayer of their curiosity. When all the evidence had been assembled, the identity of the killer stood out hard and clear. Guess who? Of course it was I, and perhaps a half-dozen like me. Those students just didn't give a damn about the things we thought they should learn. They had lost their old way of looking at things as if for the first time. Gone, too, was the delightful urge to poke into the why's and wherefore's, the mysteries. They no longer exercised the imaginative spirit that tunes itself to the wonders of the world. Somehow all of this had disintegrated, had dried up, and sifted away like chalk dust. Hadn't we, like Louisa's father, "tumbled about, within the limits of our short tethers annihilating the flowers of existence"?

Most of what we had been doing was irrelevant; we had failed to stimulate; we weren't connecting. Logic, facts, grades, I.Q.'s, word recognition, WPM's (words per minute), quizzes, final exams, percentiles, college boards, fifty-minute periods, daily homework assignments, rigid curriculums, Sputnik, a five-hundred page anthology, a coordinator of coordinators, and the guidance department had all joined forces to standardize, compartmentalize, computerize, and mesmerize us all. It was time to abandon the "establishment," or at least as much of it as possible, and go after the students. Time to give up trying to generate some enthusiasm for *Julius Caesar* by having them build model chariots, time to toss out the maps of Raveloe and the drawings of Wildfire leaping the fatal fence. Time to take down the bulletin board of "Double Duty Verbs." Time to put away the textbook, to stop playing "teacher." Time, at last, to help them discover not what the State, or the community, or the superintendent, or the department chairman thought they *ought* to know; but rather to discover what they, the youngsters, *wanted* to know. It was as simple as that. Ask them what they *wanted* to know; worry about what they *ought* to know later. Although my subject happened to be English, the same approach could be used in any course. The "what do you want to know" approach was not to be another of those thinly-disguised, forty-minute motivating devices. Nor was the question tailored to lock them into a particular subject area. I didn't plan to ask them what they wanted to know about English, or history, or science, or art, but what they wanted to know, period. Answers or partial answers can be found in all of the disciplines. I planned to couple the subject to the question only when it could be done without straining or forcing.

From the beginning I had decided that this was to be an honest program; no strings, no bait to tempt them back into the wilderness of subordinate clauses. I had also made up my mind not to back away from any question as long as it seemed to be a sincere one. Young people can spot a trap or a phoney from two miles out.

I introduced the "What Do You Want To Know" unit to a class that had just read "The Monkey's Paw." We began by talking about wishes. If they had three wishes that they knew would be granted, what would they wish for? We discussed secret wishes—the things they wouldn't want anyone to know they had wished for. This led to some talk about the public self and the private self and which of the two was more honest, which was closer to the real self. I asked them to write their private wishes, whatever they were, no hedging, flat out, right down the line. They handed them in on unsigned slips of paper. I had expected to be shocked. They didn't disappoint me. The wishes gave me a startling view of their world, a first glimpse of the vast distance that separated us. How naive I had been. How much I had underestimated them!

From three wishes, it was an easy step to three questions. "If you could have the answers to *any* three questions, what would those questions be?" They were urged to let their private selves ask the questions. The questions did not have to do with English or school subjects at all. I wanted *honest* questions, no matter how unanswerable, controversial, or silly they seemed to be. They were given two days to think about their questions, to make and revise lists in class, to look inside themselves in an effort to discover what they really wanted to know. Finally, the questions were to be written out carefully on notecards which, again, were left unsigned. On the third day they rose from the dead. In came the questions.

Let me list some of the questions that I have received over the past few years. They're presented here just as they were submitted:

1. Hell is down, Heaven is up. What is out? Where does it end?
2. Why do I have blemishes and other kids don't?
3. The President lies about Vietnam. The cops lie about LSD and marijuana. Teachers lie about how important grades are. Why do adults lie so much?
4. What is true love?
5. Should I go all the way with a boy twenty-nine years old?
6. Does it take more courage to burn your draft card or go to Vietnam?
7. How will I know when the right boy comes along?
8. How do people keep happy with each other after they're married for awhile? Or is it impossible?
9. How can a basically shy person make and keep friends?
10. What makes good kids turn bad?
11. How can you break a bad and dangerous habit?

12. Are birth control pills dangerous? How much is known about side effects?
13. What comes after life?
14. Why do people want to keep on living even when life is so terrible?
15. Who is right about the creation, science or the Bible?
16. What makes people believe that their religion is most sensible and best?
17. Why are there different races?
18. Why does God sometimes make babies suffer and allow people to be born who are crazy or who have crippled bodies?
19. Will there always be wars?
20. Will we ever be able to live together without prejudice? If so, how do we start?
21. Where do things get their names?
22. Why are we here anyway? What is it all about?
23. What is the real meaning of average?
24. Why is it important for people to belong somewhere?
25. What makes a person a success?
26. Why do people (kids especially and young adults) take drugs?
27. What makes us appear as we do? Why are our features what they are?
28. Are there ghosts?
29. What is time?
30. Was it really smart to invent the atomic bomb?

The list is only a partial one, but it indicates the range and depth of their interests. Since each discipline has something to say about those things that are fundamental, the majority of the questions, with perhaps some rewording, could be handled in most classes. It is significant that many of the questions are the universal ones. Most important, however, these are the students' questions, not the teacher's or the textbook's or the CEEB's. It doesn't matter if some of them are unanswerable or that others lend themselves to a variety of answers. It's enough for youngsters to know that questions vital to them have been bothering man since he climbed down out of the trees. It is important for him to discover that the scientist, the historian, the poet, and the musician have all been puzzled about,

"Why are we all here anyway?" It's important, too, that someone lead them toward some answers about the problems of love and marriage. (One of my groups compiled a list of the most famous quotations about love and marriage and then spent a week discussing them, often violently, with the rest of the class. Wilde and Shaw never had it so good. As a matter of fact, the library had a run on these two gentlemen that lasted for the entire year.) These are the things they *want* to know. The school's job is to provide them with the time and the means to discover for themselves.

What next? We prune the list of questions and then revise it. The need to write correctly and clearly is evident and so is the desire. Committees are formed, sources of information are listed and discussed, resource people in the school and community are interviewed, independent research projects are assigned, questions subdivided, teams formed to debate those that are most controversial, films ordered, books consulted, relevant charts, models, graphs, exhibits, pictures, dramatizations, recordings collected or constructed. Something is happening. Eventually each committee gets a day or two or a week or two to nail down its answer or to examine a number of possible answers. These reports are seldom dull. Because the students want them to be good, they plan, organize, and rehearse. Everyone contributes. Other faculty members help; adults from the community are asked to speak. Conclusions are drawn and records kept.

The project is never really dropped. The initial questions seem to generate more. The answers always lead to other ideas worth exploring. Quite often they lead back (perhaps forward is a more accurate term) to the very things we had abandoned. *Silas Marner* makes more sense when it is linked to "Why is it important to belong somewhere?" Join *Antigone* to "Does it take more courage to burn your draft card or go to Vietnam?" and both the question and the play come alive. The "What Do You Want To Know" project has a tendency to grab them all: the Ivy Leaguer with the wrong questions, the budding hippie with the unasked questions, the manicurist with no questions.

I don't mean to imply that simply by asking students what they want to know we're going to solve all our problems. I offer it only as a way to make a connection, a way to tune in to what is relevant, a way to narrow the communication gap.

What's happening? Youth is happening. They are where the action is. When we become less concerned with the length of their skirts and their hair and pay more attention to the breadth of their knowledge of their environment and the depth of their understanding of themselves, both of our worlds will be made somehow better. For each of us, the journey through life is dark and difficult. Missed connections only make it more so.

THE CURRICULUM
GAME

Arthur Daigon

Address to the NEATE at its fall conference in Burlington, Vermont, on September 27, 1968.

"Patterns for English" is an ideal theme for such a professional conference. It so handsomely accommodates the talents of all those who participate. For the attending membership it provides rich opportunities for the exercise of the verbal virtuosity unique to the English teaching tribe. Every English teacher—well, every conference-attending English teacher—is an articulate polemicist, and what better subject is there for heated argument than that vague, amorphous, up-for-grabs phenomenon, The English Curriculum, along with questions relating to where it has been, where it is going, and where it should go.

Our theme also provides much verbal grist for the guest speaker, who can thrash about during his allotted time (and more), tilting at windmills of every make and design before he comes up with his final, sure-fire formula which will organize, articulate, and sequence the mishmash we commonly identify as "English."

Let the ritual begin, then. Now, what shall I attack first?—the narrowness and the irrelevance of linguistic systems, new and old, or the super-eclecticism of the humanities? the vagaries of the spiral curriculum or the fragmented precision of programmed Skinnerian behaviorism? the iconoclasm of the multimedia madmen or the security blanket orthodoxy of The Great Books? the formalism of "the disciplines of English" approach or the platitudinous pedagogy of "meeting the needs of the learner?" Shall I attack the curriculum that is literature-centered, composition-centered, language-centered, theme-centered, experience-centered, or student-centered? Shall my

From *The Leaflet* (November, 1968) pp. 30–43. Reprinted with the permission of *The Leaflet* and Arthur Daigon.

Arthur Daigon is a professor of English Education at the University of Connecticut.

initial target be Northrop Frye, Noam Chomsky, Jerome Bruner, B. F. Skinner, or Marshall McLuhan? ("Blow wind, come wrack, at least we'll die with harness on our back!") No—none of these, I think.

If curriculum is ever to break the shackles of precedent, vested interest, and hard sell, those who talk about it will have to spend their allotted time (and more) addressing themselves to the realities of English classrooms, rather than to the fantasies created in university seminars by both Professors of Education and Professors of English. Indeed, I would exclude from all curricular discussion and return unopened all curricular contributions of those who did not have some significant experience in primary or secondary school English classrooms. I would banish the university professor of English or linguistics, however brilliant, unless he were willing to go into the schools and submit his subject matter disciplines, his ideas about the structure of language and literature to the disciplines and structures of learners and teachers, and to the goals of primary and secondary school instruction. The English of the academic professors and the English appropriate for the full range of students in our schools are light years apart, although the unfortunate trend is toward making the two Englishes indistinguishable. Too many classroom teachers relish the role of junior professor and regard the new canons of erudition as proper stuff for their learned harangues.

I would exclude professors of education from curricular consultations unless they had demonstrated substantive success as teachers of young people and were maintaining ongoing, working relationships with the schools.

I would, and I do, turn to those English teachers who have experienced success in affecting the language behavior and the literary behavior of students for insights into the directions English curriculum should take. I would ask them to be the final evaluators of the new academic-educational bandwagons which clatter by every few years.

The recent linguistic madness, for instance, surely was the result of a promotion worthy of Batten, Barton, Durstine, and Osborne. From the academic bluebloods, testimonials; from the textbook hucksters, snob and fear appeals generously laced with scientific mumbo-jumbo—and the bandwagon began to roll, convincing thousands of English teachers that linguistic salvation was to be found inside a box—a newer box, a bigger box, a more attractive box—but a box nevertheless. Administrators and supervisors all over the country were leaping onto that bandwagon, afraid of being left behind without even a pilot program to call their own or, at the very least, an addendum to the old curriculum to show for it.

And in literature too, the bandwagons roll: close reading of the best in literature, literary history, symbol and archetype orgies, literary criticism—secondary school replicas of the colleges' failure to make literature come alive for their students. *Responding to* has long since been abandoned for *learning about*, as the secondary schools meekly accommodate the imperious injunctions of the removed, generally well-moated fortresses of higher education in the hope such acquiescent association will somehow add luster to their names.

The neat, academically spawned K–12 curricular system inevitably fails in the public school, and you in this room well know why. When this conference is over and the experts and the authorities have packed up their notes and their speeches, when the last *English Journal-Media and Methods* based arguments have subsided, what happens to the word-weary English teachers, department chairmen, and coordinators, impatient to implement K–12 curricular revolutions in their school systems? They return to colleagues who are either apathetic and cynical or are so busy doing "their thing" in the classroom that they cannot muster the necessary enthusiasm for significant curricular change. The in-service course you have managed to arrange is resented by most of the staff, especially if attendance is forced. It complicates the very burdensome schedule of the English teacher, especially if the already emasculated composition program is not to be completely abandoned. Besides, the campus based instructor of the course doesn't seem able to translate the "system" into the dynamics appropriate for real students in real classrooms, and he resents the teachers' constant harping on "application" and "practicability." He says he can't be bothered with "nuts and bolts." Anyway, it will produce a swell looking printed curriculum, which will just fit into that bottom left-hand drawer. After all, that's what the principal is really interested in—the printed curriculum—certainly not what goes on in individual classrooms. Besides, four members of the department are leaving this year. (Four left last year too.) The chairman spends so much of his time breaking in the new ones, and I hear that the Teachers' Association is demanding extra pay for curriculum sessions, and the town will probably turn down the school budget. If only the teacher-training institutions would do a better job—all that talk and no practice. The new teachers aren't much better than some of the students. Half of them aren't even English majors. It takes at least two or three years to make teachers out of them. Then they leave to get married, or have babies, or worse, to become reading specialists or guidance counselors. But even the experienced English teachers are getting tired of the regular curriculum sessions with the usual listing of objectives, skills, names of books, definitions, and concepts to be learned, and are demanding descriptions of specific practices and activities. If you think about it, though, the kids in school are changing too. This new curriculum would have been just right for the ones we used to have. Somehow the kids today just don't appreciate how logical and sound the new system is. You know, "Pearls before swine," and all of that. Really, I loved every one of the novels we put on the required reading list. I remember reading them in that graduate course on the modern novel. The kids hated them, but what do they know? And when I think about my planbook with all of those plans, and all of those study guides to the old novels and short stories, and all of those quizzes and examinations I worked so hard to prepare, and all of my favorite sure-fire activities, I am not so sure about this business of curriculum change, especially that new technical stuff about deep structure. I know grammar is very important for the kids, and I really enjoy attending those linguistic workshops, but to tell you the truth, I learned all the grammar I know during my first year of teaching, so whatever happens, I'll stick to Warriner's. Anyway why knock ourselves out over a new curriculum. There's another conference coming up next year, and who knows what will be on sale then—curriculum-wise, that is. They say that hot, new professor up at State University who is going to speak has come up with something that *really* gives all of the answers.

Despite all of those varied and profound circumstances which militate against the success of the usual comprehensive K–12 curriculum overhaul, such activity is not a complete waste of time. It provides a harmless diversion for tired academicians and retired educators, and provides both with the excuse for staying away from the schools, where the action is, and where they probably would be in the way anyhow. It supplies grist to fill otherwise empty pages in the professional journals. It serves those like the Laputans encountered by Gulliver, on his third voyage, who lived high in the sky, removed from other men and who gloried in the creation of systems and theoretical constructs which bore no relation to the way things really were. Elaborate and formalized K–12 curriculum planning, usually based on the single over-arching organizing principle, also provides much needed therapy for teachers who feel that somewhere there must be some underlying meaning, some coherent answer to the absurdity of the current English Universe. Rather than waiting for Godot, many are waiting for Chomsky or are waiting for Frye or are waiting for McLuhan. The tragedy of our times is that Godot will never appear to point the way to aimless travellers. The tragedy of our profession is that the directions pointed to by the demigods only take the already disoriented traveller even further from where he should be going.

Yet, I am convinced that significant change in the teaching of English can be achieved. It can be achieved if the English classroom is viewed as the humanistic center of the school and of the community, if the English teacher is viewed and behaves as a humanistic driving force, and our subject is viewed as a complex of disciplines and modes which have value *not*, I repeat, *not* in themselves, but as they contribute in their very special and very unique way to expressing and perceiving the whole phantasmagoria of internal and external events important or potentially important to those who populate our schools.

If significant change is to be achieved, we are obliged to determine, as realistically as possible, what we want our subject to do to and for students. Do we want our students primarily to know about the workings of literature and language or do we want primary emphasis on response to literature and increased proficiency in language behavior? The argument that academic knowledge about leads to interest and participation in, is a specious one, and has been used to justify preoccupation with a mass of academic irrelevancy, of abstruse and transient language concepts and systems beyond the intellectual, linguistic, and experiential purvey of most of our public school population. A better principle is that students are prepared to gain knowledge about what is or what can be important to them.

Generally, our literary stance has been to hand on the literary heritage by dispensing knowledge about it to students who couldn't care less. We expose them to what adults feel to be quality in literature in the hope it will win the students away from trash reading or non-reading. Generally, we have conducted a museum tour of literature up the straight and narrow corridors of chronology or into the neat and symmetrical alcoves of genre, repeating the college ritual *we* had experienced. Unfortunately we teach the way we have been taught. For the most part, our achievement has been to produce two species of bibliophobes. The outspoken literary boor vocally and unequivocally rejects literature as saying nothing to him and saying it in a deliberately roundabout and rather dull way. The bright college bound student (and who isn't college bound these days?), our future cocktail-party-literary-name-droppers, pass our tests, join in our discussions, and fill notebooks, but see knowledge about literature as an accoutrement of culture, important only for social and vocational advancement. They conceal their indifference to literature behind a verbal barrage of second hand critical commentary or paraphrases of teacher-delivered lectures. Few go to literature for the special feeling—knowledge and understanding it offers about the phenomenon of living.

Why then bother with literature at all? Certainly the literary tradition is dying or is already dead in the minds of all but a select group of teachers, critics, and intellectuals. Why expose students to great works if such exposure only develops immunities to great works? Are we prepared to accept the proposition that literature does not occur in books, but in the experience readers have with books? If we can accept such a proposition, we must provide the materials, however grating they are on our refined literary sensibilities and tastes, which will seriously and pleasurably involve students on, or near, their own levels of literary response, as a first step in ascending the ladder of literary discrimination.

For the most part, our language teaching strategies stress mastery of a grammar system, that is, a formal explanation of what most speakers of the language have already learned to perform intuitively. Those who need language help are further confused by the system (whichever one happens to be fashionable). Only those who already have no need for it seem able to master it. The linguists defend such ongoing concern with the formal structure of the language because such concern is right and proper unto itself, a sort of linguistic aesthetic of language for language's sake. The resulting classroom reality is the repeated review of what was not learned during the previous year—and we are starting the awful process earlier and earlier in the grades. Thousands of students all over the country are reviewing the parts of speech, or form classes, or active to passive transformations, or phrase-structure rules, and such study and such review generally bear not at all on their linguistic performances and are an affront to the priorities shrieking for our professional attention.

I keep having a nightmare in which a class I observed three years ago is happening over and over again in secondary schools all over the country. The ninth grade class had twenty-two boys in it. Half of them were non-English speaking; all were extreme discipline problems. They were shouting to one another, pushing, and running around the room. At one point a shoe flew by. And the teacher stood at the chalkboard, poised, unruffled, demonstrating with a certain flair, how to diagram noun clauses in complex sentences. After class, when I asked him to reveal the very subtle strategy he must have been using during his remarkable performance, he sighed and confessed that the lesson had no bearing on the language needs of these students. However, he justified the lesson by reporting, "It was in the curriculum, and it had to be covered." The point is *not* that this was an outmoded grammatical system. These students were acting out, in extreme, what almost all of the others feel about formal grammar systems of any vintage, taught by the most skilled teachers. They feel that the rituals must be gone through every year for reasons that are beyond their province to fathom. The average and the bright ones take notes, do the assignments, pass the examinations—and very quickly forget what they presumably learned, but never really incorporated into their own operating language systems.

Even the English majors who go on to college and enter English teacher preparation programs must be retaught those formal grammar systems which they are soon to inflict on all of those non-English motivated students. These students need more than rituals of formal definition, prescriptive descriptions, or linguistic equations to sensitize and activate the language potential such activities so effectively stifle. Rather than filling in Warriner's blanks or performing Roberts' transformational litanies, they ought to be working with their own and each other's sentences, enlarging, changing, substituting according to the requirements of the speaker, the subject, the occasion, and the audience. Students can inductively learn the operating characteristics of various kinds of linguistic structures without the aid of elaborate descriptive systems. They have been doing it all their lives. Verbal economy and sentence complexity can be studied and used in students' writing without parsing sentences, without immediate constituent analysis, without transformational exercises.

That such new systems do indeed describe the language more accurately, that they do indeed give linguists certain tools which help them to systematize certain heretofore haphazardly arranged phenomena, are beyond doubt. One must, however, have strong reservations about demanding mastery by public school students of systems which are soon forgotten, systems which even when mastered affect no one's language behavior, systems which are more appropriate to graduate seminars for the specialist, systems which steal time from the humanizing experiences English should be providing.

Let us turn from the gloom of past and current disasters suffered in English classrooms and consider one alternate curricular possibility for grades seven through twelve (because I know these grades best). What coherent, sequential English activity should fill these six forty-week periods?

And here the nagging question "What is English?" must be faced, for one's view of what English is will determine the kinds of experiences one plans for students. Long meditation and serious study punctuated by alternating fits of melancholia and galloping hysteria finally produced what was, for me, an eminently satisfactory and delightfully simple answer to the formidable conundrum.

English is *anything*, yes *anything*, that requires disciplined employment of the language, for speaker, or writer, or reader, or listener. To claim the valid domain of our subject is English itself is, to me, absurd, for certainly we must English about something. To teach literature well, for instance, we must deal intelligently with a myriad of supposedly non-English disciplines. When we talk of human behavior, or mores and motives, of stereotypes and precedents, of passions and values, we are talking psychology, sociology, anthropology, history, and philosophy, the New Critics notwithstanding. It must be stressed that this is not abandoning literature to the social sciences, but using interest in the human situation as a means of making connections with literature. Literature and humanity's predicaments are inseparable. In its own unique way, literature addresses itself to the phenomenon of living, and concern with appropriate phases of living is our most promising means of engaging readers who are able to find eloquent answers or eloquent silences not ordinarily available. Also it is our most promising means of approaching the otherwise unapproachable literary disciplines relating to image and meter, plot and character, archetype and symbol, irony and ambiguity.

What then do we English about? The parts of speech? Phrase-structure rules? The definition of a sentence? The English phonemic system? Or should we be talking and writing and reading about those things that are important to talk and write and read about in the context of some realistic disciplinary framework? I can only view the English class as the Forum for Ideas, as the physical coming to life, the incarnation, if you will, of the library and media center, where all disciplines and all subjects lie dormant on the shelves and racks, waiting for a curriculum and inquiring students to bring them to life.

Our real problem then, as we face those six school years, is to find those somethings to English about. These somethings are the pivotal ideas, issues, interests, and concerns, important and interesting or potentially important and interesting, to adolescents. Further, these pivotal ideas, issues, interests, and concerns should lend themselves to exploration through the reading of novels, plays, poems, short stories (old and new, easy and difficult), newspapers and magazines, through viewing films and television, through listening to tapes and records, through in-school and out-of-school experiences, through individual, group, and whole class activities. These ideas, issues, interests, and concerns should permit oral and written reporting, debate, discussion, and interdisciplinary involvement.

If the special disciplines of literature and language are ever to take shape in the cognitive machinery of our students, it surely will happen in such a liberal arts context, a context of active inquiry and liberation, rather than the self-serving, elitist packaging process it seems to have become. Much legitimate college student protest is focussed on academic irrelevance and lockstep learning. Unfortunately the secondary schools have too often been guilty of aping the bad instructional examples set by the colleges.

Is it English when a class investigates black-white disintegration in our country? Is it English if students interview their peers about the morality of the fraternity system? Is it English when a student wants to discuss a novel about a teenage pregnancy? It is English when a seventh grade student gathers information about an exotic animal that has caught his fancy? My answer is, of course, an emphatic "Yes." It is more defensibly English than students enumerating the syntactical functions of words, of noting and memorizing the five characteristics of romanticism, of extracting nothing but masterplot equivalents from the unappreciated gems of the literary tradition.

Using the ideas and issues approach to English, we increase insights into the vital areas of living, that is, we perform the humanizing function with language and other media as our means. Simultaneously, we improve proficiency in manipulating language and the other media using students' interest in themselves and the worlds they perceive.

All very well, you say, but who will prepare such a curriculum? How will it operate from grade to grade and ability group to ability group? How will it fit into the five class, thirty student per class, three preparation school framework? What about the implied interdisciplinary activity with its suggestion of team approaches? Where do the skills fit?

Let me offer for your consideration a not so wild scheme encompassing not only English as just defined, but team teaching, a bit of ungradedness, and a quasi-elective system, all in the delightful context of a four class, two preparation load. What is more, no teacher would meet with a given group for more than ten weeks during a given school year, thus providing for welcome change and variety for both students and teachers. (Moving targets are always harder to hit.)

Here is how it would work. First, I would divide the school year into the following five time segments. From early September to the end of September—3 weeks for introductory, overview, testing,

guidance activities; from October 1st to the Christmas vacation—
10 weeks for Course I; from January 2 to March 15—10 weeks for
Course II; from March 16 to June 1—10 weeks for Course III; from
June 2 to the end of the school year—3 weeks for remedial work,
individual integrative projects, field work, review, examinations.

I would pool students in the eleventh and twelfth grades into one
group, and would do the same for ninth and tenth grades, and
seventh and eighth grades. Let me describe how I would combine
the students, the schedule, and the curriculum using the eleventh
and twelfth grades as examples.

A large comprehensive high school might have approximately
600 pupils in each grade. If we combine the eleventh and twelfth
grades, we have a pool of 1,200 students. If we assume (only assume)
30 students per class, we must make provision for 40 classes. Assuming (again only assuming) 4 classes per teacher, we must have 10
English teachers to teach 1,200 combined eleventh and twelfth
graders.

The year, or the semester, or the summer before such a revolution
would begin, these ten teachers would have been grouped by two's
to form 5 working curriculum teams (two teachers on each of 5
teams). Each team would be responsible for the production of at
least one, preferably two, full resource units, or courses, based on
the exploration of an idea, issue, interest, or concern important, or
potentially important, to eleventh and twelfth grade students. Let us
assume we have, as the product of such a curriculum building
process, 6–8 rich courses, each planned to fill a 10 week time period.
Each pair of teachers would know at least one, probably two courses
quite well, and would learn another which seemed appropriate to
their skills and interests. Courses fitting for 16–18 year olds might
include: 1. Traditions and Innovations; 2. The American Experience;
3. Violence; 4. Contemporary Media—Film and TV; 5. Dissent—
Social, Religious, Artistic; 6. Minority Groups; 7. Help Wanted
(careers) and so on.

The course of Violence might include reading *The Iliad, Medea,
The Gospels, Morte D'Arthur, All Quiet on the Western Front,*
Hemingway, James Baldwin, Martin Luther King, Shakespeare,
*Hiroshima, The Lottery, Durango Street, The Cool World, Manchild
in the Promised Land, I'm Really Dragged but Nothing Gets Me
Down,* newspapers and magazine articles, crime statistics, gun law

controversies, violence in comic books, in popular ballads, on television and so on. Students could write letters to congressmen, newspaper editors, and TV stations. They could write editorials and poems. They could write about violence they have observed and the dialogue of violence they have heard. One group could investigate war as violence, another crime as violence, another morality of violence. One student could look into violence on television, another in contemporary poetry, another in contemporary slang, another in the Greek myths, another in advertisements, another in the Bible. Students could prepare questionnaires addressed to members of the community, teachers, or other students. Others could study and report on the traditions of violence in America's frontier past. Biographies of violent men and the consequences of violence could be added to the instructional grist. Biological and psychological themes explaining the causes of violence might provide better equipped students with additional challenging assignments. New and ghastly frontiers of violence could be opened for scrutiny as new weapons and the morality of their employment become the subject matter of instruction, and so on depending on the imagination of the course creators. Much class time would be assigned to learning the disciplines and skills relating to the materials and activities which were undertaken.

All eleventh and twelfth grade students would be given the opportunity to elect three such courses per year, to be taken during the three ten week periods set aside for course work. That is, during an academic year each student would select three separate courses, given by three separate teachers, and his classmates in any of his courses would be either eleventh or twelfth grade students. He would see one teacher and one group of students during the first ten weeks, another teacher and group of classmates the next ten weeks and still another teacher and another group of classmates during the third ten week course. Each teacher would teach four classes during a given ten week period, say two classes of the American Experience and two classes of Contemporary Media. Perhaps a course such as Minority Groups could be made mandatory for all students, and one like Traditions and Innovations could be reserved for honor students.

The eleventh graders, having finished three courses, would elect in their final year three additional courses from the pool of eight or so created by the curriculum teams and the process would be repeated. Ample opportunity for across-the-board scheduling of the same courses would enable several classes simultaneously to view a film, listen to a speaker or debate, exchange views, or work with several teachers. Back to back scheduling with social studies classes would permit flexibility of period length and synchronized activity with social studies teachers. The same strategies could be used with grades 9 and 10 and grades 7 and 8. Perhaps those in the lower grades would have fewer elective choices. Perhaps all three courses during a given year might be prescribed.

Sequence would be accommodated by leitmotifs of theme, skill, and activity, woven into the fabric of this six year curriculum. Running through the courses from the lower to the upper divisions would be familiar leitmotifs of themes: gaining personal autonomy, variations among people, personal creativity and interests, functioning in society, and so on. Another kind of continuity would depend on similar activities: individual and group study, writing for specific purposes, reporting, reading novels, plays, poetry, articles, and so on. The skill leitmotif would include producing increasingly fluent sentences, learning speaking and writing conventions, improving vocabulary and spelling abilities. Thus, the activities and the skills would be ongoing and would vary in complexity depending on the demands of the subject being explored. A class writing a letter for information in the 7th–8th grade would learn the required letter conventions, and the 11th–12th grade group writing a letter of criticism to a TV station would learn the conventions required in the more demanding letter writing activity. All skills and activities would be subject to constant review and could be deleted or expanded depending on the experiences teachers were having.

Undoubtedly, there would be problems with such a system. Scheduling probably would require the services of a computer or of several very smart administrators; teachers would have to become familiar with other courses, so that they would not be teaching the same two, three times a year; the scheduling of other subject areas could possibly be affected; some school systems have 7–9 and 10–12 divisions, making 9th and 10th grade pooling difficult. These are relatively minor objections and could be accommodated by time and space modifications.

More serious objections would be raised by the academic critics. The academicians would protest the use of English as a "tool" subject. They would insist that English be studied for its own sake, apart from other subjects, as a separate and unique entity, having its own justifications, and its own separate and unique disciplines and conventions. My reply would be that English is in fact, a magnificent tool, an instrument able to do things to and for people no other instrument can. But only as the learner perceives, through his experience that the language tool does indeed do magnificent things, that it is indeed special, will he be prepared to examine seriously and systematically its separate parts and unique characteristics. The position, for instance, that the literary work exists out there, removed from the affairs of men, to be appreciated for its own sake, is untenable—unless "for its own sake" means for the special way it addresses and illuminates some phase of living or some shred of an idea.

If you have been listening attentively (some infernal study or other reported that at any given moment only eighteen percent of any given audience is really listening), in any case, if you had been listening attentively, you would have noted that I had fulfilled all of the requirements of a talk on the English curriculum. I have done considerable thrashing about and windmill tilting during my allotted time (and more); I have offered my own panacea for all English teaching problems, and I have provided an irrefutable answer to our mandatory question about the nature of English.

Having done all of these, I consider my assignment to be completed and wish you all a delicious conference filled with interesting propositions, rebuttals, and protests, but most of all with undying vows to create a new and better English (K through 12) the very first thing come Monday morning.

WHY NOT?

Ray Scofield

Why not say that school is for kids
rather than teachers or janitors
or secretaries or cooks
or architects or even principals?
Why not say it and believe it.
Why not abandon required homework
and put a few kids on the streets
or reading books or watching tv
or talking with a friend
or waiting for a sunset
or picking pimples
or just sitting?

Why not throw out
mandatory homework
and find another way
to intimidate kids?
Why not bite your tongue hard
and justify all the busywork you've pawned off on kids
under the guise of "excellence in education."
Why not eliminate homework
and find a better way to teach
cooperative cheating?
And if all else fails
Why not try to excite, stimulate, energize, or inflame a kid
and let the homework take care of itself?

Why not build a humanities cafeteria
with an *a la carte* line loaded with goodies.
Perhaps a student will learn to serve himself occasionally
without always waiting sheep-patiently for the waitress
to push the well-cooked curriculum *du jour*
into his hands into his head
into his heart

From *Media and Methods* (September, 1968), cover, 1, 3. Reprinted with permission of the publisher.

Ray Scofield teaches junior high language arts in Eugene, Oregon.

the leftovers into his intellectual garbage can.
Why not advertise the delectable and diverse dishes
from language and lit and composition
and LIFE and maybe
just maybe
MR will be better known as Motivational Research
than as Mentally Retarded.

Why not stop drawing and re-drawing the floor plans
of our homemade curriculum prisons
with every fetter in place
anchored securely with the cement of whatever's current
from the past?
Why not (indeed) stop drawing fresh plans of old prisons
and start tunneling or scaling or vaulting
or even scratching a little.

Why not try to find relevance
between what goes on in class and something else
anything else?
Why not ask a parent for help or a teacher
or a curriculum consultant
or the United States Commissioner of Education?
Why not ask a life guard
                    or a truckdriver
                              or a poet?

Why not retire the miniature federal reserve board
in every school
that controls the banking practices in classrooms?
A kid earns a credit and puts it into the bank
and once it is safely deposited
he throws away all of his notes and admits
original innocence
just another virgin brain
with thirteen credits in the bank.
Earn another credit and put it in the bank
earn still another credit and put IT in the bank
earn them, bank them, forget them
earn 'em, bank 'em, forget 'em
findem, earnem, bankem, forgetem
Why not claim language as our rightful stock-in-trade
our raw material
and also our finished product
Why not help a kid take pride
in the power of language personal and social

Why not help a kid use language to communicate
with an editor a draft board
                              a girl
or to discover the nobility of man?

Why not dissolve the red ink communion
(the grades that DEgrade)
Why produce self-satisfaction grade mongers
judging their worth by OUR standards
that make credit bankers out of philosophers
that make us teach multiplechoice knowledge
and that convince kids
that the dung beetle
who collects the biggest cognitive ball is best.
Why not try to evaluate kids honestly
individually
Why not try to find what a kid learns from you
rather than what he hasn't learned from his past teachers.
The difference between a student and a teacher
should be something more than a grade book
                              or an answer book.

Why not make attendance optional?
If the multi-mediaed McLuhan is right
and going to school interrupts education
Why not entice with connections to life
not plague with demands for inconsequence.

Why not take our eyes off the rearview mirror long enough
to think September 6, 1999
What will IT be?
                 pain?
                    vitamin-enriched soma??
                                 darkness???
Why not look into a crystal book or ball and find out
and at the same time find out how our classes can
let a student want to learn throughout life
or make him mankind-sensitive
or let him see his choices and decide
or show him how to love himself
or prepare him for more leisure time AND for cybernation
one cyber Nation, under IBM
indivisible
with conformity and structure for all.
Maybe.

GROWING UP ON
MECHANIC STREET

Peter Schrag

It is impossible to think of those adolescents without a strange mixture of affection, apprehension, and fear. To imagine them at all, it becomes necessary to shoulder aside the black/white clichés of youth-talk—about middle-class revolt and ghetto rebellion—and to perceive a grayer reality. I am not writing here of affluent suburbs or what others have called blacktown, but about the children of those whom Americans once celebrated as workingmen. Again sociology fails us; there are no definitions or statistics. If there were, the matter would be better understood.

Phrases like "the forgotten man" and "the silent majority" are too political to serve as normative descriptions, but there is no doubt that there are forgotten kids who are, indeed, genuine victims: children of factory workers and truck drivers, of shop foremen and salesclerks, kids who live in row houses above steel mills and in ticky-tacky developments at the edge of town, children who will not go to college, who will not become affluent, who will not march the streets, who will do no more, no less, than relive the lives of their parents.

We have all seen them: the kids on the corner with their duck-tail haircuts; the canvas-bag-toting types, lonely and lost, lining up at induction centers; kids in knocked down cars that seem to have no springs in back, whose wedding announcements appear daily in the newspapers of small towns (Mr. Jones works for the New York Central Railroad—no particular job worth mention—Miss Smith is a senior at Washington High) and whose deaths are recorded in the weekly reports from Saigon—name, rank, home town. On the south side of Bethlehem, Pennsylvania, just above the mills, there is an alley called Mechanic Street; once it was the heart of the old immigrant district—the first residence of thousands of Hungarians,

From *The Saturday Review* (March 21, 1970), pp. 59–61, 78, 79. Reprinted with permission of *The Saturday Review* and Peter Schrag. Copyright 1970 Saturday Review Inc.

Russians, Poles, Mexicans, Germans, Czechs, and Croats. Most of
them have now moved on to materially better things, but they
regard this as their ancestral home. Think of the children of
Mechanic Street; think of places called Liberty High and South
Boston High, of Central High and Charlestown High, and of hundreds of others where defeat does not enjoy the ironic distinction of
the acknowledged injustice of racial oppression.

They exist everywhere, but convention has almost wiped them
from sight. They are not supposed to be there, are perhaps not really
supposed to believe even in their own existence. Thus they function
not for themselves but to define and affirm the position of others:
those who are very poor, or those who are affluent, those who go to
college. In visiting the schools that they attend, one must constantly
define them not by what they are, but by what they are not, and
sometimes, in talking to teachers and administrators, one begins to
doubt whether they exist at all.

The fact that defeat is not universal makes the matter all the more
ugly. The record of college placement and vocational success, which
schools so love to celebrate, and the occasional moments of
triumphant self-realization, which they do not, obscure—seem, in
fact, to legitimate—the unexpressed vacancy, the accepted defeat,
and the unspoken frustration around and beyond the fringe. When
we see a growing number of students from blue-collar families
going to college we begin to assume that they all go, and that they
will all be happy and successful when they get there. Yet it is still a
fact—as it always was—that the lower ranks of the economic order
have the smallest chance of sending their children on, and that
those who fall below the academic middle in high school tend to
represent a disproportionate percentage of poor and working-class
families. It seems somehow redundant to say all this again; but if
it isn't said there will be no stopping the stories of blissful academic
success.

The social order of most white high schools—the attitudes that
teachers and students have about other students—is based (in
proper democratic fashion) on what people do in school, on their
interests, their clubs, their personalities, their accomplishments.
(Students from blue-collar families with serious college ambitions
associate with the children of white-collar professionals, and share
their attitudes, styles, and beliefs, which tend to be more liberal—

politically and personally—than those of their parents. A few
participated in the Vietnam moratorium last fall, and a handful, unknown to their fathers, have gone to the local draft counselors. But
they represent a minority.) It is possible to leave Mechanic Street
through school achievement—to community and state colleges, to
technical schools, to better jobs—yet it is hardly universal. Fewer
than half actually go. What kids do in school tends, as always, to
be predetermined. The honors class is filled with the children of
professionals, kids whose parents have gone to college. The general
course (meaning the dead end) and the vocational track are composed of the sons and daughters of blue-collar workers. The more
"opportunity," the more justified the destiny of those who are tagged
for failure. The world accepts the legitimacy of their position. And
so do they. Their tragedy and the accompanying threat lie precisely
in their acceptance of the low esteem in which school, society, and
often their parents regard them, and in their inability to learn a
language to express what they feel but dare not trust.

Imagine, says a school counselor, that you could become an animal,
any animal. What species would you choose? The secret heart would
choose freedom: Eagles soaring over mountains, mustangs racing across
the plain, greyhounds loping through fields. Freedom.

Dreams are to be denied. The imagined future is like the present
without parents. Jobs, domesticity, children, with little joy, seen in
shades of gray. Coming out of school in the afternoon, the boys
already resemble their fathers when the shifts change, rows of dark,
tufted mail order house jackets, rows of winter hats with the ear
flaps laced above the head, crossing the road from the plant to the
parking lot, from the high school to the waiting buses and the bare-
wheeled Chevies. The girls, not yet stretched by pregnancy, often
trim in short skirts and bright sweaters, will catch up with their
mothers, will be married at eighteen or twenty, will often be engaged before the tedium of school is at an end. "Unwanted kids,"
says a school administrator, "kids of guys who got girls in trouble,
kids of Korean War veterans and veterans of World War II who
didn't want the first child, and before they knew it they had two
or three. All their lives their kids have been told to get out of the
way, to go watch television. They don't have anybody to talk to.
There was a recent survey that indicated that 72 per cent of the

first children of this generation were unwanted. These are the kids."

They sit in rows of five, five by five in the classroom, existing from bell to bell, regurgitating answers, waiting for the next relief. The mindless lessons, the memory and boredom, and the stultifying order of cafeterias and study halls—no talking, sit straight, get a pass— these things need not be described again. From bell to bell: English, mathematics, history, science—and, for some, release to the more purposeful and engaging activities of the shop: auto mechanics, data processing, welding, wiring, carpentry, and all the rest—some relevant, some obsolete, but all direct. There is an integrity, even joy, in material behavior—a sharp tool, an engine repaired, a solid joint—that the artificial world of the conventional academic course rarely allows. Material things respond; theory is applicable and comprehensible—either the thing works or it doesn't; it never prevaricates or qualifies, while words and social behavior, metaphors and politics remain cloudy, elusive, and distant. You see them wiring an electric motor or turning a machine part on a lathe, or fixing a car: pleasure, engagement, or, better, a moment of truth. The Big Lie, if there is one, will be revealed later. ("No," says the director of a vocational school in an industrial city "we don't tell the students that the construction unions are hard to join; it would discourage them in their work. They'll find out soon enough that it helps to know someone, to have a father or an uncle in the union. . . . But after a kid manages to break in, he's proud of what he learned in the school of hard knocks, and he'll do the same thing to the new guys.")

From class to class, from school to home and back, there is a sort of passing-through. What is learned is to defer—to time, to authority, to events. One keeps asking, "What do they want, what do they do, what do they dream about?" and the answer is almost always institutional, as if the questions no longer applied: They go to school; they have jobs—in the candy factory, at the gas station, in a little repair shop, in a diner—and they ride and repair their cars. Many of them live in a moonlight culture, a world where people have second jobs, where mothers work, where one comes home and watches whatever is on television, and no longer bothers to flip channels in search of something better.

Some distinctions are easy and obvious. Schooling certifies place; it selects people, not only for social class, but also for geographic mobility. The college-bound students speak about moving somewhere else—to the larger cities, to the West Coast, wherever events still permit the fantasy of a better future, or at least of change; the more national the college, the more likely they are to move. Among those who don't go to college there is little talk (except in depressed towns) of moving on. Academic losers stay put. "I know this is a dreary place," said a high school senior in Bethlehem. "But I like dreary places." It wasn't meant to be a joke. Big cities, they tell you again and again, are dangerous. (And in the cities they talk about protecting the neighborhood, or about how they still live in a good neighborhood.) Some places, they say, you can't walk the streets without getting knifed—by you know who. You hear it from sixteen-year-olds.

The instrument of oppression is the book. It is still the embodiment of the Great Mystery; learn to understand its secrets and great things will follow. Submit to your instinctive and natural boredom (lacking either the skills to play the game or the security to revolt), and we will use it to persuade you of your benighted incompetence: "I didn't want to write a term paper, but the teacher said it would be good if I did; when I handed it in she made fun of it; so I quit school." The family knows that you should stay in school, that you should go to college and "get an education," but it does not know that often the school doesn't work, or that it works principally at the expense of its own kids. One of the tragedies of the black revolt is that it frequently confused the general incompetence of schools with racism, thus helping to persuade much of the blue-collar community that its children were in fine shape, that the educational system was basically sound, and that complaints came either from effete intellectuals or ungrateful, shiftless blacks. Teachers who purported to represent genuine intellectual achievement (The Book) were thus allowed to continue to conceal their contempt for both kids and brains behind their passion for conformity and order, and to reaffirm the idea—already favored among working-class parents—that schooling was tough, boring, vicious, and mindless.

The school is an extension of home: In the suburbs it is rated on college admissions, on National Merit winners, and similar distinctions; in the working-class neighborhood of the city it tends to be judged on order and discipline. Either way, the more talk there was nationally about the need for technologically trained people, the more the school was able to resist challenges to its own authority.

"Technological complexity" replaced naked authority as the club of conformity in the school.

What the school did (and is doing) was to sell its clients, young and old, on the legitimacy of the system that abused them. Of course there were exceptions—students, teachers, schools—and even the drearier institutions are sufficiently equipped with the paraphernalia of *fun*—sports, bands, clubs—to mitigate the severity and enlist community support. It is hard to find schools that do not arrogate to themselves some sort of distinction: the state championship marching band, league leadership in football or track, a squad of belles who twirl, hop, bounce, or step better than anyone else in the county. A girl makes her way from junior pom-pom girl to cheerleader or majorette; a boy comes from the obscurity of an ethnic neighborhood to be chosen an all-state tackle. There is vitality and engagement and, for the moment, the welding of new common-interest groups, new friendships, new forms of integration. It is the only community adolescents have, and even the dropouts sometimes sneak back to see their friends. And yet, many of these things come to a swift and brutal end: a note in the yearbook, some clippings, a temporary sense of value and distinction convertible into an early marriage, a secretarial job, an occasional scholarship. The most prestigious activities of high school have no lasting value; next year, or the year after that, there will be no band, no football, no pep club. Too often life reaches its highest point at seventeen.

It may well be that even white working-class parents are becoming more suspicious of the mediocrity of their schools, more aware of their crimes, and less taken by the joys they offer. The imperious contempt of large-city administrators is not limited to the complaints of the black community, and the increase in number of defeated school bond issues and tax overrides is hardly a sign of growing confidence in the school people who propose them. And yet, the things that have been preached by the best people for a hundred years (and which many of them no longer believe)—order, hard work, self-denial, and the general legitimacy of schooling—these things die hard, or die not at all.

It is too easy to forget the faces, too hard to forget the crowd. American youth, Edgar Friedenberg wrote, are "already deeply implicated in the deeds and values of their culture. . . . They go along with it and sincerely believe that in doing so they are putting down trouble-makers and serving the best interests of their community."

That was, of course, before Berkeley and Columbia, before revolt had reached sufficient mass to be called a "counterculture." For the children of Mechanic Street, however, nothing changed, except that it added yet another demon to the many others that could not be faced. The kids·of the lower middle in the order of the school had always known that they don't have much to say about anything; they have been put down most of their lives by parents, contemptuous teachers, and by fellow students. (The blue collar is still stigmatized; in the school the vocational students are fender-benders, and occasionally a particularly nasty remark is answered with sudden, explosive violence: "He called us grease monkeys, so we pushed him right through that glass door. We stick up for our rights.") What they do have to say is often directed against the most threatening invitations to independence and the most obvious examples of freedom, which constitutes the secret dream. They would—most of them—not permit demonstrations against the Vietnam War, would prefer that their teachers maintain the very order that puts them down, are resentful of anyone that can be called a hippie. ("It's not the parents that cause that," said a student radical, "it's the school. It teaches people to be uptight.") If the war continues at the present rate, several in each of their high school classes will be dead before they ever have a chance to live; of course, they would rather not have the war—and a few have joined peace marches and demonstrations—but, they tell you (in tones of a text they wish they could remember with more confidence), we have to Resist Communism, have to stand up for our rights. What about Mylai; what about the massacre of women and children in Vietnam? Most of them aren't much disturbed, haven't thought about it, or been asked about it, and haven't discussed it. You hear about someone's cousin or brother, over in "Nam," who talked about how those crazy people even had kids throwing grenades at our convoys. It's war, and you never know who's going to try and kill you. But the agony of the reply, the painful speech, in class after class, makes it impossible to press too many questions; the Hard Line plays back no better than a Shakespearean sonnet or a Euclidean theorem never worth learning. You do what you're told. Propaganda and schooling are the same thing. You ought not, you tell yourself, to pick on kids.

There is no place to go. No place now, no place ever. For the lower half of the school population—the general course, the voc-ed course, the yet to be certified losers with their low-C grades, the high school is like a refugee camp, a camp for displaced persons waiting for something to happen. The central fact of existence is not school or home of the great institutions of American rhetoric, but the automobile, the one place where life can proceed apart from those institutions, the one place where the stunted remains of the dream of freedom can grow. We have heard all this many times before—the drag racers, the hot rods—sometimes in amusement, sometimes in indignation, but we haven't come close to understanding how much it means. The car, quite simply, is everything. It is the only place where adult experimentation is tolerated: experiments with sex, with self-realization, with independence, with courage, with change, with death. The car shuttles within the city limits, sometimes to McDonalds' or the Burger King, sometimes to the drive-in movie (Clint Eastwood, John Wayne, *Easy Rider*), but rarely beyond, rarely even to the next town.

There is no place to go, except to the car itself. The radio—and the heater—thus become essential accessories, and parking becomes an all-purpose word for sex. It is the thing you do on a date. For the affluent, who have large houses and some privacy—and parental tolerance—to entertain, it may also be an invitation to turn on; sex at home, pot in the car. For those who are not rich, the car represents almost every level of reality. It is something you work on, something useful (or superpowered) that you maintain, it is a place to live, it is escape, it is privacy. It is hard to get through high school without at least one accident, perhaps even harder to become a man without being able to claim one close call—out on the spur route, or in the empty parking lot of a shopping center late on a Saturday night. Someone pulls alongside, you give the engine everything, and for a few brief moments you feel speed and power and triumph. People don't grow up with cars; they grow up in them.

There is much talk, in town after town, about having places for "young people to go," about teen centers and recreation halls (the chaperoned dances having been abandoned by all but junior high students), but that concern seems to reflect a deeper despair about the community, about *place*, and about the future itself. As the old ethnic and regional culture breaks up, the culture of aspiration— what we used to call the mainstream—should grow in its power to attract and hold. But often, needless to say, it does not. In the smaller towns and in the hyphenated neighborhoods of cities, traditional patterns and institutions—food, family, the church, the Ukrainian Hall, the Polish-American Club—become increasingly tenuous; church membership grows older, the neighborhood more bland, the swimming hole more distant, the culture more thin. The local mill, the mine, the plant, once ferocious and mythic in its demands on men, in its economic unpredictability, in its brutality, is tamed by unions, by government, and by corporate management itself. The kids don't remember the last strike, the last layoffs, let alone the last fight with the Pinkertons, the National Guard, and the company dicks. Every year a few more landmarks disappear, another memory dies, another set of roots is destroyed.

For most parents, there is still the hope of a better place, and almost every one of them does his best to get his kid to go. But the ebullient romance, the Alger myths, the dream of adventure and enterprise—all those things have been inundated by size and technology, and abandoned by the very people who invented them in the first place. The fact that things are less manageable, that the country and the world no longer respond the way we once imagined they should (or that they have become unmanageable altogether) may not be as traumatic for the ethnic and social underclass that had never controlled much of anything anyway—but it does reduce the interest and the fun of trying to join. One of the striking things is that many kids are not ambitious for power or possessions. "My parents," said one, "never had what they wanted; they couldn't get along on what they had. But we can." And yet the life that he and many others imagine is almost identical to the life of the present. As today opens up a little—a better home, a car, a television set, and a steady job—tomorrow seems to close down. Modesty in achievement and ambition is matched by an inability to visualize anything richer—in experience or possessions, or in the world at large. The generation gap—for rich, for poor, for all—is precisely this: that many kids, for the first time, are growing up without a sense of the future. And that, for America, is new.

They are people who have lost one country and haven't yet found another. Some of them are at least marginal participants in the counterculture; the hair on the boys grows longer, the hard rock is universal, and drugs (pot and pills), now prevalent among the swingers—college prep, affluent, or black—are beginning to infiltrate the middle, often with the tacit acquiescence of the cops who

know that they have lost some of their troublesome adolescent clients
to the euphoria of pot, and who are, in any case, powerless to stop
it. There may still be high schools in America where drugs aren't
traded, but they are probably scarcer than dry towns. At the same
time, the potential for revolt, for repression, for violence, random
and directed, remains. In one high school, a senior—long hair,
mustache, articulate—speaks about his plans: When he graduates
he will join the Marine Corps, go to Vietnam "where the action is,"
then return home and become a state cop. "I'll cut my hair before
they get to it," trading one form of expression for another. Perhaps
there are few alternatives left. Perhaps Vietnam remains one of the
viable ways to become a man, or to become anything at all.

"Maybe," said a sophisticated high school teacher, "we better
leave everything alone. If these kids ever become politically conscious, who knows whether they'll join the SDS or the brown shirts."
There are signs that they could do either, just like anyone else. Some
of them have harassed peace demonstrators, heckled civil rights
marchers, and have beaten up black kids in integrated schools or
on the periphery of changing neighborhoods, and have been beaten
up in return. And while middle-class, college-oriented students—
and blacks—have made the papers with their activism, there also
have been, in some of the inner cities, self-styled protofascist gangs
hunting blacks, hippies, and other signs of vulnerable liberalism.
In the 1968 election, the major support for George Wallace within
the labor movement came from younger members—the older
brothers of the kids now finishing school.

Who is to say how things are learned? For the children of
Mechanic Street—as for all others—the classroom has rarely been
more than a marginal place. Except for minimal literacy and a few
tricks picked up in a home-ec course, the girl who marries at
eighteen was educated at home, though she may well have used the
school to find her husband. Except for the certification that schools
bestow on good behavior and acceptable habits, the boy who takes
a job immediately after graduation (or who, with a fifth of his peers,
never graduates at all) takes little from his school, except perhaps
a vaguely unexpressible sense of defeat.

And yet, something is learned—perhaps from television, perhaps
from the school community itself. The well-publicized tension between generations seems to have given language and content to the

specific tensions between parents and children. Which is to say that "student revolt" or "youth revolt" seems to be applicable even where there are no students and no "youths" who identify with larger causes. Even politically conservative and/or apathetic kids now seem able to articulate differences with their parents. Many of them revolve around nothing newer than the company they keep, the people they date, and the time they have to be home at night. Nonetheless, the atmosphere of revolt provides new strategies for all (long hair, for example), opens new possibilities, and offers new ways of rationalizing old ones.

Marshall McLuhan's notion of the global village may still be more vanity than reality; yet it is accurate in one major respect: The media—television, radio, and records—are creating communities where none existed before. Media are creating bonds of style, age, and interest that transcend the particularities of locality and background. The surface manifestations of a style may themselves satisfy the longing for place and identity, providing alternatives for neighborhoods, rituals, and traditions that no longer exist. In this sense "revolt" is the opiate of the masses. High school reform and protest may never go beyond the abandonment of the dress code. But the media may also be creating the possibilities both for the development of new forms of consciousness and culture and (for the same reason) centralized political management and control. Unless Americans are prepared to revolutionize their educational system— providing far more intellectual and cultural freedom and diversity than they are currently willing to allow—the high school will, in fact, be no more than a huge amplifier for the signals that the media are willing (or permitted) to transmit. Considering the unbelievable boredom of the slow track in the average high school, and the treatment accorded its students, no "educator" can berate TV without being laughed off the stage. If there is any escape from that boredom, it is in the car and in television itself. The children are moving away from Mechanic Street. But where will they go?

TEACHING ENGLISH
WITH A FOCUS
ON VALUES

Howard Kirschenbaum
Sidney B. Simon

There must be some reason that we assign all of those compositions, read all of that Shakespeare, and work our way through such
a vast quantity of novels, short stories, essays, plays, poetry, and
other gems of the English teacher's repertory.

One possible explanation for what we do is simply that we ourselves love the literature and relish the excitement we have known
through reading and writing. We know that writing is an authentic
way of achieving better self-understanding. We have tasted the
adventure of trying to communicate our ideas and feelings. We have
seen literature open up whole new worlds of experience and
deepen our insight into ourselves, our fellow man, and our society.
We agree with Camus that literature "illuminates the problems of
the human conscience in our time." For many of us, leading young
people to the edge of these discoveries is what teaching English is all
about, and why we are in it.

Yet, sometimes we forget, and, in the pressure of our day-to-day
teaching, we often allow a giant gap to develop—a gap between
what we say and what we do. It is in this gap that the realm of
values lies. John Holt asked a college student who had received
straight "A's" in high school English if he could see some of her high
school compositions. She answered "What would I save any of those
for? I never wrote anything which really mattered to me for
English." She probably echoes the thoughts of more students than
we may care to acknowledge, for until we make the search for

From the *English Journal* (October, 1969), pp. 1071–1076, 1113. Reprinted
with the permission of the National Council of Teachers of English, Howard
Kirschenbaum, and Sidney B. Simon.

Howard Kirschenbaum teaches in the Division of Educational Psychology,
Temple University, and Sidney B. Simon is a professor in the School of Education, University of Massachusetts, Amherst.

values a consistent and persistent objective (and a behavioral one at that), we will witness all too many students going through the motions without writing or reading much of anything which really "matters" to them in English classes.

There are many things an English teacher can do about values.[1] We, however, want to discuss one particular strategy for clarifying values which we have found especially productive. It is called "The Values Sheet."

A values sheet is simply a ditto upon which is written a provocative, perhaps even threatening, but always value-laden statement. For example, with one of your own classes, try this rather eloquent example taken from Russell Baker's "Observer" column in the *New York Times*.

Values Sheet # 1. Under the Sway of the Great Apes

Edwin P. Young, an uncelebrated philosopher, once observed of football, "After all, it's only a game that kids can play." This is no longer strictly true. If it were, the networks would not have bought it up as a vehicle to sell cigarettes, cars, and beer.

The evidence suggests that it satisfies some inner need of the spectator so completely that it can rivet him to his chair through a holiday in disregard of family life or bring him to his feet howling for (Allie) Sherman's head when the outcome fails to gratify.

If sports have ceased to be only games that kids can play and become psychotherapy for the mob, it is too bad, especially for kids who will grow up hating them or busting gussets to achieve professional excellence.

What is worse, though, is the distortion of values that radiates throughout the society. For thirty minutes of farce, Liston and Clay can earn more than the entire faculty of a public school can make in a decade.

—January 5, 1965

That first part of the values sheet is the stimulator. It can come from essays, quotations, definitions, poetry, cartoons, etc. Anything the teacher is imaginative enough to find or create can involve the students in serious consideration of some area of values—politics, religion, money, love, work, friends, family, death, leisure, and so on.

---

[1] For background on the theory and for other suggestions for working with values in the classroom, see Louis Raths, Merrill Harmin, and Sidney Simon, *Values and Teaching* (Columbus: Charles E. Merrill Books, 1966).

The second half of the values sheet asks a series of directed questions which help the student to clarify his thinking about the values problems raised by the stimulator. The emphasis here is upon "you" questions. What we are after is what the student himself thinks, and not what he believes is the answer the teacher is looking for. Our questions must never be moralizing ones, and we must do everything possible to see that there are no implied right or best answers. For example, we would never ask the question: "Don't you think man should help his fellow man?"

Here are some questions of the "you" type which could be used with the "Under the Sway of the Great Apes" values sheet: (1) Did you watch football on New Year's Day? (2) Is it a pattern of yours? Are you proud of it? (3) How would you answer Mr. Baker? (4) Do you think the publishers of *Harper's* or *Atlantic* could benefit from taking ads during the televising of a football game? Comment. (5) Does this sheet make you want to do anything different in your life?

Using this general form, an English teacher can make use of values sheets to lift his subject matter beyond the factual and conceptual levels and raise it to a third level which we call the "values level." The values sheet is particularly useful in making poetry lessons more relevant to the search for values. Here are examples of the values sheets being used in two poetry lessons.

The essence of the first lesson is a comparison between the points of view expressed in Tennyson's "Charge of the Light Brigade" and E. E. Cummings' "next to god america." The first poem illustrates one kind of patriotism ("Ours is not to reason why . . . Ours is but to do or die."), while the second satirizes it ("what could be more beautiful than these heroic happy dead . . . they did not stop to think they died instead . . ."). Which attitude is the better? What are the alternatives? We believe that this is for the student to decide for himself. The following values sheet immediately *involves* the student in the poetry and in this important area of values.

Values Sheet # 2. Patriotism[2]
(The following statements, except for the last, are from the *NEA Journal*, January 1967.)

[2] This values sheet is from the work of Dr. Merrill Harmin of Southern Illinois University.

1. "To me, patriotism is one's love or devotion to one's country. Having its roots in religion, it includes respect for our leaders, honor for our heroes, belief in our ideals, and a stout defense of the integrity of America."—J. Edgar Hoover

2. "Many men have assumed that blind support of their country 'right or wrong' is the very essence of patriotism. But I agree with the view that 'he loves his country best who strives to make it best.' Our schools will produce true patriots capable of saving this nation and all that makes it dear only if they turn out youngsters alert and alive to our society's shortcomings and weaknesses; only if they instill in our children a social conscience, a fervor for righting old wrongs, defying old fears, surmounting old prejudices, and banishing old social taboos."—Carl T. Rowan, former head of the United States Information Agency

3. "We love our country, in the final analysis, because it is *ours*, because it is an extension of ourselves, and because we love ourselves. . . . But the highest ethical command is to love others as we love ourselves. The best patriotism, then, does not exclude and despise the foreigner, but gives him the love and respect to which all men are entitled."—Steve Allen

4. "To me, strong 'national patriotism' is undesirable. What we need is devotion to self and all mankind. Rather than more persons blindly loyal to a particular group, we need more persons who see that in this shrinking world all humans must share responsibility for each other's trouble and joy."—Tamaji Harmin

---

1. Which of these four statements sounds like things you were taught about patriotism? Put an "O" (for old) or an "N" (for new) next to the statements which seem old or new to you.

2. If the world's people chose one of these statements rather than the others as its position on patriotism, which one or two statements, in your opinion, would lead to the best kind of world? Discuss fully.

3. If all the world's people chose one of these statements rather than the others as its position on patriotism, which statement(s) would lead to a world that was most undesirable? Discuss fully.

4. According to the definition of patriotism which appeals to you the most, are *you* a patriotic American? Discuss. (Here you might want to write down *your own* definition of patriotism if you think it more meaningful than any of the four above.)

This values sheet may be used by the teacher in a number of different ways: (a) If used as a prelude to the reading of the poems, the values sheet is an excellent motivational device, which also focuses students' attention on the major ideas in the poems. (b) The questions can be assigned for homework before or after reading the poems. (c) The second question on the values sheet is guaranteed to start an exciting classroom controversy, which could lead directly to the reading of the poems and the values question: "Which poet's point of view do you prefer?" (d) A composition assignment: "Now that we have discussed patriotism in reference to the values sheet and have seen what two poets with different ideas have had to say on the subject, write a composition on what patriotism means to you . . ." (e) A follow-up activity: "Which statement about patriotism on the values sheet would Tennyson most likely subscribe to? Support your answer with specific references to the statement and poem. Which statement would Cummings most likely subscribe to? Support your answer.

The values sheet is no gimmick. It is a meaningful way of encouraging careful reading and critical thinking and of helping the poetry to come alive for the students.

Here is another poetry lesson following the same pattern. John Donne's "No Man is an Island" is an excellent contrast to the popular folk-rock singers Simon and Garfunkel's song-poem "I am a Rock (I am an Island)." The students read the Donne poem and, as they hear the recording, read the words to the Simon and Garfunkel song. The following values sheet can be used with these poems in similar ways to those outlined.

Values Sheet # 3. Minding Your Own Business vs.
                        Helping Those in Need.

1. Some people say that man is basically selfish, that one must watch out for himself, that it's best to serve your own purposes, avoid hurting others, and "Mind Your Own Business."

2. Other people say that men must stick together and help one another, or they will fall separately, that no man is an island, that each man's fate is intertwined with other men's fates, and one should "Help Those in Need."

---

1. What label might be appropriate for each position?

2. Is this a case of "either-or," *either* you support one position *or* the other? Can you think of other possible positions one could take concerning this issue? If possible identify some of these positions.

3. Professor Laurence Hopp of Rutgers University suggests that per-

sons who have experienced social injustice, who have experienced feelings of being unfairly treated, are likely to take the second position. Would you agree? Have you any evidence for your ideas about this?

4. Read each of the situations below and try to identify *what you would do* in each case. Although not all the information is complete for any of the situations, make the best estimate of *what you would do if you were faced with situations like these in the future.* Try to be as realistic as possible in your choice of actions. When you are finished, try to summarize *your* position regarding the issue: Minding Your Own Business vs. Helping Those in Need.

Situation A

You are walking down a busy shopping street in the middle of the afternoon. You hear screams across the street and see a man choking a woman in a doorway. Several persons on both sides of the street notice, but nobody moves as the woman continues to scream and as the man tries to drag her indoors by the throat.

Situation B

You are in a group of persons with whom you would like to be friends. Two members of the group begin to tease a nearby girl who has some awkward physical characteristics. Others in the group join in, although a few are silent.

Situation C

The young married couple that lives next to you has a little boy, three years old. During a friendly visit with them, you observe that they are energetically teaching that boy to hate a minority group.

The top of a values sheet can serve both as the motivation for and the subject of a composition assignment. If we want our students to write a composition on patriotism, we could easily say, "Write a composition on what patriotism means to you." But how much more effective it is to distribute that values sheet on patriotism, provoke a heated discussion, and use *that* as the starting point for the composition. The students, then, have thought about the topic and can use the composition to put down the ideas they wanted to get across in the discussion, when they hadn't as yet formulated their thoughts or where they didn't get a chance to speak.

This principle works for any topic. If the composition were to be on *courage*, a values sheet on courage could be used. The questions, if possible, could come from the class' readings.

Value Sheet # 4. Courage.

"Courage is to fight when someone insults you, no matter who he is."
—A gang leader

"True courage is to do without witness everything that one is capable of doing before all the world."—La Rochefoucauld

"Ultimate bravery is courage of the mind."—H. G. Wells

"Courage is . . . when you know you're licked before you begin but you begin anyway and you see it through no matter what."—Harper Lee

(Add more. Include your favorites. Make them up yourself, appropriate to your needs. Have the students give *their* definitions.)

---

1. Consider the different acts of courage which are part of the above definitions. Which kind of action, in your opinion, takes the *most* courage? Why?

2. Do you think everyone possesses courage? How? If not, why not?

3. Describe a time you acted courageously? Why did you?

4. Describe a time you acted without courage? What would you do if the situation arose again?

From this, the teacher can devise a variety of composition assignments. We have used a similar approach with a composition assignment, for high school students, on the draft. For the top part of the sheet, we presented many *different* views on the Selective Service System—it should be abolished, no college deferments should be granted, it is fine as it is, women should be drafted for non-combatant service, etc. In this case, we did not ask any questions, but went right into the composition assignment: "Choose *one* position, and support it by. . . ."

A poem might serve as the top half of the values sheet. The questions, then, would refer to values areas raised in the poem. For example, if the top half were "The Road Not Taken" by Robert Frost, the questions might go something like this:

1. What was the *most important choice* in *your* life that you have had to make between two divergent roads?

2. Which one was the "grassy" one that "wanted wear"?

3. In what way(s) has the choice made a "difference" in your life?

4. Are you proud of your choice? If yes, why? If not, why not?

5. Was there any adult who could have given you good advice at the time? Any of your friends?

6. Are you at *or* are you coming to any new forks in the road? How do you think you'll choose? What are the pros and cons of either choice?

Such questions get the student to personalize the major issues in the poem, to focus on specific words or phrases, and to look more deeply into his own values.

Instead of a special top for a values sheet, you might simply write: *Silas Marner*, Chapter 6. Your questions will relate the subject matter with the student's own experience. (a) Briefly characterize the major people you meet at the Rainbow. (b) Do you know any people who are similar to those at the Rainbow? Discuss briefly. (c) Consider the topics of conversation at the Rainbow. Do those topics persist to this day with the people you know? How much of your discussions involve those topics? (d) How would *you* define gossip?

Another top for a values sheet could be some *moral dilemma* which is relevant to the literature your class has read. The dilemma might be about money or women or man's relation to the state or a question of ends and means or a dozen other problems. Questions: (a) How would character *A* from book *X* solve this dilemma? Support your answer based on . . . (b) How would *you* solve this dilemma? Why? (c) In what ways are you and character *A* similar? (d) In what ways are you and character *A* different? A variation on this idea would be to present a situation, not necessarily a moral dilemma, and ask the student to consider how he and the literary character would probably act in that situation.

Now take another type of approach toward teaching literature, that is, teaching literature in *thematic units*. Your values sheet, on the particular theme, could precede or follow the unit. If, for example, you are concluding a literary unit on "Man and God," and have read books with different points of view on the subject (*Oedipus, Book of Job, Rubaiyat of Omar Khayyam, Crime and Punishment, The Plague*), you might devise a values sheet with some controversial statement and then ask questions which call for the student to compare and/or contrast his *own* views on the statement with those of the various authors. So it goes with other thematic units—"courage," "patriotism," "man's relation to his fellow man," and so on.

For whatever objectives—language arts, ideas, motivation, etc.— you hold a class discussion, values sheets are an excellent way to begin. If students are required to answer the questions for homework first, you will find that you get much more participation, because the students all have had time to formulate their ideas. Below is an example of a values sheet I have used in just that way.

Values Sheet # 5. Speak Up.

"In Germany, first they came for the Communists, and I didn't speak up because I wasn't a Communist. Then they came for the Jews, and I didn't speak up because I wasn't a Jew. Then they came for the trade unionists, and I didn't speak up because I wasn't a trade unionist. Then they came for the Catholics, and I didn't speak up because I was a Protestant. Then they came for me—and by that time no one was left to speak up."—Pastor Martin Niemoller

---

1. Which category are *you* in? When would they have come for you?
2. Is there something in your school, some "injustice" about which you might well speak out?
3. Why stick *your* neck out? Why not?
4. If you decide to speak up, how do you go about it? What are the best ways?
5. Some people say: "We need to value what we do and to do something about what we value." Do you agree? If not, why? If so, what have you done lately?

SUMMARY: It will come as no surprise that most of our students do not care as deeply about English as we would like them to care. On the other hand, if there is one subject they do feel passionately about, it is themselves and their attempts to develop clear, viable, and sound values in a confused and confusing world.

The values sheet is one excellent way of bringing these two concerns—the personal and the academic—together. Values sheets involve students personally in the reading and writing adventure, and help them, through increased self-awareness, to make better, wiser, and more thoughtful choices in life.

If we had to choose but one objective for our teaching, it would be to help students search for values. The English teacher with his unique, value-oriented subject matter can do more about values than almost any other teacher in the school. Values are the stars by which men steer their lives, and luckily enough, most of us who teach English are born star-gazers.

IF YOU'RE NOT SURE WHERE YOU'RE GOING, YOU'RE LIABLE TO END UP SOMEPLACE ELSE

Ed Cohen

The question of what "good teaching" is almost always begins with the premise that the teaching act is crucial and that the issue is how to develop the "best" or most effective instructor by examining his methods. How the faculty performs in the presence of learners is often considered to be of greater importance than how learners perform as a result of teaching.

The behavioral objective or systems strategy for learning mastery questions the usefulness of this approach for solving today's educational problems. The more important question has become,

"What can the learner do as a result of instruction that he couldn't do before?"

This proposed alternative approach to the teaching-learning process assumes certain fundamental things:

1. *Teachers are change agents,* in addition to their responsibility for reinforcing previously learned material. That is, unless teachers produce specified behavioral changes in their learners, they have not "taught" and no new learning has taken place. Behavior itself is

From *Media and Methods* (March, 1970), pp. 39–41, 70, 72–75. Reprinted with permission of *Media and Methods* and Ed Cohen.

This article forms part of a study, "Faculty for Teaching-Learning." Ed Cohen is former director of the Division of Two Year Colleges, New Jersey Department of Higher Education.

The author wishes to acknowledge the substantial assistance of Dr. Rita Johnson, Regional Educational Laboratory of the Carolinas and Virginia in the preparation of this aspect of the study. Her ideas and language form much of the basis for his article.

defined broadly, in Ralph Tyler's terms, to include "thinking, feeling and acting," while educational objectives refer to "change in pupil behavior."

2. *Teachers must specify clearly for themselves, their students, and their supervisors the learning objectives and behavioral changes they seek,* and must do this before they begin to plan an instructional sequence. They must then order sequentially and implement these objectives, on the basis of selectively designed methods and materials. Afterwards they must check the extent to which these desired changes have actually occurred in their students, measuring them in terms of mutually understood minimal performance units. The evaluation procedures help further define what the student is expected to be able to do once the course is completed, and these in turn enable both student and teacher to know when instruction has been effective.

3. *Teachers also must be prepared to modify their objectives and teaching techniques in order to improve future instruction,* on the basis of feedback from this total process.

What has been just described is an aspect of a systems approach to education. Once objectives are stipulated, the teacher backs up to design activities calculated to accomplish them. Student progress is monitored throughout the teaching-learning process. A feed-back mechanism and loop is built in that permits verification whether the prescribed activities indeed accomplish the objectives. Students can logically be permitted to skip learning they already possess by using diagnostic procedures to ascertain if they have reached predetermined standards of achievement. Students who initially surpass these levels on the basis of previous experience and performance on achievement tests or "challenge" examinations, should be given credit and/or placed in a more advanced course. The criteria for evaluating certain learning objectives will not always or necessarily be quantifiable, moreover, even though they should satisfy reasonably objective standards of another sort.

Utilizing such behavioral change approach to building academic programs will not automatically assure the achievement of all desirable learning objectives. Insufficient evidence exists to support such a claim. However, neither is it excluded that with greater experience in its use this will be possible in time. Even the minimal advantages it offers, and the centrality of some such instructional technique to the learning mastery strategy proposed, support its inclusion in learning programs.

The technique proposed need not (and of course should not) limit itself to the achievement of minimal terminal performances by students, but at least *does* set itself the goal of achieving those.

Moreover, it is as well prepared to go beyond concern only for factual subject matter content, to seek to stimulate creativity, "discovery learning," problem-solving, student self-actualization and other cognitive, affective and value objectives, as any other instructional technique. It can posit such objectives with greater honesty.

This technique uniquely demands of its users that they explicitly define and state all objectives, and devise methods and tests to ascertain that the behavioral changes consequent upon achievement of these objectives, have taken place. Used in conjunction with individualized instructional modes, it can provide students with an efficient base upon which they can be motivated to build their own higher, individually defined goals.

It cannot be denied that there are dangers and problems involved in the use of this, as any, technique. It should not be permitted to become a fetish, or lead to situations as described to this writer by one correspondent, "where a teacher cannot enter a classroom without having written down his behavioral objectives." But until a superior alternative is available, this approach should serve. Not the least of its advantages is that despite its high concern for the product of teaching-learning activity, it can be a self-correcting mechanism for improving the process as well. Following is a summary of the advantages it offers for improving faculty performances.

1. *The teacher becomes an inquirer into the teaching-learning act.* He becomes an investigator or a sort of "hypothesizer of change." He can perform in the classroom in ways he hypothesizes will produce the changes he's after. He can stop and check the learner to see if the changes took place as planned. If not, he can modify his teaching design until he gets the results he's after. This entire investigative process can only take place because he has written his objectives and therefore knows what he is after.

2. *The procedure encourages exploratory use of a greater range of alternative objectives, methods, materials and strategies, as well*

as criterion measures or tests. Instead of becoming wedded to one
favorite test, method, or medium, for example, because it is considered to be "best" or most commonly acceptable, the approach
prods the teacher to select from a broader variety available to him.
Teachers can discover whether favored activities advance learning,
or are merely time fillers; whether they get the material across, or
are merely perfunctory exercises. This is not to assert that faculty,
as a necessary consequence of adopting this methodological technique, will thereby automatically become more creative. It is not
improbable, however, that as a consequence of asking faculty to
plan clearly and sequentially about what and how they teach in
relation to outcomes, one may well generate certain "Hawthorne
Experiment" type effects. For the approach itself generates excitement about the subject and the process through which it is transmitted. Teaching effectiveness is enhanced when the teacher is
stimulated and can transmit a sense of that excitement. That certain
outstanding "lead edge" scholars are so often cited by students as
their "best" teachers, would seem to be due to their own commitment and involvement with the subject, striking off sparks which
ignite student interest. But most teachers, by reason of interest,
ability or opportunity, are not that type of person. What kind of
activity do they then engage in that can bring alive for them, class
after class, year after year, a similar involvement to be felt by their
students?

3. *There is an increased possibility for self-evaluation and self-
direction on the part of the teacher.* Within the overall curriculum
framework set by the school, it is the teacher who selects his own
objectives at the instructional level and specifies the changes he is
after in his learners. Furthermore, he can determine the extent to
which he has accomplished them on his own. In all fairness, an
external person, such as a dean, chairman, supervisor or parent can
only evaluate the effectiveness of teaching after full knowledge of
the intended changes in the learners, and in light of any evidence
collected to support such changes. On the other hand, the teacher,
without the aid of outside judges or evaluators, can begin to systematically improve his own teaching by collecting such evidence
of change and examining it himself. In this way, he can become more
self-reliant and autonomous.

4. *When instruction is unsuccessful, the instructional program
itself, i.e., the process, methods, materials, or techniques employed,*

can be recognized as sharing some of the responsibility for failure. Faculty and administrators will, of course, be responsible for improving the instructional program from one semester to another, and serious blame for continued failure can be laid on those who are unable, or unwilling, to make improvements. Likewise, students are not necessarily exonerated from the stigma of failure, since they are actors in the learning process and not neutral objects. When a student does not change, however, no longer may he be comfortably classified as slow or lazy. The student may not have been properly motivated, the learning objectives may have been unrealistic, the methods may have been inadequate. The approach enforces attention on all the contributing elements in the teaching-learning process, and discourages the laying of false burdens of guilt on students or anyone else for that matter.

5. *The approach is more humane in that it forces educators to focus continuously upon students, rather than exclusively upon the teacher's technique.* Student response is still the most significant aspect of the educational endeavor.

What a student does to show what he is thinking and feeling becomes the target of change. His performance or behavior prior to, during, and after instruction becomes the focus of everyone's attention.

Observations of specified aspects of his behavior produce the evidence gathered upon which to base future instructional decisions.

This means that student apathy, boredom, resistance and unrest could be defined as significantly important, though unintended, instructional outcomes. A teacher could attend to these or any other outcomes of his instruction with an eye to their modification.

6. *The teacher can also improve his selection of objectives and thereby improve the quality of skills being mastered by the students.* All too frequently, conventional test scores are not sufficient unto themselves as indices of learning. With the use of behaviorally oriented tests, an examination of the teacher's objectives may reveal that scores were high, but on the *wrong* types of items. That is, the student may have learned to memorize well, but the more important items which involve higher-level or complex cognitive tasks were missed. In other words, behaviorally oriented procedures permit specifications of multiple objectives, and programming for

each. The teacher may ascertain whether other objectives such as the complexity and transfer value of a task, and a positive attitude towards the subject has been gained, as well as the quantity or speed of student performance, or the accuracy with which a student solves, for instance, a specific kind of math problem.

7. *Finally, by establishing learning objectives and thresholds of desired student behavior, the teacher is prevented from being so permissive that the classroom degenerates into what some commentators have referred to as a form of sublimated gratification for faculty.*

THE ABNORMAL CURVE AND TESTING

The title of this section is meant to be more than a playful phrase; it is also a description of the more appropriate goal to set for student grades, and the related use of tests, under a learning mastery strategy. Bloom notes that "we have for so long used the normal curve in grading students that we have come to believe in it." The consequences of this acceptance he sums up succinctly:

Each teacher begins a new term (or course) with the expectation that about a third of his students will adequately learn what he has to teach. He expects about a third of his students to fail or to just "get by." Finally, he expects another third to learn a good deal of what he has to teach, but not enough to be regarded as "good students." This set of expectations, supported by school policies and practices in grading, becomes transmitted to the students through the grading procedures and through the methods and materials of instruction. The system creates a self-fulfilling prophecy such that the final sorting of students becomes approximately equivalent to the original expectations.

This set of expectations, which fixes the academic goals of teachers and students is the most wasteful and destructive aspect of the present educational system. It reduces the aspirations of both teachers and students; it reduces the motivation for learning in students; and it systematically destroys the ego and self-concept of a sizable group of students.

The previously described requirement for defining outcomes and constructing evaluation instruments, actually makes an implicit distinction between the teaching-learning process and the evaluation process. The former is intended to prepare the student, the latter to appraise the extent to which he can achieve in desired ways, but they are *separate* processes. Lumping them together results in achievements measures designed only as sorting instruments, which do no more than detect differences among students in their mastery of subject matter, however trivial. Achievements are then usually signified by distributing grades "normally," classifying students into five levels of performance categories relative to one another. A small percentage of the students receives an "A," balanced by an equal proportion who are failed, with the latter frequently determined by group ranking rather than failure to grasp the course's essential ideas. Administrators often reinforce the practice, admonishing teachers who are "too easy" or "too hard" in their grading. The grading practice convinces students that "C" or "D" work is their speed, as does the very system of quiz and progress testing, with teachers also confirmed by such circular "evidence" that only a minority of their students can fully master what they are there to present.

The normal curve Bloom skewers with the remark that "it is the distribution most appropriate to chance and random activity." If education is purposeful activity and if it is effective, grade distributions should reflect that and forget about establishing refined pecking orders. In fact, Bloom states, "we may even insist that our education efforts have been unsuccessful to the extent to which our distribution of achievement approximates the normal distribution."

A first essential to breaking with established grading lies in treating testing associated with the teacher-learning process separately from achievement testing, and assigning the former the functions of diagnosis and progress measurement. Bloom borrows the term "formative evaluation" from Michael Scriven to describe this sort of testing, which seeks to identify the areas of student difficulty, and the elements in a learning hierarchy that a student still needs to learn. Formative testing becomes an intrinsic part of the teaching-learning process, providing diagnostic feedback to the teacher, and pacing the students' work and helping motivate him to make effort at the appropriate time. Bloom finds that students respond best to the diagnostic results when they are accompanied by specific prescriptions for instructional material or processes to help them correct difficulties. He believes formative tests should not be used as part of the evaluative grading process, but merely marked to show whether mastery is being accomplished.

At some point in time, evaluation tests based on learning objectives to produce behavioral change (or criterion reference tests as they have been termed by Glaser), should be employed to measure the results of teaching and learning. But these should not be essentially competitive, judging the student in terms of his relative group position—and thus encouraging learner preoccupation with evidence of group standing. While competition may be a spur to some students, Bloom believes "that much learning and development may be destroyed by primary emphasis on competition." Instead, he advocates setting standards for mastery and *excellence*, predetermined with respect to desired performance levels, rather than relative standards. Students are judged as to how well they meet the performance levels, regardless of how well others in the class do. Bloom does not recommend national achievement standards, *but rather realistic performance standards developed for each school or group.* The kinds of instructional procedures previously described should then be used to bring as many students as possible up to this level.

In conclusion, the point of these proposals regarding grades and tests, perhaps was summed up in an academic vice-president's letter to the writer: "If we're going to go on grading, let's discover what it is and for what we are grading." The suggested approach rejects the use of tests merely as successive hurdles to be overcome in a certification process. The grades earned by students should not derive their meaning sheerly from competitive standards or requirements for a mechanical accumulation of credits.

CHALLENGE OF TECHNOLOGICAL INNOVATION

The focus of this approach to learning suggests immediately that innovations in instructional technology are to be regarded only as tools in the achievement of that goal. (As with Roueche and Herrscher the term instructional technology is used both generically, and with reference more to processes than the restricted connotation of hardware.) Too much current characterization of approaches and programs as innovative is mere indulgence in the penchant to be fashionably novel. Garrison has rightly noted that "there are durable and vexing problems in instruction that do not yield to novel solutions." In addition, the easy replicability of instructional media has fostered extensive research with, and facile applications of, certain approaches and equipment. While this supports the treatment of teaching as a valid field of study, these explorations also often suffer by their abstraction from the human world of students and faculty.

Some abstraction, of course, is essential to any research inquiry aiming at the development of theory as well as practical solutions. Complaints that people and their needs seem to get erased in much of this exploration, are not without foundation however. The results when this occurs are ultimately counterproductive for the teaching-learning process. For this reason, and in contrast to the panacean importance which some proponents attach to certain modern media, methods and machines, the behavioral approach views their use pragmatically. They should be judged strictly in terms of their contribution to more effective, efficient, individualized, and not depersonalized, student learning. A certain measure of technological innovation, is nevertheless an indispensable concommitant to the success of the learning strategies proposed. The challenge lies in keeping their contributions in perspective, overcoming purely Luddite-type resistances to their use, and assisting interested institutions and faculties to stay abreast of developments.

Regarding the two last problems, the Hale Report on University Teaching Methods noted that an "overindulgence in lectures should be classed as a drug addiction on the part of both giver and receiver," while Allan Cartter in his contribution to the ACE study on Improving College Teaching stated that: "using talented manpower as 'talking books' is a shameful waste in most of our colleges and universities today, and tends to keep the student a permanent adolescent. The student's umbilical cord must be severed at graduation in any event, and we should take the responsibility of playing midwife at an earlier age."

Of greatest import, therefore, will be a school's ability to assist future and present faculty in enabling them to cope with and make full use of recent and yet forthcoming technological innovations. Considering the rapidity with which changes are being suggested in educational technology and methods, moreover, an important asset for any teacher will be the possession of some analogue to the scientific method available to investigators and applied workers in the natural sciences. The strategy and techniques thus far outlined may constitute such a self-correcting evaluative framework of pedagogic values, attitudes and analytic techniques. In any case, some such evaluative approach will be required to judge new developments as they arise during the 35 or so years of a beginning teacher's professional career.

Perhaps the strongest argument for the use of technological innovation is derived from its facilitation of individualized instruction that is otherwise impractical in a mass education setting. Students with access to technological devices for instructional drill purposes can diagnose and overcome their own deficiencies. If their use is properly structured, a dehumanization of the teaching-learning process need not result, since by relieving faculty of direct responsibility for repetitive drills and other mechanistic tasks, they release time and energy for that personal instruction and contact for which no mechanical aid can substitute. Today whole curricula are being designed wherein faculty contact and technological devices are carefully combined to take maximum account of individual student needs, interests, learning speeds and styles. Moreover, libraries are exploding in size and content under the impact of technological innovation. Once the teacher merely orchestrated books, manuals, films and tapes. Today, the learning resource center, with its data retrieval banks multi-media aids and multi-purpose rooms and space, allocations is available to challenge and offer him significant assistance.

Mounting evidence that academically marginal students, in particular, learn best when a variety of sensory stimuli are utilized, should encourage the imaginative use of such handy devices as microform techniques (microfilm, fiche and ultra-microfiche), recorders and cassettes, magnetized tape, slides and transparencies, especially as this equipment becomes increasingly compact, portable, adaptable and less expensive to purchase and maintain. Most encouraging with respect to these devices, is that it is possible today to eliminate the one-way communication characteristics of older audio-visual methods, and build feed-back mechanisms into technological aids in very sophisticated ways.

But more important than the devices are the new or refurbished instructional methodologies. Imaginative use of a "mix" of seminars, workshops, academic gaming, large and small group instruction (including "eight pack" student team approaches which seek to maximize intra-group cooperation and mutual counseling), can contribute to the search for learning modes adapted to the differences in students, and those needs not solely cognitive in nature. Independent study of programmed materials, including electronically assisted tutorial programs of individually prescribed instruction, seems particularly relevant to the problems engendered by massive and diversified enrollments at any school level. Moreover, both textbook and multi-media approaches seem feasible for programmed instruction. Less complex audio and video programmed instruction appears to offer more opportunity and to be more practical at this time than computer assisted programming, because of the relatively high costs and low state of the art of the latter.

The writer also believes that faculty should be at least acquainted with the concepts of systems approaches to instruction and educational administration. The learning for mastery strategy is itself an attempt to approximate some of those concepts, and such approaches can be expected to characterize academic activity increasingly in the future.

In summation, the use of any and all technological innovations should be justified by their demonstrable potential for reaching learning objectives and causing related behavioral change. While traditional schoolroom patterns, particularly those based exclusively on high verbal and reading abilities, must be examined and questioned by teachers regarding their continuing applicability, conclusions should *not* be foregone that all are undesirable or even of lesser worth than more recent experimentation. What is important is that these various approaches, old and new, be examined and subjected to critical assessments of their strengths, disadvantages, costs, efficiency and appropriateness for current situations and demands. Faculty must be given familiarity with the range, characteristics, and qualities of technological innovations, so they can make informed choices as to whether and how to incorporate them in their teaching-learning programs.

ON HUNTING
AND FISHING
AND BEHAVIORISM

Robert F. Hogan

There's hunting, and then there's fishing. Sometimes they differ in marked ways. The hunter knows exactly what he is going after, what its usual habitat is, and what its season is. Moreover, there is a conscious fit between the equipment he carries and the kind of animal he hunts. A sixteen-gauge shotgun is fine for hunting quail but not much good for Kodiak bear. But the typical fisherman on the pier at Morro Bay hunches that there may be some stray rock cod, but more likely some small sea bass, or halibut, or smelt, or maybe nothing. But even if it's nothing, there will surely be the good sea air, some sunshine, and a few other fishermen. If the fish aren't biting, it is a matter of small consequence to the fisherman on the pier at Morro Bay. He'll come back tomorrow, or as soon as he can.

What worries me about the current hard push for behavioral objectives in English teaching is that it stems almost wholly from the hunting mentality and leaves precious little room for fishing. The unfeeling behaviorist might observe that the catching of fish only seems to be the point of the activity, and that the affective response to the sun and the sea and the fellowship is really what brings the fisherman back. He might thus conclude then that it would be a lot simpler if the fisherman forgot about his pole, tackle and bait. Think of the money the "fisherman" would save if he didn't have to buy gear; after all, cost accountability is important. The experience he is after would be cheaper if he left out the equipment.

Missing from the purely behavioristic approach to education is acceptance that some things difficult to identify, much less to name and measure, are essential to the satisfying life and, if the educational process is to have any connection to life, essential to the

From *Media and Methods* (March, 1970), pp. 43–44. Reprinted with permission of *Media and Methods* and Robert F. Hogan.

Robert F. Hogan is Executive Secretary of the National Council of Teachers of English.

educational process as well. Like what, except in Freudian terms, does the pole mean to the fisherman, who doesn't care very much whether he catches anything? Or how can we measure the degree of success or the outcome of a window shopping excursion with one's family, a solitary foray into a secondhand bookstore, the browsing together through the Sears catalogue by two small girls deciding which of the dolls each would rather have and which of the pretty models in the fur coats each child is? The only point of the activity is the activity itself, the satisfaction that the experience generates, plus, in the case of the two small girls, practice as using language, at imagining what it would be like if things were different (long before we hit them with the subjunctive mode), learning how to stand up for what you want, and learning in a fairly safe setting how it is to yield to someone else something you want yourself. But to judge the success of the Sears catalogue experience in terms of the child's generosity and selflessness in other situations is to think, God help us, like an adult.

I worry, too, about the tight tidiness of the task force model, of the no-nonsense, mission-centered mentality. Take, for example, the second grade teacher who has as one of her missions the encouragement if not establishment of subject-verb agreement in the language of her pupils. There may be much more important things to do for second grade children, but that is a subject for a different article. The goal is clear and its approximation is measurable and a fair segment of the community thinks it a defensible goal. And consider this teacher who asked her children to draw a picture about how they felt and to write underneath the picture some words to explain it. And consider the child, carrying out this assignment, who drew a picture of a tombstone with his initials on it and under that wrote "sometimes I wish I was dead." And consider this teacher whose response was to cross out *was* and to write in *were*. That teacher's clarity (and singularity) of purpose is precisely what kept her from being the teacher she could have been in that setting with that child at that moment.

The roots for the current movement are varied. For example, there is the undeniable success of programmed learning in teaching certain kinds of activities, particularly where the learning actually does consist of changes in observable behavior and where approximations to the desired behavior can also be measured. The "systems approach" has worked in such enviable fashion in some cases that others understandably seek to adapt it to their purposes. What more remarkable validation can there be for the "systems approach" than the first landing on the moon, even though it did cost us 24 billion dollars, or perhaps because those who wanted that moon shot wanted it enough to invest 24 billion dollars of our money in its execution.

But the success of the mission-centered and systems-based industrial complex in the Northeast is diminished somewhat when one considers what has happened to Lake Erie and what is happening to Lake Michigan and to the atmosphere from Chicago to Boston. Apparently, that sudsy mill stream that powers the grinding mill across the road from the Wayside Inn at Lincoln-Sudbury falls outside everyone's PERT chart. The colossal irony is that while a foundation supported by one industry has worked to restore the Wayside Inn and the other buildings in that setting, another industry is polluting the stream across the way. This phenomenon and that in the second grade classroom cited above differ one from the other only in scope. Once the mission is identified and the task defined, what falls outside is likely to be ignored.

Mandates for a curriculum based on behavioral objectives have led to crash programs to produce such curricula. Some of the more generous schools recruit teachers from various subject fields to write such objectives during the summer or on released time during the school year. But everywhere one looks, teachers are writing objectives—in July, on Saturdays, or after school and far into Wednesday night.

In the meantime, though, without ever putting them down in scientific terms, the children are constantly establishing and modifying their objectives. And theirs will almost invariably contaminate ours. We can, if we choose to, set for a ninth grade class taking a six week unit in expository writing this objective: that 90% of the students will be able 90% of the time to write an acceptable five-sentence running outline for a expository composition of approximately 250 words. Meanwhile, Jennie has discovered "Annabel Lee" and would really prefer to write poems about star-crossed lovers. And Walter, whose father is editorial writer for the local newspaper, knows that his father writes to whatever topic the editorial is about and is really quite curious to see how it is going to come out.

Fred's girl friend has missed her period for two months running. Georgia's parents have been divorced and she is now living with her aunt and uncle, and the latter is trying to seduce her older sister. Talk to them about five-sentence running outlines!

Having said all this, which is too much and too little, let me concede that a great many well-intentioned but muddle-headed English teachers have for years wasted their efforts, their children's time, and the taxpayer's money in fruitless pursuit of unreachable or unstated goals, in the examination of subject matter for its own sake. Except for what they've done to children, though, they are not too culpable. After all, it was the vocal and voting community that once placed a premium on memorizing pretty phrases from *Evangeline*, or diagramming sentences that began with a nominative absolute, and on studying the spelling of *vicissitude*. That vocal community, or another community who has found a louder voice, has veered its course and changed its expectations. And the schools have some responsibility to veer, too. If the schools are going to enjoy anything like the support given to the moonshot, then those who control the money are going to have to be persuaded that the schools are worth it.

But while we must respond to the community, we cannot in conscience capitulate to it. Some areas of our instruction may well yield to statements of performance standards. The success of most of our grammar programs—if success is measured by changes and presumably improvement in the language use of children—is modest at best. Overall improvement in performance through the secondary school years may rest more on one fact than on any other—on the fact that a third of our students, including some of the poorest, drop out between grades nine and twelve and thus change the nature of the population being examined or tested. If it's language propriety we are after—and *that* is a subject for a different article, too—surely we can specify some of the changes we seek and admit that past programs have not brought about those changes.

Actually, we have long been loosely framing behavioral outcomes for the simpler skills—e.g., spelling, penmanship, vocabulary growth—and even for some of the more complex skills—e.g., reading to detect and understand irony. All that the behaviorists are doing now is urging us to state the goals more clearly. Assuming that 100%

mastery by all pupils' on all occasions may be too much to expect, what level of performance do we seek for what percentage of students in what period of time at what grade level?

But given the present low level of sophistication in measurement, we are asked to determine from secondary clues some manifestation of change in affective behavior. (Appreciation of the same poem by different students may be revealed by vigorous participation in a following discussion, by stunned silence, by tears, or by a sudden connection six months later with another poem, or by none of these.) But we are not told what clues count nor all the clues that might count. And we are badgered by those who do not know our field to write objectives to their specifications or to admit that we don't know what we're doing. What they do not understand is that even when we do not know what precisely we are doing, we know what we are doing, and why.

Sometimes we are fishing. We don't know if we are going to catch anything, or what it is we will catch if we do make a strike. Today we are going into class with our gear: "Stopping by Woods" and a couple of questions we hope will spark a discussion which will enliven for the students and ourselves the experience of that poem. After school, we'll stop by the lounge with our fellow fishermen and swap stories about how it went and maybe we will trade suggestions about bait and try again tomorrow. Next week I am going hunting —I am going to try again to set up a discussion in which 90% of the students (that is, except for two incurably shy ones and Georgia, who is still living through her private hell) will respond relevantly to the comments of their classmates (90% of the time) and loud enough for everyone to hear (100% of the time) with a minimum of intervention from me (their comments to exceed mine by at least four to one). But tomorrow—tomorrow I am going fishing. Because to teach English is to spend part of one's time fishing.

(Tonight I am going to try again to teach my youngest daughter to brush her teeth up and down. I am also going to kiss her good-night and nuzzle her a little. I would like her to grow up with clean, strong teeth. I'd also like her to grow up nuzzled. I have the feeling it will make a difference, even if I can't tell how that difference will manifest itself.)

INDEPENDENT STUDY: TRANSFUSION FOR ANEMIC ENGLISH PROGRAMS

David W. Berg

I've got too many kids in my classes Jane just sits there all day and does nothing Billy's too smart for the rest of the class Sally isn't too bright but she sure is a good worker Sandy is very bright but she sure isn't a very good worker Sammy could care less about anything but cars if that kid smarts off one more time either he goes or I go half my class didn't even bother to bring their books. . . .

So goes a typical English teacher's conversation in the lounge or at the lunch table or to his spouse at dinner. And under the typical English curriculum these complaints are only too valid. The sad but unavoidable fact of pedagogical life that causes most of our problems is the much abused concept of individual differences, and the even sadder fact is that we are not even coming close to providing for these differences. At best, we make a feeble attempt at coping with the situation by so-called ability grouping for our English students. What we are actually accomplishing, if this is our approach, is simply eliminating gross disparities among the students in a particular track, usually on the basis of IQ. This by no means confronts the reality of individual differences in the classroom.

For example, consider one of your own English classes for a moment. Look at Jim, sitting in the corner because he's a troublemaker. Half his school career has been spent in corners or in hallways. Have we compensated for his individual difference? Next compare Suzy, with her love of poetry and romance, with Bill, the captain of the football team. They both have similar IQ's; they both have similar scores on English achievement tests; they both qualify

From the *English Journal* (February, 1970), pp. 254–258. Reprinted with the permission of the National Council of Teachers of English and David W. Berg.

David W. Berg teaches in the University School of Northern Illinois University in DeKalb, Illinois.

for the "regular" track in our system of ability grouping: therefore they both shall read and study *Great Expectations* for four weeks this year. Are we providing for their individual differences? Are we providing for the difference between Julio, an extremely bright boy who fled from Cuba without a knowledge of English, and Mike, a boy with an IQ of eighty and a court record, when we put them both in our "basic" track and give them both the same book? In your "honors" track you have above-average plodders who make it on the basis of hard work and good study habits; you also have brilliant students who gain nothing from a comparative study of Cyrano and Romeo. These are only a few of the real, nitty-gritty individual differences that we in the profession are not providing for. These are differences not in IQ or reading ability or English skills alone, but in personality, interests, and learning styles.

"But I have thirty-five students in my classes. The best I can do is teach for the middle of whatever range I have." So goes the pitiful cry of the English teacher. And I sympathize. I agree that you have too many students. But I maintain that it's a pathetic excuse, one that can no longer be accepted. English teachers have too long used this as a crutch and, having justified themselves to the world and cleared their consciences, wait for the never-never-land when school boards will suddenly listen to the NCTE and give them four classes of twenty-five students each. So what do we do in the meantime? We have two rather obvious choices: we can sit back on our dangling modifiers and continue to bemoan our unlucky fate, *or* we can use a little imagination, free ourselves of our individual and professional anachronisms, and do something with what we've got.

Specifically, I would propose launching a program of Independent Study in English for virtually every student in Grades 7 through 12, and I would start by throwing out the curriculum guide and burning the course of study. Unless yours is an exceptional school system, these are outdated and irrelevant anyway.

Why on earth should every tenth-grader—or every tenth-grader within a given "ability" range—be forced to study *Silas Marner*, for instance? Because it's good literature? Perhaps it is, but so are many other novels that are infinitely more relevant to today's youth. Even more significant, a novel that is relevant to one individual may well be meaningless for the student sitting next to him. Are there any inherent values in *Silas* that cannot be found in other books? I doubt it. Our professional judgment of what is or is not "good literature" fades to insignificance if it results in a distaste for this good literature, as it often does. Our omnipotence in decreeing what is good for all simply does not face up to the realities of modern society. Similarly, it is no more justifiable to prescribe *Hot Rod* for an entire low-ability class than it is to prescribe *Great Expectations* for an entire "regular" class.

Another lame rationalization that we offer to defend our literature offerings is that unless the students are exposed to ———— (Dickens, Shakespeare, Twain, Eliot, Faulkner, or whoever) in school, they will never get this exposure. I think the realistic approach here is to admit first that for some students it will never matter one iota if they don't get exposed to this type of literature. I also believe that the students who will benefit from this type of exposure will arrange to fulfill this need at the appropriate time. Our mission as teachers would better be to encourage and make available this exposure—to offer it rather than force it.

The second stumbling block in the English curriculum is grammar. My personal prejudice on this topic is that grammar should not be taught on the secondary level at all, except to those students who might benefit from a humanities approach to the English language. I find the study of our language fascinating and rewarding; this is one reason why I am an English teacher. I do not expect all my students to feel this way, however. I also cannot believe that intensive study of grammar year after year will help a student write better. There is no other subject that a student encounters for as many school hours with as meager results as grammar. If you feel that you must teach grammar, go ahead. But do one of two things: either teach it for the same values that we teach art or music—as a humanities course and not as a shop course—or individualize your approach so each student is studying the specific aspects of grammar in which he is deficient. Don't force half your students to sit through material they already have mastered for the benefit of the other half who probably won't learn it again this year. An individualized approach fits in well with an Independent Study program, since it will involve diagnosis and prescription for each individual student. You will have students who will do no work whatsoever on grammar this year, because they will demonstrate that they have already mastered that material. You will have other students who will be doing considerable work on grammar, starting with the basic rudiments. If you do feel that grammar must be a part of your class, this is the only realistic approach.

Think for a moment about how your English classes went today. How much involvement was there? Was the day exciting or enjoyable or meaningful for your students? Did you have a good time and end the day satisfied with what went on? Now consider this: What would happen if tomorrow you came into class and said, "Beginning next week you may elect to work in any area that interests you. Since this is an English class, the only requirements are that whatever you work on should include some reading and writing." What would happen? You would at first be greeted with stunned disbelief. Never in their entire school career of seven or nine or twelve years have they been offered this kind of choice, and chances are they will never have the opportunity again. It will no doubt take some of them quite awhile to realize that you really meant it and to realize the full implications of such a "non-assignment."

What will they do with this golden opportunity? Some will start by doing nothing. So be it. These are the do-nothings anyway. One advantage to this approach is that they are electing this option of their own volition. A major learning experience for them will be that, come grade time, you can say to them, "You elected to fail." For once in their life you have stripped them of the excuses "The-teacher-doesn't-like-me" or "I-just-don't-understand-this-junk." You are also removing the rebellion motive from this type of student. You must accept their daily option of not doing anything as a legitimate choice, as long as they don't interfere with the rest of the class. Your responsibility to them is to encourage them to take a more desirable option, by suggesting more attractive alternatives. A second advantage of this approach with this type of student is that you are not asking any student to do the impossible. It is literally impossible to threaten, cajole, or in any way convince certain students that it is to their advantage to do some of the things that are required in the traditional English class. And I'm not sure that they aren't justified in rejecting things like how to write a friendly letter, or what is a participle, or what are the conflicts in *Great Expectations*. Why *should* they bother with these?

On the other hand, I doubt very much that you will find a single student who has no interests at all. They may not be what we would consider teaching in English class, but they are interests that are real and vital to that individual; therefore, they are important. If you have a student who is interested in cars or dogs or snowmobiles or airplanes or whatever, why can't you use that interest to accomplish whatever it is an English teacher is supposed to accomplish? Do you want them to read? Then let them read a car repair manual or a book on maternity care if this is what they feel a need for. Do you want them to write? Then let Suzy write a poem and let Joe write an essay on deer hunting. The day may come when Joe too will write a poem, and you many certainly encourage and suggest it, but don't sit him down on a Friday afternoon and tell him he has to write one.

If you do elect to try Independent Study, you are not abdicating your rights and responsibilities as an English teacher. You are in fact taking on more responsibilities and work than in a traditional classroom. You are basically readjusting your philosophy to serve more realistically the needs of your students. You are for one thing a source to whom the students can turn when the need arises. Does Ken want to learn about the 1970 car styles? Then you might suggest that he write a letter to General Motors requesting some pictures and brochures, and you would show him where to find out how to write a business letter. Is Sally enthusiastic about what she found out about her topic? Then give her the opportunity to tell the class or part of the class about it. Has Harry found a book on animals that is too hard for him? Encourage him to improve his vocabulary and his reading comprehension, and show him how to do it. He will respond, because he knows he needs it. He will learn because the motivation comes from himself, not from a teacher who says, "You need help in reading. Report to the remedial reading teacher for nine weeks."

If you do accept the rationale behind an Independent Study program for your classes, there are several approaches you might adopt. After explaining what Independent Study is and the responsibilities it involves, you might begin by allowing those who have met certain criteria to proceed. You should, if you follow this procedure, encourage every student to become involved eventually in the program as soon as each one meets your standards of behavior.

You should also be very specific about delineating the path to follow to qualify for the Independent Study program, and make it very clear that it will not be restricted to the smarter students.

A second approach would be to assume that all your students are capable of pursuing Independent Study and allowing all to begin simultaneously. Although you would realize that your assumption is very probably false, this approach has the psychological advantage of not isolating those about whom you may have reservations—the less mature student or the discipline problem. Your expressed expectation that they all will succeed is a much more positive approach than beginning by implying that they could not succeed at this either. It would however entail your keeping a close eye on those students and revoking their Independent Study privileges if the occasion should arise. After a suitable waiting period you should by all means give them a second and a third chance if necessary. A primary objective of this type of program is to develop the ability to work and learn independently, and as with any other skill it will take more effort to develop it with certain individuals than with others.

As the year progresses, you will be able to encourage and develop greater sophistication in the students who are involved in the program. If a student's written work indicates a need for work on sentence structure or spelling, for example, you can both point out the need and its importance and encourage him to undertake independently a course of action that will remedy the problem. If he does elect this course of action, you will of course need to have resources available and you will have to show him how to find the information he needs. You might also have one of your students who is skilled in this area tutor him by mutual agreement only in that specific skill area. This could very well serve as an Independent Study project for both students. You could further expand this idea by asking different students to become "experts" or resource persons for various skill areas, if they so desire.

Perhaps the most fascinating aspects of an Independent Study program in English are the limitless ramifications and possibilities it offers both the teacher and the students. Intensive reading in one area or by one author may lead one student to other areas. Reading short stories may lead another student to investigate how to go about writing one himself. Having the opportunity to read about hot rods (and pass English at the same time) may bring a potential dropout to the realization that school does not have to be a threat, and there is something here of interest and value to him after all. The sense of accomplishment of a slow student at achieving his own set of objectives may encourage him to try harder at whatever his next project might be.

What are the logistics of implementing an Independent Study program in your classroom? The major requirement is a wealth of materials conveniently located in the classroom. To accomplish this does not necessarily involve the expenditure of a large sum of money. A "wealth of materials" should include as wide a selection of paperbacks as you can accumulate (ask the students for donations; ask the PTA for a paperback drive; put an ad in the local paper—you'll get hundreds); it should include a variety of textbooks from all subject areas (check the textbook storeroom; ask your fellow teachers; send for sample copies); it should include a variety of practice materials (make some yourself; take apart sample workbooks and staple the lessons in manila folders; ask other teachers to run off a few extra copies of a lesson each time they make one; use magazine articles for reading comprehension exercises, stapling them in folders and writing a few questions for each; have your students help in any way they can).

If you are including skill materials as options for Independent Study, and you should, diagnosis is the order of the day. Again, use sample materials such as tests, or make your own diagnostic tests. They don't have to be of professional caliber; they should be designed to indicate to the student areas that he might need work on. Your practice materials should then be keyed to the diagnostic test, so the student can see that if he does poorly on section one of the test he can find help in a specific place. Used in this way, your classroom becomes more an English laboratory than an English classroom.

Individual conferences are a necessity to operate successfully a program such as this one. These can be held during class time for some, before or after school for others, and during homerooms or study halls for the rest. If you object to seeing students before school or during your planning period or even once in awhile during your lunch period, you probably aren't the kind of teacher who would be willing to try a program like this anyway. You might

be pleasantly surprised though at what might happen if you asked
one or two of your students to bring their lunches to your room and
talk over their projects with you.

What are the possible outcomes of such a program? These might
be a few: more fun for you as a teacher, excitement and enjoyment
for your students, skill development for those who need it, enthusiasm, interest, and a much-needed revitalization for your English
curriculum.

PROFESSOR BECOMES
HIGH SCHOOL TEACHER

Eugene H. Smith

For one full year I voluntarily abdicated my teaching responsibilities at the University of Washington to become a rank-and-file high school English teacher. I emphasize: it was a voluntary act. It was not a quixotic nor a neurotic but, I think, a pragmatic act. My chief reason for writing about it is not to restore my damaged ego, though I did suffer several psychological bruises. Rather, I simply want to testify to this means of comprehending the task that faces high school English teachers; especially may this be true for college professors who are directly engaged, as I am, in the preparation of English teachers.

It is no ordinary high school; it is the chief central area high school in Seattle which is most embattled by Black Power advocates and all the contradictory pressures that the movement arouses. The school year 1967–68, when I was there, was the one that veteran teachers in the building described as the worst yet. We had no riots and few skirmishes that involved physical violence (I heard about only one attempted knifing in a study hall), but we had constant tension and frustration among many of the students and teachers. Academic accomplishment was at low ebb. I don't think I could have had a better opportunity to experience—in the fullest sense of that word—the contemporary crisis in American education. That is a pompous-sounding phrase. Or it was until I felt it firsthand. And feelings are the chief legacy of my experience. I *felt* what it is like to teach in a large urban high school.

I did not volunteer to teach in Seattle's most difficult high school because I have a martyr complex. I feel my social responsibilities keenly, but I don't think I have a need to submit to pain and unpleasantness because it will bring me into closer union with the

From the *English Journal* (March, 1969), pp. 360–62, 367. Reprinted with the permission of the National Council of Teachers of English and Eugene H. Smith.

Eugene H. Smith teaches English at the University of Washington.

downtrodden. And I don't particularly aspire to be a social worker; I did not have the attitude that I was going to the school in order "to do good." Nor did I aspire to become a hero: to show that my superior strength and integrity could be submitted to test-by-fire and thereby qualify me for the hero's laurels. Yet I must admit that now, months after that school year, I am aware of a certain admiration among many of my professional associates. Some of them have told me it was a fine and brave thing to do. As nearly as I can define my motives, though, that is not what I was counting on.

Maybe the most significant thing I can say about the year—along with a good many other teachers—is that I got through it. I even enjoyed parts of it. I sensed warmth from several of my approximately 155 students. I touched several of them mentally (and maybe emotionally), and they were a little different because of their association with me. I have little tangible evidence of that, of course, although there may be some significance in the fact that one of the students scratched these words in the varnish on the door of one of my classrooms: "Mr. Smith is cool." I take the anonymous compliment at face value, though I do not overestimate the number of students who may have shared that view. But mostly I felt little real satisfaction from teaching there. I was seldom aware that the students understood me, or I them; that they valued what I had to offer; that my selections of literature or composition exercises or discussion topics had any real bearing on their lives. Massive indifference to English was the response I most often saw. That was very disturbing to me, of course, because I'm supposed to be an expert on English teaching. I am supposed to be able to show prospective teachers how to mediate the world of scholarly English study and the world of American adolescents. I seldom felt like an expert. More periods ended in sorrow than in exhilaration.

If my experience is relevant to any other teacher, it will probably seem so only through specific references to work that I attempted, reactions I saw, and tentative conclusions that I reached. Here is a sampling.

Our options for a curriculum in English were limited to two: either follow the available textbooks (e.g., *Adventures in American Literature, English Grammar and Composition, Guide to Modern English*) or make it up yourself as you go along. Those of us English teachers who were really concerned about having successful English

classes met occasionally to talk about curriculum and method, but
our efforts were neither strong nor concerted. Most of the literature
we taught was just not relevant. The anthology selections deal with
worlds so different from the one these adolescents knew and could
understand˙ that involvement was usually impossible. I tried some
Langston Hughes, some war poems, and finally, ignoring the usual
book selection regulations, inveigled paperback copies of *Invisible
Man*. All of these were late in the year. Ellison got to them! There
was much that they could not understand about his technique, but
with very few exceptions the students agreed that there was literature that was relevant.

I asked each of my seniors to read books outside of class—first,
at least four books from a list of suggested titles and authors; later,
at least two books entirely of their own choosing. For at least half
of them, *any* assignment to read outside of class was too much. They
were not oriented toward using leisure time for reading; many of
them had jobs which did not allow time for homework of any kind;
they could hardly imagine themselves ever reading all the way
through a book. I also asked for written responses to the books they
read, urging them not to restrict themselves to summary but to
respond to the books. Alas, this was a request that they could not
fulfill, sometimes because they had never done it before and sometimes because they had no coherent response. Even the bright ones
had much difficulty in producing anything like a critique of a book.

I wanted to help them learn how to read literature in our classes
—to discover the structures, textures, and subtleties of literature. I
did not expect analysis of a high order, but I thought we could make
some progress beyond merely superficial reading. We did do that
with "Do Not Go Gentle into That Good Night," with "The Unknown Citizen," and with parts of *Invisible Man*. Usually it happened when I divided the class into groups of five or six and set
them to discussing two or three questions that I put on the board.
As I walked around listening to the discussions and contributing a
remark or another question here and there, some sharp perceptions
appeared. More often, though, I got withdrawal—what the students
themselves would call a cop-out. I watched the eyes of many of
them. They would glaze or stare vacantly or disappear behind
heavy lids. I sensed the unspoken questions: "Why does he want
me to think? What does he want me to say? Why should I pretend

to be interested? What are we talking about this stuff for anyway?" I often get rather excited when I am leading a discussion, but I am afraid many in my audience regarded my excitement as eccentricity rather than as enthusiasm that they could share.

Most of the students I taught did not know how to discuss an idea. When it was Black Power, we had lively participation from the extremes: the Stokleyites and the white racists (only a few of them manage to find their way into such a school). But it was not ordered or controlled discussion. Despite my efforts, it was haranguing. Ideas from literature with more nearly universal significance seemed not to interest them, though I knew that the ideas touched their lives. What especially saddened me was that many of the black students simply resigned themselves to seeming not to understand, saying nothing or "I don't know" instead of contributing even a crumb of response.

I had devised a rhetorical sequence for composition assignments. They were clusters of essays, first drawing directly upon their own experiences, then moving to other sources of evidence and to considerations of audience, voice, and organization. Several assignments were tied closely to the literature we were reading. Each successive essay was designed to reinforce and extend the skills demanded by the previous one. The assignments came at about once-a-week frequency. The papers I received came much less frequently than that! As I talked with the students about their writing, they told me that this was not only more writing than they had ever been asked to do before but also it required too much thought. And thinking was something they felt ill-equipped to do. Never had I had more concrete evidence of past and present failures to teach composition.

Much of the classroom performance of the students distressed me, the organization and morale of the other English teachers worried me most. While I was fully aware of the difficulty of remaining cheerful and optimistic in a high school like that, I thought that at least the English department could be a band of humanists whose appreciation for diversity in life and literature would sustain them. Instead we had cynicism, frustration, and even despair. As a department we had no cohesion, no concerted means for innovating, for making this an exciting experiment with language. Instead, I saw lecturing, usage drills, textbook-question-answering, and only occasional flashes of imaginative teaching. And it wasn't because the teachers there were not capable of imagination. But strong leadership had not appeared, and the exigencies of simply coping from day to day were too much. Here was clear evidence for me of the tremendous need for a magnetic English department chairman; genuine discussion among English teachers about what they are doing in classes; abundant and varied books; and searching discussion of purposes, assessment, and curriculum. If I had been swept into continuous discussions of that sort among the teachers, I am sure my disappointments would have been fewer and my satisfactions more numerous.

Now I am back at the University, again teaching the methods course for prospective secondary school English teachers. The course is not the same as it was before last year's experience. The content is not so different, but my feelings about it are. I have to try to communicate to these idealistic college students something of what high school teaching really means. I think I have made a little progress toward bridging their four years of academic training and the world that adolescents live in.

MEDIA

In classrooms where once the venerable Miss Gearshift's steady cadences "illuminated" *Evangeline* and young Archie Artless squeaked Antony to Bobby Bashful's stammering Brutus, sounds of acid rock now fill the air while strobe lights flicker, cameras whirl, and tape moves smoothly from reel to reel. English teachers have discovered media. They have discovered that it is possible to compose with a camera as well as with pencil and paper, that it is as necessary, and desirable, to learn to "read" a film as it is to learn to read a novel, that the instruments of mass communication can easily become the instruments of social control, in short, that the medium *is* the message.

Not all English teachers have been convinced of the value of media study. Some reject such activity as being superficial, intellectually barren, and unworthy of classroom attention. Others are inclined to give it a try but hang back because they feel inadequate when faced with equipment they have never used or because they fear the cost involved. It is primarily to these teachers that the writers in this section address themselves.

Robinson's candid account of his own "conversion" describes a teacher in transition. He relates how, through an honest appraisal of his own interests and those of his students, he moved from a "love" of new grammars to a concern with contemporary issues, "language situations," and media. (Incidentally, this essay could have—perhaps should have—been placed after Postman's "Linguistics and the Pursuit of Relevance." It will be profitable to reread Robinson's essay after reading Postman.)

Higgins also makes a plea for a multi-media approach. Disparaging the old "audio-visual aids" concept of media, he describes how (and why) a communications course can integrate a variety of media into a significant, exciting experience for kids.

The Carrico and Devine articles, taken together, constitute something of a beginner's manual for teachers who would bring film making into the English class. They answer most of the questions posed by beginners and give explicit directions about what to do and why. Carrico, particularly, discusses different approaches and philosophies and describes a number of programs in high schools across the country. While there is some overlap between the two articles, they are more complementary than repetitive. Even when describing the same procedure, they vary sufficiently to make reading both worthwhile.

Katz, however, contends that film making "seems impractical in many schools and for most teachers" and argues that the most fruitful approach is the integration of film with the study of literature. He discusses the similarities and differences between film and literature and then goes on to describe a ten week unit that investigates "ways in which each medium handles a particular theme."

While many English teachers are willing to accept a multi-media approach and film making (as well as film study) as appropriate for the English class, far fewer are willing to approve rock music for classroom use. Aside from an occasional Simon and Garfunkel recording to "enliven" a poetry unit or a Bob Dylan piece to illustrate the continuity of the ballad, they shun this music as "unworthy." Morse argues, convincingly, that this music *does* have substance and is itself worthy of study. While many of the songs and albums he refers to are no longer current, his approach to the study of popular music remains fresh and vital.

Decker explores the form of mass media with which English teachers are most familiar—the newspaper. Most students are "exposed" to a newspaper unit at least once in grades 7 through 12 (and probably before). This article provides an abundance of ideas and techniques to help the teacher with limited background in journalism make such a unit come to life.

The final article in this section deals with drama, a subject that may appear at first glance to be inappropriate in a chapter on media. Yet if one considers drama as a medium of expression, a way of saying and being, rather than a literary form, then its relationship to other media becomes apparent. Heathcote offers valuable advice to all English teachers, but particularly to those who see student expression and self-realization as primary concerns of the classroom.

A MULTI-MEDIA
APPROACH IN ENGLISH,
OR THE CONFESSIONS
OF AN EX-AXIOM-EATER

Bruce Robinson

"Linguistics, it is now clear, has fallen into the hands of the grammarians. Nothing, of course, could be worse news for the children of America who now seem condemned to continuing irrelevance in their English classrooms." (Neil Postman, "Linguistics and the Pursuit of Relevance," *English Journal*, November 1967.) Neil Postman said this recently, and hurrah to him for saying it. For now, having found an ally in the exalted academic establishment, perhaps I can speak openly of my own disenchantment with grammar and invoke the spirit of rebellion among others.

Five years ago I was introduced to the new grammars, and I immediately fell in love with them. It must have been something like what Galileo felt when he discovered the "new stars" around Jupiter. In consequence, I spent the next three years assiduously pouring over the handiworks of Paul Roberts, Harold B. Allen, James Sledd, Noam Chomsky, and numerous other worthies until my brain was fairly split into its minutest IC's.

Meanwhile, my students, long since comfortably inured to the grammar of Robert Lowth, were getting thoroughly traumatized by my pseudo-scientific classroom eclecticism, and every piece of literature we studied—from Homer's *Iliad* to Faulkner's "The Bear" —was reduced to its K-terminal strings.

Last year, however, I grew weary of it all. The frustrations I had experienced—cramming to make up for my own ignorance of the new linguistic sciences, raging at the humanistic indolence of my tradition-directed colleagues, bristling at the insolence of authori-

From the *English Journal* (October, 1968), pp. 1005–1008. Reprinted with the permission of the National Council of Teachers of English and Bruce Robinson.

Bruce Robinson teaches English at Union College, Cranford, New Jersey.

tarian parents, and appalled by the lack of improvement in any of my students' writing—all these were just too much to take. So last year I quit the grammar bit, grew a big hairy beard, and tried what Postman would probably call "the rigorous study of language situations."

Of course, I didn't know at the time that was what I was doing. It was just a hit-or-miss experiment; I was merely playing a hunch in frantic desperation. What I did was to take a good look at the world around me; I considered my own experience of that world. Much to my surprise (and not a little to my dismay) I found that I was watching a good deal of television, that the editorial pages of *The New York Times* and the latest art films made much more interesting "reading" for me than *The Idylls of the King* or *A Tale of Two Cities*. I even came to realize that the obnoxious behavior of Alan Burke was more intellectually stimulating for me than the brilliant dialect studies of Raven McDavid. Having made these observations about myself, I could not help thinking that as a teacher of English not only was I a dismal failure, but much worse— I was an unconscionable hypocrite.

In an attempt to rectify the situation, I culled through my personal library a few weeks before school began and came up with titles like these: Arnheim, *Film as Art* (University of California Press, 1958); Bluestone, *Novels into Film* (University of California Press, 1961); Chayefsky, *Television Plays by* . . . (Simon and Schuster, 1955); Eisenstein, *Film Form and the Film Sense* (Grove Press, 1960); Knight, *The Liveliest Art* (New American Library, 1957); Kracauer, *Theory of Film* (Oxford University Press, 1960); McLuhan, *Understanding Media* (McGraw-Hill, 1965); Postman, *Television and the Teaching of English* (Appleton, 1961); Spottiswoode, *A Grammar of the Film* (University of California Press, 1950). I inferred from this that I had a more than usual interest in and perhaps understanding of television and motion pictures. I decided, therefore, to teach these media.

Then I remembered how much excitement the debating club's activities had always generated among the students at my school. I noted that the National Forensic League's topic for 1966–67 was "Resolved: That the United States government should limit its foreign aid to non-military assistance." "Wow!" I thought to myself, "this is dynamite." I also remembered that this was to be a year of drastic change at my school—many of the faculty (including myself) were leaving for greener pastures, and a new head man was coming in the next year to try to put some pizazz into the old place. "What fertile soil for a maverick classroom newspaper!" I diabolically concluded.

Thus, when the first day of classes came around, I was armed with reams of dittoed questionnaires, reading lists, and project study guides. During the first semester, my students did their English homework by watching shows like *Bonanza, Gilligan's Island,* and *U.N.C.L.E.* For reading material they had the literary prototypes for such popular TV entertainment—books like Wister's *The Virginian,* Lewis' *Babbitt,* and A. Conan Doyle's *The Adventures of Sherlock Holmes.* To guide their viewing and reading, I provided them with a list of cross-media analysis questions similar to those suggested in Postman's *Television and the Teaching of English.* The day following each assigned TV broadcast we sat together in a circle and discussed the transformation from book to TV production.

Of course, there were many who didn't read the books assigned, and some didn't even watch the TV shows (their parents didn't approve). But it didn't matter. In the course of a few minutes' discussion each week, we all learned much from each other about the dangers of generalization and the weakness of *clichés.* As a culminating activity, each student wrote a letter of criticism (saying whatever unobscene thing he wanted) to the producer of this favorite or most detested TV program. We papered one whole wall of our classroom with the forty-seven copies of a form letter we got back from ABC. I had been a cad and hadn't told them about that. But it was a valuable lesson in mass communication—one they never would have learned out of a textbook, I fear.

After the TV unit was over, we studied motion pictures. We read and discussed Clark's novel—*The Oxbow Incident*—again with a list of pertinent cross-media analysis questions as a guide. Then we saw the Wellman film adaptation of that novel and compared the two. As a culminating activity to this unit, I passed out fifty feet of 8mm black and white film to each student and suggested that the students make their own motion picture shorts—a project due during the last two weeks of school. I also gave them a reading list of books on film-making, like Spottiswoode's *A Grammar of the Film* (University of California Press, 1962). Since many of their families had

8mm motion picture cameras and the film cost less than $3.00 per pupil (including processing)—this did not seem to me an extravagant assignment for a group of students who were largely from the upper-middle-class.

During the first half of the second semester, we were somewhat more sophisticated. I gave my classes some lectures on the history of theater; we studied Sophocles' *Antigone, Everyman,* and Marlowe's *Dr. Faustus*—all of which, of course, we read together *in class only* while listening to recorded professional productions. At about that time, the motion picture version of *Billy Budd* was being shown on television. So most of us watched that. Then we read and discussed parts of Melville's novel (in the undigested form!) and wound up taping our own laboratory production of scenes from the Coxe and Chapman stage adaptation, *Billy Budd* (Hill and Wang, 1965).

Every Friday throughout the year—we had a formal debate, using the NFL topic and strictly adhering to all the NFL regulations. As every experienced teacher knows—Friday classes among adolescents can be deadly. But I can't recall one Friday last year when the feathers didn't fly in my classroom. We even had a member of the local chapter of the John Birch Society call the school and demand that I be fired (though perhaps my beard had something to do with that).

The student essays written for my final examination questions last year made very interesting reading. But most important of all, those last two weeks of school were a veritable pedagogue's dream. Three individuals and four different teams of students (out of a total number of sixty) screened original 8mm films—three of them with sound tracks. Of course they were amateurish, and in some cases really bad. But, in at least three cases, they were really good; in fact, one of the students was admitted to a special film study program given at the Horace Mann School in New York City last summer. And they all made up for their mistakes with a demonstration of cooperation, industry, enthusiasm, and imagination I have never before witnessed in student work anywhere.

But I had placed no limits on what my students could do during those last two weeks of school. So two of them wrote and performed original ballads for the guitar, one did an abstract oil painting in which my wife (herself a professional artist and teacher) saw great promise. There were dramatic readings, carefully prepared debates, models for stage sets, original poems, advertising displays—all sorts of "crazy" goings-on in my classroom during those last two weeks.

Oh yes—I almost forgot. My students also turned out four issues of a classroom newspaper during the course of the year—a little publication which set the whole school on its ear, initiating several important reforms in the school's student government. It was an exciting year, to say the least; and the administration was glad to see me go when it was over.

But we must have been doing something right, because last summer I got the following letter from one of my former students:

Dear Mr. Robinson,

I would like at this time to express my appreciation for all you have done for me and my classmates. Others may not say so, but many believe as I do. During the 1966–67 year . . . especially in English, I learned to think . . . [sic] for myself. You helped open up new horizons for me. . . . Knowing you, as others will attest, was an experience; and an experience many are not soon to forget. . . .

Sincerely,
Paul K——

Do I sound proud? Of course. And why not? After all—didn't we prove that Postman is right—that "language *is* a current event"? Who knows, maybe even Marshall McLuhan has something when he says "the medium is the message." So far as I can see, anyway, the only thing that made my students get my messages last year was the fact that, for the first time in their lives at school, they were involved in media.

But these are dangerous ideas, some will say. They are a threat to our Great Literary Heritage. They project a world in which the human consciousness is expanded to frightening dimensions, far beyond the understanding of our own historically defined experience. In short, some will say, they are alien to our culture and they must therefore be suppressed.

To such abjurations I can only answer by borrowing from my betters. And so I cite the words of a great contemporary thinker— a mathematician:

If we adhere to . . . tabus, we may acquire a great reputation as conservative and sound thinkers, but we shall contribute very little to the
further advance of knowledge. It is part of the scientist—of the intelligent
and honest man of letters and of the intelligent and honest clergyman
as well—to entertain heretical and forbidden opinions experimentally,
. . . (Norbert Wiener, *God & Golem, Inc.*, M. I. T. Press, 1966, p. 5).

TOWARD MEDIA
COMPETENCE

James J. Higgins

Perhaps the movement toward media based instruction is not a revolution, and perhaps its opponents are not inclined to issue such sweeping indictments. It sometimes seems, however, that the *mis*use of media is a calculated machination designed to discredit any but the pencil and paper approach. Educational television and its big brother, the instructional film, provide the most glaring examples, but this misappropriation often exhibits itself in the use of all the vehicles which have been parked under the banner, *educational media*.

Take a boring, 6′2″ math teacher, stuff him into a 24 square inch box and what do you get? Nothing more than electronically proliferated boredom, reduced to scale. This "shrink it and spread it approach" is somewhat like tacking wings and propellors on a space ship. Not that making a master teacher available to greater numbers of students is a poor objective, but it is valid to join Miss Lee in asking, "Is that all there is?"

Much of what is happening is directly traceable to a case of elliptical logic. Someone, somewhere along the line discovered that outside of school the kids are subject to seven trillion inputs (whatever that is) per month, while in school the kids receive less than half an input per year. Since kids are energetic out of school and lethargic in school, it was easy to conclude that increasing the in-

From *Media and Methods* (April, 1970), pp. 34–36, 40, 42, 43. Reprinted with permission of *Media and Methods* and James J. Higgins.

James J. Higgins, the author, is currently writer-researcher for Project Information Exchange for the Philadelphia School District. Rebecca Smith and Luther Randolph are teaching at the West Philadelphia Free School and working on a Doctorate in Black Studies at Howard University, respectively. James Morrow, the fourth member of the team, is enrolled in the MAT program at Harvard University.

The authors wish to thank Benjamin Turner, principal of Vaux Junior High School in Philadelphia, without whose support the project would not have been possible.

school input count to a zillion trillion would immediately electrify the kids. It is true that the kids were shocked. It used to be that the hallways belonged to them. These were the only places in the school where they could speak and be heard. Now they have to compete with the audio-visual aide who pushes his clinkety-clank projector cart from room to room during class change.

The film titles often tell the story, especially when they range from *Telephone Manners Matter*, to *How to Eat a Banana Without Peeling the Skin*, or the omnipresent, *This Is Your City*, winner of countless Academic Awards. No matter what city or town this film concerns itself with, it always has a hypnotic, dreamlike effect. After five minutes, even the most suspicious viewer begins to imagine he has drunk one too many holiday toasts and has zonked out on the model train platform, right under the fountain in the center of Plasticville's town square.

So what *can* the machines do to help? Can the machines teach? It is equally as absurd to ask if a teacher can teach, because neither teacher nor machine can do anything more than facilitate learning. Going back to prehistoric times, even before the coming of the Carousel projector, the role of the teacher was to stimulate the students, cause them to question, then help direct them as they searched for answers. Mass education has helped eliminate the first two steps and limited the third to providing a textbook page number. It is still the teacher's responsibility to find the most effective method of performing all of his services. If a multi-media approach is to be a part of this method; it must move in two directions. It must first become quality rather than quantity conscious. Secondly, it must help free the kids from their desk-prison and make it more possible for them to investigate their world.

As to the first, David A. Sohn, in the February, 1969 issue of *Media and Methods*, suggested a "Multi-Sensory Approach to Writing, Reading and Discussion." He was concerned in his article with only one medium, "sensitive, imaginative film art," but his method is applicable to all media since what he advocated was: (a) stimulating the kids with a powerful aesthetic experience, (b) allowing them to react dynamically, then, (c) helping them to respond creatively. This is an example of the movement away from the tendency to use films, filmstrips, slides, etc. only as information dispensers and as rewards. To be totally effective, however, this kind of approach must be joined with one that will allow the machines to facilitate a two-communication process.

Imagine if the telephone operated in such a way that only one-way communication was possible. In other words, the caller could speak but not be answered, and the receiver of the call could listen but not speak. Now imagine that, instead of being gradually exposed to it, growing as it grew, you were born into the world of instant information. From the day you were born you were inundated with sounds and images. How do you respond to your environment? Man prefers to respond in an eye for an eye kind of way. In the old days, a student would read a book and respond with a poem, story or essay. The pace of his world was slow, his response was slow. How does today's kid respond to his EasyRider-AgnewMansonLennonPeaceDraftWarWallaceCleaverJonesSupremes MyLaiPillCancer kind of world? He might speed up his responses with LSD or slow the world down with marijuana, but he won't look for help in school. He could. And he should be able to. But the surest way to choke off a kid's interest in the learning to respond process, is to bind his hands and feet, imprison him in a desk and tell him to keep his ears open while all the information he will need for the rest of his life is funnelled into his brain, very slowly. When print was an only child it was sufficient for the schools to prepare kids to respond by teaching print literacy skills, but it is time someone tells educators that the stork has paid numerous calls on the communications family. Kids today require new kinds of literacy. They need to learn the how behind the howl.

Does this mean the schools should relax in their effort to teach reading and writing? Not at all. In fact, by expanding teaching approaches to include many media, the teaching of these skills could be made easier. Students must see reading and writing as tools, not products. In a multi-media situation they can be made aware of this reality since these skills are *used* to write a radio play, a TV commercial, or a script for a slide-tape or film. This is language in use rather than language usage.

1. 600 students; up to 35 students per class
2. Three teachers and one student-teacher
3. Up to six periods per week—one period four days with one double period

4. 22 Instamatics
5. 2 Super-8 movie cameras
6. 8 portable cassette tape recorders
7. 1 stereo tape recorder

The above broth, concocted at Philadelphia's Vaux Jr. High School, went by the name of "Communications." The teachers sought to discover if in-class multi-media learning could be implemented under conditions which face all teachers in overcrowded schools. They classify their program as a tremendous success, but readily admit to moments of horrendous failure. They did not discover a panacea for all of education's ills, but they did learn some things which might be helpful to others who are experimenting with multi-media learning processes.

First off, the structure of the classroom had to be changed. It had to be possible for the students to move at their own chosen speed, and the large group structure inhibited this. Each class, consequently, was divided into sub-groups of four. This small group structure also made it easier for the teachers to individualize their instruction but they had to abdicate their position as dictatorial dispensers of information and assume instead the role of guide.

The initial activity aimed at getting the kids involved in mediating information in some way other than with the mouth—which they knew how to use—or the pen—which they were often afraid of or confused by. It was important to help them discover the inter-relatedness of the media at their disposal. Each team was told to pick a topic about which they knew something that they could communicate to others. They were given a series of steps to complete in preparation for their first experience with a multi-media project.

1. Decide what topic your team will investigate.
2. Write a list of at least 25 ideas, opinions or facts about the topic.
3. Compare fact sheets. Make a master copy listing the 20 best ideas.
4. Make a list of pictures, describing one picture which you think best explains each of your twenty statements.
5. Write an original poem, play, short story or song which in some way deals with the topic you have chosen.

The students were given absolute freedom in their choice of topic they wished to explore, but since each group was allowed only one topic, arriving at a consensus provided them with insights into the machinations of back room decision-making. A lot of important deals were swung. One girl, obviously tuned in to the fine points of compromise, traded her vote for a date to a Halloween party. The final choices covered a wide range of subjects, from Fashions, to Sports to Gangs to Race. Not one group picked sound distortion as their topic, which was surprising given the sound level in the room.

It was not unusual on a given day to have one group in a corner rehearsing the fight scene in its play about gangs, and another group role-playing fashion models. The teacher rotated from group to group helping the students clarify their direction by keeping the topics in focus.

The photograph and taping followed the written work. The ideas were taped first. Each member of the group was given the responsibility for getting five of the twenty pictures. These were later matched to produce a rudimentary slide-tape. The poems, plays, short stories and songs were recorded as the group performed or read them to others in the class. If it was a play, stills were taken during the performance and later synchronized with the tape. For a poem, story, or song, visuals which matched the meaning or feeling had to be created and photographed.

Each group had a folder into which all completed written work was to be placed. No member of the group was permitted the use of any equipment until each member of the group had completed his assignments. This requirement produced some interesting side-effects. There was a tremendous amount of peer pressure, relieving the teacher of the responsibility of establishing and enforcing a deadline. It wasn't even necessary to impose time limits. In most groups a spirit of teamwork developed. Students who were embarrassed about spelling or other reading or writing skills were helped by the more literate members of the group with little of the usual teasing or scoffing. And, not least important, the students were able to get a preliminary evaluation of their work before handing it over to the teacher. These peer evaluations were usually more direct, yet less threatening, than those of the teacher. The most serious problem was the need to maximize the availability of the limited amount of useable hardware.

EQUIPMENT

Each of the three teachers carried a full roster, which meant that over six hundred students were taking the Communications Course. The maximum equipment supply consisted of 22 Instamatic cameras, two Super-8 cameras, eight portable tape recorders and one stereo tape recorder. The diverse kinds of learning situations created by the teachers for their courses presented other problems. Some assignments required the students to do after-school photography or taping. Other assignments required the availability of equipment during school time. The solution was the introduction of a lending library. Students who had completed their assignments could come after school, present their work and sign out a camera or tape recorder. They were expected to return the equipment before class on the next school day. It is interesting to note that this lending service was set up in a school where most textbooks were not permitted to leave the building. It is safe to say that the kids were surprised to be trusted with this equipment, but they reacted in exactly the way you would expect kids to react: not one piece of equipment was damaged and, through the whole year, only one camera was lost. Perhaps the medium *is* the message.

MOBILIZATION

Some assignments made it necessary for entire classes of students to leave their classrooms, or even the building. Therefore, in fifty minutes, hall passes (!) had to be issued, equipment had to be distributed, the students had to complete their assignments and the equipment had to be collected again.

One class got involved in the concept of the relationship between the school and the community. What was the attitude of the community toward community control. Did the parents think their kids were getting a good education? Were schools in other neighborhoods getting preferred treatment? The kids wanted to find out. They decided to produce a slide-tape that would present a survey of community attitudes.

Planning this project was like looking down a seemingless endless row of hurdles. The kids jumped at the chance to leave the building during school hours, but the logistical problems involved in making it possible were not so easily cleared. Since they would be leaving and re-entering the building and moving through the community without direct teacher supervision, preparations had to be made to insure against possible detention by teachers on Highway Patrol or, on the outside, the real police. The community had to be informed so its support could be enlisted. Equipment would have to be issued and then collected again. And, most importantly, a reasonable amount of time for the actual work—interviewing, taping and photographing—had to be assured. Fortunately, the Great Roster Maker in the Sky had assigned this particular class six periods of Communications—one period four days with a back-to-back double period on Wednesday afternoon. The double period automatically became production day.

The first task was to inform the community and enlist its support. Each student wrote a "Dear Neighbor" letter explaining the project. The letters were read to the class and a composite of the best sections of several letters was drawn up. This process, incidentally, included instructions in formal letter writing taken directly from the standard ninth grade text. These moments of "traditional" language arts instruction were not opposed by the kids. In fact, they welcomed them since they wanted a document that would represent them to the community to be correct in every way. At the bottom of the letter, below the complimentary close and signature, spaces for the reader's response were provided. They were asked to give their name and address and to indicate whether or not they would consent to an interview on a particular date at a certain time.

The letter was approved by the students and then duplicated. It was time to face the reality of freeing the kids from the building and getting them into the homes. The class was again divided into eight small groups. As a preliminary measure, each group selected a block near the school to be canvassed by its members. They would go door to door presenting their letter and waiting for a response. A document that would serve as both a hall pass (!!) inside the school and identification card outside the school had to be provided. For the teachers to write a pass for each student would have been too time consuming. A mimeo form wouldn't serve the needs since the students' names would have to be entered anyway. Each group, instead, was given a 3 x 5 index card when they entered the room. They were instructed to copy the following information, in the same format, onto the card:

Group #_____ Community Action Project Vaux Jr. H.S.
Date_____
Time_____
Student's Names:

Space remained at the bottom of the card for the name stamp of the Principal, who, indispensably, not only supported but encouraged the project. This canvassing operation usually took place on Monday, during a single fifty minute class period. Ten minutes were allotted for preparations, thirty for the actual work, and ten for re-grouping and getting back into the building. The teacher collected the filled-in appointment slips and saved them for Wednesday, making sure each group had at least one appointment. Tuesday's class time was spent practicing interviewing techniques, reviewing photos, or listening to and analyzing the prior week's tapes.

Wednesday, production day, required careful planning. The equipment was brought in and arranged before the class came to the room. One tape recorder, a reel of tape, a take-up reel, a camera, a cartridge of film and sufficient flash cubes were set aside for each group. The class filed in, formed groups and filled out 3 x 5 cards. When the card was completed, the captain of each group had it signed, picked up his appointment slips signed out equipment and led his group from the building.

The teachers had learned from an earlier project that matching a box of slides to one of six hundred kids could present problems. The kids were instructed, therefore, to put their section and group number on the cartridge *before* loading the camera. The reel of tape was marked, too, with a strip of masking tape containing the same information. It was possible to re-use the same five-inch reels of tape week after week by transferring each Wednesday's result onto both sides of seven inch reels.

MOVIE PRODUCTIONS

Scope magazine originally published Daniel Keyes' short story, *Flowers for Algernon*. It was later expanded to a full-novel, and later adapted into the movie, *Charly*. *Scope* also contained a comparative analysis of the story and the film. The kids read the story and the analysis and many questions arose as to the mechanics of each medium. It was a good way to analyze the tools and methods of the creative writer. By extension, if the kids themselves could be involved in the process of moving from print to film, what was learned in discussing the two forms of Keyes' story could be reinforced and enhanced.

Each student wrote a short story. All of the stories were read, either by the author or by the teacher, to the entire class. One story was selected to be the source of the first production of the *9–16 Soul Communicators, Inc.*, a quickly organized motion picture studio. From the teachers' point of view, the major problem in such an endeavor was to see that each child was involved in some way most of the time. Everyone had seen the "brightspots" of an English class read a play for the benefit of the lessers who were confined to their desks.

The first step was to script the film. The story was read to the class once more, this time with particular attention to the possibility of transferring each section to film. It became clear that certain parts of the story— e.g. a section involving a trip to Europe would have to be altered. A technique called the *flashback* was invented by one of the students to fit the need for communicating the murderer's motive to the audience. The script, as it developed, was written on the chalkboard by the teacher and copied by the students.

When the script was completed, each student was assigned a job. Those with artistic talents worked on making the sets, which included the interiors of one kitchen, two living rooms and one art museum (changed from a super market because of the availability of pictures and paintings). Those who could print made the credits and scene change indicators— e.g., "Earlier That Day." Props were gathered, serviced and stored. The author was director. There were sound men and cameramen and a light crew. There were actors and actresses, too.

The rear of the room, with desks cleared away, was the actual "set." Those who were not actors stood around the perimeter during actual production. The actors rehearsed each scene for the benefit of the camera- man and light men, who were using twin beams on a hand bar. When the Director yelled "Quiet on the Set," that's what happened. "Lights, Camera, Action!" The *esprit de corps* developed during this production was fantastic. Scenes well played were applauded. Good camera move- ment was noticed. The cooperation of the spectators was something all involved were most often proud of.

The most difficult task was synchronizing the sound track with the film. The "sound unit" was a portable, single-track tape recorder. No one was completely satisfied with the results of the hand synching but it worked and it pleased people. The film was shown to other classes, assemblies, community groups and educators. The *9–16 Soul Communicators, Inc.* was a success. And the kids knew it.

A lot of things that could be called learning occurred as a result of this project. The people of the community learned that a school can be interested in and responsive to their needs. They also learned that their kids are concerned and alert and interested in learning. The teachers discovered that most of the parents already knew this, but they also learned that the kids were even *more* responsive when given an opportunity to deal with matters that are pertinent to them.

The kids learned, too. They gained a new perspective on them- selves. Changes in their self-image and self-confidence can be de- tected from even a cursory review of the tapes. But things of a more strictly academic nature were learned as well. There were for example discussions about the 1954 Supreme Court ruling on segregated schools, the structure of the city government, the role of the police in the community, and what level of education is required for certain types of employment. There were examples of vocabulary development and changes in things like sentence structure, word order and subject-verb agreement.

STUDENT: Do you think your son would hurt anybody?
PARENT: I don't think so. Not unless he was provoked into it.
STUDENT: Provoked?
PARENT: You know, stirred up. Annoyed.

❋   ❋   ❋   ❋   ❋

STUDENT: What do you think about the racial problem in the United States?
PARENT: Well, so much has happened in the last ten years, I think it's time to take inventory.
STUDENT: (No response)
PARENT: Inventory. Like a guy who owns a store has to count the stock he has on his shelves so he knows what he needs.

❋   ❋   ❋   ❋   ❋

Changes were evident in things like sentence structure, word order, and subject-verb agreement. For example:

STUDENT: Was your kids students at Vaux?
PARENT: Were my kids students at Vaux? Both of my boys went to Vaux. Later interview, same student: Was your kids . . . I mean, were your kids students at Vaux?

But perhaps the most important thing learned was the potency of trust as a medium. Students, parents, teachers, and administrators discovered the satisfaction inherent in working together toward the same, meaningful end.

Ever since Eve taught Adam about her apple, man has been hungry for learning. Schools should be a veritable banquet for kids, and the table set with all the proper utensils.

STUDENT FILMMAKING
WHY & HOW

Paul Carrico

When most people think of movie making, a dense image fallout bombards their minds: the big Hollywood feature, underground movies, news footage on TV, home movies. They rarely think of filmmaking as a part of the ordinary academic experience of thousands of students, and if they did, their response might be "So what?" or "Why?" But regardless of anyone's reaction, students assisted by sensitive teachers have discovered filmmaking as a whole new way of seeing and of telling about the world around them. Dozens of student film festivals regularly draw dozens to hundreds of youthful filmmakers, their films, and their teachers. A lot of excitement and mutual critical respect is generated by these meetings. Beyond the incandescent enthusiasm and the long sessions of looking at badly exposed and fuzzily-focused images to find significant scenes or films, thoughtful educators are asking each other what it all means.

With the exception of a few schools, filmmaking is the newest baby in the media-in-education family. Like any new baby it is fawned over by some, not taken seriously by others, and the object of intense jealousy by a few. But the questions about its purpose and its parentage come and must be dealt with if progressive teachers are to avoid administrated infanticide or filmic birth control. A cynical question: "Since local TV stations have shown an interest, is filmmaking simply a device to rescue a few teachers and students from the gray world of the classroom to the grayed world of comercial TV?" A serious question: "Is it a glory-road cop-out for teachers who have failed to come up with a viable consumer rather than a creator-oriented film study program?" (After all, film

From *Media and Methods* (November, 1969), pp. 41–45, 72–74. Reprinted with permission of *Media and Methods* and Paul Carrico.

Paul Carrico, presently a doctoral candidate in Cinema Studies at New York University, was involved in filmmaking at Notre Dame High School, Niles, Illinois, for five years and has written extensively on the subject.

study is more difficult and more valid than film production!) Two
pragmatic questions: "Doesn't it take valuable study time away from
the 'hard' (and therefore important) subjects that students must
take? Where will all the money come from?" A silly question and the
one I encountered at Notre Dame High School: "What about all
those kids who 'sneak back' into school to edit their films; after all,
they're spending entirely too much time in the building!" My own
reaction was that if schools are to have problems, this is the kind
of problem they should have.

These questions remain; new ones will be invented. The best
answer to them is to be found in the films themselves and in what
happens in the students who make them. Heightened awareness
expressed in a creative act transcends nit-picking and even serious
questions. What follows here may serve as an answer or a least an
approach to answers to some admittedly valid questions as well as
a guide to getting started.

Even with a scant five years of production experience behind me
(I am therefore a "pioneer"), I have often wondered why making
films has not always been a normal part of the student experience
instead of a marginal activity for a few. Hardware problems, the
usual scapegoat, have never been a real no-no. Unfortunately, however, education is a conservative institution, and only recently has
the establishment been able to recover from the abortive attempts
at film education based on moral indignation in the forties and
recognize and treat intelligently the film as an artful and occasionally
artistic form of communication. The best student films I have seen
have grown out of imaginatively conceived and well-executed film
study programs. A friend once noted, "If you teach people to read,
some of them will want to write." Teach students to "read" films and
the same fortuitous problem will appear. Thus, lack of imaginative
film study programs has dampened activity in filmmaking.

At first the desire to make films is amorphous and young film-
makers conceive their first efforts on the scale of something as grand
and daring as the sequel to *The Ten Commandments*. But with
well-sequenced exposure to the short film form, they find there the
proper idiom for expressing their view of the world. Occasionally
well-made student films are produced in relative cinematic isolation
since some teachers are fearful that too much exposure to the work
of others can be too formative and a hindrance to the purity of the

individual's expression. No matter. Under the guidance of a competent teacher, either the saturation or the starvation philosophy can be successful, depending on the visual sophistication and motivation of both student and teacher.

ROLE OF THE TEACHER

The film teacher is nearly always a producer-critic, not a creator. The average teacher (even the average film teacher) has had his once glimpsed creativity either educated or "production-lined" out of his system and is "dead at the top." Despite tutorial fantasies, filmmaking is an area in which most students are clearly superior to their print-oriented teacher. Such superiority in a creative venture does not eliminate the teacher but it does modify his role.

A teacher-producer knows the creative process but rarely participates in it. His job is to assemble people and materials and to assure the proper atmosphere for creative people to work. The critic assesses the final product. Students rarely need their teacher for this role, since by the time they finish the film, it has been screened so often that they know exactly what is wrong with it. But students are not arrogant and often appreciate someone's telling them what is right with their work.

I have long been convinced that creativity and criticism are separate functions; at the end of the second semester I used to take a band of young filmmakers and their films around to other schools, PTA's, or to any group who would consent to be an audience. Such exposure provided the response and the feedback that every incipient artist needs and took care of the critical function experientially.

Creativity cannot be taught but only given a chance to grow and to be channelled. The most perenially successful film teachers try to avoid "inspiration" as such and set up as neutral a creative situation as possible. Active inspiration is "hot" and puts the teacher's trademark on student work. Unless the appeal comes from the medium itself and the student's own need for self-expression, then his movie is not worth doing in the first place and becomes the same sterile exercise as the traditional term paper or as teacher-stamped as a yearbook. The "cool" film teacher perceives himself primarily as an adult advisor, hardware expert, or the one who makes film stock, camera, editing equipment and production facilities available and leaves the student censor-free to deal with reality around him as best he can.

Freedom from censorship implies that students should also solve their own creative problems such as scripting, sound selection, movement, and pacing with the teacher refraining from any but technical advice. Students have the right to make their own mistakes. A sign of success in this "hands off" pedagogical method is not only the quality of the production (sometimes rough but really honest) but especially the fact that the name of the teacher is almost always omitted from the screen credits, so much do the students see the film as completely their own.

A few teachers, notably David McKendall, formerly at New Trier High School in Wilmette, Illinois, have employed the "apprentice" method, whereby the teacher controls every aspect of a film that is primarily his own. Students assist the teacher in the production and experience all the skills, thrills and frustrations of having participated in a well-made film. Such an approach tends to be craft-oriented but the rare creative teacher who employs it can usually deter students from a preoccupation with hardware, a problem that becomes acute in the case of some industry technicians. Such a technique is used more usually with small highly-selected classes devoted almost exclusively to production.

Other teachers see themselves in the role of carefully guiding the student step by step through the maze of mechanical skills involved in successful filmmaking before permitting the student to express himself fully on film. This approach is very much like teaching grammar as a way of helping a student learn to write. Exercises in the use of the camera—the ability to choose the right lenses for a particular shooting situation, panning correctly, tracking, handholding a camera, photographing for texture and effect—are carefully outlined for the student. Often professional filmmakers are employed to criticize each student attempt. Other aspects of filmmaking are just as carefully organized and orchestrated to teach basic skills. The most highly-publicized program of this type is a federally-financed experiment in Demarest, New Jersey, run by teacher, Rodney Sheratsky.

A variation was used by the author at Notre Dame High School in Niles, Illinois. In an elective course for students who completed at least a semester in film criticism, young filmmakers were required to submit four projects. The first was a film made without a camera —abstract figures drawn on raw 16mm film stock with magic markers or aniline dyes. The second was a student-conceived exercise in animation using solid objects such as toys, balls, clay, etc., paper and string, or line drawings. The third was the automatic discipline of a mini-film (a film exactly one minute long) or a commercial, a form that students know well. The fourth project was a film which constituted a major work of the semester; here there were no restrictions whatever. This method put the emphasis on the medium as a self-disciplining form rather than on the teacher as guide. Students quickly discovered the limitations of the medium and of themselves; rarely do they need a businessman-producer, a censor, or a teacher to tell them what they cannot do.

Other teachers such as Bob Johnson at Sir Francis Drake High School, San Anselmo, California, and David Coynik at Notre Dame High School, Niles, Illinois, use a completely free-wheeling approach, adopting whatever method is suitable to the students they have. Both are competent filmmakers in their own right and know how to respect the independence of their students.

More important than the attitude that a film teacher takes toward the young filmmaker, is the attitude of the school officials and the other teachers. Outside of extracurricular activities such as sports, the school play, or an engaging music program, students rarely are involved in any experiential way in academic life. Filmmakers— especially during the editing phase—often forget to call parents, to eat, or to be overly concerned about the next morning's algebra assignment. The more creative students tend to be mercurial and forget the school structure. Ideal weather conditions sometimes lure them from the school corridor to the street, camera in hand. Authoritarian schools find such activity intolerable and respond in a repressive way; modern schools are more flexible regarding individual differences.

Worse than repression is the penchant of some administrators to exploit students (and their film teacher) to make "useful" promotional films for the school. Such films turn out to be dry, stilted, and "talky" since the subject matter is not suited to the film medium. The only exception I have seen to this is a film made by David Coynik's students, entitled *A Thousand Days*. The students were subsidized by Notre Dame High School but left free to choose "cinematic" material and to "tell it like it was." *A Thousand Days* is one of the most honest (and best) promotional films I have ever seen because it tries hard to be truthful rather than to impress.

A film can successfully be made by a class. Sister Bede Sullivan formerly at Lillis High School in Kansas City, Missouri, divided a class into teams in order to make a long film about student leisure. But for a school administration to use a film class as a self-conscious adjunct to its public relations program is downright unfair. Film production succeeds best when it is used as a free authentic vehicle of student expression.

Finally, administrators and academic counsellors who demand measurable results find the classroom film experience impossible to understand. But some of their questions are valid. Does film override or replace traditionally accepted forms of student expression? Is there a carryover of enthusiasm when a student is confronted with more pedestrian but necessary academic courses. Do ACT or CEEB test results improve? Unfortunately the only guide to answering these questions at present is human judgement.

In school where filmmaking is a potential part of every student's experience, teachers not a proliferation, almost an explosion, in other forms of expression, especially poetry. Such a release of energy comes with discovery. Through filmmaking many students come to terms with their own vast viewing experience. Such personal "structuring" frees them from the amorphous, and hence poisonous effect of previous media intake and releases fantastic psychic energy.

There is as yet no empirical way to measure carryover but often students find information-centered classes boring after a bout with film. Modern educators agree that no course need ever be one in which "the tedium is the message." "Turned-on" students demand more of teachers; any teacher who can respond need never fear the stimulating effect of a filmmaking or film criticism course. Indeed, at many schools, teachers in sociology and religion classes are accepting the "term film" along with the traditional term paper.

Testing programs, extrinsic to the school, have not caught up to the film student as yet; tests would be geared to subject matter deemed academically respectable by college entrance committees. To date no one has suggested that students excited about learning score lower on "objective," corporation-administered tests.

THE CONTENT AND FORM
OF STUDENT FILMS

Generalizations cannot be photographed and unlike research term papers, student films are made out of bits of the filmmaker's own world. In inner-city schools the films tend to be about people, interacting with other people. Affluent students make more abstract films replete with alienation and protest. Although student films make general statements about human relationships, violence, or the hypocrisy of organized religion, such statements are formed out of the stuff of the photographable real world. Still shots lifted from magazines and images from TV are often incorporated into environmental and action shots to render an experience or to make a statement.

The films are rarely humorous. Heavy-handed contrast editing (a plush suburban church juxtaposed with a mangy dog in a ghetto street) suggest the blatant irony of many student films. Many are lyrical and impressionistic, evoking experiences rather than narrating them. Most narrative films demand action-matching the shots in a scene, a form of editing students find technically too sophisticated. Financial considerations demand that the films be limited to ten or fifteen minutes; a student film longer than thirty minutes is rare. Screen humor, especially purely visual humor, requires sophistication, split-second timing, and a certain emotional distance; hence it is not too surprising to find such humor almost totally absent from student films. Besides, the world they see is painfully close to Benjamin's in *The Graduate*: full of adult phoniness at home, war abroad, and ready for revolution everywhere. Student preoccupation with alienation, death, authenticity and sober involvement may shock demure adults, but to an educator such concerns are quite understandable.

THE EQUIPMENT OF FILM PRODUCTION

FILM STOCK

The cost, size, and often the quality of film equipment is determined by film stock width, measured in millimeters. 16mm stock, especially since the rise of silver prices in March 1968, has made production in this format almost prohibitively expensive for the average school. A typical price for a hundred foot role of black-and-white 16mm film including processing is about $8.00. At "sound" speed (twenty-four frames per second) a hundred feet will last about 3.2 minutes. Good color film stock with processing varies from $12.00 to $14.00 a roll.

So it comes as no surprise that students usually stay away from 16mm film and favor much less expensive 8mm or super 8mm film stock. Black-and-white film in these sizes is hard to come by since the market demand has traditionally been for color, but most professional film laboratories stock it. Unlike the price differential in 16mm film stocks, the price of color film is very close to that of black-and-white. A typical price for fifty feet of ordinary 8mm film with processing is $3.25; $3.75 for a super 8mm cartridge of film. At "silent" speed (sixteen or eighteen frames per second) fifty feet is equivalent to 4 or 4.5 minutes of screen time. These prices can represent quite a saving over 16mm film. Often stock can be bought more cheaply than the above mentioned prices, but let the buyer beware! Sometimes bargain film is full of splices, is flawed, or overage. Our intention here is not to discuss the wide variety of film stocks available. Any reputable laboratory, camera store, or film manufacturer can supply all the technical information necessary.

The advantage of 16mm is the extremely sharp projected image. The stronger light source in 16mm projectors also permits the film to be projected under marginal blackout conditions which would "wash out" anything in 8mm. The individual frame size is also 400% larger than standard 8mm (twice as high and twice as wide). Editing is therefore easier and it is possible to recognize each frame without running it through a viewer magnifier each time, a necessity with smaller size film. The difference between standard 8mm and super 8mm film stock is not in the width of the film but in the size and spacing of the sprocket holes, which permits an image fifty-six percent larger than the one on 8mm film. Under similar conditions, super 8 will project a larger, less grainy picture.

The advantage of super 8 over ordinary 8mm is not only in the projected image but in the ease involved in the shooting process. Almost all super 8 film is packaged in cartridges and easily inserted in the camera, thus eliminating the need to thread the film through the camera shuttle and attach it to another reel. As soon as the film is inserted, the ASA speed of the film (a chemical speed that indicates the film's sensitivity to light) is automatically locked in with the photoelectrical mechanism in "electric eye" cameras. These features make the average super 8 camera virtually foolproof to operate.

The disadvantages are not so obvious since the industry rarely mentions them. American-made film cartridges, as pioneered by Kodak, allow the film to run in one direction only, a feature which eliminates the possibility of "in camera" addition of lap-dissolves and superimpositions, a procedure possible in many reel-to-reel cameras. Reel-to-reel super 8 cameras are made by only a few companies and are generally very expensive. Some foreign-made cartridges, particularly the Fujica, permit the film to be reversed but must be used only with the Fujica system and not in cameras designed for the American-style cartridge. While the American-style cartridge is not a disadvantage to the occasional camera user, it can be inhibiting for a student who needs dissolves or superimpositions in his movie.

Overall considerations dictate the super 8 route for most film classes. Standard 8mm is becoming obsolete but if the production and editing equipment is available at a really low price it should not be rejected. Super 8 is here to stay, is easy for even the slowest student to use, and more economical than 16mm. As manufacturers become more sensitive to the student market, improvements will be made in equipment and lab services. Local film labs are becoming somewhat responsive to the needs of the student filmmaker, and in general it is safer to do business with a competent local lab rather than an unknown processor in another part of the country.

SHOOTING EQUIPMENT

The basic hardware of filmmaking is divided into two categories: shooting (or production), and editing. Besides properly chosen film stock, a camera, lights, tripod, and a meter for measuring light intensity are basic tools for a filmmaker to get images on the film.

Cameras in every style and price range superabound. Some teachers whose schools make cameras available to students prefer having a lot of low-priced cameras to one or two expensive models. While it is true that great instruments by themselves do not make great artists, a better grade of camera can enhance young talent. Desirable qualities for any camera are: *simplicity*, *durability*, and *versatility*. Cameras in a school will receive rough usage, so delicate knobs and fragile bodies are not generally "student proof." Simplicity of operation is necessary, especially for a student with a viable idea for a movie but hampered by a "hardware hangup." This seems to be especially true of female filmmakers, though not limited exclusively to them. A camera should be versatile enough to allow the advanced student to do virtually anything his imagination might suggest. Ease of maintenance is also an important consideration.

Valuable features include (1) a zoom lens, (2) a variety of speed changes (frames per second) (3) a photo-electrically operated iris or diaphragm, (4) a stop frame mechanism for animation, and (5) reflex viewing.

A *zoom lens* is a lens with a variable focal length, which in effect means that the viewing angle can be changed. If one looks through a piece of water pipe only one inch long, he can see a lot of world, but the same pipe eight inches long will narrow his view of the same world. A zoom lens has the same effect but is in addition variable over its given range. At its narrowest angle or "zoom in" position, the lens also tends to compress distance; at its widest angle or "pull back" position it tends to expand distance. At the 25mm (one inch) stop the lens will "see" subjects in relation to each other pretty much as the eye sees them.

The zoom lens has a bad reputation because of its abuse by home movie makers. The world is a mighty disappointing place as seen through the viewfinder and the amateur filmmaker tries to compensate by excessive panning and zooming. The effect on a viewer is irritating and cinematic seasickness. If students can learn to use the infinite framing capabilities of a zoom lens and to choose details with discrimination, it will prove a valuable tool and eliminate numerous camera setups.

Slow motion and *accelerated motion*, too often used as gimmicks, should be available to a filmmaker. Professional cameras have a great range of speeds from just a few frames-per-second to sometimes several thousand. For students, a range close to the camera's normal speed is usually adequate. Closely related to this feature is the ability to expose one frame at a time, essential for animation.

The *photo-electrically operated iris* which controls the amount of light that reaches the sensitive film is useful where light conditions are even. But because the photo-electric cell "reads" the most intense or "hottest" light available, a device for overriding the photo-electric cell for marginal or special lighting conditions is desirable. In such an instance a light meter, either the one built into the camera or one specially designed for the purpose can be used. Good photography is the art of painting with light and a little care here can save the frustration of over-exposed or under-exposed footage. Light meters are inexpensive and easy to learn how to read, a sometimes necessary tool for any filmmaker.

When selecting an "electric eye" camera, the buyer should make sure it has the capability of accepting many different sensitivities as measured by ASA speeds. The cheaper cameras have a much more limited range. ASA speeds should range from 40 for Kodachrome II to at least 160 for Tri-X Reversal. New films coming out (Four-X, for example) will demand even wider ranges.

These films will allow students to shoot scenes at night, in subways, and in other areas where heretofore there just was not enough light to get an exposure.

Interior lighting is the most serious flaw common to almost all student-made films. Camera mounted lights are rarely of any value, yet these are the ones—called "sun guns" or light bars—most often supplied or recommended by manufacturers. Most student "sets" can adequately be lighted with three well-placed and inexpensive photoflood lamps. Some schools find it within their budget to purchase a kit of Quartz-iodine combination flood-spotlights. Advice on lighting setups and the proper choice of bulbs of the correct color temperature (measured in degrees Kelvin) is available from film manufacturers, cinema labs, or local professionals. Adequate lighting can be learned by anyone in a relatively short time and is as important to a good production as rhetoric is to a good theme paper.

Reflex viewing means that the camera operator sees through the camera lens itself instead of a optical system parallel to it. The photographer literally sees what the camera sees. This feature is especially valuable on close work such as titles where faulty framing is extremely annoying. Reflex viewing automatically eliminates the problem of faulty framing as well as the problems of fuzzy focus or a finger in front of the lens. The operator is enabled to positively select focus between subjects in the foreground or background. Some directors today use a shift of focus as an effective substitution for cutting.

Few people can hold a camera steady while shooting, especially if the bulk of the weight is behind the camera grip. Unsteadiness or jiggling is particularly noticeable to a viewer on long shots. Professional cameramen as a rule use a tripod whenever possible. A tripod should be chosen which is sturdy and designed specifically for a movie camera. Tripods for still cameras are generally too flimsy and do not allow the operator to pan smoothly. The camera must be held rigid when shooting animation; there is no substitution for a tripod here.

EDITING EQUIPMENT

To anyone conversant with the film medium, it is all too obvious that editing is the most important aspect of filmmaking. On the editing table discrete scraps of film are transformed into statement; it is the part of filmmaking students find most rewarding. The necessary pieces of equipment include at least one projector, pairs of rewinds, a viewer-magnifier, and a splicing block with film cement or splicing tape. Alternate equipment might include extra takeup reels and a synchronizer complete with a pair of long-shaft rewinds (16mm only).

A projector is listed as a piece of editing equipment because every filmmaker makes his final decisions whether to cut or not to cut on the basis of how the film will look on the screen. For some filmmakers the process of editing is endless and they will nibble away at their creations long after the films are in release. This is especially true of students who change their films almost every time it is screened for a live audience. The editing projector should be one that the student loads and threads manually. Automatic or "self-threaders" and splices rarely mix. A "freeze" or "stop" frame mechanism and when possible a manually operated film advance clutch is useful for analyzing individual frames and necessary for accurate timing and sound synchronizing. . . .

Rewinds are simple crank-operated mechanisms for transferring film from one reel to another. Motor-driven rewinding is possible on almost every projector but a separate pair mounted on the editing table or on either end of a wide board is a necessity. Between a pair of rewinds most of the actual cutting is done. A viewer-magnifier through which the film can be pulled by the rewinds is necessary, especially during the initial stages when the pieces of film are seen for the first time. Some manufacturers incorporate a pair of rewinds into the viewer mechanism itself but these tend to be fragile and unable to withstand constant use. Professional editing equipment, designed for day-after-day usage, is definitely preferable for a school.

The splicing block should, when possible, be mounted between the rewinds for easy access and for the protection of the block. Blocks employing either liquid cement or mylar splicing tape are available. Students find tape easier to use with standard 8mm or super 8mm. Applied with care it provides an adequate bond. The block should feature a straight cut parallel to the frame line of the film instead of a curved cut popular on some home movie units.

Synchronizers and their associated long-shaft rewinds are for use only with 16mm film at the present time. Using this equipment means that the student can on the editing table add fades, dissolves and superimpositions to his film, but the equipment is relatively sophisticated for young filmmakers.

After the film has been cut into pieces, it should be labelled and stored safely while editing proceeds. The preferred way is to hang the film by one end on a "clothesline" or on a light rack built over a bin or a drum lined with a plastic bag. The soft lining along with careful handling prevents scratching. Egg crates can also be used to store the tiny rolls of film where preferred storage is not available.

After the film is edited, it can be returned to the lab for splice-free printing. If a print is not planned the film should be inspected for faulty splices and cleaned with a linen cloth moistened with film cleaner before projection. In most student productions, the many steps in the film assembly process are omitted for economic reasons and the original footage becomes the work print, the answer print and the release print.

The most important service a school can provide the student is free and easy access to equipment, especially editing material. It is difficult for anyone to create "on cue," and school structure should not for a film class become stricture.

SOUND EQUIPMENT

An apparent deprivation, the technical inability to tightly syn-
chronize sound and picture, becomes a negative but important
advantage for both teacher and student. Even with the most
sophisticated equipment, adding sound is tedious. Sound, too, is so
fascinating for young filmmakers that their creations might well
become a series of highly verbal set pieces accompanied by pictures
"in synch." At present, there are on the market several camera-tape
recorder combinations which can be electronically locked together
during shooting. On the surface these combinations look like an
instant solution to the sound hangup but they present problems in
editing. The freedom to edit film is basic to filmmaking and a
freedom that a filmmaker should never relinquish. Any salesman
should be required to demonstrate the advertised ease of editing.
Of the two systems for interlocking—optical or magnetic—magnetic
is presently preferable. The optical system now in distribution requires eleven separate meticulous steps to remove a scene. The
magnetic system is also complicated but simpler and more flexible
than the optical system.

Separate recording units can be used, but non-professional tape
recorders and projectors rarely "track" at the same speed every time,
thus making simultaneous sound difficult to achieve. Sound such as
music or voice-over narration is then used to underline or reinforce
the visuals. During the screening the projector speed can usually be
manipulated to slow down or speed up the film to permit closer
synch. However, the lack of any easy way to add simultaneous sound
in student films puts emphasis on the proper aspect of filmmaking,
the *visual*.

An encouraging new development is a new line of super 8 projectors which permits recording directly on a magnetic strip chem-
ically bonded to the edge of the film. This feature has long been
available in 16mm but the excessive cost of the projectors and
mediocre sales promotion has kept these units out of the average
schools. While this system is not always suitable for the tight "lip
synch" sound of the speaking face it does assure exact "as recorded"
synch during projection-playback. When audio-visual budgets are
drawn up it is advisable to order one projector that can record the

sound—these are relatively expensive—and one or more less expensive projection-playback units. . . .

CONCLUSION

Why permit or even encourage students to make their own movies? If the purpose is to turn out junior size film technicians, the activity is not worth serious academic attention. Students can acquire these skills more effectively at a professional cinema school or on the job in the industry. Nor should filmmaking be used as a substitute for a film study or appreciation (a *verboten* word in academic circles) course that failed because of teacher inadequacy. But used in conjunction with such a course, it is an invaluable way to give the student a new way of seeing that's more important than what they see) and a real feel for the medium.

Few films, even ones made by great film artists, are ever realized perfectly. Sometimes a film never gets off the ground. A group of my students (marginal kids with long hair, a beat-up convertible—jointly owned—and levis), back in the days before those things became quasi-fashionable, decided to make a film about Chicago's vertical slums, or "public housing." After dozens of interviews, run-around from politicians, and harassment from gangs, they decided that the movie was impossible to make. A teacher dedicated to education-as-product rather than process might have given them a failing mark. I gave them an "A" for all they learned about sociology, government, politics, each other, and goodness knows what else. Filmmaking courses are one of the few places students can succeed through failure.

Some final precautions: not everyone is capable of making a film, no more than everyone is capable of writing a good poem or short story. To force it on the half-willing student as an assignment is a sure way to kill its vitality and richness. A few students, too, find film such a personal medium that they almost literally pour out their souls. Such outpouring can approach psychodrama, and while there is undoubtedly a great deal to be said about the value of channeling one's amorphous subconscious into an intelligent and disciplined form, a great deal of psychological harm can result when a teacher becomes inordinately fascinated with self-revelation. Often such revelation is not apparent either to the creator or to other students; he simply feels that he has "gotten something out of his system" and an adult with critical insight will frequently find it necessary to keep such insights a professional secret. Filmmaking like any other humanizing activity has its prudential as well as its financial limits.

FILM-MAKING BELONGS
TO ALL DISCIPLINES

Tom Devine

The practical goals and courses of action for advancing film education in elementary and secondary schools are four-fold: (1) To provide the simplest kind of guide to the various aspects of film production, (2) to enable future film-makers to become acquainted with the different departments in film-making so that they may see where their talents lie, (3) to encourage the spirit of creativity and craftsmanship, and (4) to show the relationship between film and the other forms of communication.

The process of showing, discussing, teaching, and making films has had many positive results this year. At Champlain Valley Union High School film-making has started to explode other curricula, and now other classes (English, social studies, art, and science) are accepting film term papers or film projects as independent study contracts. That is, students may elect to produce a short film in lieu of a term paper or a research project for independent study.

Film-making appeals to students because it is something that they can make their own. A student film-maker can quite literally, by means of the lens of a camera, frame his own world and re-order his own environment.

As educators we have realized the impact that media have had on the curriculum; and with the excellent, inexpensive, amateur film-making equipment that is now available, and with film-making being recognized as a bonafide educational activity, we must start to take advantage of the film as a tool of education.

There is no magic formula or packaged film program that is available for mass consumption. Each teacher must decide for himself what the objectives for the program and for the students will be. In whatever discipline film-making is being employed, the over-all

From *La Mancha Plus One* (May, 1969), pp. 24–27. Reprinted with permission of La Mancha Project and Tom Devine.

Tom Devine teaches English at Champlain Valley Union High School, Hinesburg, Vermont.

objectives should be (1) to develop new sensitivity to visual language through the making of films, (2) to foster greater personal sensitivity to the world we live in by examining it through the lens of a camera, (3) to expand the students' knowledge of the media, and (4) to stimulate creativity.

In order for these objectives to be achieved, the teacher needs to take into consideration the materials and facilities available. Speaking from experience, it is well to take an inventory of film-making equipment that is owned by students or their families. Most of the equipment that we now use at Champlain Valley is now owned by the school department.

Where should one begin? There are many approaches to film-making that may be used. You can work with an entire class, in small groups, or with individuals. The first ingredient of any film is an idea. Some teachers believe that the ideas perceived by students should be verbalized and scripted. If a student is verbally able to express himself, it might indeed be helpful for him to outline his idea to story-treatment to scenario to a precise shooting script. For the less verbal or less print-oriented student, writing could be a problem, and the project would never get off the ground. In this case the student should not be asked to conceptualize his ideas verbally but should be allowed to develop them on film.

The story board usually is used as a means of transmitting the idea for a film onto paper. As a technique in the conception of a frame-by-frame development of a film, a student may by means of sketches or photographs taken with a Polaroid camera translate his ideas into concrete form.

The next step is to bring to realization the ideas of the film-maker, and this brings us to the actual shooting and editing of film. Each situation must produce the formula for achieving the footage desired. It is important for the successful filming of any sequence for the film-maker to concern himself with the continuity, the shooting location, and the equipment; what lenses, film speed shooting apparatus, etc.

As in the art classroom a student is trained in techniques so that he may create as an individual, so, too, the film-maker must prepare himself for the final act of individualistic creation.

If it is possible, students should be given the opportunity to view and discuss experimental films made by such film-makers as Andy

Warhol and Norman McLaren. Films by experimental film-makers will demonstrate as wide a variety of techniques as possible to stimulate students.

After viewing and discussing experimental films, allow the students a chance to produce something of their own. The following examples illustrate possible assignments that would be given to beginning students:

1. Using 100 feet of film, begin practicing the various techniques such as wipe, lap dissolve, fade in, fade out, etc.
2. Take a shot that is correctly exposed.
3. Shoot one stop over-exposed.
4. Shoot one stop under-exposed.
5. Shoot a scene exposed for background.
6. Shoot a scene for foreground.
7. Shoot a scene for backlight, etc.

The list can be as long or as sophisticated as the teacher wants to make it, depending upon the needs of the students.

When the teacher and the students view the rushes, it is easy to see concrete results of what has been learned. After shooting (and usually reshooting), the student is ready to edit. It is very difficult to teach editing as it is an activity that must be done by the individual. A teacher may assist students and instruct them, but it has to be on a one-to-one basis. It is best to instruct students in cutting and then let them find their own way. A *must* on the recommended reading lists of young film-makers and teachers should be a book on how to edit. Two books that students have found useful are *How to Edit* (Focal Press, $2.50) and the Kodak book on editing.

An interesting exercise in editing is to give each member of a class three or four hundred feet of processed film which the students are to reduce to one hundred feet. Processed news footage usually can be obtained at no cost from local television stations. It is amazing to see what students using identical footage will create through the process of editing.

Sound can be very important in film-making. Composing and editing sound tracks are useful ways of developing sensitivity to sound. Syncronous sound tracks at the elementary or the secondary level are prohibitive because of the technical complexity involved and because of the cost. Nevertheless, students do have a number of avenues open to them. The tape recorder, if used with imagination, will enable students to become quite creative with sound. The only limitation involved here is the potential and creativity of the user. The "what" a student tapes can be anything that produces sound— from human beings to machines. "How" one tapes has variations also. Sounds may be taped at various speeds, sounds may be superimposed on one another, or sounds may be arranged in sequence to symbolize a certain aspect of life.

Specific assignments that may be given for starters are:

1. Taping normal conversation—interviewing people on a controversial topic and then editing the tape into a finished product.
2. Taping the sounds that people make—laughing, talking, breathing, crying, snoring, walking, running, skipping, etc.
3. Using sounds to tell a story—placing sounds in sequence for meaning: the alarm clock, the shower, noises in the kitchen, the school bus, the bell at school, noise of students passing from class to class, sounds in class, the cafeteria, classes, bells, bus, TV, dinner dishes, the dishwasher running, TV clicked off, brushing teeth, getting into bed, snoring . . .
4. Using sounds to create certain moods or themes.
5. Music can be edited to create certain moods.

Films may have sound tracks that require simple narration, sound effects, or a musical accompaniment. We see here once again the possibilities of involving students and personnel from various disciplines.

All educators would agree that it is what is learned and not what is produced that is important. We should not be interested in producing the next great epic, or in working for the sole purpose of final screening or film festival. We should be working to get students involved in seeing film as a mode of expression.

English, science, history, art—indeed, any of the disciplines could integrate film-making into their course of study. In all of these areas there are three basic kinds of film that students can produce: documentary, narrative, and animation. The documentary is perhaps the most popular with young film-makers. They can film documentaries for social studies classes, using cut-outs from magazines and then filming them. A tape recorder then can be used to provide the narration. In the chemistry or the biology classes students can film actual experiments. The "how to do it film" has many possibilities in a variety of classes. For students who are not print oriented, it is a way in which they may become totally involved in the learning process.

The type of film that students see on television and in the movies is the narrative. It is the form that they usually will try to imitate. This form is more demanding as it does require an idea that has been transformed to story form and then scripted. The transformation of an idea to a visual story board requires skill and extensive work. The shooting of a narrative also requires preparation, for the work is precise and demanding. This is where the story board becomes so important and valuable a tool to the film-maker. It is here also that we see that the student film is a creative process involving time, skill, and work and that it does differ from the "home movie" type of endeavor.

The third type of film is animation and it requires separate techniques and skills. This type of film is one of the easiest to produce and may be made inexpensively. Students in elementary as well as secondary schools can experience a great amount of success with the animated film. Simplified animation is within the grasp of any student who is able to take pictures one at a time.

Using the animated camera, the following types of exercises can be easily animated:

1. Teachers can start their classes by making "scratch" films; the students simply scratch on leader, and when it is projected on the screen the scratches form patterns of light and design.
2. A one-day magic marker "happening" is another type of project that is easily done with students of all ages. You can remove all the emulsion from junk stock or simply provide clear leader for your classes. Allow the students to draw on the film with paint, magic marker, or crayon. (Warning!—Make sure the projectionist cleans the gate on the projector after a film like this has been screened.)

3. The collage film is easy to produce, using bits of junk stock that can be decorated by scratching or painting. The students then re-splice the film to form a new one.
4. Cut-outs or photographs can be mounted on cardboard and moved from place to place to simulate movement.
5. Models made of clay can be easily re-arranged and are easy to use in an animated sequence. Figures made out of papier mâché are also easy to use in an animated film because they can be moved about quickly and easily between shots.
6. Flipcards can consist of a series of drawings or sketches that are made on flexible cards. As the student flips through the cards, the drawings appear to move. The flip cards can be filmed individually for a couple of frames, or the camera can simply film the effect of manual manipulation of the flipcards.

There are many books available that describe the simple operations of animation. The nice thing about this technique is that it is very inexpensive, requiring only a camera with single frame capabilities, some lights and the material to be animated, imagination, and film stock.

Ultimately the finished documentary, narrative, or animated film will require an audience. Film-makers are anxious to have their work screened. Film festivals on the high school level are becoming very popular. The Forensic and Debate Tournament held annually at the University of Vermont has made it possible this year for young film-makers to have their films screened at this state festival.

Many instructors feel that the film should be a personal and private matter between the instructor and the pupil. Others screen films only in groups concerned, while a few schools have public showings of various nature, going all the way to the ultimate, the student film festival.

Concern has also been expressed about the effect of film-making, film study, and competition in general on the psyche of the student. It is felt that there are no more dangers encountered in these areas than in any of the other creative and academic competitive situations to which a student is exposed in his school years.

Many critics and educators express concern over the place of film education and film-making in the curriculum. Miss Pauline Kael, noted film critic, takes the view of today's youngsters and urges keeping film outside the curriculum:

> It's only a movie. What beautiful words. At movies, you're left gloriously alone. You say it stinks and nobody's shocked. That's something you can't do with a Dickens novel or a Beethoven symphony or even a poem by Browning and because you can't, because they're all preselected and prejudged and geared for greatness, you don't talk about them with the other kids the way you do about movies.[1]

While I do not agree with Miss Kael, I certainly can appreciate her concerns. Film-making or film study should not be restricted to a particular class within a structured grade setup. Film-making does work within the school, and it is a process that students as well as teachers find exciting and valuable. We are now faced with the problem of proving that it works.

One of the problems confronting teachers is that we are desperate for sources and resources. We need information, training, and equipment. In-service programs are certainly an important measure for preparing film-making teachers. One of the tragedies in our present system is that teachers know primarily one type of film—the "educational film." We need to broaden this scope. As the teacher of writing must write if he is going to be truly effective with his students, so, too, the film teacher must make films if he is going to work efficiently with students in this creative process.

Discussion and debate about the shortage of facts and the surplus of generalizations by those who offer solutions could go on forever. It is a fact that film is the "now" medium, and if we are going to be a valuable part of "what's happening" we must take advantage of and let our students become involved with the phenomenon of our times—the moving image. As every teacher is concerned with print as a mode of communication, every teacher must come to regard film as an equally important method of communication.

[1] Pauline Kael, "It's Only a Movie." *Film Study in Higher Education*, by David C. Stewart, (Washington, D.C.: American Council on Education, 1966), p. 133.

AVANT-ROCK
IN THE CLASSROOM

David E. Morse

Rock and Roll, as any teacher knows, commands high interest among exactly those students whose juices run most contrary to school. A student who has been "turned off" all year to Serious Literature is suddenly "turned on" by the Beatles. Knowing this, most of us are clever enough to give the Beatles a few spins to introduce our favorite literary dreadnoughts; or during a unit on poetry we turn to Simon and Garfunkel ballads for comparison. But beyond these opening gestures, our courage fails. We lumber ahead with Romantic Poetry or whatever, aware that the lethargy has returned by degrees.

And no wonder. For the trick is too obvious. It comes apparent to the canny Unreachable that what he had suspected all along was indeed true; the music was mere camouflage for some dreadful Serious Work. He is confirmed in the cynical belief that English class offers nothing to him.

Yet this need not happen. Not if we take time to consider that during the past three years, Rock and Roll has outgrown its earlier doggerel form. Although the popular doggerel still receives the most play on radio, in experimental quarters the more recent folk rock and electronic rock artists have borrowed from everything from Gregorian chants to avant-garde electronic composition techniques, Medieval modes and pentatonic scales and Indian ragas. Serious musicians increasingly have commented that the boundaries between art and rock music are growing less defined. Cathy Berberian, noted avant-garde singer for whom Igor Stravinsky and John Cage have written works, recently recorded an album of Beatle songs, and commented that "Eleanor Rigby" was one of the most beautiful she had heard in years. Aaron Copland was quoted by *Look* as saying, "When people ask to recreate the mood of the sixties, they will play

From the *English Journal* (February, 1969), pp. 196–200, 297. Reprinted with the permission of the National Council of Teachers of English and David E. Morse.

Beatle music." Leonard Bernstein on CBS-TV called the best of the new rock "irresistible." Writing in the *Columbia University Forum*, Joan Peyser calls "Sergeant Pepper's" "an extraordinary work, not just comparable to a new sonata or opera, but far more important." Rock and Roll—or, if you prefer, avant-rock—has become an exciting new art form. Not only the Beatles, but the Mothers of Invention, the Fugs, and the best of lesser groups such as the Doors, the Vanilla Fudge, and regional groups—some of them proliferating only within the past year—include poets of the third and even second rank. For the new art is in large part *verbal* in intent. "Eleanor Rigby" is a satirical word-sound portrait of loneliness.

Paul Simon, of the Simon and Garfunkel team, typically reverts to the ballads, as in "Sound of Silence:"

> In restless dreams I walked alone
> Narrow streets of cobblestone,
> 'Neath the halo of a street lamp
> I turned my collar to the cold and damp
> When my eyes were stabbed
> By the flash of a neon light
> That split the night
> And touched the sound of Silence . . .[1]

The new albums increasingly resemble multi-media novels or plays. The new *genre* has not yet found an adequate name; but the records come packaged as portfolios, with photographs and printed text, all centering around a theme which is as much literary as musical. Sometimes the effect is avowedly lyrical and poetic, as in Donovan's *A Gift from a Flower to a Garden*.

Other albums present a mosaic of sound, juxtaposing musical themes with word-images, bizarre sound effects and dialogue. Allusions to other groups abound, in a cross-dialogue reminiscent of the Eighteenth Century coffee house cliques—Donovan alluding, in one song, to the Jefferson Airplane; the Mothers of Invention in their whole album, *We're Only in it for the Money*, parodying the Beatles' *Sergeant Pepper's*, in a package complete with album photos and paper cutouts. In a more sedate vein, Simon and Garfunkel interject conversations taped at various homes for the aged along with the

---

[1] From "The Sound of Silence" by Paul Simon. © 1964 Charing Cross Music. Used with permission of the publisher.

songs in their *Bookends* album; and Joan Baez in her recent album, *Baptism*, alternates songs with readings from poets including Donne, Whitman, Lorca, and Yevtushenko.

The whole avant-rock movement clearly challenges the traditional notions of what is literature, in much the same way that Elizabethan drama challenged the earlier definitions of theater. And as always, for a time the new will tend to be disruptive to the old. The teacher of English, even if he finds the new poetry palatable and wishes to bring it into the classroom, will quite naturally have to ask himself the question: Can traditional poetry coexist with the new form, in English class?

The answer will vary of course with each teacher's style and intent. But beyond this, the key factor is the wide range of songs all loosely called Rock and Roll. If we begin with the cruder popular sounds and work toward the more esoteric and complex, by the end we have entered a medium demanding the same critical attention which any serious art demands. If we succeed in this, then far from setting music and poetry up in competition, we have brought many students who were content before merely to tap a foot or react sentimentally to maudlin ballads, into a meaningful engagement with the art of their culture. In that profounder competition which exists always between the spurious and the true, the best of the new sounds can win adherents to the best of the old; they are in the same camp. And let us not forget that all poetry is, first of all, sound.

Comparison itself can be valuable. Consider Matthew Arnold's "Dover Beach." Certainly few poems capture with greater beauty the shuffling cadences of the sea contained in the first three stanzas. But listening to the Fugs' rendering of the fourth stanza in their song, "Dover Beach," who can find it any less haunting, with their introduction of the martial snare drum and Byzantine lilt? Certainly a child is entitled to listen to both. For if you could see in your classroom—as I have in mine—the faces of those *Quasi*-Unreachables (I should qualify the term, for the truly Unreachable student is as bored or hung-up at home as in school and has no interest in Rock and Roll)—if you could see their response, you would be in no doubt as to which version laid a whole claim to their senses. Too often we kill literature for children, by a process for which none of us can be held singly responsible and through which twelve years of school narrow around the academically talented, the very students who have cut themselves off from their senses and who are left with only an intellectual response. I insist that insofar as art is concerned with evoking a whole response, *for the average student the Fugs are more alive than Matthew Arnold can ever be.*

Of course the comparisons go both ways. I have had students who, taking apart the grammar and noting the dependence on parallel structure of "Baby Light My Fire," and noting that the song by the Doors contained essentially the same three-part rhetoric of "To His Coy Mistress," preferred the latter. Marvell's poem, although it is three hundred years old, was said not only with more wisdom and beauty, but with greater clarity.

Such value judgments are occassionally helpful. But to me the process of comparison is most useful when the two works inform each other. For instance, students may find that the original version of "Richard Cory," by Edward Arlington Robinson, allows the reader more latitude for interpretation and uses words with more sensitivity, while the Simon and Garfunkel version, by tightening the point of view and by using the heavy drumbeat to accent the final couplet, obtains a more immediate emotional response. Each produces a slightly different portrait of Richard Cory. What is more, the reinterpretation brings new life to the original. Just as the poetry of Joyce and Pound serves to revivify Homer, so do the ballads of Arlo Guthrie and Bob Dylan bring fresh relevance to the American ballad tradition; and for that matter, the Vanilla Fudge in their slowed-down version of "Eleanor Rigby" cast a weird and ominous light on the Beatle tune.

But we must not stop at comparisons, whatever their value, or we are guilty of merely exploiting new young artists who deserve space of their own in the curriculum. We cannot wait fifty years for them to be enshrined along with the second- and third-ranking poets of the nineteenth century, in the anthologies. Not when our world is changing so violently. Not when the idea of the anthology itself is already virtually obsolete. On artistic grounds alone their inclusion is defensible. On pedagogical grounds, it is almost mandatory. Even for the college-bound, how can we expect to teach Dryden or Whittier —-while excluding Paul Simon, Leonard Cohen, John Lennon, and Paul McCartney—and at the same time expect anything in return

from the academically talented student, but hypocrisy and cynicism?
It is precisely our systematic exclusion of the relevant which is
attacked by the Mothers of Invention:

> Mr. America walk on by
> Your schools that do not teach
> Mr. America walk on by
> The minds that won't be reached
> Mr. America try to hide
> The emptiness that's you inside
>
> . . . Philosophy that turns away
> From those who aren't afraid to say
> What's on their minds—
> The Left-Behinds
> Of the Great Society[2]

Bob Dylan, also using the second person, attacks the traditional
"book" education of the over-25 generation, in his "Ballad of a Thin
Man." The well-read "Mr. Jones" is made to wander through a nightmarish carnival freak show, in which he is told with repeated sarcasm
that something is happening but that he doesn't know what it is.

All very well, you may say. But just how does a Mr. Jones find out
what is happening? Assuming he is willing to try avant-rock in his
classroom, how does he overcome his distaste and—let's face it—
fear of the new sounds, and venture onto a strange turf which his
students know better than he?

The answer, for me, was not to push too hard. Offensive as I
found some of the new sounds, I at least tried to give them a fair
hearing. I let my students know I was experimenting; they took me
in hand; and in much the same way as I lead them from one good
book to other, more challenging books, so they began leading me
to the more radical sounds. In no time I was surprised to find myself contributing—drawing from the analytical tools with which I
had been poking around for years in my "print-bound" world of
books—and bringing to my hangers-around a richer understanding
of structure and rhythm, and techniques such as alliteration, ironic
inversion, and dramatic monologue. Literary concepts which were

---

before mere articles of pedantry to most students, to be memorized along with other irrelevancies, suddenly became exciting and useful tools. All this happened quite naturally, without my ever trying to force myself to like all of what was played for me; just by giving it a fair hearing.

Listening to records at home, I discovered—as you will—parallels from my own store of poems. The titles themselves occasionally provide a clue; on other occasions, while listening you may recall a similar theme, or make a connection on the basis of style or subject or mode.

This began happening to me. I was listening to Dave Van Ronk's "A Little Man," when I began thinking of Frost's "Death of a Hired Man," and then some of Ring Lardner's short stories. The next thing I knew I was grabbing for books, typing ditto masters, tearing out newspaper clippings, plying students for new records as soon as I had taped the old. Soon I had built up enough of a repertoire that the songs began grouping themselves independently of printed works. Although I chose to include poems and stories in the unit, as it turned out, it was a significant breakthrough in thinking that permitted me to view a song as a work having integrity of its own.

The unit that emerged happened to concern the theme of "Dropping Out." We were using the phrase in the broad sense of dropping out of society, including the hippie alienation and the often similar motives underlying the decision of many students to quit school. "Dropping Out" came to assume a number of meanings. To me the subject was a vital one, for I know of so many talented youngsters who have dropped out in one sense or another. I will not describe the unit in detail, however. You will have your own ideas for units. And anyway, the important thing is the organic process I have already tried to describe in part, involving the combining of materials brought in chiefly by students.

We began with human relations as a sort of touchstone, depicting love and the breakdown of love. Since this is almost the sole subject matter of the most popular Rock and Roll, it was easy to begin by appealing to the grossest music tastes—songs such as "Baby Light My Fire," "Ode to Billy Joe," and "Skip-a-Rope," which by now have passed into limbo. Interspaced with these were "To His Coy Mistress," "Lord Randall," and "The Love Song of J. Alfred Prufrock."

We dealt next with efforts to escape loneliness, through religion, as in Ed Ames' song, "Who Will Answer?," in "Sound of Silence," and in Melville's poem, "The Berg"; then with the resort to stereotypes depicted variously by Pete Seeger, Ray Charles, W. H. Auden, Simon & Garfunkel, Thomas Hardy, and the Beatles; finally with the recognition of human isolation and subsequent alienation from society which culminated in the process of "Dropping Out."

Within the process of "Dropping Out" we followed a cycle, the first half of which began with the rejection of the mores and politics of "Straight" society in favor of tribal companionship, magic, and the euphoria of drugs, ending at the bottom of the cycle in a state of dehumanization. It will be useful here to show the exact progression of songs:

"A Day in the Life"—the Beatles
"Hungry Freaks, Daddy"—the Mothers of Invention
"Ballad of a Thin Man"—Bob Dylan
"Tune In, Turn On, Drop Out"—the Fugs
"Yellow Submarine"—the Beatles
"Strawberry Fields Forever"—the Beatles
"Itchycoo Park"—the Small Faces
"The World Is Too Much With Us"—Wordsworth
"I Am the Walrus"—the Beatles
"The Fool on the Hill"—the Beatles
"Just Dropped In"—the First Edition
"2,000 Lightyears from Home"—the Rolling Stones
"Blue Jay Way"—the Beatles (George Harrison)
"Strange Days"—The Doors

We found at the bottom of the "Dropping Out" process a kind of dropping on "through"—through the bottom, into a rediscovery of isolation and a new blurred and terrible sense of loneliness. The progression of songs was a powerful one; the effect, experiential. Talk was kept to less than 50 per cent during this phase of the unit; the rest of the time was spent listening to music. As an added option some students chose to read a nonfiction story in *Harper's* by Joan Didion, entitled "The Hippie Generation."

The second half of the cycle is characterized by an effort to return to human compassion. In this light we discussed the interest in

Indian gurus, Hare Krishna, and the professed aims of the Love Generation along with their inconsistencies; but most of all we listened to the newer Beatle songs, including "A Little Help from my Friends," "Norwegian Wood," "Within You Without You," and "Getting Better"; also to Ray Charles' "Peace of Mind." Finally, we discussed Frost's "Death of a Hired Man" in terms of its multiplicity of feelings, and for a "hard" view of affections in which, nevertheless, compassion transcends self-love.

Sources for the unit included the mass-circulated magazines, as well as various underground publications which are hawked in most large cities. Rock magazines such as *Crawdaddy*, *Cheetah*, *Eye*, *Rolling Stone*, and *Discoscene*, will prove to be useful sources of critical commentary, as will *The New York Times* and the *New York Review of Books*, on occasion. *Downbeat* keeps a critical ear posted to Rock. Again—students will bring in their own materials!

It took us three weeks to go full circle, on the average. I did the unit separately with three eleventh-grade classes of widely varying abilities, altering the content only slightly. Girls in typing classes volunteered to transcribe the lyrics onto ditto masters. I used Perrine's *Sound and Sense* for most of the poems. We were lucky enough to have the use of a small assembly-room, which permitted full volume; but for those not so fortunate, any sound-absorbing material such as moveable bulletin boards placed strategically in a classroom will improve it acoustically. Boys acted as "engineers," hooking up an extra speaker I brought from my stereo at home, and locating songs on the tapes.

One small indicator of the success of the unit was the number of students who had open periods and chose voluntarily to sit in. I even caught my most recalcitrant student listening secretly through a door left ajar in the rear of the room, on a day when his class didn't meet.

FIVE DOZEN IDEAS
FOR TEACHING
THE NEWSPAPER UNIT

Howard F. Decker

Teachers, not students, too often have a mental block against using the newspaper in the English classroom. The complaint I have heard most often is, "It sounds like a good idea, but I really don't know enough about newspapers to teach them."

But teaching the newspaper itself is not the purpose. Instead, the newspaper should be used as a tool to teach vocabulary, reading improvement, and composition. When teachers approach the newspaper unit with this idea in mind, their fears often evaporate.

I have used the newspaper for several years with both accelerated and remedial students in both sophomore and senior classes. The results have always been good. Never have I heard a single student complain that the unit was boring or irrelevant or "the same old thing I had last year." To borrow a phrase from current adolescent slang, I have always found that every student was definitely "turned on."

Surprisingly, very few students know anything about newspapers. They read the sports section, they glance at the comic pages, and a few search the classified ads for bargains in the "Automotive—Used" columns, but most of them will be exploring virgin territory when you introduce the unit.

To help teachers present the newspaper unit, I have compiled a list of sixty ideas which I have found to be practical. Not every idea will work in every classroom, but surely enough of them can be adapted that it will be difficult to dismiss the newspaper unit on grounds of not having enough information about teaching it.

From the *English Journal* (February, 1970) pp. 268–272. Reprinted with the permission of the National Council of Teachers of English and Howard F. Decker.

Howard F. Decker is Chairman of the English Department at Morton Township High School in Morton, Illinois, and is the author of the filmstrip series "The Newspaper in America," produced by the Society for Visual Education, Inc., and *Newspaper Workshop*, a language arts workbook produced by the Globe Book Company, Inc.

INTRODUCING THE UNIT

1. Call your nearest daily newspaper and arrange to have enough copies of the newspaper for each of your students sent to your school every day for one or two weeks (or even the whole semester). Some newspapers furnish copies to schools free of charge, and others sell them for as little as five cents each.
2. Show filmstrips or movies about newspapers. Numerous companies offer worthwhile audiovisual programs about newspapers. To find a rather complete listing of such materials available, consult the *Index to 35mm Educational Filmstrips* and the *Index to 16mm Educational Films*, both published by McGraw-Hill and compiled through the efforts of the National Information Center for Educational Media.
3. Point out the "masthead" of the newspaper, and show students that in it the newspaper announces its management and lists its subscription rates.
4. Point out that a "by-line" is simply the word *by* followed by the name of the reporter who wrote the story. Have students find by-lines in the newspaper.
5. Point out that a "dateline" is the name of the city and state where a news story originates. Local news stories carry no datelines. Have students note which stories are local and which are not.
6. Point out that the letters AP and UPI are the initials of the two major wire services—Associated Press and United Press International.
7. Give your students a half-hour to read the paper leisurely. Then have each student tell which item, news story, column, editorial, he appreciated most.
8. Clip several headlines from the newspaper and show them to the class, assigning students to write down the section of the paper in which they think the story probably appeared.
9. Have your students keep a scrapbook in which they include examples of dateline, by-line, cutlines, streamer headlines, local news story, wire service news story, syndicated news story, local columnist, obituary, etc.

IMPROVING VOCABULARY

10. Assign each student to find five words in the newspaper which he does not understand. Then each student should look up the words in a dictionary and use the words in original sentences.

11. Find numerous examples of abbreviations used in the newspaper (CIA, FHA, UAW, NATO, etc.). Have students circle these initials and then find the proper name for each set of initials.

12. Before class, find several words which you suspect your students might not be able to define. If your students have difficulty explaining the meanings of these words, show them the sentences in which the words appear and point out that words are almost always easier to understand when they are in context.

13. Assign your students to turn to one particular section of the newspaper and make a list of the words used more frequently in that one section than in any other section of the newspaper. In sports, for example, they will find such words as *inning, pennant, coach, gridders, referee, league, overtime, score,* etc.

IMPROVING READING ABILITY

14. As a weekend assignment, tell your students to read the Sunday edition of the newspaper and make a list of the differences they notice between the Sunday paper and the weekday issues. Then conduct a class discussion on the subject.

15. Assign the class to read the comic strips for ten or fifteen minutes and then conduct a class discussion of the types of humor: slapstick, wit, irony, satire, sight jokes, puns, etc.

16. Before class begins, write down twenty or thirty questions about the contents of the newspaper and assign the students to find the answers (e.g., What is tonight's weather forecast? When was Joe Smith born? What is showing this week at the Rialto? How much are Early American sofas at Ward's?).

17. Choose a dozen or so news stories and clip the headlines off.

Then challenge your students—particularly slow readers—to match the stories with the correct headlines.

18. Clip a feature story which contains several examples of a reporter's interpreting or editorializing. Assign your class to identify the passages in which the feature writer exercises a freedom of expression denied to the writer of straight news copy.

19. Clip several news stories which contain errors overlooked by the proofreaders. Assign your students to find these errors.

20. Many daily newspapers feature a weekly news quiz. If your newspaper does publish such a news quiz, assign your students to take this quiz.

WRITING ASSIGNMENTS

21. Type several examples of news stories which have errors in spelling, punctuation, and factual information. Assign your students to act as copyreaders and find the errors.

22. Have your students read the editorials for several days. Then assign them to write an editorial of their own on any topic they wish.

23. Assign your students to study the stories of weddings and engagements on the women's pages and then write an imaginary wedding or engagement story about any two of their classmates.

24. Write a classified ad, using an abundance of words. Assign your class to rewrite the ad in as few words as possible without eliminating any information.

25. Assign each student to choose an advertisement from the classified section and write a letter in answer to it.

26. Assign the class to write a letter to the editor of the daily newspaper or the school newspaper, stating their beliefs on any topic of interest to them.

27. Write a news story in which you insert numerous examples of editorializing. Assign your students to rewrite the story, eliminating all editorial comments.

28. If your newspaper carries such advice columns as "Dear Abby" or "Dear Ann Landers," instruct your classes, as a

composition assignment, to read the questions in the letters and then answer as if they were the "expert."

29. Assign your students to choose a news story and use it as a source for writing a poem or a short story.

30. Assign your students to interview another member of the student body and then write a feature story about him. Their stories should include many quotations, background information, physical description, and interesting facts.

31. Assign your students to write a "how-to-do-it" feature story. Similar to a demonstration speech, a how-to-do-it feature can discuss such topics as "How to make a tea ring," "How to ride horseback," "How to treat a victim of shock," "How to make paper flowers," etc.

32. Clip several news stories, cutting off the headlines. Then assign your class to write headlines for each story.

33. Pretend that you are a news source and have your students hold a "press conference" in which they interview you. Then they must write a news story.

34. After your students have written the news story as described above, tell them to exchange papers. Now they are copy-readers and must find the errors in their classmates' work.

35. Assign your students to cover a news story in your school. Make up a list of possible news sources so that each student has a different assignment: club sponsors, club presidents, coaches, committee chairmen, administrators, etc. Your school activities calendar should help you to find ideas.

36. Choose a well-known piece of literature such as "The Highwayman" or *Spoon River Anthology* and assign your students to write a news story based on the literary work.

37. Pretend that you are a "legman" and "call in" a news story to the newsroom. Have your students act as rewrite men and take notes. Then assign them to write the news story in polished form, ready for publication.

CLASS DISCUSSION

38. Have your students search through the newspaper, noting stories which they feel were either phoned in by readers or

sent in as news releases rather than being written by staff reporters. In class discussion have them explain their reasoning.

39. Telephone the local newspaper office and ask that the newsroom save several samples of the wire service news copy from the AP or the UPI so that you may show them to your classes. Then discuss with your students the many interesting features of wire service news copy.

40. From your school's newspaper sponsor borrow copies of newspapers mailed in from neighboring schools. After your students have examined several other papers, conduct a class discussion in which you compare your school's paper with the papers from the other schools.

41. Ask the faculty adviser or the student editor of your school's newspaper to participate in a question-and-answer session with your class.

42. Call the editor of the nearest daily newspaper to see whether one or more members of his staff would be willing to speak before your class.

43. Find examples of news releases from large organizations and have your class discuss the merits of such publicity releases. Are they newsworthy items? Or are they merely advertising disguised as news?

44. Give your students dictionaries and find the page which lists proofreader's marks. Discuss these marks with your class.

45. Ask the editor of a nearby newspaper whether he can provide you with any interesting tools or materials which you can show to your students: mats, slugs, galley proofs, press plates, etc.

46. To illustrate the differences between big city dailies and small town weeklies, bring samples of both types to class and discuss them with your students. Later let the students spend some time on free reading with both types of newspapers.

SPECIAL PROJECTS

47. Take your entire class on a tour of the nearest newspaper plant.

48. As a one-week assignment have students clip all stories from the newspaper which they think will be historically important in one hundred years. In class discussion, ask them to explain their choices.

49. As an extra-credit assignment, ask your more artistic students to draw political cartoons suitable for the local daily or for the school newspaper.

50. Early in the newspaper unit, assign your class to keep a scrapbook in which they follow a current news topic for the entire unit. Help them to choose a news topic which will "keep" for several days or weeks (e.g., a political campaign, a court trial, a world crisis, a drought or flood, etc.). To conclude the assignment, each student should write a report.

51. After explaining the stock market listings, assign the class to pretend to "buy" a few stocks and to follow the market every day, computing their gains and losses at the end of the unit.

52. Acquaint your students with the school library's resources regarding newspapers: microfilm copies, current subscriptions to daily newspapers, biographies of famous journalists, journalism career books, journalism fiction books, etc.

53. Assign your students to produce their own classroom newspaper, which you can produce using a ditto machine, Xerox copier, etc.

54. On any given day have students make a list of the news stories which they think will be continued the following day. On the following day, have them make a checklist, noting which stories were continued and which were not. Conduct a class discussion on why some stories were continued and why some were not.

55. Assign students to find various types of feature stories: news background, biographical sketch, filler stories, how-to-do-it (or advice) features, and historical features. Then have the students trade clippings and identify the types of feature stories they are given.

CONCLUDING ASSIGNMENTS

When the newspaper unit is finished, have your students write briefly on one of the following topics:

56. What have you learned from the newspaper unit?
57. What do you think the value or importance of a free press is in a democratic society?
58. What effect would a nationwide newspaper strike have on our citizens?
59. Why is editorializing in news columns regarded as a bad thing?
60. What is the value of having a school-sponsored newspaper?

DRAMA

Dorothy Heathcote

Dramatic activity is concerned with the ability of human beings to 'become somebody else', to 'see how it feels', and the process is a very simple and efficient way of crystallising certain kinds of information. Human beings employ it naturally and intuitively all their lives. 'Put yourself in my shoes' is a readily understood request, and one easily complied with, though some are more capable than others of achieving deep insight by this means. It has been turned into a complicated and therefore often misunderstood subject in school, by teachers (perhaps those who see childhood as merely the time spent waiting to become an adult, and deny the value of a child's experiencing *being* a child?) who have replaced the real experience with 'exercises for' the real experience. The underlying assumption is that children are not capable of experiencing 'the real thing', so substitutes in the form of watered-down and emasculated exercises are employed instead. This, together with a lack of understanding of the relationship between so-called 'improvisation' and 'theatre' experiences, and a paucity of adequate generally accepted vocabulary to order the thinking, has caused much confusion. A further complicating factor is that a 'good' drama experience cannot either be preserved or transferred easily, so that those using drama intuitively in the classroom or club find it difficult to communicate what they *do* to achieve their ends, or the means they employ to learn *which ends* are relevant at that time and in that particular circumstance. Most good infant teachers are able to judge *when* they may venture to join children at play, especially wendy-house play, but many would be at a loss to explain *how* they judge.

Like many human learning experiences, drama is at once a *subject* area for research opportunity—for example theatre skills—and a *tool* for personal development—in personal role-playing. Because drama is concerned with the kinds of associations and conflicts which

From *English in Education* (Summer, 1967), pp. 58–63. Reprinted with permission of the publisher and the author.

Dorothy Heathcote teaches at the University of Newcastle on Tyne.

people in their public, personal and religious lives enter into, it offers two unique opportunities to the teacher:

1. The fact that for its expression it always demands crystallisation of ideas *in groups,*
2. It can employ the individuals, *working as a group,* to conceive the ideas, area, and level of interest in the first place.

Therefore, even as the group—because such is the nature of groups—constantly modifies and gives form to its ideas, expression and sentiment, employing the natural laws of drama, it is also a direct result and expression of the interpersonal relationships of the group, and the individual strengths and weaknesses of those in it. A team-game or class project will also reflect these. The factor special to drama is that it achieves these in 'heated' not 'cold' circumstances, for it draws directly upon the individual's life and subjective experiences as its basic material, and achieves this in circumstances which are unique—that is when 'a willing suspension of disbelief' applies, and when those concerned are using their subjective world to illuminate and understand the motivations of others through role-playing.

Dramatic activity is concerned with the crises, the turning points of life, large and small, which cause people to reflect and take note, and its functions within the following disciplines:

1. It must use man in his total environment. That is, employing his experiences *before* the event in question, all his knowledge factual and subjective, his abilities, failings, blind-spots (skills, *together with what he would not know,* his particular character and personality to assist in revealing this man's ability to face the crisis chosen to confront him at the present time.
2. Human beings (or animals or creatures possessing human qualities, or attributes of man) must in action and situation be placed in some kind of emotional relationship with others, even if the topic and reason for their meeting is an intellectual one,—for example, two doctors discussing the technique of a brain operation is *not* dramatic, but the same two doctors, both in love with the woman whose brain is damaged, is dramatic.

3. The statement achieved must be achieved *in the present* and must be seen to occur (drama means 'living through'), so that the personalities must behave at a 'life-rate', performing those acts and saying those words which would be relevant to the situation and period in time, and, as in life, show no future or advance knowledge of what will occur as a result of their actions—unless they are Gods or superhuman beings.

4. The achieved final statement must have 'form'. That is, everything irrelevant to the main issues must be lacking, and the relevant material must achieve order and style, so that what is revealed is a refined distillation of all the ideas embodied in the chosen material and *considered by the group to be relevant*. So form in this case is conceived as a sliding scale and related to the standards the group are able set themselves and perceive as required in the first place. The infant child, the ESN child and the sixth-former will all require to 'in-build' rules for their work as they develop it, though these rules will be vastly different in each case.

5. Drama must in its most refined condition be capable of being shared by others who participate in a different way—the audience, which may consist of only one person carefully chosen for some quality such as sensitivity to the actors' needs (for example teacher or head mistress), or the mixed mass of persons who pay to have the experience in the theatre.

Often the child's drama and that of the theatre are seen as being in opposition. The terms 'informal' and 'formal' drama suggest this. They do in fact spring from the same roots—the need of people to role-play, to enable them to measure themselves and their own experiences and viewpoints against those of others, not only in order to see where they are *different*, but also to discover wherein they are *alike*, so that they can achieve a sense of belonging, especially in those areas of living which are not capable of being communicated by words alone. Theatre in its most complex form (say a highly skilful presentation of 'Lear') is related to the child's first groping attempts to improvise upon an idea in that there is a natural progression from the tentative meeting of the group's ideas, through the group's achieving with those ideas a statement with form to a theatrical presentation of a group's ideas. 'An ordered sequence of

events in which one or more of the people in it are brought to a
desperate condition, which it must always resolve, and must if
possible explain'—Kenneth Tynan.

One further general point: dramatic expression can only be
achieved through the six elements

total darkness	—	light
total stillness	—	movement
total silence	—	sound

used in all the infinitesimal gradations and mixtures possible between these poles which together constitute man's living environment.

DRAMA AND EDUCATION

Let us look now at some of the opportunities, and some of the
demands, of drama. First of all, it allows children to—

employ their own views of life and people,
use their own standards of evaluation,
exercise their own terms when expressing and tempering these
ideas.

It also subjects children to the demand to communicate clearly and
specifically both in discussion of the ideas, and the dramatic expression of them. The linguistic demands alone may range from
academic discussion of a factual point, to an emotional outburst
such as a king in defence of his kingdom might make (public language) or a tramp at the door of a rich man, justifying his existence
might be called upon to make (private language).

Drama cannot properly function unless the children agree to
tolerate generously, and *put to work*, differing personalities, points
of view, information, speed of working, and levels of attention. A
sixth-former recently, while working as a member of a self-chosen
after-school drama group, when asked what was affecting him most,
replied 'I never really *saw* a D-streamer before; I never realised what
it must be like not to understand what is said the first time I hear

it. This bloke learns about life in a totally different way from me, and I'm not sure that my way is the best way'.

It gives instant feedback for assessment and rethinking. E. V. Taylor in Experiments with a Backward Class, quotes the example of a little boy role-playing a Greek guard who said 'By gum, it's cold'. His classmates protested that 'Greeks don't talk like that'. He modified after some thought to 'By *ye* gum, it's cold', which passed their critical surveillance.

Drama begins at any point of the children's interest and experience. A group of four years olds were interested in an 'old' map, and decided to travel its roads and seas. They chose to go in a 'Yellow Submarine'. The song was 'Top of the Pops' that week. The approved school boys who chose to kill a president were interested to see how much latitude the (new to them) teacher would allow them in their gang-warfare. A group of Borstal boys sitting in overcoats on hot pipes in protest against a cold classroom chose a pub 'where everybody's cold and sitting on the pipes' as their beginning of an improvisation.

Finally drama is also at the service of the other areas of the curriculum simply because, when man is put, in the act of living, in his environment, the area of study regarding this many may be as varied as the man's character or his environment. Fisherfolk living in the Outer Hebrides may be of interest either because of their isolation, their fishing boats and particular skills, their religious and moral beliefs and attitudes, their homes, stories, folk-lore, understanding of the tides, means of communication, spending or voting power, hobbies or a multitude of other facets of their lives. Set them in another century and the possibilities are doubled. Which of these aspects is to be isolated and brought to special notice, depends upon the teacher's present purpose.

AIMS AND ASSESSMENT

Because of the many purposes to which drama may be oriented, it is often difficult for teachers to discover how to plan progressive work, and how to recognise progression—indeed it is impossible to do the latter unless aim and assessment are kept firmly together in the teacher's mind. All too often the aim is too vaguely defined, and the assessment based falsely on 'showing' rather than 'experiencing' aspects of the work. Teachers find it hard to observe what is the real experience for the children inside the overt action which has been stimulated. An example of this was seen when some 17 year old boys chose a theme of 'Mods, Rockers and Drugs'. They finally decided that a gang owning motor-bicycles should meet in a garage to draw lots to decide which man should do the 'ton-up' on the M 1 in order to carry urgently-needed blood plasma (and incidentally to collect some purple hearts en route). They used chairs as motor-cycles, and spent most of the drama session discussing plans and arguing in a corner of the hall (the garage). The teacher (looking for development of the drama—the shape of the play) was frustrated and felt that session to be a failure. What she failed to notice was that the boys' real experience during this session was that of owning a motor-bike. One can sit on a chair and it becomes the finest vehicle in the world—to have to wheel it out of the garage and drive off would be to turn it once again into a chair. The boys knew this for they were *inside* the situation, while the teacher remained outside. This kind of misreading of children's drama occurs all too often.

One of the broad aims of education is to help people to achieve the fullest and most varied and subtle changes of register in relating to others. These changes of register must be in reference to

role-capabilities,
language, and
physical relations.

It is in this field that dramatic activity is of most direct help, whether at the 'wendy-house' play in infancy, or the socio- and psycho-drama of adulthood, together with all other types which lie between these two extremes.

THE ROLE OF THE TEACHER

The skills required to understand how to employ drama to these ends are not so shrouded in mystery as might be supposed. They would seem to be as follows:

1. To acquire an understanding of the six drama elements and how they combine through contrasting with and supporting each other to make statements. This will be explained more fully below.
2. Vivid pictorial and aural imagination.
3. Empathy to sense the general mood of a group.
4. Capacity to put the children's needs before the teacher's plans.
5. Sensitive changes of register in verbal communication with group.
6. Ability to employ changes of register in the teaching role. This too will be explained more fully below.
7. Ability to *look*—to perceive the real situation.
   Ability to *listen*—to perceive the real statement.

Understanding the six drama elements. In drama the feelings of people and their motivations must be made clear, but they must be revealed in action through contrasts in terms of positions of persons in relationship to each other (stillness—movement). For example, a mighty king, if isolated or placed at a different level doesn't need to be able to act to reveal his *kingness*—the grouping makes the statement.

Texture of sound, whether vocal or musical or elemental is a further means of communicating the relationships and feelings of people (silence—sound).

Time of day and quality of light make not only factual statements but mood and style statements. (darkness—light).

CHANGES OF REGISTER IN THE TEACHING ROLE

The teacher's role is often seen as a consistent one—that of 'he who knows and can therefore tell or instruct'. This is too limited a register, and a barren one to boot, except in certain circumstances. In drama the teacher must be prepared to fulfil many roles:

the deliberate opposer of the common view in order to give feed-back and aid clarity of thought.
the narrator who helps to set mood and register of events.
the positive withdrawer who 'lets them get on with it'.

the suggester of ideas, as a group member.
the supporter of tentative leadership.
the 'dogsbody' who discovers material and drama aids.
the reflector who is used by the children to assess their statements.
the arbiter in argument.
the deliberately obtuse one, who requires to be informed, and the one who *'believes that the children can do it'*.

THE NEEDS OF THE CHILDREN

If children are to see their ideas function adequately the material must be so structured that *without anyone interfering* they are seen to *work*. The nonverbal child should never be placed under a verbal pressure which is too great for him to cope with—it is the teacher's task so to plan the expression of the idea that the child's strengths are used, not his weaknesses. No teacher would dream of asking children to try to make pictorial statements with badly mixed paint, and exactly the same must apply in drama work. As with art, he need not be a fine artist but he must be sensitive to the possibilities of the medium.

It is urgently necessary that some means should be evolved of training teachers to use drama progressively during the child's school life—drama which is not always related to theatrical standards but which considers the children's changing needs both as individuals and as members of groups. Then experimentation can take place to discover which kinds of group drama most efficiently serve which *present* need in the children. All too often we press the future on them and leave them with insufficient time to experience the present. An example of the kind of error we fall into was seen when a lecturer in education watched a group of nine year olds struggling to find which statement was the important one for them in the struggle between Pharoah and the Israelites. In discussion sitting round the teacher they knew that they wanted their freedom to return home, but in drama all they could say was 'Give us more food'. Each time they ask and the Pharoah refused, more children became involved, and 'changes of register' began to be available to them in this difficult verbal situation of kings and soothsayers, prophets and slaves, past civilizations and remote climatic conditions and costumes. The education lecturer thought that 'movement might have been a better approach'.

CONCLUSION

In small groups, all people whether children or adults, wise men or foolish, verbal or non-verbal types, employ the taking of roles (sometimes through individual day-dreaming, reliving of situations, reading of books, watching television and films) *when it best serves the ends they require.* To harness this to the classroom learning situation would obviously be common sense, even at some loss of the individual's ability to do what he pleases when he pleases. Rules do not restrict, they aid, if they are good and pertinent rules. The old-fashioned (and false) rules of theatre such as 'face the front', must be replaced with rules which artists have always employed when creating, such as

'use your ideas and talents honestly, serving the disciplines of the medium'.

There is no 'free' art and there can be no 'free' drama. Instead there is a discipline which once respected frees the individual to discover all the possibilities within that discipline. It is impossible to make it easy for a child to paint: all that can be done is to free him by the atmosphere and lack of external pressure to discover what he may about it. The same applies to drama.

AN INTEGRATED APPROACH
TO THE TEACHING OF
FILM AND LITERATURE

John Stuart Katz

For many English teachers the teaching film is an exciting idea. To demonstrate this, one need only point to the work of such organizations as the National Film Board, the American Film Institute and the British Film Institute, as well as the numerous articles on film in journals in the teaching of English. We have every reason to believe not only that film will continue to be taught in the schools, but that its use will increase. Teachers and other educators should, however, be wary of jumping on a bandwagon. There is still a great need in screen education for extensive research curriculum development work, and the training of teachers. Those who wish to deal successfully with film in the classroom must understand the medium and why they are teaching it.

One can identify at least four current approaches to the teaching of film, each of which has its own rationale and educational implication. Although these approaches are not mutually exclusive, they do exemplify divergent attitudes prevalent in screen education. The first two approaches illustrate what I believe is a dysfunctional use of the medium. The third approach would probably do most justice to film *per se*, but seems impractical in many schools and for most teachers. The fourth attempts to integrate film study with the knowledge and curriculum realities of both teachers and students without ignoring film's essential uniqueness.

Film has been used in the schools primarily as an audio-visual aid. Students studying Shakespeare are rewarded with, or subjected to, a filmed version of the play being studied or an "instructional" film on the Elizabethan theatre. In such cases film acts merely as a

Reprinted from the *English Quarterly* (Winter 1969), pp. 25-29, with permission of the author and the editor.

Dr. Katz is Assistant Professor of Education at the Ontario Institute for Studies in Education, University of Toronto.

"hand-maiden" to the material in which the teacher is really interested. It is unlikely that this approach to film has resulted in
enhancing student's appreciation of the medium. In fact, it has
probably done just the opposite.

Another approach to film study was spawned by McLuhan and
his disciples, whose incessant bombardments are sometimes called
the Marshall Plan, or McLunacy by those less generous. At its extreme, this approach manifests itself in attempts to inundate the
students in media. Don't interpret. Don't analyse. Just fill the classroom with films, TV, records, strobe lights, and let the students
react as they will. The teacher using this approach acts as a non-
interfering anthropologist watching the *primitifs* perform rites which
we outsiders from the pre-electronic generation can never fully
understand.

Thirdly, are two approaches, cinema arts and film-making, which
I consider here as one, because they frequently are combined in the
classroom and tend to treat film in a highly specialized way. The
cinema art approach usually concerns itself with the history, aesthe-
tics, appreciation and even the economics of film, while the film-
making approach deals with technique and production. Too often,
however, these courses see film as if it had sprung full blown from
D. W. Griffith's head and with no relationship to any other art form.
Moreover, these courses find themselves under the rubric of English
for what appears, to both teacher and student, to be no reason other
than expediency.

The fourth approach integrates the study of film with the study
of literature. It is this approach I find most viable. To me, film is
an art form, like literature, and is worthy of study *in* and *for* itself.
Paradoxically, despite its uniqueness, the study of film when integrated with the study of literature allows students to see how each
medium works and to explore the similarities and the differences
between the two media. When students study film and literature
together, they are able to understand not only the meaning or
message of a particular work of art, but also what each medium is
forced to do, what it is able to do most successfully, and what it
seems unable to do.

Let us, for a moment, look at some of the similarities and differences between film and literature which are worth pursuing with

secondary school students. The relationships to be discussed reflect what has happened historically in the mainstream of film and literature—although recent films, like many recent literary works, have attempted to overcome these conventions and limitations. But even if one must use the exceptions to prove the rule, there is value in comparison and analysis of the fundamentals of the two media.

In 1897, in his Preface to *The Nigger of the Narcissus*, Joseph Conrad said, "My task which I am trying to achieve is, by the power of the written word to make you hear, to make you feel—it is, before all, to make you *see*." Fifteen years later, the film-maker D. W. Griffith said, "The task I'm trying to achieve is, above all, to make you see." Griffith was not necessarily commenting on visual perception. He was referring to the same task as Conrad—that of enabling the reader or viewer to go beyond apprehending to comprehending, to go beyond visceral reactions to an understanding of the sense of the work.

Both literature and film are liberating arts; they are part of the humanities. They make the viewer or reader aware of outward realities and of his own inward life. Both, as Northrop Frye says of literature, develop and educate the imagination. Both film and literature present to us an artist's ordering of the chaos of human experience. With the possible exception of "l'art pour l'art," the poet, the novelist, the film-maker uses the pen or the camera to express a particular attitude towards some aspect of human experience.

Literature and film are similar also in that both tend to be content oriented. With some exceptions of course, both media make extensive use of the narrative mode. Both require cognitive participation in order to have the reader or viewer understand them. Finally, both film and literature frequently offer some form of entertainment. These last two components, understanding and entertainment, are reminiscent of the *utile et dulce* of which Horace speaks in defining the function of poetry.

When exploring relationships between film and literature, one must also examine the basic differences between the two media. To state that words are the fundamental tool of literature and pictures that of film is to make, for all of its obviousness, an important distinction. Just as a picture of a horse is not the horse itself, so the picture is also different from that image evoked by the word "horse," no matter how many modifiers the word may have. The imagination educed by literature is qualitatively different from that educed by film.

Film, because of its immediacy and its appearance of concreteness, usually deals more successfully with actions than with thoughts. Literature, on the other hand, deals with thoughts and abstractions just as easily as with actions. For example, Meursault, in Camus' *The Stranger*, has a detachment and an inwardness which are reflected in the way he recounts his story. Although he quotes directly the words of others, the judge and the priest for example, he seldom relates to the reader his exact words to them. Meursault tells the judge *that* it was by chance he had the gun and returned to the spot in which the Arab rested and similarly tell the priest *that* he does not believe in God. In the film, however, Visconti must transform the essence of what Meursault tells us *about* into something we can see, hear, or both. Visconti's Meursault, therefore, enters the realm of action.

One further difference between the two media lies in their handling of time and space. Whereas literature tends to convey time by the use of tense, film tends to convey time by the manipulation of space. In film, everything, even a flashback, happens as we watch it. The filmed version of the Ambrose Bierce story, "Occurrence at Owl Creek Bridge" by Roberto Enrico has immediacy because it is presented to us on the screen in the only way it can be shown— before our eyes, always in the present tense. But, as we learn at the end of the film, it only *appeared* to be in the present and actually was a subjunctive. The short story, in contrast, is written in the past tense, with only the description of Farquhar returning home rendered in the present. Then the sudden switch to the past tense to describe his death creates the sharp contrast which the movie achieves by showing action as it happens.

As an example of this approach which compares and contrasts film and literature, I would like to describe briefly an experimental curriculum now being developed by the Ontario Institute for Studies in Education at the University of Toronto. The curriculum is a ten week "unit" being taught this year in three pilot schools in Ontario to eleventh grade academic and technical students. The course integrates the study of film with the study of literature by investigating ways in which each medium handles a particular theme. The curriculum treats film as film and literature as literature while exploring ways in which each medium deals with certain aspects of the theme which we selected to work on this year—man's relationship to machines.

We approach the theme of man's relationship to machines in three ways. First, we consider works of literature and film which depict man in the absence of, or unaffected by machines, including some Utopian and pastoral works. Secondly, we consider those works in which the machine is praised or even apotheosized for the role it plays in man's existence. And finally, there are those works in which the machine is shown as the physical or spiritual destroyer of mankind.

The students are involved in three activities related to this thematic approach. They see films, discuss them, and write about them; they read books in an individualized reading program, discuss them, and write about them; and they make movies and discuss them. The films seen and the books read are in our judgment worthwhile works of art; no film or literary work is used only because of its theme.

The students begin the course by discussing how film and literature portray man in the absence of machines. They view short films such as *Sky, Nahanni,* and *Leaf.* At the same time they have available to them, for individualized reading, literature such as *Walden, Erewhon, Who Has Seen the Wind,* and nature poetry. The students write on the theme as well as on the ways in which film and literature deal with the theme. As a corollary to the writing, they are given Kodak M-14 Super 8mm. cameras, some technical instruction, and are set loose in a rural or natural setting to make a short film. The course does not attempt to make professional film-makers of the students. We are more interested in the process than in the product of film-making. But by making a filmic statement, the students are forced to consider some of the medium's basic aspects such as camera angles, lighting, perspective and editing. They are, in short, as is the writer or the film-maker, ordering the chaos of their experiences. They are learning to appreciate what is involved in making a coherent statement in either medium.

Students then consider the works which take an objective or positive viewpoint towards machines. They view and discuss shorts such as *N.Y.N.Y.* and *Skyscraper* and features such as Robert Flaherty's

Louisianna Story and Eisenstein's *The Old and the New (The General Line)*. Simultaneously, they read and discuss such books as Saint Exupery's *Night Flight,* the poetry of Carl Sandburg, and science fiction by writers such as Ray Bradbury, Isaac Asimov and Jules Verne. Again, the students are given the 8mm. cameras and film, and set loose, this time in the middle of the city or a factory.

Next, the students see films and read books which deal with the machine as the spiritual or physical destroyer of mankind. Included here would be the short films *Day After Day, 21/87, Very Nice, Very Nice,* and the features—Godard's *Alphaville,* Kukrick's *Dr. Strangelove,* and Theodore Flicker's *The President's Analyst.* Books the students might be reading at this time include *Brave New World, 1984, A Canticle for Leibowitz, Hiroshima, Octopus* and *The Grapes of Wrath.*

As a final project, students are given the opportunity to work in a group on the production of their own 16mm. film, including the script writing, acting, directing, shooting and editing.

We are now attempting to devise ways of evaluating the success of the program, indeed, of any program in screen education. This model for a curriculum is still in the formative stages and will be for at least the next year. We are developing and testing a flexible approach which, I believe, will enable the student to "see" better, in the Griffith-Conrad sense. While it is only one approach to the study of film, it does seem to be a viable way of incorporating an important medium into the school curriculum.

LITERATURE

Why literature? Why spend hours of class time reading and reviewing the fictions and dreams of others? Why not learn of people and events from texts uncluttered by figure or fancy obscuring truths we must all come to know?

For Louise Rosenblatt, and for thousands who have looked to *Literature As Exploration* as their teaching touchstone, literature's place in the classroom is justified only as it engages students in the literary experience, that special interplay between active reader and printed text that results in a personal evocation—at once pleasurable and enlightening.

John Rouse suggests that this *responding to* rather than *learning about* literature can best be encouraged by reexamining the works we ask our students to read. He maintains that much of what we call "trash" may provide students with more opportunities to have the literary experiences described by Rosenblatt than do conventional survey, "close reading," or "great book," based programs.

Edward Gordon considers various trends in the teaching of "The Humanities" and deplores the interdisciplinary presumptions and intellectual flabbiness of curriculum makers. His criticism of elitist concentration on books "selected for their greatness, rather than for their effect on the emotional and intellectual life of a student," complements the positions of Rosenblatt and Rouse.

The four commentators on black literature confirm the importance of making connections between the lives and experiences of readers and the books they are asked to consider. Keneth Kinnamon says "blacks now want the schools to inculcate black group awareness and pride . . . ," and he presents four practical suggestions for teachers who teach black literature courses to black students.

Although Robert Bone believes in the affective potency of literature—"black literature has a revolutionary thrust,"—he is much more concerned with making "the study of black literature just as serious, rigorous, and intellectually demanding as the study of Shakespeare," a position which Kinnamon, Rosenblatt, or Rouse might see as an academizing and consequent defusing of that affective potency fundamental to the study of any literature.

Both Barbara Dodds Stanford and Miriam Ylvisaker emphasize literature as affective rather than academic experience. Miss Stanford believes that black literature in the classroom ". . . will force us to find ways to deal with and use strong feelings in the classroom." Miss Ylvisaker, stressing literature as a moral instrument insists that "Black students *must* have a curriculum more relevant to their lives," and provides a basic book list.

All of these articles suggest that literature can inform, can move, can give unique pleasure to students who have been disenchanted by the books and activities associated with traditional instruction. They further imply that reading books is not antiquarian activity unsuited to anti-linear times, but that in too many English classrooms literature has lost the battle to the joyless academics and to those frightened of meeting today's world in the books their students are eager to read.

A WAY OF HAPPENING

Louise M. Rosenblatt

What should be understood by the term *literature* when we speak of the literature program or of teaching literature? Underlying assumptions about the nature of literature will profoundly affect the organization of the literature program and the day-to-day procedures for carrying it out. Especially important are the implicit assumptions about literature prevailing in the colleges and graduate schools, since these ideas will influence the character of the literature curriculum down to the earliest levels. That shockingly few graduates of our schools and colleges are readers of literature is a frequent criticism of our educational system. Efforts are therefore being made to produce new literature curricula. Unfortunately, the theories of literature prevalent in the colleges and universities today fail to provide sound theoretical bases for literature programs that will educate a reading public capable of participating in the benefits of literature.

What, then, should be understood by *literature?* What do we teach when we teach literature? A personal experience may provide a springboard for discussion: As I was leafing through a poetry text, I came upon the old Scottish ballad, "Edward, Edward" and found myself drawn into rereading it.

In the dialogue between Edward and his mother, he reveals the fact that the blood on his sword is that of his "Father deir." He expresses his desperate, remorseful decision to do penance wandering over the seas, leaving his towers and halls to fall into ruin, his wife and children to beggary. I found myself reliving the step-by-step revelations of the crime and its aftermath. As I finished the poem, it was as though I had been participating in a Greek tragedy in capsule. Associations with Oedipus and Orestes were a measure of my emotional involvement. And then, I turned the page:

From the *Educational Record* (Summer, 1968), pp. 339–346. Reprinted with the permission of the American Council of Education and Louise M. Rosenblatt.

Louise M. Rosenblatt is Professor of English Education at New York University.

1. What is the name of this kind of poem?
2. What was the effect of the refrain?

The shock of these questions drew me away from all that I had lived through in reading the text—the structure of feelings called forth by the pattern of events, my darkening mood as I evoked the image of the destruction of the family through the son's desperate crime and terrible penance, the horror of the final interchange between the two voices.

Is this not typical of what often happens in literature classrooms at all levels? Out of the best intentions in the world, out of misguided zeal, the student is hurried as quickly as possible into some kind of thinking and discussion or writing that removes him abruptly —and often definitively—from what he has himself lived through in relation to the text. Often, he is asked to destroy the actual effect of the poem, novel, or play through focusing his attention on a reduction of it to some clumsy paraphrase of its "literal meaning." Or he may be involved at once, as with "Edward, Edward," in classifying the work as a ballad or a lyric or an epic. Or, again as in the question about the refrain in "Edward, Edward," the effect of the work may be taken for granted and his attention focused at once on a totally analytic consideration of the function of various technical devices or underlying images. Or he may be asked to write on the theme of the work. All of these may be respectable questions about the poem, but only in their appropriate place. And their appropriate place is decidedly not as a substitute for, or an evasion of, the actual experience of the poem as a work of art.

NEGLECT OF ESSENCE

The danger is that at all levels, from kindergarten through the graduate school, in some such way the essence of literature is neglected. W. H. Auden, in his elegy on William Butler Yeats, provides powerful reminders of the essential quality of poetry (and *poetry*, for our purposes throughout this discussion, can be used interchangeably with the terms *literature, literary work of art*, and *imaginative literature*). Auden writes, "For poetry makes nothing happen: . . . it survives, a way of happening." We forget that literature is "a way of happening."

Certainly, in 1939, Auden had no notion of the newest use of the word "happening." The Random House dictionary includes this latest meaning of "a happening" as an event, and then adds that often the audience is also participating in what is going on. This seems to add another level of meaning to Auden's phrase. Yet, perhaps this meaning was already, to some extent, implicit. The poem is a happening, an event, because of the participation of the reader or the listener. The reader *makes the poem happen* by calling it forth from the text. This is why Auden, earlier in the poem could say of Yeats, "he became his admirers."

But, one may object, this is true of all readers, the reading of any kind of text, scientific, informative, as well as imaginative. In all kinds of reading, the reader is active. He must bring his own past experience to bear on the text, and thus "make something of" the symbols, the little black marks that he sees or the sounds that he hears. Because this is true, much that we say about the reading or teaching of poetry or imaginative literature has implications for the teaching of any kind of reading.

Auden's phrase reminds us, however, that poetry is a particular way of happening. Poetry, he says, *makes* nothing happen—that is, poetry is not a tool, an instrument for accomplishing some end or purpose or task beyond itself. Informational, expository, argumentative writings are instrumental in that sense. When we read such a text, our attention is focused on the outcome, on what will be left with us when the reading is over. Hence, a paraphrase or a summary of a piece of information often is quite as useful as the original. Someone else can read the newspaper or a scientific work for us and summarize it quite acceptably. But no one can read a poem for us. Accepting a summary of a poem, an analysis of someone else's reading or interpretation of experience of it, is analogous to having someone else eat your dinner for you. You can use someone else's summary of a biology text, you can benefit from the rephrasing of the technical language of a law, but a work of art, as art, must be a personal experience.

ACTIVE PARTICIPATION

This "way" of a poem or any literary work of art is what differen-
tiates it from ordinary reading. In other kinds of reading, we are
simply concerned with the information or ideas that will be left with
us once the reading has ended, as, for example, when we are reading
a text that gives us directions about how to do something. In reading
the poem, we not only bring about the "happening" by responding
to the verbal symbols that make up the text, but also our attention is
focused on the qualities of the very happening that we are bringing
to pass. We are directly involved, we are active participants in the
"happening." We are aware of what the symbols call forth in us.
They point to sensations, objects, images, ideas. These we must
pattern out of the material that we bring to the work from our past
knowledge of life and language. And these in addition call up in us
associated states of feeling and mood.

The text is the guide and control in all this, of course. We must
pay attention to the order of the words, their sound, their rhythm
and recurrence. Our attention oscillates between the texture of the
sound and rhythm of the words, and all that these evoke in us. We
vibrate to the chiming of sound, sense, and associations. We focus
on this electric charge set up between the text and us. The verbal
symbols stir much more in us than is relevant to the text; we must
crystallize out and organize those elements that do justice to the
particular words in their particular places.

This live circuit between the reader and the text is the literary
experience. Literature is, first of all, this sensing, feeling, thinking,
this ordering and organizing of feeling, image, and idea in relation
to a text. The quality and structure of the reader's experience in
relation to the text becomes for him the poem, the story, or the play.
The task of teachers of literature is to foster this particular "way of
happening," this mode of perceptive and personal response to words,
this self-awareness in relation to a text.

The sense of literature as "a way of happening," then, must be
central to any sound literature program. An underlying and pervasive principle, important for every stage of the program, from the
earliest years to the last, should be this: No practice or procedure,
no pattern or sequence, should hinder the student's growth in

capacity to create literary experiences for himself. Constant alertness is required to avoid methods and programs emphasizing concerns that may become substitutes for, rather than aids to, the sense of the personal meaningfulness of the literary experience.

TO ENRICH RESPONSE

This in no way denies the responsibility of the reader to the text: On the contrary, the literature program should be directed toward enabling the student to perform more and more fully and more and more adequately in response to texts. This means fostering both the capacity for literary experiences of higher and higher quality and the capacity to reflect on these experiences with increasing insight and maturity. Literary sensitivity and critical maturity, it will be seen, cannot be divorced from the individual's rhythm of growth and breadth of experience.

Ironically, at this time, when there is a laudable impulse towards a general revision of the literature curriculum, certain influences have tended to obscure these fundamental considerations. Current critical theories, on the one hand, and current educational theories, on the other, converge to reinforce an analytic, theoretical approach to literature.

One needs only to recall the various schools of critical theory that have prevailed in our universities and literary circles during the past half-century. All of these are reflected in some degree in the litera-ture programs and the approaches to the teaching of literature in our schools and colleges at this time. There is the didactic and moralistic approach, which stems from a long and flourishing tradi-tion, but is perhaps now most in eclipse in the universities. There is the still widespread emphasis on viewing the literary work as a document in literary history and in the author's biography. There is the approach to the literary work as a document reflective of political, social, and economic developments. There is the psycho-logical approach, treating the work as symptomatic of the author's psychic structure or as an embodiment of archetypal patterns or myths.

In recent decades, the general approach associated with the label of the "New Criticism" has, in some quarters, become a literary orthodoxy. The "New Critics" have looked upon the literary work as a self-contained system of words, and they have emphasized technical and stylistic analysis. The "Chicago group" have diverged somewhat from this, emphasizing especially the approach in terms of Aristotle's categories, but they also are mainly concerned with analysis of literary types and the author's methods. Despite the extremely valuable contributions of these and other critical schools, and despite their differences among themselves, they share with the older approaches the tendency to divert attention from literary event, the individual literary "happening" itself. The personal involvement of the reader, the engagement in the actual process of bringing the work into being from the text, has been taken for granted. All, no matter what their emphasis, usually consider the work as given—as an object for study and analysis.

DISREGARDING THE READER

Thus, the New Critics' concern with "the work itself" led, unfortunately, to disregard of the reader's contribution. Perhaps the model or the competing image of the impersonality and systematic objectivity of the sciences lurked somewhere in the background. At any rate, these critics did not work out a sound theoretical basis for relating their formalist or contextualist method to the other approaches, especially the psychological and the social. Even more important, they did not work out—or even see the need for—a thoroughly developed theory of the relationship between the reader and the text.

Hence, current critical doctrines could not offer an adequate theoretical framework when the educational environment generated a much-needed impetus toward rethinking of the literature curriculum. Jerome Bruner's *The Process of Education*[1] can be cited as one of the most influential of the various expressions of the need for cumulative and sequential curricula. A number of his formulations have become part of the general vocabulary of the field. Starting with the assumption that any subject could be taught effectively in

[1] Cambridge, Mass.: Harvard University Press, 1961; see also Bruner, *Toward a Theory of Instruction* (Cambridge, Mass.: Harvard University Press, 1966); and Bruner *et al.*, *Studies in Cognitive Growth* (New York: Wiley & Sons, 1967).

some intellectually honest form to any child at any stage, Bruner developed the notion of the "spiral curriculum," in which the fundamental structure, the basic ideas or principles, of a discipline would be taught from the very earliest level and would be encountered repeatedly in more and more complex forms throughout the years. This curricular model was admittedly based on experimentation in the sciences and mathematics.

The dominant emphases in the theory of literature fostered a rather uncritical application of this model to the development of literature curricula. The laudable effort to build up sequential and cumulative literature programs has been largely vitiated by the tendency to structure the spiral around a set of broad theoretical or intellectual concepts. Too little attention was paid to the fact that, unlike disciplines such as mathematics or the sciences, literature does not present itself as a structure of generally agreed upon basic concepts. Intent on finding something analogous to, say, the concepts of *number* or *set* in mathematics, curriculum planners have fixed on theoretically-formulated concepts such as, to illustrate the range, *form*, or *irony*, or *tragedy*. Based on one or another critical approach, structuring concepts have been drawn from subjects or themes or patterns treated in literature, from the genres or types into which they can be classified, or from the techniques or methods that can be analyzed.

BACK INTO ABSTRACTION

Thus planners of a literature curriculum build a spiral program in which *satire* is to be studied at various levels. Menippean satire is a unit in the third grade, for example, and increasingly complex units on satire are encountered at intervals throughout the subsequent nine years of the literature program.[2] Such planning tends to develop more and more complex theoretical formulations, classifications, and distinctions. Because these curricula have been produced by people of literary culture, one encounters at times evidence of a need to

[2] These comments are intended to characterize a general weakness in the patterns of various sequential curricula produced in recent years, especially by the Curriculum Study Centers sponsored by the Office of Education. I have seen a number of these at various stages, and have consulted the materials distributed by the Materials Center of the PMLA. No program is singled out here,

protest the importance of taste, of the intrinsic value of the work itself. But the absence of a theoretical basis for handling this seems to throw the planners back into the realm of abstract or theoretical concepts as the sign of progression—i.e., a progression based on concepts or information *about* literature apart from readers.

In a lecture at New York University in March 1967, the great psychologist, Jean Piaget, referred to Bruner's contention that any subject could be taught to any child at any stage, and then remarked that, after all, the child as well as the discipline has a sequential development. Even the child's ability to grasp concepts in mathematics or physics, Piaget's work has demonstrated, follows a growth process—a series of stages of development—that may, perhaps, be accelerated (if, he added, this is desirable) but cannot be bypassed.[3] If this is true for logical reasoning, how much more important it is to consider the emotional, intellectual, and social equipment of the student in planning the sequence of the literature program! The "way" of literature should not be ignored; the literature program deals with literary texts which primarily represent—not a structure of intellectual concepts to be assimilated—but a body of potential literary experiences to be participated in.

UNHEEDED WARNINGS

Surely, much more searching consideration should have been given to the question: In what sense can the study of literature be

---

since any one curriculum should be accorded a full study of its strengths and weaknesses. Individual units and sections are sometimes more adequate than the weak theoretical scaffolding of the total sequential program.

Stoddard Malarkey, "Sequence and Literature: Some Considerations," *English Journal*, March 1967 (*56*), pp. 394–400, is typical of the kind of theoretical weakness discussed here.

[3] Bruner, in his chapter "Readiness for Learning," in *The Process of Education* also recognizes the need for further research on the problem of tailoring material to the capacities and needs of students, but much more attention has been given to his idea that a spiral or sequential curriculum can be devised once the basic concepts or forms are established.

No attempt is being made here to deal with the extremely complex relationship between the work of Bruner and Piaget. See Bärbel Inhelder, *et al.*, "On Cognitive Development," *American Psychologist*, February 1966 (*21*), pp. 160–64.

viewed as a theoretically structured discipline? Bruner's use of the terms *idea, principle,* or *basic concept,* derived from the example of mathematics and the sciences, is not applicable without qualification to literature, for which the intellectual or theoretical concept does not have the same kind of fundamental priority. Bruner's own tentativeness about his extrapolations to literature—his references, for example, to tragedy, comedy, and farce, or his comments on *Moby Dick*—should have been taken more seriously, and his few warnings about the difference between the sciences and other disciplines, such as literature, should have been heeded. Instead, often under the influence of the New Criticism or of theoretical classifications such as those found in Northrop Frye's *Anatomy of Criticism,* the tendency has been to assume that theoretical categories provided the basic pattern for a spiraling complexity of analysis and classification in the literature program.

But should this program be conceived as a body of concepts to be learned and applied in increasingly complex ways? Is satire—to return to an earlier example—to be thought of as primarily a concept to be clarified? Certainly a most challenging critical problem is the formulation of a clear definition that will do justice to all the works thus designated. But prior to such a concept, should not satire be *experienced*? Is it not basically a way of viewing represented personalities, situations, and behavior in the light of feelings about what they should be and are not? Even a very simple satiric animal story requires the relating of different planes of thought and feeling about personalities and behavior. This is a complex operation involving ideas and emotional attitudes, rather than primarily an analytic, reasoning, classifying operation. Under certain conditions, even young children are able to have such an experience, but the emphasis should be on the actual literary event or happening, on a vivid evocation of image, action, and attitude from the text. We need to discover the emotional and intellectual structure of such a literary experience. Generalizations *about* it, even about its satiric meaning for human beings in general, may be beside the point, to say nothing of theoretical notions about a label called *satire.* Satiric works, whether in the ninth grade or in college, should be read primarily as structures of experience which have present meaningfulness for the student reader. Given the capacity to organize experience in this way under the guidance of the printed page, the concept of *satire* can emerge ultimately as relevant to actual literary experiences and a useful way of designating them.[4]

INTUITIVE LEARNING

Instead of a structure or sequence of theoretical concepts to be achieved through analysis of literary works, the literature program, then, should be seen primarily as a structure of modes of linguistic and literary experience. The focus should be on what the child or youth may be equipped—sensuously, emotionally, intellectually, and linguistically—to evoke and organize from the spoken word or the printed page at each stage of his development.

In opposition to the pressures toward the analytic and theoretical approach to the literary work, I should like to suggest the principle that throughout the entire literature program, the primary emphasis should be on an intuitive acquisition of literary habits and literary insights. I am using the term *intuitive* in the manner of students of language who tell us that the child acquires a language intuitively.[5] By the time he comes to school, if he has been exposed to users of English, say, he will have acquired a command of the basic structure and the signal system or cues of that language. Theoretical analysis, diagramming, labeling of parts, as the experimental evidence indicates, have little relation to his actual original acquisition of the spoken or written language. Once he possesses the basic structure of the language, as a mode of behavior, he can understand a system of grammatical analysis that may be taught him·as an explanation of what he already does. First, we are told, let the child acquire intuitively the habit of the structure of the language and its way of generating sentences. Then later (if necessary) he can learn in-

---

[4] The nature of relative complexity in literature also requires much fuller study through systematic research in the classroom.

[5] Bruner and other scientists use the term *intuitive thinking* to designate "hunches" or sudden insights into the solution of a problem, which has been preceded by logical analysis of the problem and for which logical proof must subsequently be developed. This tends to stress the absence of logical analysis. In the discussion above *intuitive* implies of formal analysis, but includes also conscious attention to responses to verbal signs and their organization into a mode of immediately apprehended experience. Theoretical analysis may be applied to this kind of intuitive event, but should not be equated with it.

tellectually and theoretically to analyze or describe this linguistic behavior.

MORE SENSITIVE EXPERIENCES

In the same way, in literary training, the prime essential is the intuitive development of habits of responding to the literary text. The literary "way" of responding to a pattern of verbal signs has to be firmly assimilated. This, we have seen, is not only learning how to relate word and referent into a meaningful organization, but also learning how to look at, to savor, the structure of image, idea, feeling, attitudes, during the process of evoking it from the text. Out of the feelings and experiences with life and language which even the young reader brings to the text, he makes the new experience which is the poem or the story. For the youth as for the young child, there should be a continuing reinforcement of habits of sensitive and responsible organization of literary experiences. The sequence to be generated in a literary program is thus a sequence of more and more complete, more and more sensitive, more and more complex experiences.

After the reader has felt the sensuous, emotional, and intellectual impact of the work reverberating within him, he can be led further to pull his experience together and to reflect on it. This indeed is the beginning of the critical process. At any level of the curriculum, what he should study first of all is the relation between himself and the text. This is what he has to learn to be "critical" of.[6] And on that kind of critical relationship can be based later the more complex kinds of self-conscious critical activity. Surely, before the New Critic can make his refined analysis of metaphor or irony or structure, he has undergone a sensitive intuitive experience in relation to the text. This is the object of his criticism, and not some impersonal external object. The path into literary mastery will not, therefore, be primarily through analysis, the naming of parts, the labeling of types, the identifying of figures of speech, the definition of themes,

---

[6] This is insufficiently recognized in the discussion of criticism as central to the literature program in *Freedom and Discipline in English*, Report of the Commission on English (New York: College Entrance Examination Board, 1965).

the evaluation of techniques, or the formulation of aesthetic concepts. *Literary experience, intuitive assimilation and reinforcement
of habits of responding to the verbal text, should at all times provide the living context for relevant or appropriate interpretation or
critical analysis.*

Under the guidance of these fundamental principles, the contributions of both the literary and educational theorists can become
welcome grist to our mill. Critical and theoretical concepts will
need to be constantly translated into the kinds of experience and
the kinds of processes involved. Thus, we may start by bouncing
the child on our knee as we chant nursery rhymes with him, and as
time goes on expose him to more and more complex rhythms and
patterns of the language. This ability to hear the rhythmic patterns
and recurrences of verse and prose is the essential accomplishment;
the laborious counting out of syllables or naming of verse patterns
is an analytic exercise whose value, even for the older student, seems
often obscure. Again, as a story is read, the young reader must learn
to link together in a meaningful way a series of episodes experienced
through time. When one finds a high school youngster who calls an
essay a story or vice versa, is this due to failure to have taught him
the terminology, or is it not due to the fact that he has not *felt* a
narrative linkage so fully that the name of that kind of experience
becomes permanently linked with it? Or as the child grows older, he
must fix his attention on the interplay of the qualities of setting and
situation and personality. These capacities to evoke experience from
the text and to interrelate these felt experiences into a structure
surely are more basic than the naming of a "novel of manners" or
a "picaresque novel."

AN INDUCTIVE PROCESS

Recognition of the primacy of the intuitive assimilation of habits
of literary response will provide, then, the basis for building a sound
sequential literature program related both to the student's development and to the basic modes of literary activity. This also offers a
rationale for inductive learning and teaching in the literature
program. In one sense, every reading of a text constitutes an inductive process, since the student reader must through trial and error

seek to organize the many sensations, emotions, and ideas that present themselves. Any reading involves such creation of tentative interpretations which are either rejected or strengthened by the new elements encountered in the text.

But here I am thinking rather of the inductive process as it leads ultimately to the development of critical or technical concepts. The soundest inductive learning seems to arise when the student is given the conditions which lead to his asking the question for which later he discovers the solution. I have been seeking to develop the image of a literature program in which the student is given the opportunity again and again to stay close to his literary experience, to reflect on it, and to do greater justice to the text and what he makes of it. After repeated experiences in which it has been important, for example, to pay attention to who is speaking in the poem or the story, the term *persona* may become both meaningful and useful. After many sensitive perceptions of the rippling-out of figurative meanings, the concept of *metaphor* can be more than a rote learning of (usually a distorted) definition. Repeated individual literary experiences can lead to analytic insights and groupings under broader critical categories. Concepts such as *epic* or *irony* or *sonnet* represent three very diverse kinds of such conceptual groupings.[7]

Probably one of the most challenging requirements for this kind of teaching is that after creating the conditions for discovery, we should have the faith and the patience to permit this process to develop. The more insecure we are, the greater the tendency to thrust the answers and the theoretical terminology upon the student. The greater also the tendency to deceive ourselves by the kinds of questions that rush the student away from the experience and lead him into impersonal and abstract formulations. Space does not permit a fuller discussion of classroom techniques here. My principal purpose is to underline the emptiness of the current tendency to think that the way to do justice to literature is through analysis or

[7] The primary stress here on literary experience as against analytic talk about literature seems to have some analogies with the psychologists' emphasis on the stage of "concrete operations" as preliminary to developing mathematical concepts, or on experience with geometric configurations and intuitive methods of dealing with them as a prelude to grasping theorems and axioms. But in the literary context, the ability to handle the intuitive phase is central, and the theoretical insights are supplementary (although some present day critics might claim that literature exists to make critical analysis possible!).

categorizing of it. When this trend reveals itself even in the earliest grades, the need for this *caveat* is obvious. (Recent articles[8] deal with "literary analysis" of a picture book in the second grade and "literary criticism" in the third grade.) Usually, teachers of the very youngest children have seemed best aware of the individual's need to perceive and to pay attention to his perceptions—his need to feel and to pay attention to his feelings. Teachers at all levels have the responsibility of honoring such needs of all readers, if literature is to be a bulwark against the dehumanization of so much of our adult lives.

A LIFE ACTIVITY

More than ever, the contemporary world affirms our democratic dream of a society in which each human being can come to fruition as an honored individual. The Civil Rights Act has committed us once and for all to compensating for the cultural deprivation suffered by many children. In the field of literature, this has forced a recognition of something that many of us have been saying for decades: If we wish children to learn how to participate in literature, we have to be concerned about the experience the child brings to the literary work. We must offer him works to which something in his own life, his own preoccupations, and his linguistic experience may serve as a bridge.[9] Only then can he have a literary experience. Once the child or the young reader has had the literary experience, he should not be misled into thinking that the literary work exists primarily as an object for analysis and classification. He should understand it as a life activity that has value in itself and that can offer him personal satisfaction. In addition, on this basis, it should be possible for us to have the courage to present literature as a source of personal and ethical and social insights.

In a sense, practically all of our children are in one way or another culturally deprived. All, we have seen, are in need of nourishment for their powers of sensuous and aesthetic perception. (Recently,

---

[8] See *Elementary English*, January 1966 (*43*), and January 1967 (*44*).

[9] The work in literature of the Hunter College Curriculum Study Center, dealing with an inner city group, illustrates this approach.

the director of a summer program in the humanities in Connecticut found that his pupils, drawn from all socio-economic segments of the community, were equally "deprived" so far as the arts were concerned.) Or practically all may be "deprived" because of a narrow environment—whether of poverty or wealth, of a totally urban, suburban, or rural life, through immersion in an ethnic or regional subculture, or, at the very least, through lack of an international culture in this at once one-and-divided world. Literature can compensate, thus, for the limitations of time and place and class and nation; can compensate, too, perhaps, in some degree, for the limitations and the sorrows of the human condition. If we think of every reading of a literary work as a "happening," as something lived through sensuously, emotionally, and intellectually, then sequential and cumulative literature programs may indeed make an important contribution to American culture.

IN DEFENSE OF TRASH

John Rouse

I

I wish to say a few words not only in defense of trash, but in praise of it. By trash I mean popular novels and cheap fiction, the kind of thing your high school English teacher considered unfit for frivolous young minds in need of serious fare. The kind of thing everyone has read but no teacher can praise, much less introduce into the classroom, without calling into question her academic purity. This includes everything from the works of Ian Fleming and Edgar Rice Burroughs to the latest books by Irving Wallace, James Michener, and Rod Serling.

One might think such stuff hardly needs defending given its popularity and steady proliferation. The health of popular fiction is largely illusory, however, since hardly anyone reads anything, the sales of books being accounted for by an increasingly small percentage of the literate public. I would defend popular fiction, then, against teachers who do so much to discourage reading by showing contempt for the books most people enjoy. And as for praise, I intend to maintain that popular fiction has more value and usefulness in the typical high school classroom than the books now generally taught there.

First, an account of the typical literature program and how it got that way. The sad story need not be long in the telling. It began when college admissions officials met in 1899 to set down for the secondary schools their requirements for entering freshmen. At this time they established a list of "classics" that has dominated literature teaching in most of our high schools to this very day, a list including such works as *Ivanhoe, Silas Marner, Idylls of the King, A Tale of*

This article is reprinted by permission of John Rouse, who is Assistant Superintendent of Schools in charge of English Instruction at Smithtown New York Public Schools and Associate Editor of *Media and Methods*. "In Defense of Trash" originally appeared in *Media and Methods* (September, 1966), pp. 26–29, 48.

Two Cities, and *Julius Caesar*. With one exception, none of these represents the author's best work, none can be considered a classic today. What they do represent is middlebrow taste at the turn of the century. Subsequent updatings of this list have usually followed the middlebrow standard, avoiding accounts of contemporary life in favor of safe classics that only the brightest and most docile students will read.

Sometimes an effort is made to engage the attention of students by giving them easier books. These usually turn out to be either simple tales of rustic innocence, like *Old Yeller*, or abridged classics, perhaps *David Copperfield* or *Jane Eyre*. In either case the selections are usually remote from the interests of today's adolescents, who do not need easy books so much as they need books that examine, even question, life as they live it and see it lived.

Programs have been dominated, then, by the classics—and by those minor works of great authors that pass for classics with the middlebrow. I would hate, in these crass, materialistic times, to be accused of preferring utility over essence, but I doubt if many of these works have any real usefulness. Just what does *The Scarlet Letter* do for a sixteen-year-old, I wonder? Of what use are *Julius Caesar*, *Moby Dick*, *Treasure Island*, and *Great Expectations* to their adolescent readers? Such questions are irrelevant to many teachers, who apparently regard the classics as grand and good things in themselves, like war memorials. The reader is expected to come away from them, perhaps, with a sense of pious satisfaction for having done his duty. I'm afraid he more often comes away with a sense of personal inadequacy and a hatred of reading. It's a high price we pay in "passing on the literary heritage."

How can we account for the curious fact that books which have delighted and instructed thousands are often regarded by teachers as bad, whereas books that have bored generations of schoolchildren and turned them against reading are thought of as good? Such views are not taken as evidence of woolly-headedness, I am sorry to say. They derive from an abstract literary standard that treats books as ends in themselves, quite apart from any immediate interest or usefulness these books may have for the reader. It is this standard that produces classroom anthologies constructed on the principle that what's difficult or dull must be good, and lists of required reading drawn up as though every kid in the class was going on to graduate school for advanced literary training. It is acquired by apprentice English teachers in college survey courses, where they learn that good books are objects to be admired, not experiences to be enjoyed.

Suppose we try a different standard, and define as good that book which gives the student a meaningful emotional experience. Then only rarely will a classic turn out to be a good book. The pleasure that comes from experiencing ideas, attitudes and emotions the reader recognizes as relevant to his condition is provided for most people by books of less than the highest literary quality, sometimes even by trash. Anything worth doing with literature in the classroom probably depends on finding books that give this experience. To see a student interested in a book and concerned about the welfare of its people is a fine thing, whether that book is *The Red Badge of Courage* or *Road Rocket*.

II

If we are ever going to make readers of young people then we will have to turn to the fiction of contemporary writers. And this means not just the work of the best writers, but the work of popular writers of all kinds. Perhaps occasionally one of the modern classics may prove to be a useful book, but we can expect to help most students find their place in the modern predicament only through popular works within their intellectual and emotional reach. Teachers who feel comfortable only with masterpieces will find this a tough assignment, but if we believe that literature ought to serve the reader by helping him learn how to be at home in his own time, then we must turn to the books he can read.

How popular literature serves in this way can be illustrated from any period since mass education created the best seller. For example, there was Mrs. Humphrey Ward's *Robert Elsmere*, the publishing sensation of its day (1888). This story of a clergyman whose faith could not withstand the "new" skepticism was pretty strong stuff to the popular audience of the time. The critics could dismiss the author as a poor writer already out of date, a writer who relived the controversial issues of her youth long after the literary world had passed them by, but they had no more influence on the great reading public than critics do today. Certainly Mrs. Ward was not avant-garde, and judged by some strict literary standard she was no doubt a poor writer whose work is unreadable today by any audience. But the problem of skepticism and loss of faith she dealt with in *Robert Elsmere* was obviously a vital issue to her many readers, just as the recent announcement of God's demise is of general concern today. The service her work performed, then, was to give its readers an organized emotional experience with the intellectual issues that had shaped their times, and so give meaning to those times.

Ever since science and technology began transforming the social structure and value orientation of modern society, reading has played an important part in educating the emotions for life in that society. Old patterns of thought do not always fit the new conditions, and popular fiction, by giving expression to common doubts and fears, gives anxiety a tangible form and so makes it manageable. So that's what the trouble is all about! a reader may say to himself with some sense of relief. What the trouble is about, judging from recent fiction, is, for one thing, problems of moral choice. For another, it is the problem of finding one's own identity in the mass society (the search for personal identity and personal freedom having become something of a national obsession). These are the concerns that sell novels like *The Embezzler* (Houghton, Mifflin $4.95)*, *All Fall Down* (Pocket Books 50¢), *Hot Rod* (Bantam 45¢), *A Separate Peace* (Bantam 75¢), *Fahrenheit 451* (Ballantine 50¢), to mention a few.

Think of teachers going on year after year as if such concerns and such books did not exist, assigning ten more pages in the anthology (next week, the Colonial Period) and collecting book reports on *Lassie Come Home* or *Two Years Before the Mast*. No wonder students are convinced that teachers live in a world of make-believe far removed from the things that count. The girl who is worrying about the conflict between what her friends think is right and what her mother thinks is not likely to believe that *Pride and Prejudice* is just what she needs. The boy who is beginning to think that maybe he really doesn't want to be like his father is not likely to enthuse with the teacher over *Moby Dick*.

* Not in paperback.

More to the point would be *Pickpocket Run** (Harper $2.95),
the story of a boy whose only prospect after graduating from high
school seems to be working in his father's gas station and helping
him cheat the tourists on whom the family depends for a living. Or
Two and the Town (Scribners $1.45) a new retelling of the old story
about the girl in trouble. Or *Dark Adventure* (Doubleday $2.95),*
in which that lost soul, the high school dropout, searches for his
identity. These are books more apt to shape the average adolescent's
thoughts and feelings than such teacher favorites as *The Scarlet
Letter* or even *Huckleberry Finn.*

We can find classics—like those just mentioned—that explore subjects of concern to adolescents, but the trouble is that they deal
with experience at too great a remove from life as young people
know it today. *Huckleberry Finn* has been one of the most popular
books in the schools—with teachers. It has everything teachers think
a book for young people ought to have including humor, adventure,
a good "message," some literary allusions to be explained—all this
and status as a classic too. Yet *Huckleberry Finn* is an astonishingly
difficult book to teach to adolescents. They seem unable to recognize
in Huck's flights from civilization their own struggles with the
hypocrisies of adults and the pressures for conformity. The barefoot
boy on a raft floating down the Mississippi is a long way from the
booted teenager tooling along the expressway. And the humor is
quite beyond their serious, even grim approach to life. Not that they
don't need to take themselves a little less seriously, but Twain is
not an author who can help them do that—not yet. Anyone who
missed *Huckleberry Finn* at twelve cannot read it until twenty.

Young people need books in the modern idiom, then, to help them
work through—emotionally and intellectually—the concerns they
feel are important. And any book that helps them do this will be a
good book, whether or not it is admired by the cognoscenti.

III

Unfortunately, many teachers select books to satisfy their own
needs and not those of students. For example, there is the need to

* Not in paperback.

spend time (*Macbeth* can take up weeks). And the need for academic respectability. And most important of all, perhaps, is the need to keep students at a distance. Any book that touches on the actual concerns of life is apt to arouse the powerful emotional energies students bring into the classroom, and some teachers fear these as they would a riot. They need a barrier between themselves and the discomforting questions, the unsatisfied yearnings, the hostile attitudes behind those bored faces. The classics make an effective barrier and have been so used for generations. The classic is preeminently the safe book.

I take it for granted, however, that English teachers are not in the business of teaching literature, but of influencing behavior. Why teach a book at all unless it promises to change the reader in some way that makes him a more effective person? It seems to me that as teachers we should value a book above all for the help it gives us in shaping the interior world by which the student interprets his experience and guides his impulses into action. I suggest, then, that literary analysis be abandoned as a major classroom activity and that instead we spend the time helping the student explore the experience a book gives him. This means, of course, a frank discussion of real attitudes and feelings.

Some teachers will argue that after all, an inferior book may very well give a superficial or even false impression of life and would, therefore, be harmful to the student, perhaps by arousing his worst impulses. We can count on the classic, the argument runs, to be true in some deep and fundamental way. The argument sounds better than it is. First, the difference between poorly written and well written books is very often one of degree and not of kind. The difference is not simply that one book is good for us and another bad, one true and another false. Both may say something worth hearing, although one may say much more. The great themes are not found only in the great books.

Also, this argument assumes that the teacher's function is simply to explicate the book—explain the hard parts—and the student's function is to "learn" the book (in preparation for a test, no doubt). This division of labor is typical of classrooms where the great books are taught to students not ready for them. I think, however, there is no such thing as learning a book. All we can learn is what our response to the book has been, and the teacher's job, then, ought to be to help the student find out what the book means to him, and to help him test this meaning against his whole experience. In the end the student must be the one to decide whether the book is true enough for him.

The success of such teaching depends, of course, on finding books that will interest young people and that deal with matters important enough to provoke them to discussion. This is not easy. Good trash is a difficult thing to find. But not quite as difficult to find as a good classic.

ON TEACHING
THE HUMANITIES

Edward J. Gordon

The examined life is worth living, but I have doubts about whether the growing trend toward courses in "The Humanities" will allow students to examine their lives. My conclusions are based partly on my reading of secondary school courses of study. My first reaction is that a course called "The Humanities" is trying to combine two, three, or four disciplines, taught in one or two periods, and is raising already abstract ideas to such a level that "learning" can only become "remembering." Almost everything that we know of learning theory and the need for concrete experiences in schools is contradicted by most of these courses. The "answers" all seem to be determined in advance. Books are selected for their greatness, rather than for their effect on the emotional and intellectual life of a student. And given the number of books to be read, music to be listened to, slides of paintings to be examined, how does a teacher get time to teach reading, listening, and seeing? We must remember that intellectual discipline is not found in subject matter alone, a great book, but in the student's approach to the problems raised by the book, the way it is read.

Since these courses are replacing English courses, perhaps it is time to get back to some basic principles on the teaching of English, the acts of teaching that must be kept in mind as one teaches any book. From the point of view of an English teacher, what would I have to do to teach the materials that I have been reading about? When I quote, unless I indicate otherwise, I am referring to phrases that I jotted down as I read the aforementioned curriculum guides.

My next reaction was to the enormity and grandiloquence of the claims for what students would learn from taking these courses.

From the *English Journal* (May, 1969), pp. 681–87. Reprinted with the permission of the National Council of Teachers of English and Edward J. Gordon.

Edward J. Gordon is an Associate Professor of English at Yale University in New Haven, Connecticut.

One guide claims "greater fulfillment of man's highest intellectual, moral, and aesthetic aspirations." Another covers in an outline of over fifty pages, 5000 years of man's life on earth, with a bibliography of 182 items. Most of the guides that I read had no objectives at all; the teacher evidently just said, "Ready, set, go," and the race across the centuries was on.

I do think that we can not separate any curriculum matters from the nature of learning and teaching. Objectives should be realizable and evaluation should tell us how near we came to realization.

What a teacher intends a class to get out of a book should be carefully thought out. To talk of understanding "Man in the Universe" is nonsense; even to narrow this down to a unit entitled "The Search for Truth" is equal nonsense. One of the major characteristics of a short story or novel is that the leading character learns something about himself—or if he does not, the reader does. Therefore any serious piece of fiction could be put under such a heading. Any true objective should be stated as subject and verb, should be a sentence, should make sense. Looseness in nomenclature encourages looseness in thought, and encourages what I think is one of the major failings in student writing, the failure of the general statement to match the evidence. Topics for themes are insufficiently developed and topic sentences for paragraphs are given inadequate detail to support the assertions. If such looseness is built into the curriculum, it will be reflected in the writing wherein we judge what we think we have taught.

The very looseness that I am objecting to can be seen in a writing exercise, used for evaluation, that asks the student to "discuss the basic philosophy of the Orient and Near East with emphasis on the religious and literature produced (sic)." Or to take another: "Discuss how various sculptured heads from Greek examples shown, through Renaissance to Giomocetti (sic) show man's search for the truth about himself."

I cite these questions, not just to say that they are bad, but also to illustrate the high level of abstraction of most of the courses. A word or phrase is abstract to the extent of the number of ideas that it includes. Go back now to my earlier example and look at it from the point of view of a student writing an examination. "Discuss the basic philosophy of the Orient and the Near East," he reads. Is there a basic philosophy? About what? Then he reads on, ". . . with emphasis on the religious and literature produced." We can assume that religious means religions, but what religions? All those of the Orient and the Near East? Do they have a basic philosophy? What is the evidence? When he gets through discussing the *Koran,* where does he go next?

Let me be more positive; a question can be changed from a very abstract statement to a series of far more concrete ones, and be far more useful to the teacher in determining how well he has taught. Here is another question that I found in reading the guides: "Discuss twentieth century man as he was after World War I, as seen in Hemingway and Eliot, for example. Is there any relevancy today?" The question is misleading because it implies that there is a "twentieth century man"; there are only twentieth century men. It implies that all of Hemingway's characters are alike and that all of Eliot's characters are alike. The words, "for example," in the question are startling. Does the phrase mean that the student should discuss other examples of "twentieth century man"? When the question goes on to ask, "Is there any relevancy today?" what does the student say? Relevancy to what? The fact is that the question smells of the closet, one that was put together by a committee and never tried out.

Let me try to frame the question differently. Remember that my standard for an overly abstract question is one that asks the student to do too much; it refers to too many things. The last example that I used as hundreds of more concrete questions built into it; I can only guess what it means. I do not know which works of Hemingway and Eliot that the student has read, but let me make up a few questions that I would prefer to have students write about:

Describe the death of Robert Jordan in *For Whom the Bell Tolls.* In what way is his death symbolic? In what way does it act out the basic theme of the novel? Prove everything you say with specific references to the book.

If they had read "The Hollow Men," I could ask why the poem had this title.

What I am trying to get across here is that the first act of planning effective teaching is the matching of objectives with the book and with the evaluation. We are then dealing with the triad that is the only effective way to talk about teaching: that is, the relationship between the teacher, the book, and the student. An objective is what we hope to accomplish by setting problems for students to solve; we set them by the day, by the week, by the year, all on various levels of abstraction. A legitimate objective, and one only, for teaching *Oedipus*, to take an example, is such a statement as: The past has a way of reappearing in the present and has a way of tripping us up in moments of crisis. This idea is a basic tenet of Freudian psychology. It is dramatically acted out in the play, and an understanding of the idea can be tested by asking: By what steps does Oedipus discover the slayer of Laius?

Whether we start with the day's objectives or with the year's, I do not know. I suspect that the answer depends to some extent on how long we have taught and how much we see the interrelatedness of what we teach.

Let me try a further example. I say to myself that I would like to teach *Antigone*. As I read it, I find many parallels with some of the most important problems in contemporary life, especially the conflict between the power of the state and the call of the conscience. As I prepare to teach the book, I read it over several times and read what the best of our critics have said about the book and about tragedy—so that I am not misteaching it. Then I evolve a rough essay on what I think *this* particular class in *this* room can get out of the play. In doing this, I started with some objectives. I do not say "Understanding the Tragic Mode"; I do not know what such phrases mean. What understandings should a class get about what tragic mode: Aristotle's, Miller's, Shakespeare's, Steiner's, Sophocles' or Krutch's? I would rather have the student work out his own definition and keep refining it as he reads further. If we fill him with slogans, he will try to apply them. He will search for Oedipus' "fatal flaw," and will not find one. So he will make one up. So, with *Antigone*, I think out some objectives: I want the class to see that if a man sets up an absolute as a guide to his behavior, he destroys all other absolutes. I want them to see that there are people who believe that there is a higher law than that of man; a democratic government is founded on this idea.

The book is worth teaching, not only because it is a beautifully written play, but because it still speaks to our condition. Its main idea used to be called "the natural rights of man"; we justified the American Revolution by appealing to it. This particular play is a classic because it metaphorically describes a situation that is still with us. A growing number of college students are announcing that they will refuse to be drafted to fight in what they consider an unjust war. The Pentagon people will argue as does Creon. The paradox will not be resolved. The tragedy will be unavoidable.

Let me summarize a moment. A great book is one that has persisting relevance to men's lives. It acts out the continuous truth of myth. The book is a metaphor where, if we read it as metaphor, we find the great questions that man should ask himself as he lives his life. It does not offer answers, but rather *an* answer, to be accepted or not as the spirit moves us.

Now as I write this essay containing what I want the class to see in a book, what do I do with it? Because team teaching happens to be a contemporary gimmick, should I rise and offer my knowledge to an audience of fifty or a hundred and hope that they will remember what I said? When I was taking education courses, the teachers used to make fun of the lecture method. "Those college lecturers haven't heard of the printing press," the education professor would lecture.

Any teacher has the choice of asking questions or giving answers. I prefer the first because a student is learning whatever it is that he is doing. If a teacher is asking good questions, he may be teaching a student to ask similar questions. If he is offering answers, he is teaching students to remember. When a student is asked questions, his answers should follow the acts of thought that we call logical. He should make a general statement; he should expand on any key terms in his answer to make clear what they mean, and he should offer evidence from the text that proves what he says. And the evidence for the answer should be found in the text, not in vague personal opinions that the student brought with him to class. Good questions alone are not enough; relating them to the text is equally crucial. In one guide I read, under "Man's Inhumanity to Man," "What are some of the motivations which prompt people to treat human beings in an inhumane way?" Among the texts are *The Diary of Anne Frank* and Steichen's *The Family of Man*. I do not believe that the question can be answered with reference to those texts.

If we can agree, then, that questioning is the way to teach a book, what kinds of questions should be asked? When people teach important books, there is a temptation to get too quickly into the big ideas, to skip too quickly over what the author has said. We need to get first to the concrete experience being enacted in the book. To return to the teaching of *Antigone*, we might ask: What is the situation as the play opens? What does Antigone propose doing about it?

Why? What reservations are held by Ismene? After Antigone has been caught, what reasons does she give for contradicting Creon's decree? In the confrontation between Antigone and Creon, what reasons do they give for their actions? What comments does the chorus make on disaster, on the power of Zeus, on hope? As Creon and Haemon debate, what ideas are raised about the relation of a father to a son, about rebellion, about obedience? Why does Creon finally give in?

After the play gets a close reading, based not on what is said and done, but rather on the meaning of what is said and done, we can turn to the bigger questions wherein the student must take the knowledge that he has and draw general statements on a higher level of abstraction: Which of the two, Antigone or Creon, had more freedom in the choices that they made in the play? In *Oedipus* and in *Hamlet* the individual's suffering causes a change, a reform, in the world of the play. What is the effect of Antigone's suffering on her world? Comment on the following statement: The conflict between Creon and Antigone came because they wanted different things from life. As Creon tries to break down Antigone, what does he reveal of his own beliefs toward religion, law, government, and family? Does tragedy occur at the moment in which the hero is faced with two impossible choices?

Or to take a question that could be used for extensive writing, try the following:

In an article in the *New York Times*, W. H. Auden tries to show the difference between Christian tragedy and Greek tragedy. He says that in Christian tragedy the person's downfall comes because he makes a "wrong choice" which leads to the tragedy. In other words he feels that the tragedy could have been avoided if the person did not willingly make the wrong decision which eventually caused his downfall.

In Greek tragedy he feels that the downfall was inevitable. The person did not make a "wrong choice"; what happened was in no way his own fault.

Question: Discuss these two ideas on tragedy, using *Antigone* and any example of what you would consider "Christian tragedy" as Auden defines it. You may disagree with any part of the quotation.

To recapitulate, the objectives for our teaching should be whatever it is that we hope a student will get out of what we teach, and they should be stated on the same level of abstraction as that on which we intend to evaluate. The questions that we ask should have some relevance to the students' lives. A basic, recurring idea in dealing with tragedy is how much control the hero has over his own destiny. It is a question that all of us must ask of our own lives. We get perspective on its meaning when we see comparable situations, when we compare, for example, Oedipus' behavior with that of Willy Loman. We see tragedy as metaphor when we read a recent column by James Reston in the *Times*, comparing the United States Senate to the chorus of a Greek tragedy. Finally, the book we choose should have value in teaching a person how to live his life. The tragic character is always one who has been driven to the last point of human endurance. The quality of the man is what he does about fighting back. Oedipus offers the image of a man that we can admire. Willy illustrates Eliot's dictum: "This is the way the world ends/Not with a bang but a whimper."

Teaching unrelated great books is not enough. The basic purpose of the study guides that I have read is to teach the student to make connection between the various parts of his humanistic education; fine. I can see the attempts if I read horizontally across the page: *Oedipus the King* is correlated with the music of an opera on Oedipus. But as I read down the page I often lose the thread of connection. And too often the connection is forced. I taught a course recently in which a large part was taken up by Blake's poems, but when asked by a syllabus to "discuss them in relation to the philosophy of the Orient," I am lost. For many years I attended Bach festivals and enjoyed the chorales, but when asked to discuss how they were affected by "the religious conflict of the Reformation," I was stumped. I asked the music professor in the next office, and he said that he could not answer the question either. He had thought of them as expressions of Lutheran theology.

Another level of seeing connections is that within the book itself. This idea I have discussed in relation to teaching *Antigone*. I emphasized the fact that the student should find the generalities; he should not be given them by a teacher. One of the basic reasons we teach books is to show students how to read similar books. An educator calls the process "transfer." Jerome Bruner used the fine phrase "to learn how to learn." Teaching this way takes time and a mighty intimate struggle with the mind of a student.

How can we connect great books? We can look at some of the big questions that they address themselves to. *Antigone* deals in large part with how much power the government has over the conscience of the individual. Christ said, "Render unto Caesar the things that are Caesar's, and unto God the things that are God's." But we have never been able to decide which things belong to which. And consequently, Silone said, "In the sacred history of mankind it is still Good Friday. Those who hunger and thirst after righteousness are still derided, persecuted, and put to death." We insisted at the Nuremberg trials that the Nazi underlings should have opposed the path of the German government. The Americans who do so in this present moment of history are contemptuously referred to as peaceniks.

There are many books that deal with the theme of individual conscience in conflict with the state. Plato's "Apology" and "Crito," Thoreau's "Essay on Civil Disobedience," Ibsen's *An Enemy of the People*, Anouilh's *Antigone*, Shaw's *Saint Joan*, all teach well in high school. The last is valuable if only to cast some doubt on whether God *does* speak English.

Let me digress here a moment to raise another doubt about the objectives of some of the study guides I read. There is a kind of pious quality about them, a slight suggestion that great books produce better people. Sheila Schwartz, an English teacher at the State University College at New Paltz, New York, put it well, in a speech to the Conference on English Education in Athens, Georgia:

It occurs to me that the use of the great books for humanities courses is the result of a basic confusion in which it is assumed that exposure to literary excellence will lead to humanistic understanding. We know logically that this is not true. Members of the Inquisition knew the Bible and many Nazis were well read.

And, I might add, many who weep over Joan of Arc, if she offered to return to life after sainthood, as she does in Shaw's version of the story, would repeat with Cauchon, "The heretic is always better dead. And mortal eyes cannot distinguish the saint from the heretic." Only the best of them would agree with Dunois: "Forgive us, Joan; we are not yet good enough for you."

Psychologists who talk of values do say that intellectual awareness of problems must come first; this part teachers can try to attend to, but only with books that speak to students. Actual changes are more likely to come from concrete experiences.

If then we organize the books that we teach around the great questions instead of around great books, we can use different kinds of books to deal with different kinds of answers to the questions. Many of the lists of great books that I read paid little attention to the student, and the amazing repetition of key titles made me think that they were emanating from some Kremlin of the Humanities. *Twelve Angry Men* has more to say to many classes than Mill's *On Liberty.* One deals with a concrete experience; the other with a series of high level generalizations to which the reader must bring a great deal of experience.

And this brings me to another comment on the choice of books. As teachers we know that the best way to get a student involved in reading is to give him a book in which his own experience with life is involved. No one can argue against *Faust* as a great book. I taught it to some of the brightest boys at Yale and found it nothing more than an intellectual exercise for them; it did not excite them. Not one said "I liked that. Where can I find some other books by this guy Goethe?" I noticed Dante's "Inferno" on nearly all the lists. I spoke to a member of the Yale Italian department about this. He said, "We give a full year course on the *Comedy.*" But I persisted, "Assuming that it is taught only through lectures, how many lectures would you recommend?" He answered, "In Italy it is taught over three years. And why should anyone teach only the 'Inferno'? That's like teaching only the first two acts of *Hamlet.* The *Comedy* is about man's spiritual journey through life; why leave him in hell?"

As I look at the list of what some schools say they teach, I think that there is a bit of boasting going on: our syllabus is harder than yours. I tried teaching *Paradise Lost* to some of the brightest secondary school students that I ever had. It went badly because they did not have sufficient background in the allusions. When the Advanced Placement program was first set up, we avoided setting a list of books; we put our emphasis on what it meant to read a book, the kinds of questions one should ask of a particular genre. We did suggest that people not tackle such complex books as *Paradise Lost.*

Some of the guides did make admirable suggestions for books to be taught; these guides looked very much like what I would call good courses in English. Some suggested works of such low quality that they could not possibly be thought of as great books. I would not disparage this last approach if the books are organized around great questions. The basic purpose of literature is to evoke an emotional response from the reader. If the book is remote from the student's view of life, it cannot have a proper emotional impact on him. If the book does not move the student, we may be teaching him not to read.

It is difficult to make distinctions in a short space but even knowing that I may be misunderstood, I will try. I am for the humanities as a tradition and as a center for man's education. Within this tradition he may learn to use his mind and learn that human life has great values and that all humans are to be equally valued.

But I resent the idea that the humanities can be taught as one course. The trend toward doing so is the worst thing that has happened to education since the discovery of World History. Curriculum trends, especially in science and mathematics, are paying more attention to the laws of learning. Why, at the same time, are English teachers moving in the opposite direction, toward more abstract books and experiences?

If the humanities are good for all people, why are we now setting up courses merely for the elite? If we think only in terms of great books, are we also saying of the masses "Let them read *Silas Marner*"?

Why not begin our thinking with great questions, as I suggested earlier, and find books that throw light on them? Then we might adapt the book to the reader and teach the humanistic tradition to all who can read.

Over thirty years ago the National Council of Teachers of English published *The Correlated Curriculum*, and today we have "The Humanities." The impulse behind both movements was the same, and one that I applaud, to get the subject of English into the marketplace, away from its sterile concern with commas, with grammar drill, and with dull books. But gathering a fraternity of the best students and burning incense before great books is not a viable solution. Those who are enforcing their way of life with red paint, with axe handles, or with napalm are also our students.

AFRO-AMERICAN LITERATURE, THE BLACK REVOLUTION, AND GHETTO HIGH SCHOOLS

Keneth Kinnamon

Recently I received a letter from a former student of mine in her first year of teaching at a black high school in Chicago. It expresses with moving urgency the concern that our profession at last is coming to feel about the need to read, to understand, and to teach Afro-American literature:

> I was scanning the English section of the '69 U. I. timetable in the Counselor's office today and noticed your Afro-American Lit. course—and by then this pen was already in my hand.
>
> Since October I have been teaching at . . . a black inner-city school which is barely functioning at the minimal educational level expected of a secondary school. My classes are at the "Basic" and "Essential" levels— two levels below "Regular," which is deemed average—and are totally unlike anything I've ever known. There should be special training programs in college for white would-be teachers in city schools—it's an entirely new world.
>
> Having made an adjustment of sorts, I have been striving to create a modified approach to American literature (which I'm supposed to be teaching) which starts from the black contributions to our culture but as you can guess it is more than difficult for a 22 yr. old white, middle-class female to teach soul.

She goes on to ask for pedagogical suggestions and a reading list. Her letter concludes: "I sincerely wish you success in your new course and hope to hear from you (HELP!) soon."

My response to this letter was dilatory, mainly because of some very real doubts about my qualifications, for although my chief

From the *English Journal* (February, 1970), pp. 189–94. Reprinted with the permission of the National Council of Teachers of English and Keneth Kinnamon.

Keneth Kinnamon teaches in the Department of English of the University of Illinois in Urbana, Illinois.

187

scholarly interest is Afro-American literature and although I have followed the development of the black revolution with some care, I know very little about high schools in general or ghetto high schools in particular. The urgent sincerity of my student's plea was not to be ignored, however, and I offered to her and, on a different occasion, to other Illinois teachers, the following reflections and advice.

The roots of the present confusion about Afro-American literature lie in the soil of past neglect. Until two or three years ago, college courses in black writing were almost never offered except in black institutions in the South. Furthermore, a Jim Crow aesthetic excluded black authors from most anthologies of American literature (read: *white* American literature). How many English teachers read Phillis Wheatley when studying the poetry of the colonial and revolutionary periods? Probably not many, for the standard academic attitude was formulated as early as 1897 by Moses Coit Tyler in *The Literary History of the American Revolution*. In this massive work, the single paragraph devoted to Wheatley dismissed her in this fashion:

The other prominent representative of the town of Boston in the poetry of this period is Phillis Wheatly [sic], a gentle-natured and intelligent slave-girl, whose name still survives among us in the shape of a tradition vaguely testifying to the existence of poetic talent in this particular member of the African race. Unfortunately, a glance at what she wrote will show that there is no adequate basis for such tradition, and that the significance of her career belongs rather to the domain of anthropology, or of hagiology, than to that of poetry—whether American or African. Her verses, which were first published in a collected form in London in 1773, under the title of "Poems on Various Subjects, Religious and Moral," attracted for a time considerable curiosity, both in England and in America,—not at all, however, because the verses were good, but because they were written by one from whom even bad verses were too good to be expected. In 1784, under her new name of Phillis Peters, she published in Boston a poem entitled "Liberty and Peace," suggested by the happy ending of the Revolutionary war. This production, however, makes no change in the evidence touching her poetic gifts.

Yet Phillis Wheatley is as good a poet as Anne Bradstreet or Phillip Freneau, and a better one than Michael Wigglesworth or John

Trumbull. Turning to other examples of the neglect of black writing, I wonder how many of you read *The Narrative of the Life of Frederick Douglass, An American Slave* or *Black Boy* in college courses? Yet these are classic American autobiographies, as interesting and artistically successful as the *Autobiography* of Benjamin Franklin or *The Education of Henry Adams.*

The situation in the high school has been no better. You can recall your own experience in this regard. For all the recent clamor, present undergraduate students at the University of Illinois, black and white, have had little or no exposure, in the high school to Afro-American literature. Recently I conducted an informal poll in my junior-level survey of Afro-American literature. In a class of over one hundred students, twenty per cent black, two-thirds had read no black writing whatsoever in high school. Of the remaining third, most could recall only a poem or two. Two white girls, one from Peoria and the other from Boulder, Colorado, could remember reading only James Weldon Johnson's magnificent folk sermon in verse, "The Creation," but they were not told that Johnson was black!

Of the situation in grade school and junior high, perhaps it is better not to speak. Some of you may have read Jonathan Kozol's eloquent testimony in *Death at an Early Age* of the persecution he suffered at the hands of school administrators when he taught a socially conscious poem by Langston Hughes to his black pupils in Roxbury, the black ghetto of Boston, that sometimes citadel of the abolition movement. Let it not be said, however, that nonliterary contributions of black Americans have been utterly ignored in the elementary grades. I may have reached maturity before encountering the names of Nat Turner, Frederick Douglass, and W. E. B. DuBois, but I distinctly remember a fourth-grade teacher bestowing high praise on Booker T. Washington and George Washington Carver, whose acquiescence to white supremacy made them acceptable for discussion.

The reason for this scandalous neglect of black writers is not far to seek. It is merely the literary manifestation of that pervasive white racism that has corrupted all aspects of our national life from the seventeenth century to the present.

Now, however, suddenly, black literature is the thing. Black students demand it; worried administrators wonder who can teach it; white teachers wonder whether it exists, or if so, whether it is any good. Members of the school board may even be induced to condone it, especially if they are persuaded that the alternative is a school building—or a city—reduced to embers.

I am not at all sanguine about the probability of order arising from the present confusion surrounding the study of black literature in the high schools. As long as white administrators and white teachers control the curriculum in black high schools, black desires and demands will probably not be met to anyone's satisfaction. And I am not referring here to white racism, for that point is obvious enough, but to paternalistic white liberalism and old-line white radicalism, which are mainly integrationist and therefore misunderstand and fear the militant nationalism that constitutes the basic ideological premise of the black revolution today.

For most young ghetto blacks, integrationism is passé, irrelevant to the needs of the black masses and ideologically repugnant. Hence, a most serious dilemma, for the traditional function of American public education has been to socialize the child, to preach patriotism, to minimize group differences, to serve as a melting pot. But blacks now want the schools to inculcate black group awareness and pride, to expose the shams of a racist society, to prepare for black self-determination leading to some kind of separatism. Not only are blacks convinced that white America will *not* fully assimilate blacks into the central patterns of the national life, but blacks do not *want* such assimilation, for they see America as Babylon, as an avaricious, sanguinary, imperialistic, faggoty, sterile, hypocritical, racist hell. Why integrate hell?

But the present black nationalism is not merely a negative reaction to a decadent empire in its death throes, but also the latest expression of a basic historical trend. At the risk of considerable oversimplification, one may designate the two major schools of black social thought as nationalist and integrationist (or separatist and assimilationist). Nat Turner, Bishop Richard Allen, Martin R. Delaney, Alexander Crummell, George Washington Williams, Booker T. Washington in certain respects—all these were major exponents of black nationalism in the nineteenth century. W. E. B. DuBois, in his Pan-Africanist phase, Marcus Garvey, Elijah Muhammed, Malcolm X, Stokely Carmichael, Harold Cruse, LeRoi Jones, and Eldridge Cleaver are important twentieth-century spokesmen of the same philosophy.

Many definitions of black nationalism have been offered. Benjamin Scott, a black activist in Boston, lists as the essential elements unity, community, soul, and self-determination. The Black Panthers have a slogan: "All Power to the People. Black Power to Black People. Panther Power to the Vanguard." However defined, the basic thrust of black nationalism is clear: to achieve maximum black group control of black group life—socially, economically, politically, and culturally.

Thus the leaders of today's urban black students are not Roy Wilkins or Whitney (called Whitey) Young or even the martyred Martin Luther King, Jr., whom young blacks had called The Preacher or De Lawd. Their revolutionary spokesmen are, rather, Malcolm X and Rap Brown, LeRoi Jones and Eldridge Cleaver.

What are the implications of this situation for the high school teacher of Afro-American literature? They are many and complex, but I will limit myself to four practical suggestions.

First, and most importantly, be black. If you can't be black, think black, try to develop a black heart. Soul is by definition not a quality that can be willed into existence, but try. In all things be receptive and empathetic—empathetic, not sympathetic. You have much to learn from your students.

Second as teachers of literature you should recognize and respect black verbal inventiveness. Blacks love word play, "signifying." The black students in your classroom are not inarticulate; they just don't trust white people. Why should they? But they will respond to literary expressions of their rich colloquial speech. A couple of examples are in order. Soon after his arrival in Harlem, the protagonist of Ralph Ellison's *Invisible Man* meets a street vendor. This is the conclusion of their conversation:

"I thought you was trying to deny me at first, but now I be pretty glad to see you . . ."

"I hope so," I said. "And you take it easy."

"Oh, I'll do that. All it takes to get along in this here man's town is a little shit, grit and mother-wit. And man, I was bawn with all three. In fact, I'maseventhsonofaseventhsonbawnwithacauloverbotheyesandraisedon blackcatboneshighjohntheconquerorandgreasygreens—" he spieled with twinkling eyes, his lips working rapidly. "You dig me, daddy?"

"You're going too fast," I said, beginning to laugh.

"Okay, I'm slowing down. I'll verse you but I won't curse you—My

name is Peter Wheatstraw, I'm the Devil's only son-in-law, so roll 'em!
You a southern boy, ain't you?" he said, his head to one side like a bear's.
"Yes," I said.

"Well, git with it! My name's Blue and I'm coming at you with a
pitchfork. Fe Fi Fo Fum. Who wants to shoot the Devil one, Lord God
Stingeroy!"

He had me grinning despite myself. I liked his words though I didn't
know the answer. I'd known the stuff from childhood, but had forgotten
it; had learned it back of school . . .

"You digging me, daddy?" he laughed. "Haw, but look me up sometimes, I'm a piano player and a rounder, a whiskey drinker and a pave-
ment pounder. I'll teach you some good bad habits. You'll need 'em.
Good luck," he said.

"So long," I said and watched him going.

The next example is from a more recent book, Eldridge Cleaver's
brilliant *Soul on Ice*. An inmate of Folsom Prison is expressing his
revolutionary ecstasy over the Watts rebellion of 1965:

"Baby," he said, "They walking in fours and kicking in doors; dropping
Reds and busting heads; drinking wine and committing crime, shooting
and looting; high-siding and low-riding, setting fires and slashing tires;
turning over cars and burning down bars; making Parker mad and making
me glad; putting an end to that 'go slow' crap and putting sweet Watts on
the map—my black ass is in Folsom this morning but my black heart is
in Watts." Tears of joy were rolling from his eyes.

Langston Hughes' inimitable Simple stories, of which "Dear Dr.
Butts" is my personal favorite, provide an abundant supply of this
rich material. The language of the ghetto is so expressive and poetic
that you may yourself wish to learn to rap black. And speaking of
language, don't use the word *Negro*. Young blacks consider it a term
of disparagement meaning a Tom integrationist. The word is *black*
or *Afro-American*.

The third suggestion is to innovate freely. If one approach doesn't
work, try something else. In an article in the *English Journal*
(November 1968), entitled "*Black Boy* and Role Playing: A Scenario
for Reading Success," Marcia Pitcole describes how she involved
even the slowest readers in Richard Wright's autobiography through
an ingenious experiment in acting out individual episodes. There

is no accepted standard method of teaching black literature. Do your own thing!

Fourth, connect Afro-American literature as closely as possible to the lives of your black students. Thus the chronological approach should be junked. Black students at DuSable High in the inner city are not going to be able to relate, as the phrase goes, to Phillis Wheatley, any more than white students at New Trier are going to dig William Shenstone. Furthermore, to convince your black students that literature is meaningful for *them*, you will probably need to begin with militant, outspoken, candid books. "Tell it like it is" has become a tired cliché, but it has a special cogency for people who have grown up in school on white lies, evasion, and dishonesty. Unless you persuade them otherwise, your black students are going to think that literature is an esoteric game played by whites too rich and too bored to spend their time better. Three years ago I gave a lecture on Richard Wright to a group of Upward Bound students from East St. Louis. I began by asking how many played the dozens. About half the hands went up. I then asked how many knew what the dozens were. All the hands went up. I asked finally how many thought that the dozens would be a good subject for literary treatment. All the hands went down. I then read to them a passage from Wright's novel *Lawd Today* narrating a bout at the dozens. Surely any human experience is suitable for literary treatment. What are we shielding our black students from? Are we going to shock them by having them read *Manchild in the Promised Land?* On the contrary, we are going to show them that their own lives are the stuff of literature. I have specified in the first group on the following reading list some books to begin with. After establishing rapport between teacher and student and between student and literature, you can then proceed to some of the books in the second group, for which the student should then be ready.

In implementing these four suggestions—be black, respect black verbal inventiveness, innovate freely, relate black literature to black life—you may encounter administrative misunderstanding or even hostility. Courage and persistence are necessary. The social and professional stakes are so high that to forfeit the present opportunity is to betray a generation of students by perpetuating the literary racism that has characterized our past.

A BASIC READING LIST IN AFRO-AMERICAN
LITERATURE FOR THE HIGH SCHOOL

All of the books listed, except the last, are available in paperback editions.

I. James Baldwin, *The Fire Next Time*
   Claude Brown, *Manchild in the Promised Land*
   Eldridge Cleaver, *Soul on Ice*
   Chester Himes, *If He Hollers Let Him Go*
   Langston Hughes, *The Best of Simple*
   LeRoi Jones, *Dutchman*
   Malcolm X, *The Autobiography of Malcolm X*
   Richard Wright, *Native Son; Black Boy*

II. James Baldwin, *Go Tell It on the Mountain*
   Arna Bontemps (ed.), *American Negro Poetry*
   Charles W. Chesnutt, *The Wife of His Youth and Other Stories*
   Frederick Douglass, *Narrative of the Life of Frederick Douglass, An American Slave*
   Ralph Ellison, *Invisible Man*
   James A. Emanuel and Theodore L. Gross (eds.) *Dark Symphony: Negro Literature in America*
   John Hope Franklin (ed.), *Three Negro Classics* (contains Booker T. Washington's *Up from Slavery*, W. E. B. DuBois' *The Souls of Black Folk*, and James Weldon Johnson's *The Autobiography of an Ex-Colored Man*)
   Langston Hughes *The Panther and the Lash*
   James Weldon Johnson, *God's Trombones*
   Claude McKay, *Home to Harlem*
   Jean Toomer, *Cane*
   David Walker, *David Walker's Appeal*
   Richard Wright, *Uncle Tom's Children*

III. Some Secondary Sources:
   Robert Bone, *The Negro Novel in America*
   Sterling Brown, *Negro Poetry and Drama; The Negro in American Fiction*
   Margaret Just Butcher *The Negro in American Culture*

Addison Gayle, Jr., (ed.), *Black Expression: Essays By and About Black Americans in the Creative Arts*

Seymour L. Gross and John Hardy (eds.), *Images of the Negro in American Literature*

Herbert Hill (ed.), *Anger, and Beyond: The Negro Writer in United States*

David Littlejohn, *Black on White: A Critical Survey of Writing by American Negroes*

Alain Locke (ed.), *The New Negro*

Edward Margolies, *Native Sons: A Critical Study of Twentieth-Century Negro American Authors*

Negro Digest

Saunders Redding, *To Make a Poet Black*

NEGRO LITERATURE
IN THE SECONDARY SCHOOL:
PROBLEMS AND PERSPECTIVES

Robert Bone

Two developments have combined to make this NCTE meeting possible. First, the emergence in recent years of a substantial body of good writing by American Negroes. And second, the determined assault by black students upon the racist practices that permeate our schools and universities, an assault which has produced a major crisis in American education.

Without the good writing, we would have no professional concern. We might, as private citizens, support the Negro cause, but as teachers of American literature, we would have no proper role. As it happens, however, this substantial body of good writing falls squarely within our jurisdiction. Furthermore it is we, and no one else, who have been responsible for its criminal neglect and its systematic exclusion from the curriculum.

Had it not been for the courage and militancy of the black students, this disgraceful situation would have persisted to the present day. For if black literature is at long last beginning to be taught in the classrooms of this nation, it is not because teachers and administrators have suddenly seen the light, but because the black students have begun to ask, "Where am I in this setup?" So to begin with, I want to pay tribute to those youngsters whose social weight, far more than their just cause, has brought us together for these deliberations. A little black power goes a long way!

Even as I speak, a black foot is in the door. Everywhere principals and department heads, deans and college presidents, are hastily improvising courses in black history and black culture. Have they been persuaded of the academic validity of this enterprise? Not at all.

From the *English Journal* (April, 1969), pp. 510–15. Reprinted with the permission of the National Council of Teachers of English and Robert Bone.

Robert Bone teaches at Teachers College, Columbia University in New York City. This paper was presented at the NCTE Convention in Milwaukee, November, 1968.

They are responding to political pressures in a political way. They are trying to cool it.

There is nothing wrong with that. It is infinitely better than refusing to respond at all. But I sense among these educators, even as they bow to the political realities, and undertake the necessary practical reforms, a profound uneasiness. They feel vaguely guilty, as if they were violating some deep conviction, or reluctantly abandoning some cherished hope. At bottom, they remain unconvinced of the legitimacy of Afro-American studies. It strikes them as an abandonment of the integrationist ideal.

It is this ideal, as propounded by a generation of American liberals, that the black revolution is determined to discredit. For it is a curious fact, but a fact, that black literature has been excluded from our schools and colleges not by evil men, not by bigots or racists, but precisely by liberals and humanists. And the basis of their opposition has not been an open advocacy of white supremacy, but a false and meretricious universalism.

Let me give you an example. Not two weeks ago, in the city of New York, the Whitney Museum sponsored an exhibition called "The 1930s: Painting and Sculpture in America." Not a single black artist was represented. Not one. Total invisibility. The exhibition was picketed and the director of the museum, a distinguished art historian, was interviewed by the *New York Times.* Said John Baur, who, I emphasize, is a man of humanistic learning and liberal sentiment: "I certainly think they have every right to picket. But a principle that has guided us all along is that art has nothing to do with the color of skin or race."

Art, it would seem, is a lofty activity far removed from the fury and the mire of human history. It has nothing to do with time or place or circumstance, with the particularities of the human condition. It exists in some Platonic realm, fleshless and disembodied: devoid if not of color at least of skin color, and bereft of any ethnic or national tradition. I wonder what Baur makes of those famous lines of Yeats, "O chestnut tree, great rooted blossomer,/Are you the leaf, the blossom, or the bole?"

But something more momentous is at issue than a debate in aesthetic theory. I have heard some variation or other of Baur's position a thousand times. Indeed, so persistent is the argument, and at the same time, so indefensible, that one suspects an unexamined article of faith. What subconscious interest, or commitment, or loyalty could such an article of faith conceivably serve?

I have a theory to propose. A theory to account for the scandalous neglect of black writers and the resistance to their work which persists among educators even to the present day. I believe that this neglect serves the interest of the white suburban middle class, precisely the group from which the staff and personnel of our schools and colleges are drawn. This is a group which cannot afford to be openly racist, and yet which does not wish to be disturbed. It is generally happy with the way things are. It has its own beliefs about black America, and does not wish to be disturbed in those beliefs. It therefore develops a defensive armor, which will protect what James Baldwin has called its willful innocence.

How can such a group escape from the disturbing versions of the American reality now being openly proclaimed by black writers? Recall that these are not the followers of George Wallace of whom I speak. They cannot simply say, "Keep the colored books out of the schools." That would be entirely too vulgar and too crude. They desperately need a defensive armor, but of what shall it consist? Precisely of the notion that "art has nothing to do with the color of skin or race." On these lofty grounds they can succeed in banning disturbing material from the public schools and at the same time preserve their self-image as liberals and enlightened men.

Until we recognize this phony universalism for what it is—a defensive armor—we will never move ahead. Self-knowledge is the source of all effective action, and if we conceal this stalling tactic from ourselves, there will be a constant foot-dragging, resistance, and sabotage. For make no mistake: black literature has a revolutionary thrust. It will make no converts to the value system of the white middle class.

So much for the barriers and obstacles which exist within ourselves. Unless we can recognize and surmount them, we will be defeated before the enterprise is well begun. Let me turn now to problems of a more objective kind: such matters as the maintenance of standards, curriculum reform, the availability of materials, and the question of teacher education.

Fundamental to the entire enterprise is the development of a sound body of literary criticism. It is one thing to decide to teach black literature, and quite another to know what literature to teach. Richard Wright, for example, has published thirteen books, and at some point we have to discover where, in this large and uneven body of work, the permanent values lie. One recent book by a white critic suggests that serious Negro literature commences with the publication of *Native Son*. He refers to the period before 1940 as "the dark ages." He is quite wrong. There is excellent work in the 1920s and good work even in the 1890s, but the necessary sorting-out process has hardly begun.

The problem of critical standards becomes still more urgent if placed in the perspective of the current campus revolt. For behind the slogan of student power and participatory democracy we are witnessing a widespread assault on the concept of culture as such. Black students are no less guilty in this respect than others of their generation. Thus the Black Student Alliance at Yale University recently called for a sweeping reform of the music curriculum. Bach, Beethoven, and Brahms, they complained, did not have too much relevance for them. They demanded rather courses in Afro-American music.

No one will defend the exclusion of Afro-American music from the Yale curriculum. But why should this be posed as an either-or proposition? It is an act of cultural barbarism to dismiss the three B's as "irrelevant." What is the point of culture, what is the point of education, if it does not transport us beyond our time and place, beyond a narrow and parochial and even narcissistic idea of "relevance," and thus extend our sensibilities to other times and places and modes of feeling?

If black students in the first flush of self-discovery are now to chant, "No more Shakespeare; we want Wright!" then we must be prepared to respond along two lines. First, we must *insist* on Shakespeare, and above all on his relevance. Who better than a black American will understand the line, "Something is rotten in the state of Denmark"? And second, we must make the study of black literature just as serious, rigorous, and intellectually demanding as the study of Shakespeare.

The legitimate demand for black literature, in short, must not be allowed to undermine traditional literary values. Our only safeguard lies in the maintenance of high critical standards. We must turn to the best of black writing, the most enduring, the most solidly constructed, the most impressively styled, the most thoroughly crafted. At no point in our enterprise should bad writing be countenanced merely on the grounds that it is the work of a black author.

Mediocrity, of whatever origin, should be called by its right name.

Once a decision has been made to include black literature in the curriculum, the question of specific course arrangements will arise. Should this material be incorporated into the standard courses in American literature, or should a new course be designed?

The important point is that such decisions be based on sound educational, and not ideological grounds. Those committed to the ideology of integrationism, and to the phony universalism I have been describing, will argue for an "integrated" course. A separate course, they will contend, is nothing but a form of literary segregation.

If we attend rather to the nature of the material than to any social theories, we will discover that black literature, to be taught well, must be taught in sequence. Things do not happen in the arts at random, but as part of a discoverable sequence of events. They should therefore not be taught at random, but as part of a *tradition*.

To understand a literary tradition, it is necessary to observe it unfolding through time. It is necessary to place the black poets, novelists, and playwrights in their proper historical context, to trace influences, to establish trends and movements. This is not to say that the Negro literary tradition is sealed off from the white, but merely that it has its own cohesiveness, its own dynamic. All of this argues for a separate course, or at the very least a substantial unit, long enough to permit the demonstration of cultural continuity.

Anything less should be regarded as a form of tokenism. It is better than nothing to teach an occasional poem or novel by a black author in a standard course in American literature. But it deprives the black student of a systematic knowledge of his particular tradition.

We are not faced, to be sure, with an either-or dilemma. The ideal solution, in my opinion, would be a separate course in black literature, as well as a standard course in American literature which included an occasional black author. The curriculum would then reflect the cultural pluralism which, according to Ralph Ellison, ought to be our national ideal.

Once we have decided on the proper course arrangements, the problem of textbooks will arise. It is heartening to note that in recent months the publishers have begun to respond to this demand. Yet much remains to be done, and much that is presently being done is being done badly. In the torrent of materials that will soon be pouring forth, it will be no simple task to assure the preservation of the highest standards.

In the field of general anthologies I want to mention two titles, even while remarking on their limitations. The first is *Black Voices* (New American Library), edited by Abraham Chapman of the University of Wisconsin at Stevents Point. The second is *Dark Symphony* (Free Press), edited by James Emanuel and Theodore Gross of the City College of New York. Both of these are useful books. The level of taste is high, the range of selections is ample, and any high school teacher will find plenty of teachable material, if the need is for a single text.

Yet even these have the weaknesses of all general anthologies. In poetry, for example, it is not enough to have a handful of poems by a host of poets. What is needed is a sharper sense of the major figures, along with twenty or thirty of their poems, so that we can follow their artistic development. Such an anthology has yet to be produced. Still better would be an inexpensive pamphlet series—a Negro Poets Series—for the serious study and appraisal of individual achievement in the genre.

The same sort of thing needs desperately to be done for the short story, the drama, and the essay form. I speak here of materials that will give us more than scope—more than a superficial acquaintance with a large number of black writers. What is needed is a rigorous selection of the very best, arranged in such a way as to stimulate intensive study.

In the field of the novel, there are special problems. Most of the first-rate work is now available in paperback, but some good novels of the second rank should be brought back into print. Often the available editions, which were initially prepared for the general market, are printed on cheap paper, with small unreadable type, narrow margins, and flimsy bindings. Publishers should begin to consider the possibility of more substantial textbook editions, especially in the case of certain classics.

It must be noted finally that next to nothing has been done by way of preparing materials specifically for high school and junior high school students. There is a teachers' handbook called *Negro Literature for High School Students*, prepared by Barbara Dodds and published by the NCTE. But if textbooks or anthologies exist, I don't know about them.

Even with the best of textbook materials, everything in the last analysis depends upon the competence and skill of the classroom teacher. And it is precisely here, in the area of human resources, that our crisis is most acute. Decades of neglect have left us with a critical shortage of trained teachers, and even as demand increases the supply is so inadequate that it will take a generation to close the gap. Crash programs will be necessary at all levels.

To give you some idea of the proportions of the crisis, let me quote a letter from my daughter, who is a freshman at Swarthmore College: "Daddy, there's a boy here who wants to do graduate work in black literature. He wants to know which schools have the best department for that?" I'm afraid that the answer is a little startling. Not only is there no *best* department, there is *no* department, period. So far as I am aware, no *course*, much less *program*, in Afro-American literature is offered by the graduate faculty of any major university.

We are involved, in short, in Operation Bootstrap. At the top of the profession there is nothing but a gaping hole. The initiative and leadership must therefore come from institutions which are more responsive to the social need. It is the high schools and community colleges, the teacher-training institutions, the four-year colleges with significant black student populations, that must bear the brunt of social change.

Where teacher education is concerned, our difficulties are compounded by the nature of our subject-matter. The study of black literature will release a flood of "controversial," not to say inflammatory, emotions in the classroom. That is precisely its therapeutic value in ministering to the youth of a sick nation. But such teaching will require an unusual level of emotional maturity. It will also require an unusual combination of skills. To succeed in the teaching of black literature, one must possess an extensive knowledge of the black experience, and at the same time, a solid background in literary studies.

As we consider the problems of producing such teachers, there is no point in pretending to be color blind. We will have many white candidates with a good literary training and a minimal exposure to the black experience. And we will have many black candidates with an intimate knowledge of the black experience and a minimal exposure to literary studies.

The problems will be somewhat different for the two groups. The white students would no doubt benefit from background courses in history and sociology, to familiarize themselves with various aspects of black culture. They would also profit from a certain kind of sensitivity training, to discover and uproot, as far as humanly possible, those vestiges of unconscious racism from which no white American is entirely free. If they intend to teach in the ghetto schools, their single most creative undertaking would be to study, and if possible to master, Negro dialect. After all, the elementary act of respect in approaching another culture is to learn the language spoken by its people.

As for the black students, the focus of their education should be literary and cosmopolitan. For the ghetto, no less than the white suburbs, narrows and restricts and parochializes. And it remains, despite the passionate denials of the black nationalists, both economically and intellectually impoverished. The education of black teachers should be aimed at overcoming their parochialism, broadening their intellectual and literary horizons, and consolidating their knowledge of their American and European heritage. The goal must be to prevent a narrow chauvinism and insularity, to arrest spiritual myopia, and to discourage any tendency to employ race as a refuge for mediocrity.

What is required on each side of the color line is an act of transcendence, a breaking out of the rigid compartments of American life. The teaching of black literature—and the learning to teach it—is of necessity a liberating, a transforming experience. It can also be a bridging, a unifying experience, a means of repairing the fatal breach that has appeared in the nation's soul.

❁ ❁ ❁

I have been discussing what amounts to a cultural revolution. When it has run its course, America will have a new image of herself. She will no longer see herself as a white nation and a white people, but as a multi-racial nation; composed of many ethnic strains. And she will have faced herself, for the first time, at the moral center of her being. It is because imaginative literature impinges so directly on the moral and spiritual center of a culture that we must be prepared to risk, to innovate, and if necessary struggle, to implement these programs in the public schools.

AFFECTIVE ASPECTS
OF BLACK LITERATURE

Barbara Dodds Stanford

"Volcanoes of creative energy" is how my college methods teacher described high school students, and this image burns the pit of my stomach as I watch my leaden-eyed students shuffle listlessly into the room and stare blankly into space waiting for their buttons to be pushed. I am pained to see them so unhappy and bored, but I can get no more excited than they about reading *Silas Marner* or discussing elliptical clauses, parts of the prescribed curriculum. The dryness and irrelevance of school irritates me further, because I know that most of my students have real problems in communication: they continually complain that they cannot talk to their parents; they sit nervously, afraid to speak to any of their classmates except their own small circle of friends; and most of them are completely unnerved when confronted with a member of another race. These are the communication problems the English class must deal with, not the intricacies of the theory of tragedy or nominal clauses.

Black literature is a godsend to the teacher who wants his class to deal with genuine communication problems in the classroom. Writers like James Baldwin, William Melvin Kelley, Richard Wright, and Gwendolyn Brooks confront deeply, honestly, and humanly the issues that our students fearfully struggle with alone in their inner worlds. What a relief it is to recognize our own struggle to find ourselves in Baldwin's *Notes of a Native Son*, for Baldwin's frank discussion reassures us that this is a normal human question and aids us in our own quest. Robert Teague's *Letters to a Black Boy* gives parental advice to a black child, but it also gives the white reader honest reactions which will help him communicate with the

From the *English Journal* (March, 1970), pp. 371–74. Reprinted with the permission of the National Council of Teachers of English and Barbara Dodds Stanford.

Barbara Dodds Stanford teaches English in Vashon High School in St. Louis, Missouri.

blacks around him who may not be as open. Claude Brown's *Manchild in the Promised Land* shows the devastating toll of human life and happiness that the city slum takes, and students who are worried about their own friends and family—or even themselves—can gain some courage and insight from Brown's escape. Lorraine Hansberry's *A Raisin in the Sun,* James Baldwin's *Go Tell It on the Mountain,* and Paule Marshall's *Brown Girl, Brownstones* portray young people struggling to assert their own independence and identity against their parents. Most black writers deal with sex openly and without embarrassment as in William Melvin Kelley's short story "Connie," which tells of a pregnant girl who must decide what to do with her baby.

But even if we rush to our classes with exciting samples of black literature, we may still face the blank, turned-off faces of our students. Instead of vibrant communication about real issues, we may find actual resistance to discussion. What can the problem be? Obviously their silence and apparent lack of interest is not irrelevance of material as it was with *Silas Marner,* for they read eagerly and comment on how much they like the books. But during discussion they are silent and look the other way.

I began to understand my students' silence and apparent apathy better when I myself was a participant in a discussion group. In this group I found that though I had plenty to say, I was very reluctant to talk, even when the silences became uncomfortable. I hid within myself weighing each comment carefully, wondering how the rest of the group would react to my revelation. Would they dislike me or make fun of me or refuse to associate with me if I said what I was thinking about? And in this particular group I was with people I probably would not see again. How much more frightening it must be for students to reveal their feelings to classmates whom they see daily and who control their social success or failure.

Their fears are well-founded. Several weeks ago two girls from an all-white school were explaining why they did not want a certain boy to go on a trip with them. Their main objection to him was that he was prejudiced, and they based their judgment on an incident several years earlier when they had heard him call a Negro by a derogatory name. Of course, in another social group, a student could be ostracized for being too friendly to Negroes. Naturally, students are reluctant to participate in serious discussions when the social consequences can be so disastrous. Not only can a person be penalized for the wrong response by ostracism for years in the future, but he often does not even know what response his fellow classmates want.

If dealing with relevant material is so dangerous, then maybe we had better put Baldwin back on the shelf and resurrect "Idylls of the King." And that is the "cop-out" many of us use. But there are two answers to any problem in teaching: One is to give up; the other is to accept the challenge and develop new techniques and ideas to solve the problem. It may be that in the long run the greatest contribution of black literature to the English class will be that it will force us to find ways to deal with and use strong feelings in the classroom.

One of the first skills I found that I had to develop to teach black literature effectively was simply to listen. While watching my apprentice teacher imitate me, I realized that in presenting my well-developed lesson plan explaining a literary work, I was so concerned about getting my own ideas across that I could not give any of my attention to the ideas my students were generating. As an experiment, I tried going into the class every day without any preparation other than reading the assignment. I would ask a very general question such as "What do you want to talk about from yesterday's chapter?" and would wait for the students to present their own ideas. Although there were several periods of silence, the discussions were much more effective than usual, and I gained much insight into my students, and myself. Since then I have found it very effective to begin discussions of black literature or other controversial materials with such open-ended questions. With slower students, the question may need to be more focused, and the students may require some direction to be able to express their ideas. For example, after reading aloud "The Debut" by Kristin Hunter, a story which shows how a social climbing girl learns about her power over men from watching a girl from the streets handle a group of boys, I asked the students to make their minds blank and then to think about the story and to tell me which scene came to their minds.

"The girl's mother."
"What did you notice about the girl's mother?"

"The way she was trying to make the girl be something that she wasn't."
"IIow did you feel about the mother?"
"I didn't like her."

Another student added, "Yeah, she thinks she is better than anybody else," and the students continued in an effective discussion of social climbing. As the discussion began to die down, I told them that I was surprised by the statement that the mother interested them the most, for I had noticed that they all seemed to be much more attentive during the scene where Lucy Mae was talking to the boys. "Who did you like most. Judy or Lucy Mae?"

By now they were ready to quit intellectualizing about social climbers and to express their feelings about the two girls, particularly their hostility toward Judy, who thought she was better than Lucy Mae, with whom they identified. With little direction, they heatedly discussed their resentment of people who think they are better than anybody else because of money or color, and they criticized the story because from their view of the world the story was unrealistic. In their world a girl like Judy would end up tragically. They discussed the story with depth and explored on their own most of the significant themes as well as applying sophisticated critical skills.

This technique also works well with books which students may have strong reactions to. The question "What makes you angry about this book?" revealed that my students felt that the author of *To Kill a Mockingbird* was very prejudiced, and they did not understand that the comments of characters like Mrs. Dubose did not necessarily express the author's opinion. This discussion led naturally to the concept of point of view.

But an effective class that can deal with black literature needs more than a teacher who can listen. It also needs students who can listen, who can tolerate differences of opinion, and who can trust each other not to hold differences of opinion against them. The biggest aid in helping students talk to each other is letting them see that they have many ideas and problems in common.

The "Secret Sharing Game" is a very effective way of showing students how many problems they share with their classmates. For this activity, students are given identical sheets of paper and instructed to write about a personal problem. Then the papers are exchanged and the person who receives the paper must read it as if it were his problem. Usually students will see that most people have basically the same problems. I particularly like to use this exercise while reading a play like *A Raisin in the Sun* and have students extend the exercise by presenting Beneatha's, Walter's, Ruth's, Mama's, and the white visitor's problems in the same way.

Variations of role-playing activities can also help to build trust within a group as well as helping students empathize with the characters in a book. Students could be assigned to the roles of the father, mother, son, brother, and aunt in *Go Tell It on the Mountain* and asked to respond to such open-minded statements as "I am most afraid of . . . ," "I would like to . . . ," "I hate . . . ," and "I don't understand. . . ." Students then could continue by filling in the blanks as they apply to their own feelings. A discussion of this type might give students enough confidence to talk about the touchy subjects of religion and illegitimacy that the book raises.

Besides the ability to listen and a spirit of trust within the class, effective teaching of black literature requires honesty and a willingness to face painful self-revelation. We all like to think of ourselves as good, kind people; black literature forces us to recognize the murky prejudices, hatreds, and fears that lurk in our subconscious. A white girl who thinks of herself as tolerant may be horrified upon reading *Julie's Heritage* to realize that she has done the same things that wounded Julie. This revelation may be so painful that she cannot face it herself, and certainly she will not want to talk about it to her classmates. At times like this, silence may be the best sign of success.

Last year the black revolution hit our school, and I was aware of the identity crises my students faced as they both flirted with and tried to avoid militant groups. Ellison's *Invisible Man* seemed the ideal book to help them understand the conflicts within them, but the questions the novel raised were too personal and confusing for effective class discussion. This time a partial answer was dividing the class into small groups where students could explore their ideas with less threat because the group was smaller. But even here, discussions could not reach the depth of the struggle the more perceptive students were engaged in. Two of the students attempted to create order out of their chaos by their own literary efforts—one with a nightmarish short story, obviously imitating the style of

Invisible Man but dealing with the students' own problem, and the other with a very creative poem.

And isn't that what literature is all about? Isn't good literature an attempt to create meaning out of the chaos of our lives? Isn't literature a way of not only releasing our feelings, but of using them to create beauty and understanding? If we allow our students to listen to honest writers struggling to deal with this very frightening world, perhaps they will not only experience the comfort of knowing that others have faced these same problems and the insight of seeing different perspectives on the problems, but perhaps they will also see that literature can be, for them, too, a way of dealing with the world, a way of handling and using their feelings, a choice of weapons.

OUR GUILT

Miriam Ylvisaker

How long before we listen? In high schools throughout California black students are telling us—by strikes, by boycott, with violence—that the school curriculum is, to them, an enemy. Certainly the school curriculum is not the only enemy Negroes in America face, but for millions of black students what they are taught in school forces them to confront over and over again the fact that the white man's world is not theirs.

Among the demands which militant black students everywhere are making are more black history, more black culture, more black literature. If those demands are made *first* in the form of physical assaults on fellow white students and *then* verbally, it is because that is the only way whites can be made to listen. Too often we respond like parents to an aggressive child, reacting to symptoms rather than looking for causes. "How dare 'they' act that way"; " 'they' are trying to take over the school"; as teachers we make and enforce stricter rules in the name of "safety"; or our students imitate their fathers, buy guns, and surreptitiously bring them to school.

A recent Brandeis University report says that for the next few years the battleground for America's racial conflicts will be the schools. Already this is so, and in more cities each day. It may already be too late. The fact that it has only now occurred to me to write this article, that only now it is being printed, would indicate that too much time has already passed.

If it is not to be too late English teachers must become leaders, political activists if you will, leaders in the fight to help our white colleagues see that *right*, not majority rule, must prevail. Black students *must* have a curriculum more relevant to their lives, and if the battleground is to be the schools and if black America is to feel that there is any hope anywhere, then black students must win on that battleground.

From the *English Journal* (February, 1969), pp. 193–95. Reprinted with the permission of the National Council of Teachers of English and Miriam Ylvisaker.

Miriam Ylvisaker teaches English at Fremont High School, Oakland, California.

It is no accident that so much of America's most successful fiction portrays innocence and youth, for America prefers to think of itself as young and innocent, free of guilt in the most corroding area of its national life—slavery and its aftereffects. Why is *Huckleberry Finn,* which is in our times and on our terms—and to blacks—definitely a racist book, still so popular? Probably because it glorifies the kind of relationship white America still prefers to think it has with its Negroes—a simple friendship full of sentimental, condescending goodwill on the part of Huck, which in turn evokes a response of servile gratitude from Jim. And in those times the simple solution was still enough: Huck frees Jim; all live happily ever after.

But by now innocence, non-guilt, is not enough, has gone wrong. Scout, in *To Kill a Mockingbird,* cannot do anything to save Tom Robinson; Holden Caulfield knows everything is phony but cannot put his finger on why. Even *Lolita,* which critics have called a metaphor for America's lost innocence, by a not too fantastic stretch of the imagination, can be seen as a parallel of the unconscious sexual fantasies which at the same time destroy and bind together black and white America.

English teachers, if they chose, could make a difference by letting every black student know that the teacher recognizes and sympathizes with his student's feelings. (For a statement on what those feelings are, read *Black Rage* by Dr. Price M. Cobbs, the most significant book on the problems of the Negro in America since *The Autobiography of Malcolm X.*) English teachers could make a difference by persuading administrators to listen, to try to understand what black students want, and to try to help make their demands possible.

And English teachers could perhaps make a tiny difference, a small gesture of understanding by simply making available, not necessarily for the whole class but for those students, black and white, who are interested as many books as possible about the struggles of black men and women in America.

Here then, too little and probably too late are some books that have proved popular in the classroom.

A Paperback Classroom Library:
   Books by and About Afro-Americans—Titles have been chosen with these criteria in mind:

1. Books should be as current as possible.
2. The list should include some titles by major Negro writers.
3. Books should be readable, rather than primarily scholarly (Lincoln—*The Negro Pilgrimage in America* rather than Quarles—*The Negro in the Making of America*, for example; *Crisis in Black and White*, rather than *Before the Mayflower*. The list does not include Ellison—*Invisible Man* because it is too difficult for most high school students).

The list is not meant to be a definitive collection on all aspects of black culture. Since the list is limited to paperback (for economy and convenience in the classroom) this would be impossible and not particularly desirable. It is assumed further titles are available in the school library. Rather, operating on the *Hooked on Books* theory of saturation and interest, the list is designed to be a handy package of attractive, readily available books, with emphasis on fiction.

Paperback books go in and out of print fast. All titles on this list are available currently. Teachers should be aware of new titles continually appearing, such as Cleaver's *Soul on Ice* and the collection of writing by young people in Watts, *From the Ashes,* Both soon to be published in paperback.

Baldwin, James. *The Fire Next Time*, .50 Dell (2452).

Baldwin, James. *Going to Meet The Man*, .75 Dell (2931).

Baldwin, James. *Notes of a Native Son*, .60 Bantam (H2842).

*Barrett, William. *Lilies of the Field*, .40 Popular Library (PC-1027).

Belfrage, Sally. *Freedom Summer*, .75 Crest, Fawcett World (T908).

*Bonham, Frank. *Durango Street*, .50 Scholastic Book Service (T1005).

Botkin, Benjamin. *Lay My Burden Down*, $1.95 Phoenix, Univ. of Chicago (P24).

*Braithwaite, Edward. *To Sir, With Love*, .60 Pyramid Publications (X1608).

Brooks, Charlotte. *The Outnumbered: Stories, Essays, and Poems about Minority Groups*, .50 Dell (6772).

*Brown, Claude. *Manchild in The Promised Land*, .95 Signet, NAL (Q2938).

* The starred books have been found particularly popular.

Carawan, Guy. *Ain't You Got a Right to The Tree of Life?*, $3.95 Simon & Schuster (paper original).

Carawan, Guy. *We Shall Overcome!*, $1.95 Oak (082) (original).

Carmichael, Stokely, *Black Power*, $1.75 Vintage.[1]

Conot, Robert. *Rivers of Blood, Years of Darkness*, .95 Bantam (N3526).

*Davis, Sammy. *Yes, I Can*, .95 Pocket Books (95034).

DeCarara, Roy and Langston Hughes. *The Sweet Flypaper of Life*, $1.50 Hill & Wang.

Fairbairn, Ann. *Five Smooth Stones*, $1.25 Bantam (Q3576).

Fanon, Frantz. *Wretched of The Earth*, $1.95 Grove, Evergreen (E390).

Gregory, Dick. *From The Back of The Bus*, .60 Avon (S129).

*Gregory, Dick. *Nigger*, .75 Pocket Books (75091).

Gregory, Dick. *Write Me In*, .95 Bantam (extra original).

*Griffin, John. *Black Like Me*, .60 Signet (P2700).

Hansberry, Lorraine. *The Movement*, $1.95 Simon & Schuster (49411).

*Hansbury, Lorraine. *A Raisin in The Sun* (published with *The Sign in Sidney Brustein's Window*), .85 Signet (T2926).

Hentoff, Nat. *Jazz Country*, .50 Dell (4197).

Horne, Lena. *Lena*, .75 Signet NAL (T3015).

Hersey, John. *The Algiers Motel Incident*, $1.25 Bantam (Q24386).

Hughes, Langston. *The Best of Simple*, $1.65 American Century, Hill.

Jones, LeRoi. *Blues People*, $1.65 Apollo (A103).

Jones LeRoi. *Home*, $1.75 Apollo (A147).

Jones, LeRoi. *Tales*, $1.95 Grove, Evergreen.

*Kata, Elizabeth. *Patch of Blue*, .50 Popular Library (50-1059).

Kaufman, Bel. *Up The Down Staircase*, .95 Avon (N130).

King, Martin Luther. *Strike Toward Freedom*, .65 Harper-Row (P16).

King, Martin Luther. *Why We Can't Wait*, .60 Signet, NAL (P2476).

---

[1] Books without Code numbers are too recent to have appeared yet in *Paperbound Books in Print*. Announcements on them have appeared in *Publisher's Weekly* or *Cumulative Book Index*, neither of which has publishers' numbers.

Lincoln, C. Eric. *The Negro Pilgrimage in America*, .60 Bantam (HP 4038).

Mayerson, Charlotte. *Two Blocks Apart*, .60 Camelot, Avon (ZS126).[2]

*Miller, Warren. *Cool World*, .60 Premier, Fawcett World (R353).

Olsen, Jack. *Black Is Best: The Riddle of Cassius Clay*, .60 Dell (0630).

Owens, William. *Look To The River*, .50 Pathfinder, Bantam (FP4130).

*Parks, Gordon. *A Choice of Weapons*, .75 Berkley Publications (S1399).

Russell, Bill. *Go Up for Glory*, .60 Berkeley Publications (X1365).

Saunders, Doris E. *The Day They Marched*, $1.00 Johnson (original).

Shapiro, Milton. *Jackie Robinson*, .50 Archway, Washington Square Press (29009).

Silberman, Charles E. *Crisis in Black and White*, $1.95 Vintage, Random (V279).

Smith, Lilian. *Our Faces, Our Words*, $1.95 Norton (N251).

Stolz, Mary. *The Noonday Friends*, .50 Tempo, Grosset & Dunlap (4832).[2]

Styron, William, *The Confessions of Nat Turner*, $1.25 Signet (Y3596).

Thomas, Piri. *Down These Mean Streets*, .95 Signet.[2]

Waters, Ethel. *His Eye Is on The Sparrow*, .75 Pyramid Publications (T1613).

*Wright, Richard. *Black Boy*, .75 Harper & Row (P3056).

*Wright, Richard. *Native Son*, .75 Signet, NAL (T2598).

*X, Malcolm. *The Autobiography of Malcolm X*, $1.25 Grove (B146).

X, Malcolm. *Malcolm X Speaks*, $1.25 Grove.

---

[2] A few books about Puerto Ricans living in New York City have been included.

LANGUAGE

Of all the recent proposals for redesign and reorganization of the English curriculum, those dealing with the study of the English language are probably most familiar to most teachers. The terms "linguistics" and "grammar" (often used interchangeably) have provoked argument, confusion, and despair at meetings of English teachers from the departmental to the national level. Over and over the same questions are asked: "What grammar shall I teach?"— "What does transformational grammar offer my students that traditional grammar does not?"—"How much grammar at what grade levels?"—"Which textbook series has the 'newest' approach?"

As the writers in this section indicate, such questions suggest an attitude towards language and language teaching that is neither responsive to change nor aware of challenge. Such questions are essentially reactionary, attempting less to explore new possibilities than to find "relevance" in the *status quo*.

The "generalizations" of Cannon and Ives, for example, point out succinctly the enormous breadth of the field of study called linguistics, a breadth encompassing such basic questions and problems that the question of "What grammar shall I teach?" is reduced to a triviality. The inanity of such a question is pointed out more explicitly by Postman who attacks not only the functional value of grammar instruction, but also the oft-repeated (and supposedly humanistic) contention that the study of grammar is valuable "for its own sake." He proposes, instead, language study that is "inseparable from the study of human situations. . . *linguistics as the rigorous study of language situations.*"

Moran's examination of the language of education represents the result of the kind of study Postman advocates. In this essay he shows clearly how the language of teachers, especially in the questions they ask, reveals their narrow and restricted view of the nature and purposes of education.

Four readings in this section deal with dialect, an area of language study of which English teachers are just becoming aware. These articles also point up the kinds of social (indeed, political) issues

215

that underlie questions of curriculum. For example, Furbee's discussion of the study of dialects includes a description of oral drills designed to help speakers of "nonstandard" English master the "standard" dialect, and McDavid offers his checklist of significant features "as an aid to the teacher who is interested in a more efficient approach to the problem of teaching a standard variety of English—for public roles—to those who use nonstandard varieties at home." Sledd rejects such an approach, claiming that it merely reinforces existing social and racial prejudices and initiates children "into the world of hypercorrection, insecurity, and 'linguistic self-hatred.'" Griffin proposes yet another alternative that the English classroom become a laboratory (or what Postman would call a "language situation") and that the language of the children in the classroom, and that of their friends and relatives, become the subject of an analysis of the significance (social, economic, and political) of dialect in America.

Torvik argues that such a critical analysis should extend to all aspects of language use (not merely dialect) and that the study of semantics will provide students with the "critical instruments" they need. She then details a step-by-step description of an introductory unit intended to start high school students thinking critically about the role of language in human affairs.

Finally, in his discussion of the processes of language learning, Dixon summarizes what is currently known or hypothesized about *how* children acquire and master language and, in so doing, places in perspective the comments of the other writers included in this section.

SOME GENERALIZATIONS
ABOUT LANGUAGE

Garland Cannon
Sumner Ives

The following generalizations are set down with special reference to pedagogical issues and applications:

1. The term *linguist* no longer refers only to someone who has learned a great many languages. At present, it is used more often for someone whose field of study is linguistics—the study of language and of one or more individual languages. There are several branches of linguistics, such as historical linguistics and dialectology, and a few combinations with other fields, such as psycholinguistics and sociolinguistics.

2. A linguist may have no superior innate ability to learn languages, but his training makes him able to learn them more efficiently.

3. No natural language seems to be intrinsically easier or more difficult than any other. A child learns the language of his social environment, and the variety he learns is the dialect of this environment. Children seem to learn all languages at about the same rate. On the other hand, and adult is likely to find some languages easier to learn than others. For example, an Italian can learn Spanish more easily than he can learn Korean. A Japanese can learn Korean more easily than he can learn Spanish.

4. Each language is a system of symbols by means of which persons can communicate. To discuss the actual communication process, it is convenient to divide this system into at least three interacting and somewhat overlapping subsysems.

From *College Composition and Communication* (October, 1968), pp. 201–03. Reprinted with the permission of the National Council of Teachers of English, Garland Cannon, and Sumner Ives.

Garland Cannon teaches English at Texas A & M University. Sumner Ives teaches English at New York University.

In popular terms, these are the phonology, grammar, and vocabulary. In speech, an utterance is manifested by units of the phonology. If there is a writing system for the language, an utterance may be represented by units of this system.

5. When writing is used in a community, somewhat different conventions for written and spoken expression develop. Thus, learning to express ideas in writing is not simply learning to transcribe speech. It is learning to use a related but somewhat different mode of expression. Confusion occasionally results from the fact that the term *writing* has been used both for transcribing and for more artistic creation.

6. Each language reflects the needs of some community in thought and expression, and the language changes over a period of time. Such change is not necessarily improvement or deterioration. Modern English is quite different from Old English. Yet the English of Alfred's day was, so far as one can know, adequate to communicate the speaker's wishes, and great literature has been composed in each period. Literary value is not resident in a language; it results from the way the language is used.

7. So far as we know, every language has been used for artistic expression, including languages which have no writing system. Oral traditions of song and story may be rich and sophisticated. Intricate poetic forms have been used by men who were not literate. In Iceland, as late as the tenth century, the law of the community was usually not written down but carried in the memory of a trusted individual. Artistic expression and historical record-keeping are facilitated by writing, but they are not entirely dependent on it.

8. To say that a language is phonetic or unphonetic is to confuse writing and speech. The term *phonetic* refers only to language sounds. An alphabetic writing system may represent the phonology more or less consistently, and thus may be described loosely as more or less phonetic. English phonology and orthography have both changed, but the former has changed more rapidly than the latter. Several attempts to reform English spelling have been made in the past few hundred years, but these have had little effect. Thus the

letter <i> may now represent a diphthong, as in the verb *wind*, or a monophthong, as in the noun *wind*.

9. Every linguistic performance utilizes resources from both the grammatical and lexical subsystems of the language and is manifested by units from either a phonology or an orthography. Any theory of meaning, or of linguistic communication, that does not consider the interaction of these subsytems is, at best, superficial. Ideally, then, a native language program in the graded school levels should include some consideration of all components of the linguistic system and such additional information about the language as is feasible and relevant in the local situation.

10. Descriptions of a language may be developed for different purposes and may vary in completeness according to the requirements of different educational levels. These purposes may include learning a different language, developing proficiency in using the language, analyzing the linguistic performances of others (as in the study of literature), and understanding the nature of language as a medium of thought and expression.

11. The use of the term *grammar* to designate a part of the total language system precludes its use as a general term for matters of usage, which may include variations in pronunciation and vocabulary as well as in morphology and syntax. The English language is a general system, but whenever English is spoken, some dialect of English is used. Each dialect has at least two dimensions—regional and social. In the expression of intended meaning, one dialect seems to be as efficient as any other, within the needs of the group that uses it.

12. A child's language is a reflection of his social environment. A dialect can be changed deliberately only through a great deal of effort. Hence, linguistic usage is one of the primary marks associating an individual with a group. Furthermore, judgments about a social group are often assigned to the usages associated with it. For these reasons, complete rejection of these usages may be resisted, for it implies rejection of group identification, but mastery of an additional dialect

increases freedom of movement within the social structure. There seems to be no connection between race and dialect, except as race acts as a factor in social discrimination or grouping.

13. Variations in linguistic discourse may be stylistic as well as dialectal. These are the adjustments a person makes to his audience, to factors in the immediate occasion, and to his mode of expression, which may be speech or writing. A customary set of choices made on this basis constitutes a functional variety of the language. These functional varieties are resources. One's ability to choose the variety which is appropriate to the occasion is one measure of his command over the resources of the language.

LINGUISTICS AND THE PURSUIT OF RELEVANCE

Neil Postman

Linguistics, it is now clear, has fallen into the hands of grammarians. Nothing, of course, could be worse news for the children of America who now seem condemned to continuing irrelevance in their English classrooms. Naturally, one cannot blame the children for this state of affairs, but neither can one blame grammarians. Not many people will refuse work and influence when they are offered both. This is especially true of people, like grammarians, who have no large social or political value; in other words, people who have to take their work wherever they can get it. Emphatically, the blame lies with English teachers, who *do* have large social and political functions but who appear, with some notable exceptions, not up to their responsibilities. Given general dissatisfaction with traditional English teaching, given massive financial incentives to modernize, given increased communication with university faculties; given, in short, an atmosphere altogether encouraging to radical change, what have English teachers come up with for their students? What, especially in the name of linguistics and the New English, will they have their students do in the years ahead? Their answer, for the most part, is: "Draw diagrams of sentences. But, of course, new diagrams, not the diagrams of another age." And having agreed that the old diagrams must be replaced in a world of unprecedented change and turmoil, what do up-to-date English teachers gather to discuss? Why, of course, whose new diagrams are best to draw? Shall it be those of the venerable revolutionaries, the structural linguists? Or shall it be those of the heady transformationalists, whose diagrams are so mysteriously multi-directional? Or perhaps— who knows?—the future may belong altogether to the wondrous drawings of the stratificationalists!

From the *English Journal* (November, 1967), pp. 1160–65. Reprinted with permission of the National Council of Teachers of English and Neil Postman. Neil Postman is a Professor of English Education at New York University.

All in all, there has never been such sustained joy among grammarians. English teachers invite them to conferences, pretend to read their books, enroll in their courses, take notes at their lectures, and beg for their counsel. Rarely, has the pursuit of irrelevance been undertaken with such ardor. Recently, I attended a state convention of supervisors of teachers of English. The state in question has had a troubled and ugly history of racial crisis. Its people are struggling, against themselves, to adopt attitudes America desperately needs. Like other states, this one has many of its young men in Viet Nam, killing and being killed for reasons not all Americans support. Poverty is no stranger to this state. Nor is censorship, the John Birch Society, or a dozen other issues and quarrels that separate Americans from each other, and from a satisfactory meeting with the future. And since all of these problems are human problems, in one way or another they are touched, shaped, even created by language. Could there be, then, a more interesting meeting to attend than one convened by supervisors of language teachers? Early in the proceedings a man rose to ask a question about linguistics, for that was the main topic of the conference. "What we want to know," he asked the assembled experts, "is which grammar should we teach?" Now, what would you suppose to be the response of an audience of mature, responsible educators to such a question? Laughter, perhaps, at a feeble attempt at irony? Annoyance maybe, for the time it wastes? Disgust, in a measure equal to the seriousness of the questioner? There was applause—warm, fully approving applause. The man was right. That was exactly what the audience wanted to know, and the answer it received was also warmly appreciated: teach all of the grammars and prepare yourself to teach, as well, those yet to come.

As I said, the grammarians are not to be blamed, although one wishes they wouldn't be quite so pushy even in trying to keep a good thing going. Why, for example, must they tell English teachers that it is a good and humane thing to draw sentence diagrams? That, it seems to me, is a gratuitous humiliation. As if to call deliberate attention to the vulnerability of English teachers, as if to say that these are people so far removed from reality that there is no piece of nonsense one cannot get away with. Which brings us, of course, to the problem of English teachers themselves. Why have they looked to grammarians for their opportunities? Why, of all the relevant and perceptive inquiries into human problems that linguistics allows, have English teachers fixed on the abstractions of grammatical systems? In answering, one must try hard not to be libelous. But we must admit there are those in the teaching of English who are, quite simply, fearful of life. The stuffy and precious ones. The lovers of symmetry and categories and proper labels. For them, the language of real human activity is too sloppy, too emotional and uncertain, and altogether too dangerous to study in the classroom. Grammarians offer such teachers a respectable out. They give them a game to play, with rules and charts, with boxes and arrows to draw, and most of all, with right answers. Great big white Right Answers. What's more, it's scientific. You can attend meetings about it, even argue, a little and genteelly, about new theories. A grammarian recently told an audience of English teachers: "You can have a word-based grammar or a sentence-based grammar." And I do believe there was from the audience a more than slight trembling of delight at the prospect of its having such heavenly options.

Then, too, we have among us those who are fearful not so much of life as of children. These are the controllers and the syllabus-makers, who are afraid to go where the feelings, perceptions, and questions of children would take them. These are the sequence-lovers who can take you from form-classes to terminal strings in just the right amount of time because they consult the structure of their grammar books and not the structure of their students. If only we could find for these teachers a sequential or spiral student, their sequential or spiral curriculums would really work. But they, at least, do not see this as a problem. Spiral student or not, they will get to sector analysis before the Christmas holidays. In the process, what is most fertile in the young will be neglected and remain barren, but by Christmas time sector analysis will be in full flower.

There are, of course, other reasons why linguistics has been reduced by English teachers to a synonym for grammar, among them, obviously, that some teachers of English have not been sufficiently informed of any other possibilities. In any case, it is futile to count the reasons. It is also depressing. Depression leads to inaction, and I choose to believe that there is still time to rescue linguistics before it gets either all the way up or all the way down the river. In other words, I choose to believe that there are large numbers of English teachers who are not fearful of language, life, or children, and as such are concerned to find in linguistics a way in which the teaching of English can be transformed into a continuing pursuit of relevance.

Permit me, then, to suggest an alternative, one which would change the meaning and impact of linguistics in the English classroom; and of necessity would place the grammarian and his works at the distant periphery of language study, not at its center. The alternative is based on the assumption that the primary goal in language teaching is to help students increase their competence to use and understand language, especially those styles, varieties, and functions of language that most intimately affect their lives. This assumption emphatically rejects the idea that language study need not have any practical value to justify its inclusion in the curriculum. I state here categorically that no one, not even a paranoid schizophrenic, does anything for "its own sake," as the grammarians quaintly put it. Quite simply, people do things for reasons. Their activities have purpose. Granted, the purposes are varied, ranging, for example, from self-amusement to self-improvement, but to talk of human activity without human purpose is both shallow and irrelevant. I am assuming, therefore, that the teaching of English has purposes and that none is more important than helping students to manage their lives more effectively by increasing their control over language.

The alternative I will suggest is also based on the assumption, supported by 60 years of educational research and the direct experience of thousands of teachers and millions of students, that the systematic teaching of grammar does very little, or nothing, or harm, to students who need to learn what language is for, how it works, and why so often it doesn't. America's greatest living linguist, I. A. Richards, has stated the case for both of my assumptions in an article in *The New York Review of Books*. Writing of the general failure of teachers to make the study of language relevant and useful, he said: "It was *not* the badness of the grammar descriptions which caused the failure, but a simpler and deeper mistake: learning how to describe a language is not at all the same as learning how to *use* it with power and discernment. In point of fact, current efforts by English teachers to use 'transformational grammar' far too often result in glib manipulation of nomenclature—just as of old—and play with 'tree diagrams' without bringing any improved understanding of what sentences do or how they do it." Richards needs no help from me, but I think he might appreciate my saying that we have failed, because we have not seen the forest for all the trees. Richards is not often invited to conferences of English teachers, perhaps because he insists on reminding everyone that language is always produced by human beings for human purposes to share human meanings. Thus, for him, the study of language is inseparable from the study of human situations. That is exactly what so many teachers are afraid of, and, of course, that is exactly what I would propose as an alternative to linguistics as grammar: namely, *linguistics as the rigorous study of language situations.*

A language situation is any human event in which language is used to share meanings. A poem is a language situation. So is a joke. An expression of condolesce. An editorial. An advertisement. A song. There are not as many language situations as you would imagine if you conceive of them as representing patterns of human discourse. One does not have to study every editorial ever written to understand what use is made of language in them. An editorial is a language system, a human convention; above all, a human *situation* designed to permit a sharing of human understanding and feeling. It has a structure, special functions, a characteristic tone. It is written from a particular point of view and contains particular kinds of statements. The same is true of a business letter, a scientific report, a TV news broadcast, even a menu. Would it be beneath the dignity of a linguist to inquire into the language of a menu? Perhaps. Although such an inquiry would probably tell us more about ourselves and how language affects us than the study of noun clusters.

In any event, the English teacher does not have the same freedom as the linguist in choosing the language systems he wants to scrutinize. The linguist is free to choose that which is merely interesting to him. The English teacher is—or should be—governed by a sense of what is important for his students to think about. For the English teacher, linguistics must be not merely the study of language situations, but the study of *relevant* language situations.

I will come in a moment to the question of what a relevant language situation might be in today's world. Here, it is necessary to stress that, in spite of the impression that grammarians have created, a rigorous, scientific inquiry into language need *not* be confined to the phonemic or morphological or syntactical structure of language. Linguistics is not so timid as that; only certain linguists are. "Linguistics," Leonard Bloomfield wrote, "is the scientific study of language," which means that a linguist is a man who employs the attitudes and varied procedures of science in his quest for knowledge about language. Thus, a linguist may choose to study the structure of sentences in order to discover their grammatical rules. Or, he may choose to study the structure of a language situation to discover its human rules—its purposes, its effects, its tone, its style, the roles people play within it. This is exactly what Richards did when he studied the causes of misreading poetry, what Hayakawa did when he compared the effects of the lyrics of popular songs with those of blues, what Carl Rogers did when he probed into the ways in which communication may be facilitated among people who disagree, what Wittgenstein did when he tried to discover why certain philosophical questions could not be answered, what Eric Berne has done in describing the verbal games people play, what Jerome Frank has done in analyzing the language of the Cold War, what Korzybski did in describing the abstracting process. For such students of language as these, nothing could be more sterile than studying "language as language," to use the grammarian's phrase. For them, language is always a social event, a process that occurs in a human context organized for some human purpose to achieve particular effects. Their inquiries focus on the correlation between language and the behaviors language produces. For them, the most important question that can be asked by a linguist is, "What does language cause to happen?" Obviously, this implies that they are mainly concerned with meanings: how meanings are achieved or blocked, how meanings facilitate human survival or threaten it, how meanings contribute toward personal development or arrest or even personal tragedy. For these men there is no worthwhile study of any aspect of language that is not a study of some aspect of a language user and the context in which language is used. If, as a consequence, these linguists speak of phobias and prejudices instead of phonemes and prefixes, they are not the less scientific for it. They are simply, in my opinion, more relevant. That is why I believe the activities of such men as these can form the basis of a really useful New English as against the trivial, antiseptic, precious tree-sprouting we seem to have got. If we want our students to behave as linguists do, if we want them to adopt the attitudes and use the inquiry processes of linguistic science, then let us also allow our students to investigate matters that can make a difference in their own language behavior. Is there anyone here who truly believes that it matters to anyone but a grammarian how you define a noun, or what the transformational rules are for forming the passive voice or how many allomorphs there are of the plural morpheme? I will not recite for you, since you know it as well as I, the catalogue of needs, troubles, controversies, and disasters that define what we call contemporary life. Surely, linguistics and the New English have to be connected in some way with all of it, or we are wasting our students' time and maybe even their lives.

Let me pose, then, some of the questions I would judge to be in urgent need of answering for the majority of our students today. These are questions about the various language systems that impinge on their lives, indeed, that control their lives, and which they must know how to use and understand. These are questions which linguists have investigated, or may choose to investigate if they wish. These are questions whose answers can directly contribute toward helping students grow in power and discernment in their experience with language.

Consider, for example, the language of advertising.

What are its purposes? What are its most important symbols? What kinds of relationships does it maintain toward its audiences? What social values does it express? To what extent do these values reflect those of the audience? How do its metaphors work? What are the situations in which its symbolism is most effective? What standards may be used to judge its truth? In what sense can the language of advertising be "true"?

Or consider the language of news reporting:

What are its purposes? What is "news" anyway? What is a fact? What do we mean by "objectivity"? From whose point of view is news written? How can you tell? What standards may reasonably be used to evaluate news? In what sense can the language of news be said to be "true"?

Or consider the language of politics:

What are its purposes? What are its major assumptions? What are its controlling metaphors? What are its various kinds of statements? What attitudes are required to interpret it intelligently? What is its characteristic tone? What are the meanings of some of its key terms: *law, theory, defense, sovereignty, freedom, peace,* etc.?

Or consider the language of religion and prayer:

What are the functions of prayer? How does it accomplish its work? What are its rules? How is it organized? From what point of view are religious statements to be evaluated? What are their major assumptions? In what sense can religious statements be said to be true? What are their most important metaphors?

Or consider the language of science:

What are its purposes? What is its characteristic tone? What are its various levels of abstraction? What use does it make of metaphor? From what point of view is it written? What is the meaning of the phrase, "scientific truth"? How does it differ from a "religious truth"? From a "political truth"? What standards may be used to evaluate the language of science?

These are some of the questions about some of the language systems that I would commend to you as a way of connecting linguistics with reality. If the questions strike you as more appropriate to a current events curriculum, then I would remind you that language *is* a current event, a most ubiquitous and urgent current event. If the questions strike you as being in the realm of social science, I would remind you that linguistics is a social science, or at least is one when not in the hands of the Great Trivializers. If the questions strike you as politically dangerous, I would remind you that there is nothing more dangerous to the future of our country than curriculums which keep students playing with sentence diagrams while the languages of reality go swirling, uncomprehended, around their ears. It is worth noting that there are a great many political, social, and cultural leaders who have a vested interest in the irrelevance of our current curriculums. Some of them rely absolutely on the perpetuation of irrelevance to carry on their work. Finally, when I add to the language systems already mentioned, the language of song, the language of business, of romance, of poetry, of humor, or myth, if it occurs to you that I would thus destroy the tripod known as literature, composition, and language, then I would invite you to join me in saying, *good riddance.* The Tripod Curriculum is as unnatural, irrelevant, and unworkable as the metaphor is ugly. Show me in the natural environment any situation requiring the production of what we call a composition, and I'll yield. Show me how the study of literary works is not also the study of a language situation, and I'll yield again. And show me how the grammarian can help our children understand themselves and their environment, and I will yield still. Because no one has, I have felt compelled to prepare this statement, to tell you that an irrelevant New English is worse than none, to warn you that linguistics is too important to be left in the hands of grammarians, and to suggest to you an alternative worthy of our students and ourselves.

THE LANGUAGE
OF EDUCATION:
THE GREAT TRIVIA
CONTEST

Terence P. Moran

Who was the first actor to win an Academy Award in a starring role? A silver bullet is used as an identifying symbol by (a) Tom Mix, (b) the Durango Kid, (c) the Lone Ranger, (d) Hopalong Cassidy. For what studio did Humphrey Bogart make most of his major movies? Fibber McGee was famous for (a) his courage, (b) his musical talents, (c) his closet, (d) his friendship with Calvin Coolidge. Can you name two television series which featured Robert Rockwell?

Trivial questions? What do they have to do with the "language of education"? Then try these questions:

Who was the first American writer to win the Nobel prize for literature? A silver bullet ends the life of the principal character in (a) *Orpheus Descending*, (b) *The Emperor Jones*, (c) *The Silver Cord*, (d) *The Great God Brown*. Who published the first edition of Shakespeare's plays? Mrs. Malaprop was famous for (a) her beauty, (b) her patronage of the arts, (c) her misuse of the English language, (d) her friendship with Sir Philip Sidney. Can you name two plays written by John Webster?

The Random House Dictionary of the English Language defines "trivia" as "matters or things that are very unimportant, inconsequential, or inessential; trifles; trivialities." The word itself comes to us from the Latin *trivium*, a place where three roads meet and where conversation was limited to "small talk." In classical education

From *Language in America* (1969) pp. 103–113. Reprinted by permission of Pegasus, a Division of Western Publishing Co., Inc., from LANGUAGE IN AMERICA, Copyright © 1969 by Western, and also by permission of Terence P. Moran.

Terence P. Moran teaches in the Department of English Education at New York University.

students studied the trivium—grammar, rhetoric, and logic—thereby establishing the first connections between the trivium and trivia.

If the questions asked about the Academy Award, the silver bullet, Humphrey Bogart's studio, Fibber McGee's fame, and Robert Rockwell's television shows are trivial—of little importance or consequence—into what category shall we place the questions about the Nobel prize, the second silver bullet, Shakespeare's publisher, Mrs. Malaprop's fame, and John Webster's plays? Why, into education, of course. While we recognize the triviality of the first set of questions, most of us fail to recognize the same triviality in the second. Such questions are what all too frequently pass for education in our society.

The sad truth seems to be that the language of education is largely the language of trivia. It is not without significance that the current game of Trivia sprang full-blown from the minds of our university students. Karl Marx once wrote that historical events occur twice, once in tragedy and one in farce. Given the state of American education today, it seems that the game of Trivia is the farcical counterpart to the tragedy of education.

For those who find this comparison of education to Trivia a bit strained, a bit far-fetched, I invite you to recall your own experiences in school. How do you rate yourself on these questions: (1) Who discovered America? (2) Who was the first man to circumnavigate the globe? (3) Who were the first men to explore the Mississippi River? (4) Who was the first President of the United States? (5) Who was the "Father of the American Navy"?

Are these legitimate history questions or trivia? I need not labor the point that what we call "America" had been inhabited long before Columbus, St. Brendan or Leif Ericson set foot on the place. Not only are such questions trivial in nature; they are racist in spirit, in that they contain a built-in assumption that nothing is "discovered" until it is stumbled upon by a European.

If you find the question "What were the names of the three horses ridden by Hopalong Cassidy, Eddie Dean, and Gene Autry?" to be trivia, what do you make of the question, "What were the names of the three ships that sailed to America with Columbus?"

Without doubt you were made to memorize the names of Columbus's ships in school; perhaps you remembered the names of the horses from Saturday movie shows. What is it in the questions that makes one part of a parlor game played for fun and the other part of a curriculum studied supposedly for education? It assuredly is not in the forms of the questions, since they are identical; it patently cannot be in the kinds of "learning" involved, since they are identical; it can only be that educators have decided, for some mysterious reasons, that it is worth while to know the names of the ships.

But why not learn the name of Hoppy's horse? Surely that is knowledge worth having. In my neighborhood a kid could achieve a hell of a lot more status among his peers (as the social scientists like to call guys you hang around with) if he reeled off "Topper, Copper, and Champion" than if he said "the *Nina*, the *Pinta*, and the *Santa Maria*." If you answer that some facts are more important to know than others, I would agree; but I would ask you in return, "More important for what, and to whom?"

Make no mistake about it; knowledge of trivia brings fame, success, and reward in our culture. Whether it's a guy who wins beers in the corner bar because he can name the original Dead End Kids, a Charles Van Doren who achieves fame from answering questions on "Twenty-One," or a high-school student who can answer the teacher's questions about who wrote "The Highwayman" and "My Last Duchess," our entire system pays dividends for knowledge of trivia. What passes for a "good student" in our schools is usually that student who has memorized the most trivia thought important by the teacher.

I invite you to compare two sets of questions about various subjects. What differences do you find between the two sets? Which set seems more justified to be included in the curricula of our schools?

Science

1a. The scientist who first synthesized DNA was (a) Kornberg, (b) Sanger, (c) Ochoa, (d) du Vigneaud.

1b. The actor who first played Dr. Frankenstein in the movies was (a) Boris Karloff, (b) Bela Lugosi, (c) Colin Clive. (d) Basil Rathbone.

2a. Of the following, the scientist who originated and developed the system of classifying

2b. Of the following, the actor who originated the role of Tarzan in the movies was (a)

the plants and animals of the
earth was (a) Linnaeus, (b)
Darwin, (c) Mendel, (d) Agassiz.

Johnny Weissmuller, (b) Buster
Crabbe, (c) Elmo Lincoln, (d)
Herman Brix.

Social Science

1a. With which of the following
is the "iron law of wages" most
closely associated? (a) David
Ricardo, (b) Leon Walrus, (c)
Adam Smith, (d) Karl Marx.

1b. With which of the following
is the saying "a friend to those
who have no friends, an enemy
to those who make him an
enemy" most closely associated?
(a) Charlie Chan, (b) Bulldog
Drummond, (c) Boston Blackie,
(d) Sherlock Holmes.

2a. If the names Joseph Schumpeton, Wesley Mitchell, and A.
F. Burns were mentioned in a
discussion, the subject under discussion would most likely be (a)
money and banking, (b) business
cycles, (c) housing, (d) Social
Security.

2d. If the names Benson Fong,
Mantan Moreland, and Willie
Best were mentioned in a discussion, the subject under discussion would most likely be (a)
race relations, (b) the United
Nations, (c) crime detection, (d)
World War II.

3a. *Patterns of Culture* was
written by (a) Margaret Mead,
(b) Ruth Benedict, (c) Ralph
Linton, (d) Ashley Montagu.

3b. "Terry and the Pirates" was
created by (a) Hal Foster, (b)
George Wunder, (c) Milton
Caniff, (d) Ham Fisher.

At this point you may be thinking something like, "Yes, all this
may be true for history, for geography, for science. After all, there
are many facts that have to be learned in these areas. But the
humanities are different; that's where students come to grips with
ideas and concepts, where they learn to think creatively." My only
answer is to invite you to continue with the test.

Philosophy

1a. Schiller, James, and Dewey
are associated with (a) pragma-

1b. Solomon, Hercules, Atlas,
Zeus, Achilles, and Mercury are

tism, (b) deism, (c) positivism, (d) fascism.

associated with (a) *The Iliad*, (b) *The Odyssey*, (c) Captain Marvel, (d) The Ecumenical Movement.

2a. The last two hours of Socrates are described in (a) "The Two Fundamental Problems of Ethics," (b) "Phaedo," (c) "Rebellion of the Masses," (d) "Metaphysics of Morals."

2b. Freedonia's struggle for freedom is described in (a) *Horse Feathers*, (b) *Birth of a Nation*, (c) *Duck Soup*, (d) *Gone with the Wind*.

3a. "Catharsis" means a (a) purging, (b) lengthening, (c) reduction, (d) flippancy.

3b. "Ungawa" means (a) come, (b) go, (c) help, (d) all of the above, plus.

4a. One of the best known of the Cynics was (a) Diogenes, (b) Santayana, (c) Plato, (d) Rousseau.

4b. One of the best known of the Keystone Cops was (a) Milton Sills, (b) Harold Lloyd, (c) Ford Sterling, (d) Sessue Hayakawa.

5a. The Lyceum is associated with (a) Hegel, (b) Apuleius, (c) Marx, (d) Aristotle.

5b. Lompoc is associated with (a) Charlie Chaplin, (b) Stan Laurel, (c) W. C. Fields, (d) the Marx Brothers.

6a. "God is without passions, neither is he affected by any emotion of pleasure or pain"— expresses a phase of the religious philosophy of (a) Luther, (b) Spinoza, (c) Hume, (d) Emerson.

6b. "Never apologize; it's a sign of weakness"—expresses a phase in the life philosophy of (a) Richard Nixon, (b) Hideki Tojo, (c) John Wayne, (d) Ronald Reagan.

Are these the burning questions that students of philosophy should concern themselves with? Is this the examination Socrates had in mind when he said, "The unexamined life is not worth living"? To those who object on the grounds that some factual knowledge is a necessary prerequisite for more creative thinking, that details must be mastered before problem-solving begins, I maintain that few, if any, students (or teachers for that matter) ever go beyond the Trivia-Game stage of learning. Few education systems—whether on the primary or secondary, undergraduate or graduate level—spend considerable time on any aspect of education besides trivia questions.

If education is committed to trivia questions in the sciences, the social sciences, and philosophy, it is *dedicated* to such questions in the area of literature. Far from liberating the creative spirit of the students, most teachers of English sacrifice their students' creativity on the altar of the God of Trivia.

Literature

1a. "Thou shalt see me at Philippi" is the warning of (a) Hamlet's father to Hamlet, (b) Caesar's ghost to Brutus, (c) Antony to Cleopatra, (d) Tybalt to Romeo.

1b. "Even he who is pure in heart and says his prayers by night can become a wolf when the wolfbane blooms and the autumn moon is bright" is the warning given to (a) Clyde Beatty, (b) Lawrence Talbot, (c) Conrad Veidt, (d) Alf Landon.

2a. Dora Spendow, Steerforth, and Mr. Murdstone are characters in (a) *Seventeen*, (b) *David Copperfield*, (c) *Tom Jones*, (d) *Jane Eyre*.

2b. Titus Moody, Senator Claghorn, and Mrs. Nussbaum, are characters in (a) "Life with Luigi," (b) "Amos 'n' Andy," (c) "Allen's Alley," (d) "Out Our Way."

3a. A novel that presents a picture of clerical life in a cathedral town is (a) *Barchester Towers*, (b) *Middlemarch*, (c) *Wuthering Heights*, (d) *Vanity Fair*.

3b. A radio show that asked the question, "Can a young girl from a mining town in the West find happiness as the wife of England's richest and most handsome lord?" was (a) "Helen Trent," (b) "Mary Noble," (c) "Our Gal Sunday," (d) "Stella Dallas."

4a. The term "Malapropism" is associated with (a) Wilde, (b)

4b. The term "Kemo Sabe" is associated with (a) Tarzan, (b)

Sheridan, (c) Congreve, (d) Shaw.

Ramar, (c) Tonto, (d) Jungle Jim.

5a. The writer whose declared purpose was to "justify the ways of God to man" was (a) Jonathan Edwards, (b) Mathew Arnold, (c) John Bunyan, (d) John Milton.

5b. The crime fighter whose declared purpose was to "defend with equal vigor the rights and privileges of all ... citizens" was (a) Boston Blackie, (b) The Green Hornet, (c) Mr. District Attorney, (d) the Public Defender.

6a. Of the following, the author who has not written a major work dealing with Thomas à Becket is (a) Jean Anouilh, (b) Alfred Duggan, (c) Evelyn Waugh, (d) T. S. Eliot.

6b. Of the following, the actor who has not played Frankenstein's monster in a movie is (a) Lon Chaney, Jr., (b) Bela Lugosi, (c) John Carradine, (d) Boris Karloff.

I could continue *ad infinitum*, and *ad nauseam*, but I trust the point is made well enough: the language of education and the language of Trivia are identical. The only difference seems to be in what educators decide to call "significant" at any given moment in history. I fail to see how and why knowing who created the Snopes family is, in and of itself, more important than knowing who created Snoopy.

It is not that schools merely use such knowledge as a basis for further learning but that all too frequently this kind of knowledge becomes not only the means but the ends of education. From grade school through graduate school we challenge the student to become a trivia expert. Classroom tests, Regents examinations, College Board Scholastic Aptitude Tests, the Princeton Graduate Record Examination—all of these make widespread use of trivia as a basis for judging student learning and aptitude.

And the saddest part is that the students do learn: they learn how to use various study guides—Monarch Notes, Barron's Study Guides, the Made Simple series (even, Socrates forgive us, a *Philosophy Made Simple*); they learn how to prepare for specific trivia questions for each class; they learn that the rewards of education are for the

Trivia expert and the punishments for those foolish enough to hazard an original thought.

When the student has demonstrated his proficiency at playing Education Trivia, he is invited to participate in the more esoteric and demanding game of Minutiae, sometimes called "specialization" or "doctoral dissertation." In this variation of Trivia, the player attempts to become expert in some one area of study, preferably an area about which few people know or care. One of the best things about this game is that it allows the player a legitimate "out" when asked general trivia questions: "Goethe? Sorry, I'm a Beaumont and Fletcher man myself." As you can see, this is the perfect defense against a charge of ignorance.

In self-defense, I have created my own game of Minutiae called "Barnabe Googe." Strange as it sounds, Barnabe Googe actually was an Elizabethan poet. Since he is neither well known nor widely read, Googe is perfect for playing Minutiae. I am only going to tell you that he had a wicked way with the "fourteener" (two points for identifying that) and that his work is considered quite representative of English poetry between the time of Wyatt and Surrey (one point apiece) and that of Spenser (one point).

At the moment I seem to have Googe more or less to myself, but I fully expect to see any day now a monumental ten-volume study entitled *Barnabe Googe: His Life, Times, Friends, Works, Habits, Influences, Politics, Religion, Philosophy, and Followers.* Actually, I am myself considering writing a monograph on "Our Neglected Elizabethan: Barnabe Googe" and still another entitled "From Greville to Feveral to Googe." This last should be an important contribution to the Literary Criticism Trivia Game.

John Dewey once wrote, "Education is what is left after the facts are forgotten." Unfortunately, most of what is called education today is concerned more with forgettable facts than with consequential learning. So much time and effort are spent on memorizing the "facts" that little or nothing is left after the facts are forgotten. All that remain are the remnants of the game of Trivia.

For some time George Steiner has been challenging the traditional belief that the study of the humanities makes one more humane. Citing the experience of Nazi Germany—camp officials at Buchenwald and Dachau listening to Bach in the morning and gassing men,

women, and children in the afternoon, the Führer himself devoted
to Beethoven and Wagner—Steiner calls into question the entire
rationale behind the teaching of the humanities.

Actually, it may well be that one of the reasons the teaching of
the humanities fails to make us more humane is the manner of the
teaching. Go into any art gallery or museum and watch the joy and
satisfaction displayed by people if they are able to identify a painting, usually by naming the artist. That a particular painting is by
Rembrandt, Van Gogh, Pollock, or Norman Rockwell is less important than the response it evokes in the perceiver. It is the labeling, not the perception, that is the stuff of which art-appreciation
classes are made.

In similar fashion, the most common response to music is one of
identification, of labeling; whether it be a symphony by Beethoven,
an opera by Verdi, or a song by the Beatles it is the labeling that
triumphs over the response. It must be noted, however, that the
identification of a Beethoven symphony or a Verdi opera has more
importance in formal "education" than that of a Beatles song, which
only further illustrates the capriciousness of Education Trivia. There
is an old joke about a woman who listens to a recording, then reads
the album cover and exclaims, "Oh, it was the *Eroica*! That's my
favorite symphony!" This is what comes of placing labels before
responses—from choosing the letter over the spirit.

I am reminded of a story told to me some years ago by a teacher.
It seems that once upon a time there lived a successful clothing
manufacturer who had bought a house in Westchester. As a successful man, he felt that he needed a house to mirror his success. Accordingly he had built in the house a library and a hi-fi room fitted with
the latest and most expensive audio equipment. All that he lacked
was record albums. To remedy this situation, he purchased nineteen
feet of record albums—to fill the nineteen feet of space on the
shelves of his record library.

Those of us who are tempted to smile superciliously or to laugh
aloud at the gaucherie of the clothing manufacturer would do well
to examine our own consciences and library shelves. Do you own a
set of the Harvard Five-Foot Shelf? Do you participate in the Great
Books Game? How about the Book-of-the-Month-Club Game? The
Columbia Record Club Game? Have you joined the Metropolitan
Museum of Art Seminars in the Home Game?

The clothing manufacturer and the college professor are not different in kind, merely in degree. Both conceive of education as a "matching" process instead of a "making" process. Both are collectors of culture; each places a premium on the amount of labels one is capable of storing. Each is more interested in cataloguing than in creating. The art teacher who flashes two hundred slides on a screen for a student identification test of art; the music teacher who asks questions like "What instruments represent Peter, the Wolf, the grandfather, and the hunters in 'Peter and the Wolf'?"; the literature teacher who requires his students to recognize quotations from ten novels read during the term; the philosophy teacher who asks not "Why?" but "Who wrote?" about the Allegory of the Cave—each of these, and all teachers like them, are engaged not in education (in Dewey's terms) but in Trivia.

Dylan Thomas once wrote of receiving at Christmas "books that told me everything about the wasp, except why." In our schools and universities students learn everything about science, everything about history, everything about philosophy, everything about music and art and literature and life—everything *about* but little or nothing of *why*.

Edwin Land, the inventor of the Polaroid-Land camera, once asked a vital question of educators: "Where, anywhere in life, is a person given this curious sequence of prepared talks and prepared questions, to which the answers are already known?" If I may be permitted a personal definition of Trivia it is that *Trivia consists of asking questions to which the answers are already known.* And what better describes the process of education? So long as we continue to ask students to match instead of make, so long as we continue to be more interested in what and who, in when and where instead of in why, education will remain largely a Trivia contest.

As long as education remains a game of Trivia, I do wish those who plan curricula would open the field up a bit, allowing me to display my erudition in regard to Jimmy Cagney movies, pre-1950 comic books, and the film appearances of Vera Hruba Ralston. In this wish I betray my brotherhood with most educators: I want to play Trivia in the categories I know best.

Of course, there is the possibility—a seemingly absurd one, I grant—that the language of education can be changed into something other than the language of Trivia, into something that will remain long after the facts are forgotten. At the moment, all that is left are the rules of the Trivia Game instead of the important, the consequential, the essential. When the language of education concerns itself with questions to which the answers are not known, with techniques and strategies for survival, in short, with the *why* instead of the *who* and *what* and *when* of education, then, and only then, will education cease to be the greatest Trivia Game in America.

A final note on the Trivia questions in this article: those of you who feel uncomfortable about not knowing the answers to any of the trivia herein have missed the point of my argument and illustrate the validity of my comparison. By the way, whatever happened to Abner Bibberman?

THE STUDY OF DIALECTS

N. Louanna Furbee

Americans are a mobile people, socially as well as geographically. When an American moves to a distant point in the country, he usually finds that his new neighbors speak a regional dialect that is not quite the same as his own; likewise, when an American moves into a different social stratum, he often finds that the speech of his associates differs from his own. He probably, perhaps unconsciously, will try to acquire features of the speech of those around him; to do so will increase his social and economic effectiveness within his new environment. It should be obvious that the acquisition of such speech will make easier his acceptance in another stratum; indeed, it may be necessary for him to acquire the new dialect before he can be accepted. This social stratum, by the way, may be represented by several things: a job, a neighborhood, a sales contact, a promotion, a kind of vacation, all the things that represent a social class in a country such as the United States where classes are not entirely matters of inheritance but are instead based on income, accomplishment, and innumerables such as "tastes" or "prestige" that seem to defy neat definition.

A social class may be defined as any group that shares certain socio-economic characteristics; however, what may be regarded as socially significant in one community, may not be so regarded in another. Stemming from this observation is the following working definition developed by Julian Pitt-Rivers: A social class is what is recognized as a social class by the members of the community.

Recently, large numbers of lower and lower-middle class Americans from the South and from Spanish-speaking areas have migrated to distant parts of the country, usually to urban areas, often to Northern cities, in search of an economic climate that will allow them to earn more and live better. Because these people usually

Reprinted with permission of the Illinois State Wide Curriculum Study Center in the Preparation of Secondary School English Teachers (ISCPET) and N. Louanna Furbee. "The Study of Dialects" appeared originally in *American Dialects for English Teachers* (May, 1969), pp. 13–22.

move into different geographical dialect areas, it may well be that the social dialect differences in their speech have become more apparent in their new geographical setting than ever they were in their original one.

In any case, such migrations have prompted great interest in the function of a social dialect as a class marker, especially when the social dialect is one that hinders the assimilation of in-migrants by their adopted communities. Language is only one of the problems faced by the in-migrant, but it is a key one. Evidence of concern for these people may be found among educators, sociologists, anthropologists, urban specialists, and linguists of all sorts, especially dialectologists.

In 1964, a conference bringing together members of all these disciplines was held in Bloomington, Indiana, under the auspices of the Illinois Institute of Technology and the National Council of Teachers of English. Publication of the report of this conference, *Social Dialects and Language Learning*, may be considered evidence of the developing interest in dialectology as a key to what can be done about acquisition of standard dialects by speakers of nonstandard dialects.

Before going further into the problems of acquisition of a standard dialect, it is necessary to define what we mean by a dialect. First, we must agree that everyone speaks a dialect; unlike its usage among many European authorities, the term among Americans is not synonymous with rustic or archaic speech. Furthermore, dialect is not purely a matter of accent, that is, variations in pronunciation, nor does it refer just to differences in vocabulary or arrangement of words in an utterance. It is all these things and more. Every aspect of speech should be included in the definition of what a dialect is.

If we agree that everyone speaks a dialect and that all features of speech are included in this dialect, does this then mean that every person speaks a dialect different from that of every other person? After all, it is true that no one speaks exactly the same way as anyone else; more than that, it has been shown that no one person ever says the same thing twice in the same way. We can see that what was a useful concept might be sliced so thin as to have no further utility. In a sense, however, we can answer these questions with both a yes and no. To do so, we conclude that a dialect viewed at the level of the speech of a single person is an *idiolect*—the dialect of an individual. We reserve the word *dialect* for referring to those features of speech that are common to a large group of speakers, to a speech community.

In order to describe a particular dialect, then, we must identify those groups of people that share enough features in their speech to qualify as a speech community. There are two ways of approaching the problem of identifying such speakers and their dialects: One way, the geographical or regional approach, has a long history and might be said to be the traditional sort of dialect investigation. The second, although much more recent, is prime among our considerations here; it involves identifying those features shared by a social group or class, and the dialect so identified is a *social dialect*. In the United States, as opposed to other countries such as France where educated Parisian French is taken as a standard, there is no one regional dialect of such prestige that it is considered "standard." Although we speak of Standard English (or the standard dialect) as though it were a single type of speech common to all whose dialect is acceptable, in truth we are talking about a collection of dialects, varying more or less among themselves and each of which is equally acceptable. Unquestionably, these standard dialects resemble each other, especially in matters of grammar, but they are nonetheless not homogeneous.

For the most part, differences between regional standard dialects are matters of phonology; a speaker of a Southern *standard* English will be identified in a Northern community by speakers of a Northern *standard* English as having a Southern accent, or drawl, but he will, in no important way, be discriminated against; quite to the contrary, his dialect may be looked on as charming or pleasant or different, certainly nothing more pejorative than quaint. The speaker of a Northern standard English will have a similar linguistic experience in the South, and so on. But the speaker of any nonstandard dialect, whether he comes from Jackson, Mississippi; Chicago, Illinois; Las Vegas, Nevada; Beckley, West Virginia; Seattle, Washington; Cheyenne, Wyoming, or any other place, will be discriminated against on the basis of his speech, regardless of his talents, actual or potential contributions to society, or personality. It is true that social dialects, standard and nonstandard, within a dialect region share many characteristics, especially in phonology, but the pronunciation differences require specialized instruction because there is often less awareness of these differences and new muscular skills must be taught. Although similar divergences in verb forms and other aspects of morphology and syntax are more general throughout nonstandard dialects of all regions, these seem to be more easily learned.

Generally speaking, problems in social dialectology have been examined with regional dialects as the touch-stone. These regional dialects, for their part, have been studied from the standpoint of phonological differences, grammatical differences, and vocabulary differences.

LINGUISTIC ATLAS

The methods of the *Linguistic Atlas of the United States and Canada* have been applied to a study of nearly every region of this country, although only the Atlas for New England has been published. These methods involve the interviewing of speakers who are representative of the dialects of each community by a trained field worker who uses a standardized questionnaire, or work sheet. Each informant (a technical term designating the person being interviewed) is asked questions designed to elicit certain responses. These responses may be diagnostic of the phonological features, grammatical features, the vocabulary, or any combination of these three, of the dialect. All responses are recorded in detailed phonetic transcription by the field worker.

Obviously, the Atlas methods create a highly structured sort of investigation. The questionnaire for the *Linguistic Atlas of New England* included about 900 items; for just the New England area, 413 informants were interviewed, which indicates the thorough sort of coverage that such a study affords.

In addition to the *Linguistic Atlas of New England* and the *Handbook* for it by Hans Kurath, three valuable books are available, which draw on the field records of the *Linguistic Atlas of New England* and the as yet unedited Middle and South Atlantic records covering the area extending from New York to Georgia. One of these, *Pronunciation of English in the Atlantic States* by Hans Kurath and Raven I. McDavid, Jr., is an excellent source for phonological information on the speech of these states. *A Survey of Verb Forms of the Eastern United States* by E. Bagby Atwood is a grammatical study, giving the distribution of a selected group of verb forms as shown by the Atlas records. A third, *A Word Geography of the Eastern United States*, by Hans Kurath, is concerned with geographical distribution of vocabulary items elicited by the Linguistic Atlas field workers.

From these books and, even more, from the field records of the Atlas, it is possible to determine the regional differences in the speech of Americans and, to a lesser degree, the social differences since informants were selected according to the speech-type they represented—old-fashioned, common, or cultivated. Therefore, the findings of the Linguistic Atlas provide an excellent basis on which to begin social dialect investigations; because they give regional differences, they may be used in social dialect studies as a reference for what is regional rather than social.

In recent years, the questionnaire method of the Linguistic Atlas has been applied to social dialect studies, notably by Lee Pederson, who examined the phonology of Chicago speech by interviewing both White and Negro informants with a modified version of the Shorter Work Sheets of the *Linguistic Atlas of New England*. Others have used this or similar questionnaire-based techniques to study the speech of a community in depth; for example Gerald Udell applied this method to a similar examination of the speech of Akron, Ohio. These in-depth studies of single communities afford us a close look at a densely populated area in a way that the Linquistic Atlas, because of its wide coverage, could not do.

Still derivative of Linguistic Atlas methods, such devices as check lists and non-Atlas based questionnaires have also been applied to the problem of social dialects.

Currently, a second atlas-type study is in progress: *The Dictionary of American Regional English* (DARE). Under the direction of Frederick G. Cassidy, of the University of Wisconsin, the DARE project has completed most of its field work at this time (1968). The questionnaire being used is long, about 1500 items, and is concerned chiefly with vocabulary, although many pronunciation and grammatical features are being investigated also. DARE will interview 1000 informants, who represent all of the 50 states.

A third investigation, under the direction of A. L. Davis, will be a collection of tape recordings, which will sample the pronunciation of varieties of standard English in the United States and Canada.

OTHER METHODS

Some investigators have chosen to discard the questionnaire-based interview for a type of investigation that more closely resembles traditional anthropological linguistic field work in description of language. They have tried to describe social dialects, especially Negro dialects, as though they were analyzing a foreign language. Whereas the Atlas method is so structured that it involves a built-in comparison of the nonstandard social dialect to the standard (we might say prestige) dialect, the anthropologically influenced linguists wish to approach the nonstandard dialect as a separate entity so they may analyze its grammar as a system in itself, reserving until later the comparison to the standard dialect. Extensive use of tape recordings now make it possible to study hours of connected speech. Syntax can be more adequately sampled, and minute phonological features can be recognized. There is of course, much merit in examining a dialect on its own terms and without imposing the grammar of another dialect on it, even for comparison, until it has been fully treated as a separate entity. It is unfortunate that such study is lengthy, for the social problems cry for immediate answers, be it anthropological or questionnaire-based.

There are a number of current research projects, . . . which hold promise for answering at least some small part of the complex problem we call social dialectology. The standard dialect of Negro college students is being studied at Tuskegee Institute of Alabama; there is a study of the language of the District of Columbia area being conducted under the auspices of the Center for Applied Linguistics. Roger Shuy has recently completed an examination of the social dialects in Detroit. There are several studies on the acquisition of language by children, especially the development of syntax in disadvantaged children. William Labov and co-workers have recently completed one part of their study on the structure of English used by Negro and Puerto Rican speakers in New York City. Other workers are designing pattern drills to help teach standard dialect forms to speakers of nonstandard dialects. Two investigators studied the other side of the problem; they tried to identify what sorts of dialects are interpreted as being nonstandard by the community. Edward T. Hall has been working on how various ethnic groups, particularly Negroes, use space in inter-personal encounters; for example, how closely they stand to one another in various sorts of conversation and to what degree eye contact is required.

As mentioned previously, the *Linguistic Atlas of the United States and Canada* is the main source of information on the regional dialects of the United States. The published part of it, that for New England, and the three books derived from a study of its field records all established three major dialect areas, a finding made the more valid because each of the three books taking in material beyond New England concentrated on a different kind of information: one on phonology, one on grammar, and one on vocabulary. Moreover, the dialect areas all correlate nicely with settlement history for those regions.

When a linguistic geographer sets about to identify dialect areas, he examines the field records item by item for the distribution of sounds, grammatical items, and vocabulary terms. The usage of each of these by every informant is plotted on a map. If, for example, the item in question is the sibilant consonant sound used in the word *greasy*, he will plot the responses of all the informants to the question on the work sheet that yields this word. After these have been mapped, he will look for differences in usage. Wherever he finds differences, he will set apart areas where one sound predominates from areas where another sound predominates. In this way, he draws lines between regions that differ as to the particular sibilant used by a majority of speakers living there. The resulting dividing lines are called *isoglosses*, a term similar to the meteorological word *isobar*, but in this case it is a linguistic boundary for one sound in one word.

One isogloss, such as the [grisi]–[grizi] line, tells nothing by itself except that there is a geographical difference in the pronunciation of one word *greasy*. If we were to find other differences in pronunciation, grammatical items, and vocabulary items, that share the distribution of the two pronunciations of *greasy*, we have a *bundle of isoglosses* or a *dialect boundary*. And we have identified a regional dialect area.

It is by these methods that regional dialect areas have been identified in this country as in others. These major American dialect areas for the eastern states are Northern, Midland, and Southern.

THE NORTH

The North includes the following sub-dialect regions: Northeastern New England, Southeastern New England, Southwestern New England, Upstate New York and Western Vermont, the Hudson Valley, and the New York City area.

Pronunciations with [-s-] in *grease* (verb) and *greasy* and [U] in *roots* are characteristic of the North. *Pail* (rather than the Midland and Southern *bucket*) is a Northern vocabulary item; *dove* as a preterit of *dive* is also predominantly Northern, as is *hadn't ought* for "ought not."

THE MIDLAND

The Midland encompasses two main sub-dialect areas, the North Midland and the South Midland, which in turn may be divided into the Delaware Valley (Philadelphia area), the Susquehanna Valley, the Upper Ohio Valley (Pittsburgh area), and Northern West Virginia—all North Midland, and Southern West Virginia and Western North and South Carolina–the South Midland.

Typical Midland pronunciations are /-r/ kept after vowels (also Inland Northern); [ɔ] in *on* (also Southern), in *wash* and *wasp*, and in *hog, frog* and *fog*; [θ] regularly in *with*, and [r] frequently intrudes in *wash* and *Washington*. *Blinds* for "window shades" is a characteristic vocabulary item. In the grammar of the Midland dialect, *I want off* is common.

THE SOUTH

The South includes the following areas: Delmarva (Eastern Shore of Maryland and Virginia and Southern Delaware), the Virginia Piedmont, Northeastern North Carolina (Albermarle Sound and

Neuse Valley), the Cape Fear and Peedee Valleys, and South Carolina.

Loss of [r] except before vowels is the usual pronunciation in the Southern dialect region as it is also of Eastern New England and New York City. Among the many characteristic Southern vocabulary items are *tote* for "carry." In grammar the expression *might could* for "might be able" is common.

Until very recently, it was thought that the entire United States beyond these sections fell into one great dialect area, the speech of which was called General American. As the investigations of the Linguistic Atlas and related studies have been extended westward, however, General American has been found to be a fallacy resulting from lack of research.

In the dissertation of A. L. Davis (1948), the Northern and Midland boundaries were extended through Ohio, Indiana and Illinois. Certain other western extensions of the Northern Midland and Midland-Southern boundaries have been proved, but until the final work on the Linguistic Atlas has been completed, the western boundaries must be considered tentative.

Several short works on regional American dialects are available. One of the best of these is the chapter, "American English Dialects," by Raven I. McDavid, Jr., in *The Structure of American English* by W. Nelson Francis. Roger Shuy has written a short book, *Discovering American Dialects*, published by the National Council of Teachers of English. There is a good chapter on dialect geography, including both American and European dialect studies, in *Language* by Leonard Bloomfield, the usefulness of which is restricted very little by the fact that it dates to 1933. Carroll E. Reed's *Dialects of American English* has good summaries of Eastern dialect features, as well as information about the Far West.

Although poverty has become a national concern, far too little is known about it or what it means to be disadvantaged. Evidence for this fact is found in the diverse definitions of disadvantaged and, for that matter, of poverty. If we cannot even agree on what poverty or being disadvantaged constitutes, it may seem fruitless to plan programs to help people we cannot identify. To be very arbitrary, however, we can say that if a person has difficulty finding regular employment, if his children profit little from the kind of schooling offered them, and if there is unrest or instability in the environment, then there is an obvious need for help of some kind. That many of these people also have social dialects that restrict their achievement lends credence to these criteria; furthermore, the dialect problems are among the easiest to identify and, in theory, to treat.

If however, we set out to train all disadvantaged school children to speak a standard dialect, we must be very careful that in our zeal we do not set for ourselves the goal of completely changing the speech of such children from nonstandard to standard. Fortunately, this is probably an impossible task, for were we to do such a thing we would seriously undermine the child's relationship with his family and friends. Indeed, we would be making the very mistake that English teachers have been committing for decades: telling the child that his language, that of his parents and close associates, is a bad language. That it is not. But without a doubt, his dialect is not the one that will permit him the greatest mobility in society. Rather the best goal is one that would give such children a second dialect, a standard one, which they may use on appropriate occasions, for example, at school and later on, at work.

The burden of this effort falls, unfortunately, on those who are already at the disadvantage. At this early stage in social dialect work, it would seem necessary that this be so, but the best sort of program would be one that included an educational campaign about dialects directed at the general public. If the privileged knew only one fact, that the grammars of all dialects are systematic although different, their acceptance of divergencies from their own standard speech would probably be increased greatly.

So in our work, we are made to serve two masters: one of expediency and one of idealism. By educating the public now, however, we may be bringing the two closer.

There are several aids to the study of social dialects; one of these, the work sheet, is used in direct interview with each informant; usually all or many of the informant's responses must be written in phonetic transcription and then tape-recorded. For example, one item is included on most questionnaires to determine if the informant uses a voiced or voiceless *th* sound ($/ð/$ or $/θ/$) in the word *with* before an *m* sound. The frame specified for this is one that will elicit the response, "with milk," from the informant. Such questioning might go something like this:

FIELD WORKER: If you put something in your coffee in addition to
    sugar, you might say that you drink your coffee . . .
INFORMANT: With cream.
FIELD WORKER: Yes, but suppose you didn't have any cream, you
    might use something similar as a substitute and then you'd say that
    you drank that cup of coffee . . .
INFORMANT: With milk.

Field work takes skill and can be tedious. It is really the only way
to get valid phonological and informal grammatical data, however.
A worksheet questionnaire allows us to gather comparable data for
speakers most economically. The questions asked to assure the required responses vary somewhat between field workers. What is
most essential is that the field worker understand what information
is being sought.

Another kind of questionnaire is called a check list. It does not
require interviewing by a field worker, and an investigation by check
list may be conducted by mail. A series of multiple choice questions
are designed to yield responses that are diagnostic of dialect differences. Because the check list is filled out by the informant, the most
successful questions are those involving vocabulary items, choosing
from different words for the same thing. To seek phonological data
requires tampering with conventional orthography, and often an
informant will choose a standard grammatical form on the check
list even if he regularly uses a nonstandard form in his speech.

Check lists are valuable accompaniments to field studies with
work sheets since many more people can be reached than is possible
with the field worker and interview technique. When the questions
on a check list are chosen very carefully and the analysis is made
with equal care, new territory can be covered by them.

In 1966, the dissertation of William Labov was published by the
Center for Applied Linguistics. In it were two different kinds of
important information: The first is reflected in the title, *The Stratification of English in New York City*; included was a probing investigation of the speech of New York City, information long
needed. Of almost equal importance, however, was the sort of
methods used by Labov to collect this information. He was able to
use a detailed sociological study of the Lower East Side and identi-

fied five variables in speech that seemed to distinguish various social classes. These five variables (use of *r* in post-vocalic and preconsonantal position; the vowel in *bad, ask, dance, had,* and *cash*; the stressed vowel in *awful, coffee, office*; the use of [θ] in *thin*; and the use of [ð] in *then* and *the*) he investigated in a great variety of situations and styles of speech. He also interviewed a selected sample of informants with a longer questionnaire. He found he was able to do something that no previous investigator had been able to do: to predict certain changes in the speech of certain groups. His study is probably the most sociological of any to date; at the same time, it is truly linguistic.

All these methods are good. In choosing a certain technique, one must weight the resources with which he has to work and the information he seeks. It is hoped that soon there will be many more people conducting research in dialectology.

Generally speaking, those who need special dialect training will come from two main groups: Southern in-migrants to Northern cities and migrants from areas or countries where a foreign language is spoken. Of the first group, by far the largest number are Southern Negroes; another important contingent are the Southern Appalachian whites. The second major group is composed, in large part, of speakers of Spanish from any of several Spanish dialect areas, Puerto Rico, Cuba, Mexico, certain parts of the Southwestern United States, and Central and South America. In addition, any sizable group who speak a language other than English in their community may be involved: within the United States are many whose first language is one of the American Indian languages, Japanese or Chinese, or a European language, such as the French of parts of Louisiana and New England. Every major city has neighborhoods where some language other than English is the first language. It may be German, Czech, Hungarian, among others. Parts of the rural Northern Middle West have large populations of speakers of a Scandinavian language. Many of these people are not poor, but their social mobility may be hindered by their language problems.

One group must be distinguished from those who need help for social dialect difficulties; these are the people, usually school children, who have physiologically based speech problems. Too often a child with a different social dialect is either sent to a speech therapist for treatment of a physiological problem he does not have, or he is regarded as mentally retarded. Children who have physiological speech problems or who are mentally retarded need help too, but it is of an entirely different nature from that needed by the child with a social dialect problem.

Because so little has been published on the acquisition of standard dialects of English, English teachers, if they are to be successful, must really become their own investigators. There are two phases in the planning of such a program for school children, the first of which is a research phase in which the nonstandard dialect must be described. The second phase is the preparation of materials for teaching the children.

DESCRIPTIVE PHASE

A good beginning for the descriptive phase is to make an inventory of the vowel and consonant phonemes of the nonstandard dialect being studied for contrast with the same sort of inventory for the standard dialect of the region. *Pronunciation of English in the Atlantic States* is a good source of information on regional standard dialects of many parts of the country.

After the vowel and consonant phonemes of the standard and nonstandard dialects have been compared, we can note the sounds for which exact correspondences are not evident in the two dialects. This is most easily done by using the standard dialects of the region as a reference, and listing as substitutions the sounds used in the nonstandard dialects for the sounds used in the standard. Of particular importance are consonant clusters which need to be listed completely.

At the same time that the vowels and consonants are being compared, some attention should be given to the intonation patterns. Whenever they too differ from the intonation of the standard dialect, a note should be made about it. Differences in intonation will be especially important when studying the speech of children whose first language is not English, for example, Spanish-speaking children. Gross changes in grammar may also be listed, especially variant verb forms. *A Survey of Verb Forms in the Eastern United States* is a good source for information on these too.

Very often "slang" or special vocabulary will receive great emphasis. While there is no doubt that these vocabulary items are interesting and often will mystify the outsider—which is, after all, their purpose—the fact that they are vocabulary and seldom form a phonological or grammatical sub-system should not be lost sight of.

Traditional teaching of English has often failed in its efforts to change nonstandard speech to standard because, although corrections were regularly made by the teacher, there was never enough drill to make the corrections stick. This situation is analogous to that in foreign language teaching in this country until the development of the aural-oral method during the Second World War.

The aural-oral method of teaching language involves the presentation of an oral model by the teacher and its imitation by the students. The key to the method is pattern drill. Each drill is designed to teach a particular phonological or grammatical pattern, but, in order to make the pattern become unconscious habit, the student's attention is drawn to substitutions in the pattern. In this way, the student absorbs the pattern in the lesson by unconscious repetition of it. For example, if the pattern being taught were the negative construction with *isn't*, a sample drill might be:

He isn't in school today.
He isn't in class today.
She isn't in school today.
She isn't in class today.

And so on, each time the model is given by the teacher, and the students repeat it. Sometimes, individual students may be called on to repeat the model alone. Such drills can be handled with humor and snap, but the content is without a doubt not very stimulating otherwise. The important thing is however, that when the drill is finished, the student knows the *isn't* pattern for making a negative statement; he knows it in a way that reading about it in a book or writing out a sentence with it will never teach him.

These drills must always be presented orally. They lend themselves nicely to tape recording, which spares the teacher many practice hours. In that case, the model is recorded on the tape, with a pause after it for the student to repeat the model.

Following are illustrations of such a drill made up for a sound and for a grammatical feature of the standard dialect of Northern Midwestern English that differ from the corresponding sound and grammatical item of the nonstandard Appalachian dialect. It is important that the teacher present the sound, with practice on it alone, to the children before the drill. Otherwise the children many not hear the difference between the teacher's pronunciation and their substitution. In the vowel comparison for Appalachian speech and the standard dialect, the vowel sound in the word *I'll* has an ingliding to [ə] rather than an upgliding toward [I] or [i] after the main vowel [a]. This same sound in the words *life, my,* and *like* is also inglided. Taking as the standard pronunciation [aI], we first present it in isolation to the students, asking them to repeat it after us and encouraging them to follow the [a] sound with a high front [i] sound; a teacher can say, "Like the letter E," or "Like the sound in bee," to help with this, even though this is an exaggeration. After they have made something close to the sound in isolation, the drill may be begun.

TEACHER: I'll tell you a joke.
STUDENTS: I'll tell you a joke.
(repeat as many times as needed)
TEACHER: I'll tell you a story.
STUDENTS: I'll tell you a story.
TEACHER: I'll tell you my joke.
STUDENTS: I'll tell you my joke.
TEACHER: Do you like jokes?
STUDENTS: Do you like jokes?
TEACHER: I like stories.
STUDENTS: I like stories.
TEACHER: My brother plays jokes on me.
STUDENTS: My brother plays jokes on me.
TEACHER: My brother likes jokes.
STUDENTS: My brother likes jokes.
TEACHER: My brother likes tennis.
STUDENTS: My brother likes tennis.

From here on, the teacher can substitute any sort of item she likes. The drill should not last longer than 10 minutes without some sort of diversion if the children are grade school age. The teacher might then change to this form of question and answer drill.

TEACHER: I like school. What do you like, John?
JOHN: I like (bubble gum, candy, whatever he wishes to add). What do you like, Sue?
SUE: I like my dog, Dusty. What do you like, Mary?
MARY: I like vacation. What do you like, Billie?

And so on through the class until everyone has had a chance to tell what he likes. Throughout the practice the teacher should make corrections of the group and of individuals. By the time the drills are over, the children should begin to have the [ai] sound as an alternate for their [a] and [aə] sounds.

The same sort of drill can be made up for grammatical items. For example, the verb form *wunt* ([wvnt]) occurs in the speech of the Appalachian children for *wasn't*. A pattern drill for this problem might be:

TEACHER: He wasn't named John.
STUDENTS: He wasn't named John.
TEACHER: No he wasn't.
STUDENTS: No he wasn't.
TEACHER: He wasn't tall.
STUDENTS: He wasn't tall.
TEACHER: No he wasn't.
STUDENTS: No he wasn't.
TEACHER: He wasn't short.
STUDENTS: He wasn't short.
TEACHER: No he wasn't.
STUDENTS: No he wasn't.
TEACHER: He wasn't silly.
STUDENTS: He wasn't silly.
TEACHER: No he wasn't.
STUDENTS: No he wasn't.

With the "He wasn't . . ." frame, the teacher can add in all sorts of adjectives and nouns, preferably funny ones, in the final slot. She can also ask the children to do the same, something like, "He wasn't licorice," or "He wasn't a cartwheel." The last slot merely diverts the students' attention from the "wasn't" so that the pattern will become habit. Since it is a device, it can be played with. The second pattern, "No he wasn't," gives practice with "wasn't" in a stressed position; the first, "He wasn't . . ." has "wasn't" in unstressed position.

As we see, the pattern drills are not difficult to make up, although creating interesting ones does take talent. After the contrastive analysis of the nonstandard dialect and the regional standard have been completed, the teacher simply takes those items that do not match, especially the phonological items, and one by one presents them in the form of a pattern drill. Always, the drill must have the lesson of the day as a constant; the alterations in it are for diverting the attention of the student.

There are many books of pattern drills designed for teaching English to speakers of foreign languages. Some of these drills might be used by the teacher; others will lend themselves to modification. Also available are contrastive analyses of English and many foreign languages. There are teaching materials published for teaching English to speakers of Spanish and many other languages; some of these materials are designed for use with children. . . .

It is well known that children learn foreign languages rapidly. There is every reason to think that they will become bidialectal with relative ease also, although it may be that it is more difficult to learn a second dialect than it is to learn a second language since the close resemblances of the two dialects may cause interference. The points of contrast between dialects are few and do not involve many changes in meaning. In some ways it is harder to learn variations to a system you already know than it is to learn an entirely new system.

A CHECKLIST OF
SIGNIFICANT FEATURES
FOR DISCRIMINATING
SOCIAL DIALECTS

Raven I. McDavid, Jr.

As an aid to the teacher who is interested in a more efficient approach to the problem of teaching a standard variety of English —for public roles—to those who use nonstandard varieties at home, the following list of features (all of which are both systematic and significant) has been drawn up, partly from the collections of the regional linguistic atlases, partly from more intensive local studies. The emphasis is on those features of the language that recur frequently and are therefore most amendable to pattern drills. It must not be inferred that other, less well-patterned features of English are unimportant as social markers, but only that they do not lend themselves so readily to productive drill. Discriminating the principal parts of irregular verbs, such as past tense *saw* and past participle *seen,* is a part of the linguistic behavior that constitutes standard English, but the pattern *see/saw/seen* is duplicated only by such compounds of *see* as *foresee.* On the other hand, the discrimination between *I see* and *he sees* is a part of a pattern of subject-verb concord that is faced every time a subject is used with the present tense of a verb.

The list is concerned with social dialects of English and does not include all the problems faced by the native speaker of some other language. For each situation of this last kind one needs special contrastive studies like those currently being published by the University of Chicago Press. Native speakers of Czech or Finnish need to learn the accentual patterns of English; native speakers of

Reprinted with permission of A. L. Davis, editor Iscpet dialect project, and of the American Council of Learned Societies, sponsors of the Linguistic Atlas project.

An earlier version of this article appeared in *Dimensions of Dialect,* Eldonna Evertts, ed. (Champaign, Ill.: National Council of Teachers of English, 1967).

continental European languages need to master the perfect phrase in such expressions of time as *I have been in Chicago for five years*; native speakers of almost every other language need to learn a finer-meshed set of vowel distinctions as between *peach* and *pitch, bait* and *bet* and *bat, pool* and *pull, boat* and *bought, hot* and *hut*.

The origins of these features are of indirect concern here; that they are of social significance is what concerns us. In general, however, it is clear that most of them may be traced back to the folk speech of England, and that in the United States none of them is exclusively identified with any racial group, though in any given community some of them may be relatively more frequent among whites or among Negroes.

This list is restricted to features that occur in speech as well as in writing. It is recognized that regional varieties of English differ in the distance between the norms of standard informal speech and standard formal writing. They vary considerably in the kinds of reductions of final consonant clusters, either absolutely or when followed by a word beginning with a consonant. The plural of *sixth* may be /sIks/, homonymous with the cardinal numeral; *bûrned a hóle* may be /bârdə hól/ but *bûrned my pánts* /bârn mai pánts/. Similarly the copula may not appear in questions such as *They ready? That your boy? We going now? She been drinking?* The auxiliary *have* may not even appear as a reflex of /v/ in such statements as *I been thinking about it* or *we been telling you this*. In families where the conventions of written and printed English are learned early as a separate subsystem, differences of this kind cause little trouble; but for speakers of nonstandard dialects who have little home exposure to books, these features may provide additional problems in learning to write. It is often difficult for the teacher to overcome such problems in the students' writing without fostering an unnatural pronunciation.

It should be recognized, of course, that cultural situations may change in any community. To take the Southern dialectal situation with which I am most familiar, forty years ago there was a widespread social distinction in the allophones of /ai/.[1] The monoph-

---

[1] This observation was made, *inter alia*, in my analyses of the pronunciation of English in the Greenville, S.C., metropolitan area, and presented to the Linguistic Society of America at its meetings in New York City (December, 1938) and Chapel Hill, N.C. (July, 1941).

thongal [a·] was used by all classes finally, as in *rye*, or before voiced consonants, as in *ride*; before voiceless consonants, however, educated speakers had a diphthong and many uneducated speakers used the monophthong so that *nice white rice* became a well-known social shibboleth. In recent years, however, the shibboleth has ceased to operate, and many educated Southerners now have the monophthong in all positions; and the numbers of such speakers are increasing. This observation has also been made by James B. McMillan of the University of Alabama. McMillan fears however, that the falling together of /ai/ and /a/ before /r/, so that *fire* and *far*, *hired* and *hard* become homonymous, was still restricted to nonstandard speech. Yet very recently I noticed that this homonym was common on the Dallas radio in the speech of the women's editor.[2]

It should not be assumed, furthermore, that one will find no other systematic features discriminating standard speech from nonstandard in particular localities. Nor should we be so naive as to expect the speakers of any community to cease regarding the speech of outsiders as *ipso facto* inferior because it is different—even though these outsiders may be superior in education and social standing.

We are all ethnocentric after our own fashion; in our localities we may consider some differences important whether they are or not; and if enough people worry about them, some of these may actually become important. This is the traditional origin of neuroses as well as the specific origin of the proscription of such useful features of English as *ain't* and the multiple negative. Meanwhile, it is probably good sense as well as good humor to recognize that though the white middle-class Chicagoan often considers the loss of /r/ in *barn* and the like a lower-class feature the cultivated Southerner often associates the Middle Western /r/ in such words with speech of poor whites—and that the distinction between /hw-/ and /w-/, as in *whales* and *wails* respectively, is socially diagnostic nowhere in the English-speaking world. The features listed here are diagnostic everywhere, though not all of them occur in every community where differences in social dialects are important.

---

[2] The monophthongal Southern /ai/ disturbs many Easterners and Middle Westerners. Some Philadelphians, for instance, allege that Southerners confuse *ride* and *rod*; some Detroiters, that they confuse *right* and *rat*. They do not; the confusion exists in the minds of the Eastern and Middle Western observers.

PRONUNCIATION:[3]

1. The distinction between /θ/ as in *thin* and /t/ in *tin*, /f/ in *fin*, /s/ in *sin*.
2. The similar distinction between /ð/ in *them* and /d/, /v/, /z/.
3. The distinction between the vowels of *bird* and *Boyd*, *curl* and *coil*.

A generation ago this contrast was most significant among older speakers of the New York metropolitan area; uneducated older speakers regularly lacked it. It has become less important, since few of the younger speakers lack the distinction. But it should still be noted, not only for New York City but for New Orleans as well.

4. The omission, in nonstandard speech, of a weak-stressed syllable preceding the primary stress, so that *professor* may become *fessor*, *reporter* may become *porter*, and *insurance* become [šu əns] or [šoəns].
5. In substandard speech, a statistically disproportionate front-shifting of the primary stress, giving such forms as *po*-lice, *in*-surance, *ee*-ficiency, *gui*-tar, etc.

   Front-shifting is characteristic of English borrowings from other languages; in *bal*cony it is completely accepted; in *ho*tel and *Ju*ly acceptability is conditioned by position in the sentence.
6. In nonstandard speech, heavy stress on what in standard English is a weak-stressed final syllable, giving acci*dent*, ele*ment*, presi*dent*, evi*dence*, etc.

INFLECTION:

NOUN

7. Lack of the noun plural: Two *boy* came (come) to see me.
8. Lack of the noun genitive: This (is) *Mr. Brown* hat.

[3] These remarks are restricted to American English. The "wobbling *h*" of lower class British speech, as in *hell* for *l*, *eye* for *high*, would be a similar social marker.

PRONOUN

9. Analogizing of the /-n/ of *mine* to other absolute genitives, yielding *ourn, yourn, hisn, hern, theirn.*
10. Analogizing of the compound reflexives, yielding *hisself, theirself, theirselves.*

DEMONSTRATIVE

11. Substitution of *them* for *those*, as *them* books.
12. Compound demonstratives: *these here* dogs, *that (th)ere* house, *them (th)ere* cats.

ADJECTIVES

13. Analogizing of inflected comparisons: the *wonderfullest* time, a *lovinger* child.
14. Double comparisons: a *more prettier* dress, the *most ugliest* man.

VERB

15. Unorthodox person-number concord of the present of *to be*. This may be manifest in generalizing of *am* or *is* or *are*, or in this use of *be* with all persons, singular and plural.
16. Unorthodox person-number concord of the past of *be*: *I were, he were; we was, they was.*
17. Failure to maintain person-number concord of the present indicative of other verbs: *I does, he do* (perhaps the most widely recognized diagnostic feature).

Note that three third person singular forms of common verbs are irregular: *has*, does /dʌz/, *says* /sɛz/. In the last two the spelling conceals the irregularity, but many speakers who are learning this inflection will produce /duz/ and /sez/. The form *bees* is also derived from this kind of analogy.

18. Omission of the /iŋ/ of the present participle: He was *open* a can of beer.[4]
19. Omission of /-t, -d, -əd/ of the past tense: I *burn* a hole in my pants yesterday.

Note that before a word beginning with a consonant the /-d/ may be omitted in speech in *I burned my pants*. Those who normally have this contextual loss of the sound may need to learn the special conventions of writing.

Note also that the loss of the inflection extends to those verbs that form the past tense and past participle irregularly.

20. Omission of /-t, -d, -əd/ of the past participle.
21. Omission of the verb *to be* in statements before a predicate nominative: *He a good boy.*
22. Omission of *to be* in statements before adjectives: *They ready.*
23. Omission of *to be* in statements before present participles: *I going with you.*
24. Omission of *to be* in statements before past participles: *The window broke(n).*

Note that in questions related to features 21-24 the verb *to be* may be omitted in standard oral English, though it would never be omitted in formal expository prose.

25. Omission of the /-s, -z, -əz/ reflex of *has* before *been* in statements: *He been drinking.*

Note that this omission may occur in questions in standard oral English, and also that in standard oral English many educated speakers may omit the /-v/ reflex of *have*: *I been thinking about it*; *we been telling you this*. Needless to say, this omission would not occur in standard expository prose.

---

[4] The distinction between /-iŋ/ and /-in/ has no social significance. Both forms may be heard in educated speech, depending on the region from which the speaker comes and the style of discourse he is using.

26. Substitution of *been, done,* or *done been* for have, especially
with a third singular subject: *He done been finished.* In other
person-number situations *done,* at least, often occurs in
standard oral English, as *I done told you that three times.*

BI-DIALECTALISM:
THE LINGUISTICS OF
WHITE SUPREMACY

James Sledd

Because people who rarely talk together will talk differently, differences in speech tell what groups a man belongs to. He uses them to claim and proclaim his identity, and society uses them to keep him under control. The person who talks right, as we do, is one of us. The person who talks wrong is an outsider, strange and suspicious, and we must make him feel inferior if we can. That is one purpose of education. In a school system run like ours by white businessmen, instruction in the mother tongue includes formal initiation into the linguistic prejudices of the middle class.

Making children who talk wrong get right with the world has traditionally been the work of English teachers, and more recently of teachers of that strange conglomerate subject which we call speech. The English teacher in the role of linguistic censor was once a kind of folk heroine (or anti-heroine), the Miss Fidditch of the linguists' diatribes. Miss Fidditch believed in taking a strong stand. It never occurred to her that her main job was making the lower classes feel so low that they would try to climb *higher*. Instead, Miss Fidditch taught generations of schoolchildren, including future linguists, to avoid *ain't* and double negatives and *used to could* and *hadn't ought*, not because *ain't* would keep them from getting ahead in the world, but because *ain't* was wrong, no matter who used it, and deserved no encouragement from decent people who valued the English language. She did her job all the better for thinking that she was doing something else.

Miss Fidditch is not popular any longer among educators. Though the world at large is still inclined to agree with her, the vulgarizers

From the *English Journal* (December, 1969), pp. 1307–15, 1329. Reprinted with the permission of the National Council of Teachers of English and James Sledd.

James Sledd teaches in the Department of English of the University of Texas, Austin, Texas.

of linguistics drove her out of the academic fashion years ago, when they replaced her misguided idealism with open-eyed hypocrisy. To the popular linguists, one kind of English is as good as another, and judgments to the contrary are only folklore; but since the object of life in the U.S.A. is for everybody to get ahead of everybody else, and since linguistic prejudice can keep a man from moving up to Schlitz, the linguists still teach that people who want to be decision-makers had better talk and write like the people who make decisions. The schools must therefore continue to cultivate the linguistic insecurity which is already a national characteristic but must teach the youngsters to manipulate that as they manipulate everything else; for neither Miss Fidditch's dream of a language intrinsically good, nor a humbler ideal of realizing the various potentialities of the existing language in its responsible use, can get in the way of the citizenry in its upward anguish through the pecking order. The linguists think that people who do knowingly what Miss Fidditch did in her innocence, will do it more efficiently, as if eating the apple made a skilled worker out of Eve.

As long as most people agreed that up is toward Schlitz and another TV set and as long as they could pretend that every American eaglet can soar to those great heights, Fidditch McFidditch the dialectologist could enforce the speech-taboos of the great white middle class without complaint: either the child learned the taboos and observed them, or he was systematically penalized. But the damage done to the Wasps' nest by World War II make difficulties. People who talked all wrong, and especially black people, began to ask for their share of the loot in a world that had given them an argument by calling itself free, while a minority of the people who talked right began to bad-mouth respectability and joined the blacks in arguing that it was time for a real change. Some black people burned up the black parts of town, and some students made study impossible at the universities, and in general there was a Crisis. Optimists even talked of a revolution.

The predictable response of the frightened white businessman's society was to go right on what it had done before—which had caused the crisis—but to do it harder and to spend more money at it. Education was no exception. Government and the foundations began to spray money over the academic landscape like liquid fertilizer, and the professional societies began to bray and paw at the rich new grass. In that proud hour, any teacher who could dream up an expensive scheme for keeping things as they were while pretending to make a change was sure of becoming the director of a project or a center and of flying first-class to Washington twice a month. The white businessman strengthened his control of the educational system while giving the impression of vast humanitarian activity.

Black English provided the most lucrative new industry for white linguists, who found the mother lode when they discovered the interesting locutions which the less protected employed to the detriment of their chances for upward mobility. In the annals of free enterprise, the early sixties will be memorable for the invention of functional bi-dialectalism, a scheme best described by an elderly and unregenerated Southern dame as "turning black trash into white trash." Despite some signs of wear, this cloak for white supremacy has kept its shape for almost a decade now, and it is best described in the inimitable words of those who made it. Otherwise the description might be dismissed as a malicious caricature.

The basic assumption of bi-dialectalism is that the prejudices of middle-class whites cannot be changed but must be accepted and indeed enforced on lesser breeds. Upward mobility, it is assumed, is the end of education, but white power will deny upward mobility to speakers of black English, who must therefore be made to talk white English in their contacts with the white world.

An adequate florilegium may be assembled from a volume entitled *Social Dialects and Language Learning* (NCTE, 1964), the proceedings of a conference of bi-dialectalists which was held in 1964. William A. Stewart of the Center for Applied Linguistics begins the chorus (p. 13) by observing among our educators "a commendable desire to emphasize the potential of the Negro to be identical to white Americans"—a desire which is apparently not overwhelming, however, among the Black Muslims or among the young men who have enjoyed pot-shooting policemen for the past few summers. Editor Roger W. Shuy next speaks up (p. 53) for social climbing by our American Indians, who have been notably reluctant, throughout their unfortuate association with their conquerors to adopt our conquering ways. Our linguistic studies, Shuy remarks in the purest accents of fidditchery, "should reveal those elements, both in speech and writing, which prevent Indians from attaining the social status which, with socially acceptable language, they might otherwise attain." A similar desire to be at peace with status-holders is suggested (p. 66) by Ruth I. Golden, who opines that "a human being wants most of all to be recognized as an individual, to be accepted, and to be approved." Since Southern speech brings "negative reactions when heard by employees in Detroit," where Dr. Golden labors in the schools, she devotes herself to stamping out /i/ for /e/ in *penny* and to restoring /l/ in *help* (pp. 63 f.).

An admirable scholar from New York, William Labov, then agrees (p. 88) that "recognition of an external standard of correctness is an inevitable accompaniment of upward social aspirations and upward social mobility," and advises that people who (like Jesus) prefer not to take excessive thought for the morrow can probably be made to. In Labov's own words, "since the homes of many lower class and working people do not provide the pressures toward upward social mobility that middle-class homes provide," and since adults in those lower reaches are sometimes resistant to middle-class values, we must "build into the community a tolerance for style shifting which is helpful in educational and occupational advancement," and we must build into the children, "starting from a level not much above the nursery school and going on through high school, a tolerance for practice in second role playing" (pp. 94–97, 104).

Presumably Labov sees nothing wrong in thus initiating children into the world of hypercorrection, insecurity, and "linguistic self-hatred" which marks, as he has said elsewhere, "the average New Yorker" (*The Social Stratification of English in New York City*, Center for Applied Linguistics, 1966, Chapter XIII); and Charles Ferguson, the eminent exdirector of the Center for Applied Linguistics, is equally confident of *his* right and duty to remake his fellow men in his directorial image. Talking about the Negroes in our Northern cities, Ferguson says that "we have to face a rather difficult decision as to whether we want to make these people bi-dialectal . . . [please to remark Ferguson's choice of verbs] or whether we want . . . to impose some kind of standard English on these people and to eradicate the kind of substandard English they speak" (p. 116). To cite another NCTE volume (*Language Programs for the Disadvantaged* [NCTE, 1965], p. 222), if the black children of the ghetto "do not learn a second kind of dialect, they will be forever prevented from access to economic opportunity and social acceptance." Middle-class white prejudice will rule eternally.

The bi-dialectalists, of course, would not be so popular with government and the foundations if they spoke openly of the supremacy of white prejudice; but they make it perfectly clear that what they are dealing with deserves no better name. No dialect, they keep repeating, is better than any other—yet poor and ignorant children must change theirs unless they want to stay poor and ignorant. When an NCTE "Task Force" set out to devise *Language Programs for the Disadvantaged* (NCTE, 1965), it laid down a perfect smoke screen of such hypocrisy, as one would expect from persons who felt called upon to inform the world that "without the experience of literature, the individual is denied the very dignity that makes him human" (p. v) but that not "all disadvantaged children are apathetic or dull" (pp. 24 f.).

"In this report" (p. 117), "teachers are asked to begin by accepting the dialect of their students for what it is, one form of oral communication. . . ." Teachers are warned particularly that they "need to accept the language which Negro children bring to school, to recognize that it is a perfectly appropriate vehicle for communicating ideas in the Negro home and subculture" (p. 215), that it is "essentially respectable and good" (p. 227). But though teachers must not attack "the dialect which children associate with their homes and their identity as Negroes" (p. 215), they must still use all the adult authority of the school to "teach standard informal English as a second dialect" (p. 137), because the youngster who cannot speak standard informal English "will not be able to get certain kinds of jobs" (p. 228).

The most common result of such teaching will be that white middle-class Midwestern speech will be imposed as mandatory for all those situations which middle-class white businessmen think it worth their while to regulate. In the words of Chicago's Professors Austin and McDavid (p. 245), "future educational programs should be developed in terms of substituting for the grammatical system of lower-class Southern speech [read: black Chicago speech] that of middle-class Chicago white speech—at least for those economic and social situations where grammatical norms are important." Labov goes so far as to ask (*Social Dialects and Language Learning*, p.

102) whether Northern schools should tolerate Southern speech at all—whether they should not also correct the "cultivated Southern speech" of privileged children who move North.

The description of compulsory bi-dialectalism may be completed by examining the methods which its proponents advocate for perpetuating the supremacy of white prejudice. Essentially, those methods are derived by analogy from structuralist methods of teaching foreign languages—methods whose superiority has been claimed but never demonstrated and whose intellectual foundations vanished with the demise of structuralist ideas. As an eminent grammarian privately observed after a recent conference, "The achievements of the operators will continue to lie in the field of getting and spending government money. . . . They seem to have an unerring instinct for finding ways of spending it unprofitably—on conferences at which they listen to each other, for example. Now they're out to teach standard English as a second dialect through techniques that have served very poorly in teaching second languages."

High on the list of those techniques is incessant drill on inessentials. In theory, the drills are the end-product of a long process of systematic comparison of the children's nonstandard dialects with the standard dialect which they are to be taught; but since the systematic comparisons have never been made, the bi-dialectalists fall back on a simple enumeration of a few dozen "features of pronunciation, grammar, and vocabulary which can be considered indices of social stratification" (Roger Shuy, "Detroit Speech," in A. L. Davis, ed., *On the Dialects of Children*, p. 13). Professor Rudolph Troike of the University of Texas was thus simply platitudinizing piously when he told the TESOL convention in 1968 that "any instructional program . . . must begin with as full an *objective* knowledge as possible" of both or all the dialects involved. The escape hatch in Troike's statement is the phrase *as full as possible*. What is usually possible is an unsystematic list of shibboleths—the simplification of consonant clusters, the Southern pronunciations of *walk* and *right*, *ax* for *ask*, the dropping of postvocalic /r/, *ain't* and *fixin' to*, *bofe* and *mouf* for *both* and *mouth*, and the like. These innocent usages, which are as familiar as the sun in the late Confederacy, are apparently the terror of Northern employers, who the bi-dialectalists assume are almost suicidally unconcerned with such details as character, intelligence, and training for the job. The fact is, of course, that Northern employers and labor leaders dislike black faces but use black English as an excuse.

Having established, however, that a child of darkness under her tutelage says *mouf*, the pretty white lady sets out to rescue his soul. First she plays tapes of Southern speech to convince her victims, who understand Southern speech far better than they understand hers, that Southern speech often makes "complete understanding of content . . . difficult," "not readily comprehensible"—as is demonstrated by the fact that the pretty white lady would never have detected her victim's four-letter word just by listening and without watching his lips (New York Board of Education, *Nonstandard Dialect*, pp. 1, 14, 17). The difficulty of detecting him is all the more reason for fearing the iniquitous *mouf*-sayer: it proves he is a cunning devil who probably says *dentissoffice* too and who perpetrates such subversive "malapropisms" as "The food in the lunch room is not fitting to eat" (*On the Dialects of Children*, p. 23). How else *would* he spell *fitten?* But for such a hardened rogue, a good many "motivational activities" are likely to be necessary before the pretty white lady can really start twisting the thumbscrew with her drills.

Yet the drills are available, and the pretty white lady will use them when she sees her time. She has drills of all kinds—repetition drills, substitution drills, replacement drills, conversion drills, cued answer drills, the reading in unison of long lists of words like *teeth / reef, toothbrush / waffle, bathtub / alphabet, weather / weaver*. To get rid of the *dentissoffice*, she may have students debate such propositions as "Ghosts do exist" or "Formal school tests should be eliminated"; and before a really "culminating activity" like playing "Pack the Trunk" she may "divide the class into consonant-cluster committees to seek out words containing" clusters like *sks, sps,* or *kt* (*Nonstandard Dialect, passim*). At this point the class might be invited to suggest a context for a replacement drill—maybe something like "Teacher! teacher! Billy Joe say that Tommy ————— Bessy!" This last suggestion, it must be confessed, has not yet been made in the literature, but it seems considerably more stimulating than choral recitation of Poe's "Bells" (*ibid.*, p. 35).

Perhaps it need not be added that existing tests and evaluations of such "instructional materials" are something of a farce. If bi-dialectalism is really harder to acquire than bilingualism (Einar

Haugen in *Social Dialects and Language Learning*, p. 125), teachers
and texts ought surely to be superb, and judgments on them ought
to be severe; but New York City's curriculum developers can give
"highest priority" to making the children change *a* to *an* before
nouns beginning with a vowel (*Nonstandard Dialect*, p. 14), and
Texas' Professor Troike can argue the success of his methods by
showing that after six months of drills a little black girl could repeat
his hat after her teacher, instead of translating automatically to
he hat. Unfortunately, tapes do not record psychological damage,
or compare the effectiveness of other ways of teaching, or show
what might better have been learned in the same time instead of
learning to repeat *his hat*.

So much for a description of mandatory bi-dialectalism, a bit
enlivened (since the subject is dreary) by irreverent comment, but
not distorted in any essential way. In the U.S.A., we are being told,
everybody wants approval—not approval for doing anything worth
approving, but approval for doing whatever happens to be approved.
Because approval goes to upward mobility, everybody should be
upwardly mobile; and because upward mobility is impossible for
underdogs who have not learned middle-dog barking, we must teach
it to them for use in their excursions into the middle-dog world.
There is no possibility either that the present middle class can be
brought to tolerate lower-class English or that upward mobility, as
a national aspiration, will be questioned. Those are the pillars on
which the state is built, and the compassionate teacher, knowing
the ways of his society, will change the color of his students' vowels
although he cannot change the color of their skins.

It is not at all certain that the bi-dialectalists, for all their absurd-
ities, can be dislodged from their well-carpeted offices. They are
supported by the National Council of Teachers of English, the
Modern Language Association of America, the Center for Applied
Linguistics, the federal government, the foundations, the govern-
ments of a number of major cities, and by black people who have
made it into the middle class and so despise their origins and their
less efficient fellows. In the best of times our top dogs are pleased
by docility, if not mobility, among the beasts below; and in 1969 a
new ice age is beginning. Newspaper headlines tell us that the
Department of Health, Education, and Welfare has been urged to

relax its requirements for desegregation of schools immediately but quietly, and President Nixon loses his Miami tan at the thought that militant students will "politicize" our universities—as if government grants to upwardly mobile faculty had not politicized them long ago. In Lyndon Johnson's Texas the citizens of Austin vote down an open housing law, their board of education then justifies segregated schooling by the established pattern of segregated housing, and the governor of the state praises the state university as the source of brain-power to assist the businessman in the lucrative exploitation of what the governor proudly calls the "insatiable appetite" of Texans. The only revolution we are likely to see is the continued subversion, by the dominant white businessman, of the political and religious principles on which the nation was founded.

Yet though the times are bad, they are not hopeless, at least not in the small, undramatic world of English education, and the bi-dialectalists are so gorgeously absurd that the breath of laughter may collapse their card-house if only enough people can be brought to see it as it is. It is not simply quixotic, then, to add to a laughing description of imposed bi-dialectalism a more serious statement of reasons why it cannot succeed and should not be tolerated even if it could—a statement which can lead, in conclusion, to the proposing of an alternative policy.

The argument that bi-dialectalism cannot be forced is easy to make out, even, in part, from the reluctant admissions of some of its proponents. Two principal reasons have already been suggested, the ignorance and unproved methods of the bi-dialectalists. The term *ignorance* is used literally, and in all fairness. Whatever one thinks of teaching standard English by methods like those for teaching foreign languages, contrastive analyses of our different dialects are a prerequisite—but a prerequisite which has not yet been supplied. Until very recently, the principal sources of information were the collections for the *Linguistic Atlas*; but they are unsystematic, partially out-of-date, and in some respects inaccurate and superficial. Where, for example, should one go for descriptions of intonation and its dialectal variants, for accurate accounts of the system or systems of verbal auxiliaries, for analyses of the speech of ghetto children instead of rustic ancients? Such minimal essentials are simply lacking. In fact, it might be said that for all the talk about revolutionary advances in linguistics, neither the structural nor the generative grammarians have yet produced a satisfactory basic description of even standard English.

The best descriptions of all our kinds of English would still not be enough to make coercive bi-dialectalism a success. The English teacher's forty-five minutes a day for five days in the week will never counteract the influence, and sometimes the hostility, of playmates and friends and family during much the larger part of the student's time. Formal education could produce real bi-dialectals only in a vast system of state nurseries and boarding schools to which the children of the poor and ignorant would be consigned at an early age; but such establishments would be prohibitively expensive, intolerable to the people, and still not absolutely certain of success, because the most essential of all conditions might not be met— namely, the desire of the children to talk like the white middle class.

When one thinks about it in these realistic terms, the whole argument about bi-dialectalism begins to look schizophrenic, as out-of-this-world as an argument whether Lee should surrender at Appomattox or fight back. There is no evidence that the bi-dialectalists, if they actually had good textbooks, better teachers, and as much money as the country is spending to devastate Vietnam, would really know what to do with those fictional resources. Instead of clear ideas, they offer clichés, like the familiar attack on "traditional methods and approaches" or the protected pedagogue's arrogant assurance that illiterates can have no human dignity. They fly off quickly into high-sounding vaguenesses, talking (for example) about "differences in social dialect and associated versions of reality" (*Social Dialects and Language Learning*, p. 68), as if metaphysics rested on a preconsonantal /r/. At their most precise, they suggest the prudential avoidance of Southern pronunciations of *walk* and *cough* in Washington because Negroes there look down on new arrivals from Georgia and the Carolinas. They happily assume what they should prove—that intensive training in "standard informal English as a second dialect" has produced or can produce large numbers of psychologically undamaged bi-dialectals, whose new accomplishment has won them or will win them jobs that otherwise would have been impossible for them to get. When their guard is down, the bi-dialectalists actually confess that they *have* no concrete program, since "no one program at any level yet seems applicable to a significant number of other classes at the respective level" (*Language Programs for the Disadvantaged*, pp. 30 ff.).

Some awareness of their difficulties, and some uncertainty about priorities, seem indeed to be spreading among the bi-dialectalists (though it would be too much to hope that if their present bandwagon falls apart they will consider themselves discredited and resign their membership in the Society of Mandarin.) For one thing, they have become aware of the significance of reading, which William A. Stewart, as late as 1964, could reduce to the level of "socially desirable embellishments" (*Social Dialects and Language Learning*, p. 10). In his latest book, however, *Teaching Black Children To Read*, Editor Shuy announces "the simple truth that speaking standard English, however desirable it may be, is not as important as learning to read" (p. 118). His colleagues Walter A. Wolfram and Ralph W. Fasold are even closer to enlightenment. In the same new volume (p. 143), they hesitantly admit that "there is some question about the degree to which Standard English can be taught to the ghetto child in the classroom at all"; and Fasold meant what he said, for he had said it before at the Milwaukee convention of the NCTE. Though that august body was still congratulating itself on its concern with "a language component for the so-called culturally divergent," it had to bear with Fasold's embarrassing confession: "Because of the operation of social forces in the use of language," he said, "forces which are only poorly understood, it may not be possible to teach Standard English as a second language to Black English speaking children unless they are interacting with Standard English speakers in a meaningful way outside the classroom" (*Convention Concerns—1968*, p. 10). The Center's linguistician came as close as standard English would allow to saying that it is segregation which makes black people talk different and that there would be no slum children if there were no slums.

No doubt the most important of Fasold's poorly understood social forces is one which everybody but white linguists has understood for a long time: black people may just not want to talk white English. Several years ago, Labov observed that some of his more rebellious New York subjects were deliberately turning away from social-climbing New York speech toward a black Southern model (*Social Dialects and Language Learning*, pp. 96 f.), and today comment on "the new feeling of racial pride among black Americans"

(*Teaching Black Children To Read*, p. 142) is a platitude. Wolfram and Fasold go on to the quite unsurprising speculation that that pride may even extend to the Negro's speech. "If a realization develops that this dialect, an important part of black culture, is as distinctively Afro-American as anything in the culture, the result may well be a new respect for Black English within the community" (p. 143). More plainly, condescending middle-class white charity is not wanted any more, if it ever was, in language-teaching or anywhere else. We should learn from the example of the British: the social cataclysm of the Second World War, and the achievement of political power by labor, did more to give the "disadvantaged" English youngster an equal chance than charitable bi-dialectalism ever did. We are past the stage when white teachers, whether Africans or Caucasians, can think well of themselves for trying to turn black people into uneasy imitations of the whites.

The immortality of that effort is the chief reason why enforced bi-dialectalism should not be tolerated even if it were possible. Predators can and do use dialect differences to exploit and oppress, because ordinary people can be made to doubt their own value and to accept subservice if they can be made to despise the speech of their fathers. Obligatory bi-dialectalism for minorities is only another mode of exploitation, another way of making blacks behave as whites would like them to. It is unnecessary for communication, since the ability to understand other dialects is easily attained, as the black child shows when she translates her teacher's prissy white model "*his* hat" into "*he* hat." Its psychological consequences are likely to be nervous affectation, self-distrust, dislike for everyone not equally afflicted with the itch to get ahead, and eventual frustration by the discovery that the reward for so much suffering is intolerably small. At best the altered student will get a somewhat better job and will move up a few places in the rat-race of the underlings. At worst he will be cut off from other blacks, still not accepted among whites, and economically no better off than he was before.

White teachers should hope, then, that their black students will be recalcitrant, so that bi-dialectalism as a unilateral condition for employment can be forgotten. It would make better sense, if pedagogues insist on living in a fantasy world, to require whites to speak black English in their dealings with blacks, since the whites have more advantages than the blacks and consider themselves more intelligent; or perhaps we should be hard-headedly consistent in our brutalities and try to eradicate the vices which really do enrage employers—like intellectual questioning, or the suspicion that ours is not the best of possible worlds.

Indeed, the educationists' faith in education would be touching if it were not their way of keeping up their wages. Nothing the schools can do about black English or white English either will do much for racial peace and social justice as long as the black and white worlds are separate and hostile. The measure of our educational absurdity is the necessity of saying once again that regimented bi-dialectalism is no substitute for sweeping social change—*necessity* being defined by the alternative of dropping out and waiting quietly for destruction if the white businessman continues to have his way.

The reply that the educational system should not be politicized is impossible for bi-dialectalists, since bi-dialectalism is itself a political instrument. They may purge themselves of inconsistency, and do what little good is possible for English teachers as political reformers, if instead of teaching standard English as a second dialect they teach getting out of Vietnam, getting out of the missile race, and stopping the deadly pollution of the one world we have, as horribly exemplified by the current vandalism in Alaska.

One use for a small fraction of the resources that would thus be saved would be to improve the teaching of the English language. Bi-dialectalism would never have been invented if our society were not divided into the dominant white majority and the exploited minorities. Children should be taught that. They should be taught the relations between group differences and speech differences, and the good and bad uses of speech differences by groups and by individuals. The teaching would require a more serious study of grammar, lexicography, dialectology, and linguistic history than our educational system now provides—require it at least of prospective English teachers.

In the immediate present, the time and money now wasted on bi-dialectalism should be spent on teaching the children of the minorities to read. Already some of the universal experts among the linguists have boarded this new bandwagon, and the next round of government grants may very well be for programs in reading and writing in black English. That might be a good thing, particularly if we could somehow get rid of the tired little clique of operators who have run the professional societies of English teachers for so long. Anyway, the direct attack on minority language, the attempt to compel bi-dialectalism, should be abandoned for an attempt to open the minds and enhance the lives of the poor and ignorant. At the same time, every attempt should be made to teach the majority to understand the life and language of the oppressed. Linguistic change is the effect and not the cause of social change. If the majority can rid itself of its prejudices, and if the minorities can get or be given an education, differences between dialects are unlikely to hurt anybody much.

(The phoniest objections to this proposal will be those that talk about social realism, about the necessity for doing something even —or should one say particularly?—if it's wrong. That kind of talk makes real change impossible, but makes money for bi-dialectalists.)

DIALECTS AND
DEMOCRACY

Dorothy M. Griffin

English teachers need to know a great deal more about their students' dialects—and dialects in general—than they often do. Furthermore, they need to educate students in important language concepts and democratic attitudes toward dialects much more directly and relevantly than most of them feel called on to do at this time. So many of us English teachers seem to operate from the smug assumption that we know all about language—after all, it is the basic tool of our trade and we do teach some language concepts through literature and, perhaps, composition. Some of us see no reason to take valuable class time away from teaching our already crowded curriculum to deal with the seemingly obvious. We all—or most of us—speak the same language, don't we? And there are certain standards we're all conscious of and working toward, aren't there? As a matter of fact, we *don't* all speak the same kind of English, and we *don't* all accept the same standards of, "good" and "bad" usage. Herein lies a powerful source of conflict for ourselves and our students which we cannot afford to ignore in these days of social upheaval.

I think the time has come for us to back away from the daily classroom struggle as far as possible and take a long, hard look at language problems, particularly those of dialect differences, and then try to come up with some solutions that make sense to ourselves and the younger generation.

The purposes of this paper, then, will be (1) to explore the need for a directly presented, specifically focused dialectology unit in high school English classes, (2) to discuss procedures whereby such linguistic learning can be accomplished, (3) to present, briefly, some

From the *English Journal* (April, 1970), pp. 551–8. Reprinted with permission of the National Council of Teachers of English and Dorothy M. Griffin.

Dorothy M. Griffin teaches in the Department of English at Evanston Township High School, Evanston, Illinois. This paper was presented at the NCTE Convention, Washington, D.C., November, 1969.

problems facing teachers and supervisors working in this area, and finally, (4) to suggest some possible solutions.

First, a word about goals. My present goal in teaching dialectology in high school English classes is to increase students' linguistic sophistication so that they become aware of the many different kinds of language behavior that exist in our country, that they understand the reasons for these differences, and finally, that they become tolerant of speech variations in a truly democratic spirit. There are other goals and plus values to which I attach importance, but I think these will become clear as we go on.

What is dialectology? As my associates and I have thus far defined the area at Evanston Township High School, dialectology is the study of all of the regional and social variations in spoken English in this country, the different ways people talk in various parts of the country, in different situations, and on different levels of society, and the influence these language varieties exert not only on standards of usage, but on interpersonal relationships. As you can see, this is a broader than usual definition of the area, but a necessary one, I think, if the significance of dialect study as basic to major understandings of language as it operates in society is to become clear to students. Thus, we avoid stressing the quaint fine points of dialect difference (you say "fishing worm"; I say "bait") at the expense of more important linguistic principles and social concepts. In other words, we focus on all language behavior through the lens of dialectology.

But why, again, should teachers and students be concerned with dialect differences? It seems obvious to us all—even little children —that people speak differently. A ghetto dweller sounds quite unlike a suburban housewife. A Kennedy comes across unlike the recent occupant of the White House—or even the present one. Any one of us may have different dialects we use on different occasions. Clearly, a tremendous variety in spoken English still exists in this country in spite of the levelling effects of mass communication, public education, and population mobility.

Very well—granted that people do speak differently. What has this got to do with the teaching of English? And why are we concerned with *spoken* English? Isn't this more nearly the province of the speech teacher? The answers to these questions are that we are *obliged* to tackle the spoken word first if we are to reach any real understanding of our language by scientific means rather than through the avenues of intuition and tradition.

Ninety-nine per cent of human communication is verbal—at least, first—and the greatest changes in language—the innovations, alterations, and so on, as well as the most explosive conflicts—occur most dramatically in speech. Spoken language is the basic language; speech is the primary mode of human communication, whereas writing is only a partial representation of the whole. I might add here that this linguistic assumption is a real sticking-point with most of my literature-oriented colleagues and has been the cause of many hot arguments. If, however, we accept this linguistic viewpoint, it then becomes very necessary for us and our students to find out how people really *do* talk in different parts of our country and in various social situations.

And this is exactly what I have tried to do with my dialect project at Evanston High School—encourage our students to go through some of the same inductive processes linguists do to arrive at certain linguistic truths. Not that we can, or should, make junior linguists of our students, but I hope, by having them look objectively at the language of their schoolmates, families, neighbors, and community leaders—as well as the varieties of American English spoken in other regions and circumstances—I will cause them to uncover some of the truths about language which will be useful to them for the rest of their lives.

For example, in one independent project my students developed, they interviewed three speakers of Received Standard British English and compared their dialects with American speech (Chicago brand). This project led to further research into the history of the dialect divergence between British and American English, and the students concluded that languages constantly change for a number of often obscure reasons. Right here we have already opened up an important linguistic insight. Languages change and nothing can halt the process to any significant degree. If we can establish this one principle and all of its ramifications, we can get rid of the false, but still widespread misconception that some golden age of language once existed, that all we have to do is go back to that perfect state and then stand pat—resist all change—and our language will be perfect forever. Students should learn that language is a living, constantly changing organism. While we hope they treat it with respect and responsibility, neither we nor they can fix its form in some mythical perfect state, no matter what we do.

Maybe the most important concept of all that students can and should discover on their own is that there is no one standard of spoken English in America—that each identifiable speech region such as New York City or Southern Louisiana has its own standards, not only in pronunciation, but also in word choice and grammatical construction. It sometimes comes as a revelation to Evanston students, for example, that it is perfectly proper for a Southern gentleman to inquire, "May I carry you to town?" If they find out that the speaker who pronounces "fire" as "fahr" is not necessarily illiterate but may be using an acceptable pronunciation for his part of the country, then they have come a long way toward breaking down those old myths about "good" and "bad" English. If they realize that usages unfamiliar to them may be perfectly respectable elsewhere, then they are less likely to confuse regional forms with class or status distinctions. The point, of course, is to make this understanding really stick, to get the student to change long-held and deeply ingrained dialect prejudices. You will still get many questions such as, "But Mrs. Griffin! What is *really* right?" At which point, you patiently go over the ground again and throw the question back to the student. Needless to say, you, the teacher, must be familiar with standards of usage in dialects throughout the country.

At this point, too, you lead students into that bramble thicket of class distinctions. You try to get them to see that the value judgments they make as to "right" and "wrong" are usually based on the social prestige of the group speech to which they aspire. This comes hard. There are no greater language snobs than middle-class, suburban high school youngsters, and they just can't believe that the brand of speech they consider socially acceptable is just that— socially acceptable in their group, not ultimate perfection handed down from on high.

While they are groggy and reeling from this heresy, you have a chance, if you will take it, to press on and drive home a truth so important that I am tempted to say the fate of our country depends on it: you judge a man not by his speech any more than by the color of his skin; you judge him by what kind of human being he is. He may be intelligent or dumb, lazy or ambitious, crooked or honest, but he *is* a human being, alive and breathing in—of all places—a democracy. The kind of speech he uses indicates only the kind of group he grew up in. It doesn't tell us whether he is a worthwhile person or not. Students may protest that the nonstandard speaker can't communicate well, can't be understood. Oh, yes, he can—in his own speech community—and even in alien environments, if we apply a little knowledge and play fair. I think the time has come to educate middle-class young people and adults, too, in some other dialects besides their own. Since when, in this country, has it been decreed that all individual differences were taboo?

This need for tolerance of language variations brings me to something that I feel very strongly about—if I may digress for a moment —the incredible upsurge, in the last few years, of programs, heavily funded by the federal government, to teach standard English *as a second language* to nonstandard (translate that, "ghetto") speakers. Language is a human being's most personal possession. It's part of him, who he is. We cannot tell a whole generation of children that their language is so inferior they must learn another language to rise in this world. How much better it would be to educate those who hold power and their offspring in democratic attitudes and linguistic tolerance!

I understand some of the motives that have brought about this wholesale retraining activity, I think. Give the black student the white man's English, quick, so he can pull himself out of the ghetto. But, however altruistic, this is a shortsighted attitude. The problem is not so simple. For the past two years I have worked as a human relations coordinator for Evanston Township High School and my experience with our black student (about 18 per cent of the school population) has taught me a great many things. Many of our black students are thoroughly middle-class and speak a brand of standard English that would be acceptable anywhere. But I would as soon attempt to retrain the language patterns of the nonstandard speakers as I would tell them they couldn't wear their afros and *dashikis* to school. And I would get about as far. The students are struggling for a sense of personal worth and identity. One of the big problems we have now is that so many of them are turning us off because they feel the courses they take are white-oriented. Often bright students cut class, refuse to work, and get in trouble because it is more important to them to be black and belong somewhere than it is to learn white man's ways, even if this is necessary to get along in the

white man's world. If some black students react this way in a well-
to-do suburban high school, I shudder to think what whole black
schools in the inner-city will do if this kind of education is forced
on them.

But, back to the business at hand. Maybe, since I have been talking in generalities, it would be helpful for me to tell you briefly
about the kind of dialect unit I actually teach and relate it to our
overall language program at ETHS.

About five years ago, several colleagues and I set out to develop
an experimental, four-year language program for our school. After
monumental struggles, the project shaped up something like this:
for the ninth-graders, a fairly long, linguistically-oriented language
unit which gives them some exposure to transformational grammar
and an introduction to lexicology-lexicography, dialectology, and
the history of the language, all of which, excepting the grammar,
they will study in more detail as they go through school. The sopho-
mores have a two-week unit in lexicology-lexicography; the juniors
concentrate on dialectology, and the seniors study the history of the
language.

My own contribution, the dialectology unit, turned out to be an
expandable unit which can be taught in anything from three to six
weeks. As the unit is set up, the first day or so is spent in general
introduction and orientation. I like to start off with a random selection of the latest news headlines about situations where language
differences have brought about violent conflict. There are always
plenty of these:

"Thousands Die in Language Riots in Southern India"
"Puerto Ricans Riot over N.Y. Language Program"
"Language Split Grows in Quebec—Montreal a Powder Keg"

I then point out that if separate languages divide people in such
situations, dialects can be said to divide Americans. At this point,
I make a transition into some of the students' own more obvious
dialect differences. For example, I ask them how they pronounce
roof and get the expected split on this word. An even better word is
soot. If you're lucky, you get a three-way division here. I sometimes
ask them to put the verb *dive* in the past tense; this usually leads
to a spirited argument. Students seem to enjoy this kind of discus-

sion, and it leads naturally into the first principles I want to establish: that dialects differ from each other in pronunciation, vocabulary, and grammar.

At this juncture, I have in the past described the International Phonetic Alphabet and tried to establish a need for mastering it as a tool for recording differences in dialect. I am not sure I would insist on this again in the future. Maybe the thing to do is leave the option open—allow those who want to go on with IPA to do so on an independent study basis. Usually students pick up the simplified version of the IPA I give them with little trouble. But teachers with tin ears or little training in this area find phonetics terrifying.

Very soon I involve students in field research projects where they go out in the community and collect vocabulary variations. At first, I arm them with a very short check sheet patterned after the DARE work sheets. For example, they ask their informants (preferably people from other parts of the country): "What do you call the new superhighways that run from coast to coast?" When the students return from the field, we pool our results and see if any patterns emerge; they rarely do at this point. There are, however, other projects like this that get students out investigating on their own, and as their experience builds up, their accuracy improves.

When students observe firsthand some of the difficulties one encounters in trying to pin down dialect differences in the field, talk turns naturally to the methods linguistic geographers use in their research. Students read about and report on the Linguistic Atlas project, the work of the American Dialect Society, and the methods of individual linguistic scholars. Needless to say, by this time I have assembled in the resources center a considerable library of language books and other source material which they can browse through.

We next go into a more detailed examination of American regional dialects, using records and tapes and again encouraging students to investigate these differences through research or field work, and we begin to tie dialects to the geographical locations where they are usually found. Sometimes students get hooked on a certain brand of regional dialect and do such a fantastic job of researching on their own that the American Dialect Society would be proud of them. I always teach them the accepted forms for submitting material to Publication of the American Dialect Society or the *Dictionary of American Regional English* and let them know that they can, if they come up with valid findings, become part of the scholarly community.

It is probably a good idea to get everybody started on a major project of his own about this time. I suggest possibilities but much prefer letting the student find something that really interests him and set up his own goals and procedures. We make a contract. The student comes to me with his idea and then sets up his own goals, criteria, and timetable. I usually get some very original and sometimes fascinating returns on this assignment. Among the more entertaining ones last year were: "The Dialect of Abraham Lincoln," "Negro Radio Sermons," "Regional Dialect Research via Ham Radio," "William Faulkner's Use of Dialect in *The Sound and the Fury*," "A Texan Changes His Dialect" (with accompanying tapes), "Negro Folk Tales," "Alabama Talk," "The Down-Easters," and, of course, numerous up-to-the-minute surveys of ETHS slang. Nearly always, too, in a school the size of Evanston Township, we have students who have lived in other countries who can give us inside information about the kind of English—a second language almost everywhere—which is spoken by the local citizens where they were.

Now I like to introduce something quite different—a diagnostic questionnaire testing student attitudes toward the speech of others. I tried to develop this questionnaire so that it would reflect students' inner feelings about language without placing value judgments on their answers. Sample questions go like this: "If someone told me that Boston speech was superior to Chicago speech, I would (a) agree completely, (b) feel that there was some truth in the statement, (c) doubt the truth of the statement, (d) disagree completely." And another: "A person who wants to change the way he talks may be (a) intelligently ambitious, (b) a go-getter, (c) disloyal to his family, (d) wasting his time." Or again: "Having a southern accent marks a person as (a) socially superior, (b) socially acceptable, (c) belonging to a certain race, (d) socially inferior." Another: "Someone who says 'Nigra' for 'Negro' (a) is ignorant of the proper pronunciation, (b) is always being consciously offensive, (c) may be using a standard southern pronunciation, (d) is obviously low-class." There are twenty-six questions such as these, then a section where students rank different professions and occupations on the basis of need for "good grammar," and finally, a free comment section where they write on the general subject "What Is 'Good English'?"

These questionnaires are collected, tabulated, and laid aside for the time being. If there is time we now go into the questions of how and why American dialects developed and the differences between British and American dialects. Both of these areas can usually be covered best in lecture sections, and it is always fun, if you can round up a visiting Englishman, to let him present the British point of view. Or again, if we have time, we may take a brief excursion into foreign-language-influenced American dialects such as "Cajun" in the Louisiana Bayou country or Pennsylvania Dutch or Gullah speech from the southeastern coast. There rarely is time, however, for these diversions, and they are best left to independent exploration.

Going into the final phases, we come to an area I have labelled "imagistic" dialects, which simply means dialects through which we present ourselves to others in a certain role—in which we establish an image either consciously or unconsciously. I prefer to use this term rather than the term "social dialects" because it takes in a great deal of behavior which is actually associated with social and class dialects but is rarely considered with them and allows us to shift the focus slightly to a less opprobrious angle. It changes the emphasis to a certain extent in that the speech an individual uses at a given time or place may not automatically lock him into a particular social class, but may also represent the image of himself that he wishes to present. We talk about such things as levels of usage, formal and informal speech and slang, but we also look into dialects reflecting sex differences, dialects of youth and age and special interest dialects (spacespeak, computer-talk, etc.). Finally, we look into the rhetorical aspects of all dialects—the fact that we, all of us, have a number of dialects at our disposal and unconsciously shift to the one we feel is appropriate to the situation in which we find ourselves or to one that will accomplish the results we want. If you have ever had a student stop you in the hall and speak to you about an assignment using the standard dialect he thinks you expect and then have seen his lightning switch to adolescent in-slang when he hails a passing friend, then you'll understand what I mean. Now, also, it is reasonable to encourage students to learn another dialect, preferably a nonstandard one. They may discover such facts as that even nonstandard dialects may have a perfectly consistent grammar, that they are not necessarily sloppy or "bad" English, but only a different English.

When you reach this point, you are ready to cap the whole unit off with a discussion of standards of usage. What are they? What determines them? Why must we judge our fellow man on this basis? But I have talked quite at length about this before, and hope I have made my point. At any rate, now you give the questionnaire on speech attitudes a second time and compare with your students the results of both. You may have caused some changes in attitudes. I sincerely hope so.

But there are problems that arise in teaching a unit like this. And most of these problems come under the heading of teacher-resistance. I believe that this resistance has a readily traceable historical basis. English as a distinctly teachable area first arose in the latter half of the nineteenth century out of what had been departments of rhetoric and oratory which emphasized both the spoken and the written word. The development of mass journalism and the rise of the penny press, large masses of literate people, and a kind of chauvinistic interest in the writers of English, American as well as British, produced an increasing shift of emphasis from the spoken word to the written word. English departments became bastions of experts in literature. Rhetoric in the classical sense was fragmented, English departments retaining mainly the stylistic concepts which were taught largely through composition. The oral aspects of rhetoric with an emphasis on delivery became the province of rapidly growing speech departments that developed in the early part of the twentieth century.

Now in our present century, largely through the technological development of radio and TV, there has been a rapid shift away from the written word back to the spoken word as the essential instrument for shaping our society. Symptomatic of this change is Wayne Booth's call for a new rhetoric and Marshall McLuhan's perhaps premature obituary for the age of linear print and recent popular works such as John Gross' *The Rise and Fall of the Man of Letters* (Macmillan, 1969). At the same time, linguists, working, until rather recently, somewhat independently of academic policy structure, have come up with a mass of data and resulting understandings of the nature and structure of language which establish clearly the primacy of the spoken over the written word as the chief mode of communication.

If this is true, word has not filtered down to English departments in colleges—which must surely be the most conservative academic groups in the world. A look at course offerings in all but a few still reveals a heavy emphasis in literature and a perfunctory smattering of linguistics courses. Often the linguistics courses are not even part of the English curriculum, but are included in other disciplines such as anthropology, sociology, or speech.

What is happening, then, some forty years after the birth of the *Linguistic Atlas*, is that college English departments are still turning out prospective teachers who have little or no knowledge or understanding of linguistics. It is understandable, then, that these young people, as well as the vast majority of older English teachers, with a great deal of time and interest invested in literature, are extremely resistant to teaching linguistically oriented language programs along with the standard literary fare. Troubled by problems of relevance in English offerings—as we all are—most high school English teachers go to great lengths to reach the new breed of students through the only avenue they know, literature, ignoring the more immediately relevant channels of language and rhetoric. We find a proliferation of units stressing the humanities—see the world through the eyes of great books—but only a perfunctory gesture toward serious language study. Even the most progressive high school supervisor—and I happen to have one—finds it almost impossible to dent the hostility of most teachers to a linguistic program. Curriculum projects may flourish on paper, but if teachers are not knowledgeable in the area, do not really understand the rationale of the approach and feel threatened by being forced to teach subject matter which is new to them, they will usually produce only mediocre results which are then greeted as evidence that such language units won't go and so on, until the circle of evasion is complete.

I can truthfully say from my own experience in teaching dialectology to juniors for the past five years that the students have been interested in and responsive to and in a few cherished cases, stimulated to go on to further work in linguistics in college.

How, then, can language programs such as the one described gain acceptance in high schools? The solution to the problem is not simple, nor, judging from the rate of progress being made, will it be quick in arriving. The primary objective, of course, would be to work for a more realistic balance of linguistics and literature in the college curriculum. That this shift of emphasis will come about, I am confident. The question is *when*. It might be facilitated if more supervisors demanded some linguistic background from the teachers they hire. Another possibility is increased teacher retraining in linguistics for established teachers who have not kept abreast of the times. Inservice training is a third possibility and seems to me to be the most immediately available avenue open to administrators who really want to promote a language program. I should not like to see development of compromise language programs such as one I recently examined in which linguistic concepts are taught solely through literature. Dialectology, for example, is taught through pulling ideas about language from *Huckleberry Finn* and *The Grapes of Wrath*. The motives for this approach are commendable—to bypass the apathy of literature-oriented teachers to linguistics—but the end results are likely to be disastrous. The method, it seems to me, is founded on a paradox. How can one examine the wide range of living language which is relevant to modern experience through the microscope of minute portions of language abstracted in written approximations of dialects? What probably results is a killing of the literature by mangling it beyond recognition to extract linguistic truths and at the same time throwing at the student a confused mass of derived linguistic information without order or impact. I rather expect the intelligent student might rebel.

Until such time as wider understanding of linguistics and better teacher preparation in linguistics become general, I can only reiterate: teachers most certainly need to know more about their students' language and their own, too. Who knows? In the dim future we may be able to convince English teachers that teaching tolerance of others' dialects is as important as learning about life through Macbeth's character or finding one's identity with Holden Caulfield.

PROCESSES IN
LANGUAGE LEARNING

John Dixon

In general, it is a mistake to assume that—past the very earliest stages
—much of what the child acquires is acquired by imitation. This [assump-
tion] could not be true on the level of sentence formation, since . . . most
of what he produces . . . is new.

(Chomsky: *Formal Discussion*)

. . . the social structure generates distinct linguistic forms or codes
and these codes essentially transmit the culture and so constrain behaviour
. . . there will arise distinct linguistic forms, fashions of speaking, which
induce in their speakers different ways of relating to objects and persons.

(Bernstein, 1965)

In a sense a child over-abstracts at first as well as under-abstracts: he
cuts his world into a few simple categories that cover too much and
discriminate too little. . . .

(Moffett, Dartmouth)

Dialogue inside grows out of dialogue with others. This is how society
penetrates our thinking.

(H. Rosen, Dartmouth)

Because our concern is language in operation, we need to understand the processes involved in language learning. Unfortunately,
from the standpoint of theory these are still areas of ignorance rather
than knowledge. We can do little more than sketch the regions where
investigation is going on and where more should be encouraged.
Members of the Seminar from both sides of the Atlantic agreed that
there had been a failure to set up adequate research institutes for
such investigations. In the first place these needed to be grounded
firmly in the classroom, with teachers actively involved. But though
the roots should be the schools, what arises needs help from psycho-

John Dixon, *Growth through English*, reprinted by permission of the
Clarendon Press, Oxford.

linguists, socio-linguists and child psychologists, for example. An institution—a centre—is needed where teams of this kind can collect and with which teachers can keep in touch. A working relationship between the schools and the centre would help to produce working knowledge and awareness. (For "knowledge," we note, has suffered unduly from its reification.) A major function of research at such a centre would be to confirm or modify the teacher's preconceptions, to point our attention to new kinds of awareness, and to help us (when we feel the need) to make some awareness more explicit. But we teachers must ask the questions too.

THE REPERTOIRE OF STRUCTURES

Thus, as we observe the language that children use, both in speech and writing, we may wonder how much of the basic structure they have learnt. For some time the linguists have maintained that the normal child of five or six is "a linguistic adult." "He controls, with marginal exceptions if any, the phonemic system of his language; he handles effortlessly the grammatical core; he knows and uses the basic contentive vocabulary" (Hockett). Observations and analyses of children's speech and writing by Strickland, Loban and Hunt clearly support this claim and suggest that the limited structures often encountered through casual observation are probably only a small part of a latent repertoire. The achievement of this repertoire is a remarkable example of self-education which the schools do well to build on. "What the child has learned already he has learned under the pressure of the necessities and pleasures of daily living. If school is to continue the processes already started it must stir the same kind of pressure and kindle the same excitements." It seems essential to know how a child achieves this mastery; as yet, however, the best that scholars can do is to point to the likely factors affecting language development. These include "the amount, variety, and quality of language heard and used in the family (in conversation, table talk, stories, etc.); the variety of experience including much non-threatening, self-enhancing interaction with other people and opportunity to verbalize this experience; encouragement and opportunity for self expression, not only in language but in other ways"

(Loban). There is a remarkable agreement between these factors and some ideas on school independently suggested to the Seminar by David Holbrook (p. 95).

Perhaps this is the place to mention the danger, on the other hand, of restricted linguistic judgements. For instance, the repertoire of structures used in speech shows an increasing complexity as children grow older and develop more control of language. On the face of it, then, one might use growing complexity of repertoire as evidence to support a particular programme of instruction in language (given the appropriate controls). But this is to forget that complexity may be well used or badly used to organize experience. Members of the Seminar were sharply critical of claims, based on such evidence, for *sentence-stretching* by adding modifiers or by sentence synthesis.

LANGUAGE SWITCHES

Nevertheless, the effect of modern linguistic research is to reinforce our awareness of the complexity of resources demanded by modern societies. Infant speech is perhaps best thought of as "an undifferentiated matrix out of which will emerge many highly specialized language functions" (Whitehead). A major hurdle for young children with a strong local or social dialect is learning to accommodate to the standard English in which all their books are written. And we now begin to see this as only one of a whole set of language switches that a pupil must gradually learn to make as he copes with new situations and takes on new social roles. The language of home, he learns, differs in significant ways from the language of the classroom; the language of the classroom differs from that of a school assembly; stories differ from talk; textbooks about a new subject may appear to have invented a new language. It can all be very puzzling. The failure of schools to help pupils gradually to assimilate the complicated varieties of English in modern use explains why in secondary schools today so much of language "looks at pupils across a chasm."

Thus in learning to read, children are in danger of feeling a sudden discontinuity, a change from the familiar dialect forms to forms which may (at worst) have been rarely heard or which feel

alien. A linguistic barrier can be set up in this manner and in the
majority of cases it need not be. At least four stages should be
observed:

a. much enjoyable listening to standard English—assimilating it
   with satisfaction through stories told by the teacher and later
   through her reading stories too;
b. reading aloud by teacher and child of the child's own stories,
   told in his own language and preserved in that form by the
   teacher who wrote them down;
c. reading stories in standard with accompanying talk;
d. reading standard on his own.

The length of each stage will be related to the differences between
dialect and standard forms. But in any case "learning to read and
write leaves the child alone with language in a way which differs
from his previous experience. This should not be made a sudden
transition. The new activities should be preceded, accompanied and
followed by talk."

So much for learning to assimilate the standard forms written by
somebody else; but what of speaking and writing for onself? Of the
two, writing is the simpler issue, because there is, broadly speaking,
only one British form (the one used in this book) and American
standard English differs hardly at all. There are hopes (in need of
experimental testing) that under the influence of much reading, the
written forms used by a pupil will change to standard. This demands
teachers who realize that "the concept of original sin, linguistically
speaking, is untenable" (Marckwardt)—that dialect is personal and
valuable, not an incorrect version of standard. The alternative
method of writing drills seems difficult to motivate, of dubious
effectiveness, and possibly of damaging effect. Pupils need to associate standard English, whether heard or read, with pleasure rather
than with drudgery or uncertainty. And in the interim, while the
accommodation is being made, the teacher makes a decision on the
priority to be given to the human purposes in language. A West
Indian, about thirteen years old, comes to your school, for example.
Does her experience come first or the "correctness" of her English?
Suppose she writes this in answer to your assignment:

In ten years times I'll remember a picture of my dad who I haven't seen for 5 years. My dad when to America in 1958, when there and haven't been back. I when to see him there from since then I haven't seen him.

He took a picture of the family and leave it when he were going, from since then I have that picture and alway will to remember the last time I saw him and to remember those day when he were near.

That picture is home in a frame and every night before I go to bed I take up the picture and look at it sometimes a strong feeling come over me and just start to cry it make me think if the family will ever by like the old photograph which in that frame on the wall.

For some years I ask my mom why don't dad come and see us no more, she just says some day why some day I ask. In replied she just answer you have to find out for yourself. I said to her mom are you afraid of something are you holding something from me, replied no. So one day I ask my nany is mummy and daddy had a quarrel why he dont come to see me no more? . . .

Whatever our attitude to the forms of language, spoken or written, we have to leave the way open for things of importance to be said— to retain the position of trust. And that means ignoring correctness and dialect forms at such moments, because for the pupil the experience is all-important.

Why is the problem so complex? Because, though it lies in the linguistic domain, dialect is fundamentally a social matter. Language asserts our membership of a speech fellowship (Firth). To members of lower status groups, then, standard is a prestige dialect spoken by upper status groups or classes. The reverse of this view is that dialects of lower status groups are "sub-standard". In a paper too important to be briefly summarized here, Labov* has pointed to a major difference of attitude between status groups in New York. Lower class speakers showed little or no consciousness of external standards of correctness in spoken English: as one said, "How can I speak any other way than I do?" Lower middle class speakers have the highest group recognition of such external standards "as an inevitable accompaniment of [their] upward social aspirations and upward social mobility."

Notions of "correctness" and sensitivity to "correct" speech forms have a class bias, therefore. Often they will produce a counter-

* "Social Dialects and Language Learning," N.C.T.E., 1964.

pressure in the school or neighbourhood, so that "the adolescent peer group exerts strong pressure against any deviation in the direction of middle class" norms.

So, in a world of insecurity and status preoccupations, "one uses the language which helps to preserve one's life, which helps to make one feel at peace with the world, and which screens out the greatest amount of chaos," as Ralph Ellison said (S.D. & L.L.). But "if you can show me," he goes on, "how I can cling to that which is real in me, while teaching me the way into the larger society, then I will . . . drop my defences and my hostility . . ."

Let us be clear that it is a case of teachers liberating themselves as well as their pupils, and that to do so they need to draw on linguistics, psychology and sociology for a conceptual framework that will explain the processes involved. Thus:

a. A dialect often, maybe generally, carries indications of social or class status.

b. When we speak it we identify ourselves with the group who use it, whether Tynesiders or Harlem Negroes.

c. Standard spoken forms are inevitably less well defined than standard English proper (the written form); the question of acceptability is more open since there is no institution (like the publisher) concerned with producing an acceptable standard, and no simple method like consulting the dictionary, for example.

d. Both local or social dialect and standard spoken English will vary in phonology, syntax, morphology, and lexicon according to whether the situation in which they are used is formal or informal. In his New York study of certain status markers in pronunciation, Labov has shown that a workman may use the prestige form quite frequently in formal situations, and that middle class speakers frequently use unconsciously in casual speech the very form that they explicitly stigmatize. So there may be overlapping stratification of local dialect and standard, or there may not: the evidence so far is fragmentary.

e. Whatever the dialect, learning to use a regional variety of standard spoken (which even in Britain is acceptable in discourse on educational, governmental topics, etc.) involves wanting to be accepted by speakers already using it. Social segregation in more or less extreme forms exists in both countries and while it does, the children and young people who suffer from it are unlikely to see adequate reasons for changing their dialect. For example, "unless the white community shows an active will to accept and integrate the Negro citizens, they cannot possibly have a full-scale motivation for learning standard English. The school can give them only a surrogate for the teaching they should be getting from their white friends and neighbours. Those who learn standard English may still be snubbed and rejected for their colour. They have put in a great deal of effort to lose their Negro identity yet they have still failed to acquire a white identity" (Haugen, S.D. & L.L.). Social change must precede educational change in this case.

f. Where people of different social background mix fairly freely, the need to use mutually acceptable forms produces accommodations—and thus produces teachers who sometimes informally use local forms, and pupils who on more formal occasions use a variety of standard. (One can see this at work with B.B.C. television interviewers.) The sympathy, respect and emulation stirred by the school and what it stands for in such a community will provide the necessary preconditions for pupils learning to use standard forms alongside their own dialect. If the streaming or grouping system in the school accentuates social differences, on the other hand, accommodation is much less likely.

g. Most pupils who speak a dialect do learn to assimilate varieties of standard that they hear and read. In a sense, then, they have already mastered the standard forms as well as their own: all they have to do is to move on from passive mastery of standard to active use of it. This suggests that the change is not impossible. But equally, "all scholars are agreed that it is harder to keep to similar languages apart than two very different ones" (Haugen). Teachers with an adequate awareness of the problems of switching back and forth will be less concerned to penalize "mistakes" (inefficient learning after the event) and better prepared to see that the pupil is *incidentally* reminded of the standard form in the course of school work. We need more evidence on the process, the stages, and the timing involved.

h. However willing they are, some pupils may find it difficult to pick up standard forms of spoken and written. What to do next is not clear. Can drama help? Should second language drills be used—and if so, with what motivation? Experiments will help to clarify our answers here.*

RESTRICTED ROLES FOR LANGUAGE

Teachers and linguists alike have been accustomed to think of dialect in over-simple terms. Labov points out that "linguistics has made the most progress in analysing the cognitive components; but many elements in language . . . are imbued with non-cognitive values as well." Thus the dialects of the urban working classes choose certain levels and elements from experience and imply evaluations of them. Standard and social dialects are not different ways of saying the same thing—are not a set of equivalent "codes." Each style of life, implying as it does certain kinds of relationship between people and certain attitudes to experience, results in the habit of selecting in certain ways from the cognitive and non-cognitive possibilities of a language. Thus Basil Bernstein has drawn out attention to the manner of speech among some working class boys in London—how predictable their utterances are, how much relies on implicit meaning and extra-verbal signals. As one index of what is going on, he looks at the boys' use of "they": the word has a characteristic vagueness. It does not necessarily refer back to particular people, or even to groups like "the bosses." The lack of an antecedent implies that *"we"* all know what is referred to, so it would be redundant to elaborate. In a sense, therefore, "they" is being used to reinforce "the community of interests generated by we." There are some similarities with the (under) conceptualizing of young children— the way for example a toddler may use "a mummy" to refer to almost any person other than a young child. The concept looks to us highly

---

* Nelson Francis is at present engaged in such an experiment, using various methods to help college students gain a mastery of standard forms.

abstract but it felt by the child to be very concrete. Gradually he will learn to refine on this concept—to distinguish among girls, young ladies, married women, mothers, motherly people, etc. But as Bernstein comments, this development of a series of levels of abstractions seems to be missing in the use of "they" that he reports. This is only one of many features in what he calls a "restricted code".

Of course everyone uses language in this way at times, in talk with intimate friends perhaps. But pupils limited in their language strategy to such a restricted code are poorly equipped to make meaning explicit to themselves or others. Consequently they enter school with an enormous disadvantage and are unlikely to recover from it—unless we can devise teaching methods that take their special needs into account.

But the process is more than linguistic in its roots and its consequences. The linguistic limitation "originally elicits and later reinforces a preference in the child for a special type of social relation . . . limited in terms of verbal explicitness. . . ." The social "dialect" restricts the roles a child can take on, and restricts his image of himself. "A change of code involves changes in the means whereby social identity is created." As Bernstein said in the NATE Bulletin, "We [teachers] are asking a lot of these children."

"If there is an imaginative, creative, adventurous potential within our children, then there is a new responsibility for teachers of English (far more than for other teachers in the school system) which isn't a simply pedagogic responsibility, because the school in fluid societies is an agent of cultural change. New identities are being created as children become involved in the school system, and a symptom of this change in identity will in fact be presented to the teacher in terms of that child's difficulties and tensions, initially in English." We might relate this general comment from research to a statement by a seventeen-year-old Yorkshire schoolboy in "The Excitement of Writing." (American readers should note that in the U.K. only a rather academic minority of pupils normally stay on into the "Sixth Form" after reaching the age of sixteen.)

The problem of speech facing a sixth former in a working class area is only a relatively minor one. It is a reflection of the much greater complexities he faces in having to live two lives . . .

At present this is a new field. We can do little more than outline
the scope for teachers and researchers to look into the varieties of
English that pupils start school with, meet there, and need to
develop. One can think of such research as looking in three directions
(not mutually exclusive).

—First, at variations in the way children's language impedes and
   enlarges the relations in which they can stand with respect to
   experience, and in particular the cognitive and affective quality
   of those relations. Here Bernstein's present work is central,
   though it also includes other directions.
—Second, at the way language needs to vary as the form of experience changes (in the nature of the elements isolated and the
   structure and type of their relations to each other). Work
   recently set up in England and Wales under the Schools Council
   is directly related to this: at present it is designed to cover
   speech among pupils eleven to eighteen, and writing from
   eleven to eighteen in the different school subjects and for general purposes.
—Third (and intimately associated with both the others) at the
   way pupils' language varies with their social relationship to the
   listener(s) or potential reader. Here the Seminar agreed on the
   urgent need for further research into the dynamics of groups in
   class, with investigation of questions such as the following:
   a. How does children's language change in changing group
      situations, e.g. problem-solving as against gossiping?
   b. What differences does the presence of the teacher make?
   c. How far does size of group affect the style of utterance?
   d. What kinds of language emerge from the carrying out of a
      common task, self-initiated as against teacher-initiated?

The vital need is "to use the evidence of speech variation (and
varieties of writing) . . . to infer the deeper, underlying processes
which must be understood if we are to solve the urgent problems of
the urban schools" (Labov). For children come to school limited in
the social roles they can play and the situations they can cope with.
As far as language is concerned, we can see the school as a special
opportunity to meet a wide variety of situations and to take on (in
play and in earnest) a variety of roles within them. As they do so,

the children learn (under the teacher's guidance) to draw on those levels and develop those features of language that will help them to entertain and control the experience.

LANGUAGE ENABLING NEW ROLES TO BE DEVELOPED

Take, for example, the way children use language in carrying out certain tasks—a subject to which the psycho-linguistic research of Luria and Vygotsky has brought new awareness. Where the manipulations required are complex (requiring step by step procedure) and planning is called for, it seems that language has an important function: young children who can talk over the steps and operations as they carry them out have a better chance of succeeding, even when their companion says nothing. Here is Stephen, just under three but from a linguistically rich home, learning to use language in this way while playing with his trains. (His mother's responses are in italics.)

That's going on . . . on . . . on the carriages. That's going to go next to the carriages—you see?
And we shall put on the brake you see?
We shall put on the brake.
We got the diesel trains haven't we?
I play with that, then Jonathan played with that train and then I played with those two trains. And he played with Punch and Judy when Daddy was ready to go to work.
Did he? Yes, he did. . . .
. . . Then fall down like this . . .
Oh that's going to go—on this do you see?
And then it's got a [inaudible] like that.
Mine's a block engine isn't it?
And that engine is going to be on that train you see.
And if you do have a truck in there it won't work.
Won't it? No. *Why not?* Cos it won't.
There's two engines. There's lots of trains.

I want my socks off—the fire will warm them won't it?
Yes. My nose was a bit runny so wiped it on that.
Did you? That will warm it up—there—I've put them my socks on the fireguard so the fire will warm them up you see. Oh—

Look! you see? The book shouldn't be under there should it?
No! No! [etc.].

Stephen's language is already beginning to move flexibly from one
purpose to another. It precedes and accompanies his activities; it
recalls past events, putting them in a simple sequence; it helps in the
rejection of certain behaviour ("if you do" . . .)—though an explicit
cause and effect relation is evaded. His mother's presence seems
unimportant, until we think of the "you sees." Her remarks are highly
redundant; when her language *is* used for cognitive purposes, it
fails to elicit the appropriate response.

In the silent classrooms of the old infant schools, children who had
not already developed these purposes and procedures in their play
at home were probably retarded in the performance of all but the
simplest school tasks. One answer was to drill, to simplify the task
through handing the planning over to the teacher. There is something symbolic in the method: "don't teach children to plan, plan for
them." The alternative is to provide at school similar situations to
the one Stephen enjoyed. Play has long been recognized as an essential part of work in the best primary schools; what we need now is
an increased awareness of the language purposes it encourages and
develops. As part of his current research, for example, Bernstein has
developed, with the help of the teachers, experimental games and
play directed to helping young children break out of restricted codes.
This is a field where a survey of fruitful ideas already in operation
would help many infants' teachers working with children from
linguistically impoverished homes. So would a reduction in the size
of classes, which at 35–40 often make impossible the individual
attention that Stephen was getting.

We must recall that the role of English here is fundamental to
social life. Planning procedures, built on the sort of work Stephen
was doing, enter into a great deal of adult behaviour, often at points
where we are no longer aware of them, because their operation is
not conscious—as in starting and driving off in a car. And this is a
simple example: for one that is more complex, consider the child
who does not "know how to start his story." What operations has he
to develop to get under way? Will sitting silent be a help—or would
talking it over with the teacher, or a classmate, or a group of

children? What sort of nudging goes on when a good teacher helps the child to make a start?

Perhaps the switch from talking over an operation with someone to talking it over with yourself (thinking it over) is part of a general switch that many young children learn to make, more or less for themselves. Stephen's "you see" ("won't it, isn't it, haven't we") represents a half-way stage. The address to another person is becoming redundant and so are her replies. This marks an enormous gain in linguistic independence. For in conversation (the elementary form of language) a child's responses are to some extent structured (in behaviour and linguistic form) by the need to respond to what his experienced companion has just said. Conversation permits a rapid and continuous feedback of signs that show how effective language has been—signs in words and signs in movement (facial gesture particularly). Deprived of the sight of the other person's face, as in telephoning, children may find talk difficult until they learn to use the linguistic clues to response (even something as simple as "yes . . . yes . . . yes . . ."). The feedback helps us all to modify, repeat, replan or continue what we were saying. We see this at work in class discussion and, at a higher level, in Socratic dialogue. But monologue throws us back entirely on our own linguistic strategies—and this is a matter of something more than vocabulary and sentence structure (though both are included). In some way we need to internalize the other speaker in the dialogue. The child learns to take on more than one role: asking questions and answering them, one might say, or giving himself good advice. (Stephen illustrates this process.) Telling a story, writing, and giving a talk are just a few of the forms of monologue we may need to master and each will demand a set of special if overlapping strategies. And we are only at the beginning of realizing the significance to human understanding of being able to internalize the language and viewpoint of the other speaker. (Think at the university level of the simulation of international conflicts or conferences, with students taking the roles of prime ministers, generals, etc.)

One day a girl of six on her way to school saw a kitten killed by a lorry. Such an experience is hard to take, whatever way we look at it. The girl worked for a long time that day, drawing and (with her teacher's help) writing beneath each of the drawings. Strung together, this is what she wrote.

> The sun is waving goodbye to you all.
> The moon is coming out said the kitten to himself.
> Today I hear the thrushes sing on my lawn said the kitten to himself.
> The thrushes are in the garden and the kitten is in the garden.
> The kitten is coming to church said the children.
> The kitten is coming home said the children.
> Goodbye said the children.
> The kitten is coming to bed said the mice.
> The kitten is coming to town said all the kittens.
> The lorry is coming to squash the kitten said the mice.
> The lorry is coming to squash the kitten said the children.
> The kitten is squashed.
> And that is the end of my story about the kitten.

Often the heart of a child goes out to a kitten, seeing there an image of itself. But children learn to be many people, many creatures. Has this girl perhaps learnt in the end to face and suffer the kitten's mutilated death and yet to see that experience in all its variety stretches away beyond?—that life goes on; one lives in other roles.

We come here to the border country between scholarship and the intuitive understandings of observant and sympathetic teachers. Ideally the one kind of evidence should feed the other. Teachers who can help their pupils to develop through language may draw attention to unsuspected potentialities. We might recall Joan in David Holbrook's *English for the Rejected*: timid, plain, with thick pebble glasses. Her I.Q. was 76; there was nothing surprising perhaps in her primary school record—"has no originality or imagination." Yet after a year's encouragement to creative work in language and drama, she wrote this (in the course of the exam):

A poem

> A little yellow bird sat on my window sill
> He hop and poped about
> He whiseld he cherped.
> I trid to chach my little yellow brid
> but he flew into the golden yellow sun,
> O how I wish that was my yellow brid.

Work such as this has given us a new right to talk about the creative potentialities of *all* children. Consider not only the beauty but the complexity of Joan's achievement. The bird is alive, quick and jaunty; we feel her longing too. But despite its immediacy the poem surely suggests another level for the yellow bird and the golden yellow sun—a level not to be spelt out, but just as certainly to be felt. For language, like drama, has the capacity to bring elements from experience into a structure that stands for life not merely in particular but in general. Indeed it is clear that in the earliest river valley civilizations men learnt to handle generality not in explicit, rational terms, but through myth—creative stories, poems and dramas. So (perhaps?) as they develop, all pupils need to explore their power—through language and dramatic movement—to bring a new, simplifying order to the complexity of life. This might be called the poetic work of language (but an undifferentiated poetry rather than the specialized genres of contemporary society).

What we see here is one pole of a continuum. At this end, deeper levels of the self are realized and composed; at the other, language takes us out to encounter and bring to explicit order the external world. Neither is simple.

> We had the experience but missed the meaning,
> And approach to the meaning restores the experience
> In a different form . . .
>
> *(Dry Salvages)*

Pupils, like adults, need to talk over new experiences, returning to them again and again maybe, finding new elements and connections. The potential meaning of an experience—an outing, a visitor, an experiment—is not always clear at once. It needs to be worked over, "realized" again through language, shared and modified perhaps in the way we apprehend it. And new experiences are sometimes old ones seen in a new light ("Tintern Abbey"). So the toughest, least articulate teenager may be putting up a shield to keep experience at bay (as he thinks) and preserve his balance against its threatening effects. Talking it over, thinking it over, and (as confidence is gained) writing, can be natural parts of taking account of new experience (cognitively and affectively).

The processes described as "resolving inner tensions," "taking account of experience," "coming to terms with it," and so on, share some characteristics with the work of an artist. Like the artist, children engaged in these activities are adopting a special role to their selves and to their experience, the role in some sense of spectator rather than participant. How everyday and yet fundamental this role may be is suggested by an illustration from James Britton:

> I think we can distinguish two ways in which a wife may recount to her husband when he comes home what the children have been doing. The one is quite ordinary and frequent. She goes over the events because she knows he is interested: and though what he hears may inspire him to vague dispositions to act or to decide, they are so vague and so remote that they do not switch him from the role of spectator to that of participant. If hairbreadth escapes are part of the story, once he has been assured that the children are safely tucked up in bed and none the worse, he will even savour the excitement of fright about these events—an experience quite different from the fears of participant. And the wife who tells him the tale savours it now in a way she certainly did not, as a mother, earlier in the day when they were actually happening.
>
> And there are other, rarer occasions when the wife, after tactfully (and perhaps tactically) talking about other things, begins to tell a different kind of story about the events of the children's day. She tells it in a different way because she is herself still a participant, wanting to influence her husband to act this way rather than that. And he listens as a participant because he is called upon to act and to decide: he has not now the spectator's freedom to enter fully into the events of the story and savour the emotions: instead, it is *his own* role he must play, mastering his feelings if need be, and summoning his judgement.
>
> (*The Arts in Education*)

The role of spectator—of an attentive, immersed onlooker—is thus a link between the child and artist. Again we become aware of the work children have to do (through language) before they can draw on the mature writer. If their talk and writing in the role of spectator does not reach occasionally beyond the level of gossip, how can they be expected to reach up beyond that level into what the play or the novel is saying. Yet it is at the level of gossip that we all start, and with many children the classroom offers them their only chance to move towards a fuller sense of what talk and reflection can offer. For "detached evaluative responses, though less intense, tend to be more widely comprehensive than the evaluation that precedes participation. One views the event in a more distant perspective and relates it to a more extensive system of information, beliefs and values. And this detached evaluative response undoubtedly possesses the utmost importance in building up, confirming and modifying all but the very simplest of our values. . . . If we could obliterate the effects on a man of all the occasions when he was 'merely a spectator' it would be profoundly to alter his character and outlook"* (Denys Harding). When life is felt as immediate and particular, our work in this role is closest to the artist; as it moves towards generality it moves closer to the thinker. Perhaps English holds the middle ground. Certainly there are times when the two are not felt to differ: consider this passage by a sixteen-year-old girl about her mother.

. . . It is sad that I should only recently realize that sympathy she has in her, how easily I can talk to her of my feelings, and how sympathetic and understanding she is, and how willing she would be to help me out of my difficulties even though it may be against her own principles. It makes me feel ashamed that I should have less affection for her than I did as a young child. Perhaps it is the loss of my complete dependence on her and the awareness of my mental independence or the maturity of my emotion and that what I took for deep love and utter devotion in my early childhood was nothing but a superficial emotion. A young child has to love someone and I had no-one else on whom to place my affections. Or maybe we have only a certain capacity for affection and though at one time we may lavish it all on one person as soon as others come along we take from the first person to give a little to the others. I do not know the answer, only that all emotions and qualities change, develop or mature and that time leaves nothing untouched. . . . I am afraid not only of losing my physical youth but any childishness I still have. . . .

Pupils with their own experience of the role of spectator have the power, then, to draw from the artist and thinker new insights into life. When it speaks to them like their own work, the mature writer's poem or story or philosophizing helps to give new order and meaning to parts of their own experience. But as the writer realizes experience more fully, keeping the language in touch with far more of live feeling and human interaction, children who become involved

* "The Role of the Onlooker," SCRUTINY, 1937.

in his "work" (as we rightly call it), giving their share of creative work in re-enacting its processes for themselves, may gain a new richness in facing experience.

To sum up: an understanding of the processes involved in developing a mastery of language becomes vital when it sharpens the teacher's awareness of a pupil's potentialities, problems and limitations. In the pre-school years, almost all children ˙ miraculously acquire the basic resources in phonology and structure of the local or standard dialect. But some children also acquire through parents and neighbourhood a restricted strategy for the use of these resources, for behind language lies the force of social relationships and where these are critically limiting, language is too. Nevertheless, one starts in teaching from a respect for each pupil as he is, and that means for what expresses his identity, notably his language. "One of the most intimate possessions of a person is his dialect. . . . The identification of the child with his community and his relationship to it must be protected" (Wilt). The principal aim is to build on the method of language learning by which he has already accomplished so much. The classroom is a place for taking on new roles, facing new situations—coming to terms in different ways with new elements of oneself and new levels of human experience. In the course of doing so, with the teacher's encouragement and guidance, language is *incidentally* adapted to the new role, especially when the teacher can avoid serious discontinuity. Thus the movement from spoken to written, from dialect to standard, from kinds of dialogue to kinds of monologue, are all potentially points of rupture—of breakdown in confidence, in acceptance of school, and at worst in the sense of one's own identity. Each movement is therefore a source of failure—or strength.

Fortunately, and partly because English is so rooted in experience outside school, the resources for new strength are latent in all children and young people. We note particularly a resource that becomes our major concern, in the high school and beyond: the power through language to take on the role of spectator and thus to enter into and share in the work of the mature artist and thinker.

TEACHING SEMANTICS
IN HIGH SCHOOL
Solveig Torvik

Much has been made recently of the idea that the American high school has failed to represent "the real world" within its cloistered walls. One explanation bearing on this state of affairs comes from S. I. Hayakawa in "Learning to Think and Write: Semantics in Freshman English" published in the *Journal of the Conference on College Composition and Communication* (Feb. 1962):

I believe there is a good reason they [college students] were not taught semantics . . . earlier. It is that we, as parents or teachers or both, rely profoundly on word-magic, the confusion of inferences and judgments with reports, and the authority of lofty and unexplained abstractions in our attempts to control our children. Until the anxious years of high school are over for our children, most of us would rather not put into their hands such critical instruments as would enable them to expose as nonsense much of what we say to them. Hence, there cannot be much in the way of semantics . . . until . . . parents and teachers begin to be willing to treat the children as children no longer.

We educators are finely tuned to the niceties of scientific discovery; we have introduced the new math; we have redescribed the structure of our language. How is it then that we largely ignore the pressing demands on the student who hopes to survive the "verbal Niagara" represented by the mass media, sociological upheavals, political freedom, and philosophical choice? Is it ethical of us adults to avoid giving teenagers critical instruments needed for such a survival simply because we fear they will turn their weapons on us and expose our folly?

Further, how do we convince the student who senses our folly and shrugs off the adult world as a fraud eminently unworthy of his

From the *English Journal* (December, 1969), pp. 1341–46. Reprinted with permission of the National Council of Teachers of English and Solveig Torvik.

Solveig Torvik has taught English at Granite High School, Salt Lake City, Utah.

concern that we too are not speaking with a forked tongue, perpe-
trating the adult party-line nonsense, invoking authority in place of
logic? In short, how do we establish the bonds of trust that convince
a student that the real world is being represented in the classroom?

One answer, I find, is to give high school seniors a unit in semantics which is designed to force them to evaluate their own assumptions and beliefs as well as all others with which they come in
contact. We attempt to examine, in a simplified definition, "how
words affect human thought and behavior."

One heartening aspect of this admittedly Herculean task is that
the semantics unit is equally fitting for the needs of both the terminal
and the college-bound student. For the first, it is a practical necessity
to survive the political, philosophical, and commercial verbal pro-
fusion; for the second it is invaluable in dealing with the endless
"truths" which he is expected to assimilate as a member of the
educated portion of society. For both it is an incomparably effective
tool for dealing with life intelligently on his own level, and that the
latter is more quick to see its significance than the former is only
further justification for giving training in semantics more assiduously
to the former, who needs all the training he can get to develop
whatever critical power he may have simply to insure his intelligent
survival.

The unit in semantics which I present is based on Hayakawa's
text, *Language in Thought and Action* (Harcourt, 1941), and consists of seven broad sections of emphasis. In order, these are:
symbol-thing confusion; generalizations; inferences, judgments, reports; classification; abstractions; directive, affective, informative
uses of language; two-valued and multi-valued orientation.

We begin with a shocker in symbol-thing confusion. I stress the
shock element at this point, because it is vital to the success of the
unit that the student be stripped of all his previous complacent
notions concerning the function of his language; it is of paramount
importance that he be placed in a position which will implement an
immediate breakdown of his indifference to "mere words" and force
him, by instilling a momentary mistrust of them, to examine critically
the symbols, written or otherwise, which shape his reality. He has to
be shown that *words use him*, he does not "use" words, whatever
may be said for building one's vocabulary.

An effective beginning for the unit may be achieved by writing something on the board not usual to the classroom atmosphere because of its highly affective connotations; the word "hell" serves well. The teacher should make no comments concerning the word during the first five minutes of class business, but after the students have had time to notice the word, the teacher can casually step to the board and add the letter "o." The next step is to have the students write on unsigned slips of paper their reactions to the first word as contrasted to the second. As the teacher reads aloud some of the responses registering the surprise, humor, mild shock, or disdain described, the point is made for departure into a discussion of how and why *a tiny chalk circle* can change and control one's emotional responses.

Another device which is an effective opener to illustrate the pitfalls of symbol-thing confusion is to write a word such as "breast" on the board and ask individuals in the class to explain what this is. Most will react with singular embarrassment, some will refuse to answer, a few will cheerfully try to beat the teacher at his own game, others will offer safe biological definitions. It is then time to suggest that the word *is* nothing but a series of chalk marks on the board. There is often considerable relief when the students hear this suggestion, but their relief is short-lived when the students see the teacher add "of chicken tuna" to the term and are asked to explain why they now laugh or feel comfortable since nothing has been done to alleviate their discomfiture except to add more of those chalk marks which originally provoked their silly response. After a moment, they see the point and discussion can begin.

A word of caution is necessary here, I think. The teacher should choose a word of incident to illustrate the concept which he feels is justifiable for the success of the unit. However, the teacher who chooses to tell a "dirty" story or to use an "obscene" word has simply missed the point. The student himself will be the first to admit that he is made uncomfortable by and to lose his cool by the word symbols in a "foul" tale; what he needs to have demonstrated is that he is equally manipulated by the innocuous. It must be made apparent to him that words can force him to a reaction—embarrassment, anger, laughter, tears,—and that if mere hen tracks or symbolic sounds have this much control over him, it would seem imperative to discover how to control this power instead of being controlled by it while in total ignorance of its existence.

From this introduction the point is taken that symbols, be they words, markings, cloth, metal or paper, have the power to affect us as if the real thing which they stand for were being presented to us. From further exploration by means of analysis of immediate sources such as the letters to the editor, editorials, news reports, and the like should come critical awareness of the human tendency to equate the symbol and its referent, the classic example of which is the person who faints upon hearing the *word* "snake." This study should enable the student to distinguish between the symbol—the "A" on the report card—and the thing—the knowledge which the ink mark supposedly represents. And, hopefully, he will come to value the latter over the former, much as we would hope he learns to value his country above the flag which symbolizes it.

Once the concept of "You think you think, but words structure your thinking for you" has been established, we move into the area of generalizations. Students are taught that generalizations are acceptable, providing one can find 100 per cent proof to support them. The futility of providing such support is immediately apparent, and one of the first evidences of their mastery of this concept is the way in which they begin to phrase their statements in class discussions and writing assignments. The inherent flaws in statements such as "All good politicians are a little bit dishonest" are quickly challenged, and the teaching of generalizations is not for the teacher who dislikes being corrected by his students; *never, always, everybody* are words which soon disappear from their accustomed places in the class vocabulary.

As the student begins to look with new eyes at the generalized "truths" which have been handed down to him and which he has heretofore calmly accepted, he begins an often painful period of scrutiny of the moral, social, and political "facts" which support his beliefs. Normally, this questioning period does not come for American teenagers much before the traumatic freshman year away from home. It is perhaps an advantage and of some comfort to the parents, at least, that they have their offspring under their roof to advise him as best they can during his fledgling attempts to deal with the world on adult terms. Certainly it is an advantage in that the student is not yet in a position to be fully responsible for himself as an adult;

he is in a training period prior to full adulthood, and reasonably enough this training should come before the responsibility is assumed.

To introduce the process by which we usually arrive at our notions of "truth," we put on the board the following, minus the labels:

(Report): Mary Smith didn't get in until two o'clock last night.
(Inference): I bet she was out tearing around.
(Judgment): She's a worthless hussy. I never did like her looks.

The obvious fallacies of arriving at "truth" by such a method are apparent to all rather quickly, even the slower students who exhibit much sympathy for the mythical Mary Smith and are usually the first to spring to her defense by suggesting that as all things are possible, after all, Mary could have been out babysitting or helping old ladies cross the street. The terms *judgment* (a statement of negative or positive value), *inference* (a statement about the unknown based on the known), and *report* (verifiable fact) are given at this point, and the students are asked to label the three statements correctly. Further exercises such as this on serve to reinforce the differences between the kinds of statements often loosely termed as factual.

We approach the subject of classification by retelling the story of A-town and B-ville in a semantic parable found in the text. In the story, two towns of largely identical means share the same problem: unemployment due to depression. As the result of their thinking about, classifying, and handling of the problem, one town gives $200 a month to the needy with the result that the needy accept it with pride and a coherent community results; the other town gives $200 to the needy with the result that the needy resent it and becomes social problems. One town calls its $200 *insurance*, the other calls it *relief*. Once the problem of classification has been established as the reason behind the divergent reactions to an identical situation, the students are ready to come to grips with everyday complexities in assigning names to things and thoughts. They come to see that not only does no word ever mean the same thing twice, but that Mary today is not exactly Mary as she was yesterday—emotionally, mentally, or molecularly—and that it is folly at times to insist on treating her as if she were. When they understand that Negro 1 is not Negro

2 any more than mother 1 is mother 2, they have surmounted a barrier in the way of reason and logic which many of their parents are not even ready to begin to recognize. And armed with this knowledge, they understandably chafe at the adult order of things: twenty-one years equals membership into the class "adult"; one drop of "black" blood equals membership in the class "Negro"; one vote in the legislature equates aspirin with "drug" instead of "harmless" medicine.

Examination of abstractions follows closely on the classification section. Many methods are useful to introduce this concept, but I find the text illustration of the abstraction ladder and Bessie the Cow to be the most successful overall. The ladder begins at step one, the most specific and concrete, with an illustration of Bessie as a collection of atoms; hence, a scientific description verifiable in fact. It ends at the top of the latter with Bessie represented as wealthy, probably the most abstract and general term applicable in this case. Intermediate steps are descriptions of her as "cow," "livestock," and "asset," all of which delineate the progression of varying terms which can be applied to Bessie, depending on the desired generality or specifics of the description, or on one's concept of reality.

The students can then be led to see that specific referents for such words as *justice, love, evil, patriotism, good,* and *moral* are essential in actually communicating what one means to say *in this instance.* "For example" becomes a key phrase in writing and discussion, and they become impatient with teachers, administrators, parents, and politicians who bandy about reverential-sounding abstractions without the accompanying concrete illustration.

An example comes from an incident growing out of a visit by a noted newspaper comumnist-educator-politician to one of the church-owned universities in our area. The columnist observed the school and its students and later in a column praised them as seemingly the last stand of student morality and virtue left on the American college scene. The students in my classes, many of whom were pleased on Sunday by the glowing report in the paper on their favorite university, were appalled on Monday when they were handed the same article to analyze for semantic implications of the flattering argument presented. I urged them to forget their loyalties momentarily to the school and the church which supported it and to concentrate instead on noting the author's assumptions. They were asked to challenge his assumptions, not the school on its independent merits. They spent an hour listing the seemingly endless thinking traps into which the author had permitted himself to fall, and their independent and overwhelming conclusion focussed on the great lack of logic in the article. As one student told me afterwards, "I am so humiliated when I think how pleased I was when I first read the article! I even cut it out and phoned my friends to tell them that this man had given the most convincing argument why they should go to school there with me. I'm still going to school there—but not for the reasons *he* said."

The students were forced to divorce themselves from their pre-conceived prejudices—as it happened, violently pro or con—and to examine objectively the merits of the argument itself on the basis of logic. They came to see that the school itself existed independently of what anyone might want to say about it. It was a testament to their power of critical thinking that those who favored the school for the very reasons that the writer did were able to perceive the fallacy of the reasoning he used and to attack it as being unsound.

Next, we explore how social control is achieved through language. The revelation that language is designed in part to control their behavior is more distressing than illuminating to many students. From the temporary loss of faith in the verbal social structure, however, can be built an awareness of how to use language responsibly, which, of course, is the central concept behind the entire unit. The student needs to understand that language is used in an attempt to direct or influence future actions of other human beings, and therefore it necessarily only sets up *goals* of behavior, not descriptions of present behavior. Therefore, the student can learn to live with and accept "Policemen are defenders of the weak" and "All mothers love their children" as directives (expected behavior) and not as reports of facts. When he crosses this hurdle, the teenager is a long way on the road to understanding and coping with the seemingly contradictory aspects of adult values and actions.

Finally, we are ready for the concept of multi-valued thinking as opposed to the two-valued, black or white type. A simple way to open the discussion is to ask "Do you love or hate school?"—or mother, brother, etc. It isn't long before the honest student will admit that "sometimes" is the key to answering such a nonsense question. In writing, reading, and analysis (again, sources such as the letters to the editor and radio stations with call-in opinions aired are gold mines for illustration of the two-valued orientation), the students begin to understand the dangers of the "Either you're with us or agin' us" mentality, and they begin to grasp the importance of keeping a reasonably flexible approach to complex problems which do not admit to simple solutions. The more compelling the political, moral, and social beliefs in question, the more agonizing the finding of *the* answer becomes. And it is at the moment of this recognition of the complexities attendant to finding *the* answer that the comprehension of what it is to be an adult dawns meaningfully upon the student. It is, for most students of my acquaintance, an awe-inspiring and frustrating moment.

When the unit is over, the student has been exposed to the ingredients of mature, perceptive thinking (and attendant behavior). As a consequence, he is more fully prepared for responsible adult life simply because he understands the imperative necessity for awareness in using language, a source of grievous blocks to rationality and maturity in teenager and adult alike. He has seen poignant illustrations of precisely why we are learning to cope with the dangerous tool for misunderstanding and destruction which each of us has inherited: our language. The case of the Indians who chose to circumvent "reality" by calling a "blue cow" a "blue horse" so they could kill it; the case of the South African girl born of white parents who was "reclassified" as Negroid on the basis of her features; the case of the writer who berated *Webster's Third International Dictionary* for "cheapening" the language; the draft card and flag-burnings all illustrate man's monumental and infinite capacity to misunderstand the functions of his language and symbol structure.

The students find this kind of analysis exhilarating and bring their best to it, knowing that they themselves have the tools with which to bring to discover and recognize that ever-elusive abstraction, "truth." Thus, they also discover that the classroom can be a most realistic, challenging, and satisfying training ground for what he now abstracts "up the ladder" as "life." They have learned, hopefully, how judgments stop thought; they have learned to disagree with weak logic in a position with which they are essentially in sympathy; they have learned that the word *is not* the thing; they have learned, when confronted with a verbal impasse, not to shout,

"You're crazy!" but to ask, "Why do you think so?"; they have learned to preface any statement of "truth" with "In my opinion"; they have learned that there is no such thing as a *right* name for anything; they have learned that a word only *means* inside oneself; they have learned that words never say all about anything. They realize, as it were, the permanent necessity of the ETC. orientation in dealing with modern-day word magic.

All this has greatly heightened their perception of the practical as well as the philosophic. They may point out in literature study that Henry Fleming is the victim of symbol-thing confusion in *The Red Badge of Courage* or that Judge Danforth is trapped in the hopelessness of the two-valued orientation in *The Crucible*, but they will also be aware that "My mother is two-valued on the subject of sex" or that the principal suffers from symbol-thing confusion concerning the dress code. It is a dangerous knowledge we give them because they can—and do—and should use it to expose as "nonsense much of what we say to them." But it is a knowledge which is far less dangerous than the ignorance in which we would perhaps prefer to leave them—and ourselves—of the insidious nature of the verbal world.

WRITING

The teaching of writing has long been both the bulwark and the bane of the English teacher. On the one hand it has given him the primary justification for his professional existence (even the most philistine school board or reactionary administrator will admit that we must have teachers of writing in our schools), on the other hand it has been the source of a constant feeling of personal inadequacy and failure and the object of continuous criticism by colleagues, colleges, and the community at large. Everyone knows kids just can't write these days. And so, year after year, the teacher trudges to his classroom armed with handbooks, workbooks, spelling lists, vocabulary builders, one hundred sure-fire topics, a thick bundle of red pencils, and a sinking feeling in his stomach that it won't work this time either. And it usually doesn't.

The articles in this section express the viewpoints of teachers who believe that there are approaches that *can* work, that *have* worked for them. Not infallibly, not completely, but often well enough to suggest that in these methods at least there is hope. They propose, simply enough, that one learns to write by writing, that writing must be a purposeful, meaningful activity for a student, or he learns nothing from it (except, possibly, that he hates to write or "can't" write), that as in the acquisition of any skill, the learner needs constant practice, correction, and reinforcement. It is the way they propose to put these ideas into action that sets them apart from other teachers.

Moffett stresses the concept of feedback and response, but he contends "no feedback of whatever sort can help the learner if his will is not behind his actions, for will is the motor that drives the whole process. . . ." He then explains how the will to write can be developed if students write to each other, rather than to the teacher, receiving both the stimulus to write and the feedback necessary to improve their writing from their fellow students. Likewise, Murray, McLeod, and Harvey advocate the development of a sense of

319

audience in young writers and the importance of audience-to-writer feedback. Murray, for example, proposes that the teacher become a participant in the writing class, composing along with the students and throwing his efforts open to group analysis and criticism.

Nonetheless, for most teachers, particularly beginning teachers, there will be occasions when the student's writing is directed to the teacher rather than to his classmates. Often, English teachers' responses to student writing have been characterized by unbelievable insensitivity and an almost fanatic concern with the trivialities of form and linguistic etiquette. Stratta offers some advice to help teachers provide helpful rather than harmful feedback to young writers.

And, as always, there remains the question of "What is good writing, and how do I recognize it?" Christensen attempts to answer this question by defining "a mature style" in rather explicit terms, and in so doing makes some interesting comment on the effectiveness of transformational grammar as a tool for teaching writing.

LEARNING TO WRITE
BY WRITING

James Moffett

If someone were to ask you what the main way is that human beings learn to do things with their minds and bodies, what answer would you give? Don't think first about learning to write—we'll get to that soon enough. Think about learning to walk, ride a bicycle, play a piano, throw a ball. Practice, you say? Coaching by other people? Yes, but why does practice work? How do we get more adept merely by trying again and again? And what does a good coach do that helps our trials get nearer and nearer the mark? The answer, I believe, is feedback and response.

Feedback is any information a learner receives as a result of his trial. This information usually comes from his own perception of what he has done: the bicycle falls over, the notes are rushed, the ball goes over the head of the receiver, and so on. The learner heeds this information and adjusts his next trial accordingly, and often unconsciously. But suppose the learner cannot perceive what he is doing—does not, for example, hear that the notes are rushed—or perceives that he has fallen short of his goal but does not know what adjustment to make in his action. This is where the coach comes in. He is someone who observes the learner's actions and the results, and points out what the learner cannot see for himself. He is a human source of feedback who supplements the feedback from inanimate things.

But, you may say, learning to write is different from learning to ride a bicycle or even learning to play the piano, which are, after all, physical activities. Writers manipulate symbols, not objects. And they are acting on the minds of other people, not on matter. Yes, indeed. But these differences do not make learning to write an exception to the general process of learning through feedback. Rather, they indicate that in learning to use language the only kind of feedback available to us is human response.

James Moffett, author of *Teaching the Universe of Discourse* and *A Student Centered Arts Curriculum, Grades K-13*, 1968, Houghton Mifflin (Boston).

Let's take first the case of learning to talk, which is a social activity and the base for writing. The effects of what we do cannot be known to us unless our listener responds. He may do so in a number of ways—by carrying out our directions, answering our questions, laughing, looking bored or horrified, asking for more details, arguing, and so on. Every listener becomes a kind of coach. But of course a conversation, once launched, becomes a two-way interaction in which each party is both learner and source of feedback.

Through their research in the early stages of language acquisition, Roger Brown and Ursula Bellugi have been able to identify two clear interactions that take place between mother and child. One is the child's efforts to reproduce in his own condensed form the sentences he hears his mother utter. The other is the mother's efforts to expand and correct the child's telegraphic and therefore ambiguous sentences. Each time the mother fills out his sentence, the child learns a little more about syntax and inflections, and when the child responds to her expansion of his utterance, she learns whether her interpretation of his words was correct or not. Linguists never cease to marvel at how children learn, before they enter school, and without any explanations or teaching of rules, how to generate novel and well-formed sentences according to a paradigm or model they have unconsciously inferred for themselves. In fact, many of the mistakes they make—like *bringed* for *brought*—are errors of over-generalization. This ability to infer a generality from many particular instances of a thing, which also accounts for some children learning to spell even without phonics training, is of course itself a critical part of human learning. The learner's abstractive apparatus reduces a corpus of information, such as other people's sentences, to a usable rule. It is a data-processing gift that enables us to learn *some thing*, but not how to *do* something. To learn to talk, the child must put his data into action and find out what happens. Thus he learns his *ir*regular verbs when he says, "I bringed my cup," and some adult replies, "Well, I'm glad you brought it." Throughout school, imitation of others' speech, as heard and read, remains a major way of learning language forms, but conversational response is the only means the child has for making progress in speech production itself. Later, after the syntax and inflections have become pretty well fixed, the responses the learner gets to what he says are not expansions but expatiations. That is, his listener reacts to his ideas and his tone, picks up his remarks and does something further with them, so that together they create some continuity of subject.

Learning to use language, then, requires the particular feedback of human response, because it is to other people that we direct speech. The fact that one writes by oneself does not at all diminish the need for response, since one writes for others. Even when one purports to be writing for oneself—for pure self-expression, if there is such a thing—one cannot escape the ultimately social implications inherent in any use of language. As George Herbert Mead argued so well, even in our unuttered thoughts, we speak as though to another because we have long since incorporated the otherness of the social world to which language is irrevocably tied. Furthermore, we have all had the experience of looking back on something we have written earlier and of responding much as another person might do. Thus, once beyond the moment of writing, the writer himself becomes "other," and can feed back helpfully to himself.

But no feedback of whatever sort can help the learner if his will is not behind his actions, for will is the motor that drives the whole process. Without it, we ignore the results of what we have done and make no effort to adjust our actions so as to home in on the target. The desire to get certain effects on an audience is what motivates the use of speech. This is what rhetoric is all about. So the first reason why one might fail to learn is not caring, lack of motivation to scan the results and transfer that experience to the next trial. The other principal cause of failure is, on the other hand, a lack of response in the audience. One cares, one makes an effort and no one reacts. For me, the character Jerry, in Albee's *The Zoo Story* epitomizes the desperation of one who cannot get at response. To get some effect on the unresponsive Peter, he runs through the whole rhetorical gamut—chitchat, anecdotes, questions, shocking revelations, quarrelling, until finally he resorts to tickling, pushing, and fighting. It is Jerry who says, "We *must* know the consequences of our actions." And sarcastically: "Don't react, Peter, just listen."

In the February 17th issue of the *New York Times Magazine* Bruno Bettelheim, speaking from his experience with autistic children who had withdrawn and given up, touched on the importance of both initiation and response. From the very first, he says, an infant should be given the chance to communicate his needs, not have them anticipated, and be responded to when he is communicating the need, not fed according to some other timing.

It is for this reason that time-clock feedings are so potentially destructive, not merely because they mechanize the feeding, but because they rob the infant of the conviction that it was his own wail that resulted in filling his stomach when his own hunger timed it. By the same token, if his earliest signals, his cry or his smile, bring no results, that discourages him from trying to refine his efforts at communicating his needs. In time he loses the impulse to develop those mental and emotional structures through which we deal with the environment. He is discouraged from forming a personality.

But those are infants, not adolescents, and we teach our students to write, we don't feed them. Bettelheim continues:

Even among adults the joke that fails to amuse, the loving gesture that goes unanswered, is a most painful experience. And if we consistently, and from an early age, fail to get the appropriate response to our expression of emotions, we stop communicating and eventually lose interest in the world.

"But," we say, "I praise my students, I give them an encouraging response."

But this is not all. If the child's hungry cry met with only deep sympathy and not also with food, the results would be as bad as if there had been no emotional response. . . . should his smile, inviting to play, be met with a tender smile from the parent but lead to no playing, then, too, he loses interest in both his environment and the wish to communicate feeling.

Smiling, gushing, or patting the back are not to the point. A response must be real and pertinent to the action, not a standard "professional" reaction. Any unvarying response, positive or not, teaches us nothing about the effects of what we have done.

If, as I believe, writing is learned in the same basic way other activities are learned—by doing and by heeding what happens—then it is possible to describe ideal teaching practices in this way and compare them with some current practices. Ideally, a student would write because he was intent on saying something for real reasons of his own and because he wanted to get certain effects on a definite audience. He would write only authentic kinds of discourse such as exist outside of school. A maximum amount of feedback would be provided him in the form of audience response. That is, his writing would be read and discussed by this audience, who would also be the coaches. This response would be candid and specific. Adjustments in language, form, and content would come as the writer's response to his audience's response. Thus instruction would always be individual, relevant, and timely. These are precisely the virtues of feedback learning that account for its great success.

Clearly, the quality of feedback is the key. Who is this audience to be, and how can it provide a response informed enough to coach in all the necessary ways? How is it possible for every member of a class of thirty to get an adequate amount of response? Classmates are a natural audience. Young people are most interested in writing for their peers. Many teachers besides myself have discovered that students write much better when they write for each other. Although adolescents are quite capable of writing on occasion for a larger and more remote audience and should be allowed to do so, it is difficult except in unusual situations to arrange for this response to be relayed back to the writers. For the teacher to act as audience is a very intricate matter fraught with hazards that need special attention.

First, although younger children often want to write to a "significant adult," on whom they are willing to be frankly dependent, adolescents almost always find the teacher entirely *too* significant. He is at once parental substitute, civic authority, and the wielder of marks. Any one of these roles would be potent enough to distort the writer-audience relationship; all together they cause the student to misuse the feedback in ways that severely limit his learning to write. He may, for example, write what he thinks the teacher wants, or what he thinks the teacher doesn't want. Or he writes briefly and grudgingly, withholding the better part of himself. He throws the teacher a bone to pacify him, knowing full well that his theme does not at all represent what he can do. This is of course not universally true, and students may react in irrelevant and symbolic ways to each other as well as to the teacher. But in general, classmates are a more effective audience.

The issue I want to make clear, in any case, is that the significance of the responder influences the writer enormously. This is in the nature of rhetoric itself. But if the real intent of the writing is extraneous to the writing—on a completely different plane, as when a student turns in a bland bit of trivia to show his indifference to adult demands—then the effect is actually to dissociate writing from real intent and to pervert the rhetorical process into a weird irony. Much depends of course on the manner of the teacher and, curiously enough, if the teacher shifts authority to the peer group, which is where it lies anyway for adolescents, and takes on an indirect role, then his feedback carries a greater weight.

But students are not informed and experienced enough about writing to coach each other. Won't their feedback often be misleading? How does the teacher give them the benefit of his knowledge and judgment? Let's look a moment at just what students can and can not do for each other. Part of what they can do is a matter of numbers: multiple responses to a piece of writing make feedback more impersonal and easier to heed. Group reactions establish a consensus about some objective aspects of the writing and identify, through disagreement, those aspects that involve more value judgments. It is much easier for peers than for the teacher to be candid and thus to give an authentic response, because the teacher, usually aware of his special significance, is afraid of wounding his students. A student responds and comments to a peer more in his own terms, whereas the teacher is more likely to focus too soon on technique. Many of the comments that teachers write on themes can be made by practically any other person than the author and don't require a specialist. The failure to allow for the needs of the audience, for example, is responsible for many difficulties indicated by marginal comments like, "misleading punctuation," "unclear," "doesn't follow," "so what's your point?," "why didn't you say this before?," and so on. Irrelevance, unnecessary repetition, confusing organization, omitted leads and transitions, anticlimactic endings, are among the many things that anyone might point out. Again, numbers make it very likely that such things will not only be mentioned if they are problems, but that the idiosyncrasy of readers will be cancelled out. Probably the majority of writing problems are caused by egocentricity, the writer's assumption that the reader thinks and feels as he does, has had the same experience, and hears in his head, when he is reading, the same voice the writer does when he is writing. It is not so much knowledge as awareness that he needs. A student may write off the comments of a teacher by saying to himself, "Adults just can't understand," or "English teachers are nitpickers anyway," but when his fellow human beings misread him; he has to accommodate the feedback. By habitually responding and coaching, students get insights about their own writing. They become much more involved both in writing and in reading what others have written.

What help can a teacher give that peers cannot? Quite a lot, but the only time he makes a unique contribution to the problem of egocentricity is when the students all share a point of view, value judgment, or line of thought that they take for granted, in which case one can question whether the teacher can or should try to shake their position, which is probably a factor of their stage of growth. Imposing taste, standards, and attitudes that are foreign to them is futile and only teaches them how to become sycophants. But there is value in the teacher's expressing his point of view so they at least know that theirs is not universal. Where the teacher can be of most help, however, is in clarifying problems after students have encountered or raised them. Adolescents—or, as I have discovered from experimenting, even fourth-graders—can spot writing problems very well, but often they do not have enough understanding of the causes of a problem to know how to solve it. This insufficient understanding more than anything else causes them to pick at each other's papers in a faultfinding spirit or to make shallow suggestions for change. A student reader may complain, for example, that a certain paper is monotonous in places and suggest that some repeated words be eliminated. But the real reason for the monotony, and for repeating of the words, is that there are too many simple sentences, some of which should be joined. The teacher projects the paper with the comment about monotony and leads a problem-solving discussion. This is where the teacher's knowledge, say, of a generative grammar comes in—not as technical information for the students but as an aid to the teacher. Embedding some of the sentences in others involves, as well as transformations, the issue of subordination and emphasis, so that the problem of monotony can now be seen as also a lack of focus. The teacher, in other words, helps students to interpret their initially vague responses and to translate them into the technical features of the paper that gave rise to them. Notice the direction of the process—the emotional reaction first, then the translation into technique. This amounts to sharpening response while keeping it paramount, and will help reading as well as writing. While helping to solve specific writing problems, the teacher is at the same time dispelling the negativism of comments and creating a climate of informed collaboration in which feedback is welcomed.

The role of the teacher, then, is to teach the students to teach each other. This also makes possible a lot more writing and a lot more response to the writing than a teacher would otherwise sponsor. He creates cross-teaching by setting up two kinds of group processes—one that he leads with the whole class, and a smaller one that runs itself. It is in the first kind, which I just illustrated, that the judgment and knowledge of the teacher is put into play. Periodically, the teacher projects papers for class discussion, without presenting them as good or bad examples and without trying to grind some academic ax. No detailed preparation is needed. He picks papers embodying issues he thinks concern students and need clarifying, getting his cues by circulating among the small groups, where he learns which problems are not getting informed feedback. He asks for responses to the projected paper and plays these responses by alert questioning designed to help students relate their reactions to specific features of the paper before them. If they indicate problems he asks them to suggest changes the author might make. In these class discussions the teacher establishes tone and a method of giving and using feedback that is carried off into the small groups.

The procedure I would recommend—forgive my impertinence if you do this already—is to break the class into groups of four or five and to direct the students to exchange papers within their group, read them, write comments on them, and discuss them. This would be a customary procedure, run autonomously but constantly reinforced by the model of class discussion the teacher continues to lead. It can be of help *during* the writing process, before the final draft. The small size of the group, the reciprocity, tend to make the comments responsible and helpful. The teacher makes it clear that all reactions of any sort are of value—from strong emotions to proofreading. A writer should know when he has succeeded in something; honest praise is very important. Descriptive remarks are very helpful

—of what the paper seems to be or do, and of the effects it had on the reader. All these responses can be compared by talking over together the comments on each paper. Later in this discussion, the author says what he meant to do, and suggestions for bringing the paper more in line with his intentions are made if needed. The teacher sits in on the groups in rotation, acting as consultant and joining the discussion without necessarily having read the papers. After the sessions, the papers may be revised. The more use to which they are put, the better. In fact, the small groups would most of the time act as editorial boards to prepare papers for some purpose. Themes should be printed up, exchanged with other groups just for reading, performed, and many other things. Eventually they go into folders kept for each student and when the teacher has to evaluate student work for the benefit of administration, he makes a general assessment of the writing to date. No grades are given. The teacher of course may respond individually to any paper at any time during a discussion or during a conference. Whether he writes comments on the paper himself depends on several things. Do his students still need an adult to validate and give importance to their work? Is his commentary helping or hindering? Is it necessary? If a student does not want a certain paper read by anyone but the teacher (which happens less often in small groups, where trust is stronger), the teacher honors the request and serves as reader and commentator himself. For some assignments the teacher may feel that his comments are especially relevant, for others not. In any case, if student cross-commentary occurs during the writing process and is at all effective, the amount of commentary the teacher needs to make should be small, as indeed it should be anyway. Mainly, the teacher has to know the effects of *his* action, how students are taking his feedback. First-person comments are best and will set an example for student cross-commentary. A teacher should react as an audience, supplementing the peer audience. Above all, a piece of writing should not go to a dead-letter office. Both the non-response or the irrelevant response persuade the learner that nothing is to be gained from *that* line of endeavor, and the impulse to write withers.

I would like now to go back to aspects of the action-response model of learning other than the quality of the feedback. These have only been implied so far. Plunging into an act, then heeding the results, is a process of trial and error. That is the first implication.

Now, trial-and-error sounds to many people like a haphazard, time-consuming business—a random behavior of children, animals, and others who don't know any better. (Of course by "random" we usually mean that we the observers are ignorant of the reasons for the behavior.) Trial-and-error is by definition never aimless, but without help the individual alone may not think of all the kinds of trials that are possible, or may not always see how to learn the most from his errors. And if it is a social activity he is learning, like writing, then human interaction is in any case indispensable. So we have teachers to propose meaningful trials (assignments) in a meaningful order and to arrange for a feedback that insures the maximum exploitation of error.

The second implication is that the teacher does not try to prevent the learner from making errors. He does not pre-teach the problems and solutions (and of course by "errors" I mean failures of vision, judgment, and technique, not mere mechanics). The learner simply plunges into the assignment, uses all his resources, makes errors where he must, and heeds the feedback. In this action-response learning, errors are valuable, they are the essential learning instrument. They are not despised or penalized. Inevitably, the child who is afraid to make mistakes is a retarded learner, no matter what the activity in question.

In contrast to the exploitation of error is the avoidance of error. The latter works like this: the good and bad ways of carrying out the assignment are arrayed in advance, are pre-taught, then the learner does the assignment, attempting to keep the good and bad ways in mind as he works. Next, the teacher evaluates the work according to the criteria that were laid out before the assignment was done. Even if a system of rewards and punishments is not invoked, the learner feels that errors are enemies, not friends. I think any learning psychologist would agree that avoiding error is an inferior learning strategy to capitalizing on error. The difference is between looking over your shoulder and looking where you are going. Nobody who intends to learn to do something wants to make mistakes. In that sense, avoidance of error is assumed in the motivation itself. But if he is allowed to make mistakes with no other penalty than the failure to achieve his goal, then he knows why they are to be avoided and wants to find out how to correct them. Errors take on a different meaning, they define what is good. Otherwise the learner engages with the authority and not with the intrinsic issues. It is consequences, not injunctions, that teach. We all know that, don't we?

But doesn't this process lead to more failures? A learner needs very much to feel successful, to score. If he learns everything the hard way, doesn't he get discouraged by his mistakes? For one thing, trial-and-error makes for more success because it is accurate, specific, individual, and timely. For another, if the teacher in some way sequences the trials so that learning is transferred from one to the next, the student writer accumulates a more effective guiding experience than if one tried to guide him by pre-teaching. And feed-back of the sort I am advocating—because it is plentiful and in-formed—does not just leave a feeling of failure, of having "learned the hard way," in a sense of coming out a loser. When response is real and personal, it does not leave us empty, even if our efforts missed their mark. The procedure, moreover, of getting feedback *during* the writing instead of only *afterwards* allows the learner to incorporate it into his final product (as, incidentally, you and I do when we write an article). I recommend also a lot of chain-reaction assignments, such that one paper is adapted into another. This amounts to a lot of rewriting, not mere tidying up but taking a whole new track under the influence of suggestions from other students. It is with the isolated, sink-or-swim assignment that the student goes for broke. Finally, the error-avoiding approach has hardly given students a feeling of confidence and success; since it is the predominant method of teaching writing, it seems fair to attribute to it a lot of the wariness and sense of failure so widespread among student writers today.

The third implication of action-response learning follows from the last one about the futility of pre-teaching writing problems. If we learn to write best by doing it and by heeding the feedback, then of what use is the presentation of materials to the learner? Don't presentations violate the trial-and-error process? Don't they in-evitably entail pre-teaching and error-avoidance? My answer is yes. If I reject all prepared materials for writing, it is not that I am failing to discriminate among them. I know that they come in all sizes, shapes, and philosophies. It is not the quality but the fact of these materials that I am speaking to.

If there is a way to be tactful about this subject, I am too grace-less to know what it is. Practically all of us in this room have an investment of some sort in textbook materials, either as consumers or as creators. Writers, editors, and publishers put a lot of thought and experience into making them, I know, and teachers into using them. In a gathering of this sort, to speak against textbooks can only seem in bad taste, at best, and at worst, downright rude. The matter is one I have thought about a great deal, not only as teacher and researcher but as a potential author of texts who, in declining invitations from publishers, has had to soul-search a bit. But I truly believe that the intention behind textbooks is misguided and that the assumption underlying them seriously contradicts how we best learn to write.

The assumption I infer from textbooks is that the output of writing be preceded and accompanied by pedagogical input. Now, there are indeed some kinds of input that are prerequisites to writing—namely, conversation and reading—but these are very different from the presentations of textbooks. Let's look at the sorts of materials that are used to teach writing.

This material may be classified into six overlapping sorts, all of which might appear in any one unit or chapter. The first sort consists of advice, exhortation, and injunction. It is the how-to-do-it part, the cookbook material. Here are some fabricated but typical samples. "Make sure you allow for your audience." "Catch the reader's interest in the first sentence." "Make sure your punctuation guides the reader instead of misleading him." "Connect your ideas with linking words that make transitions." "Write a brief outline of the points you want to make, then write a paragraph about each point." "For the sake of a varied style, it is advisable to begin some sentences with a main clause and others with subordinate clauses or phrases." "A vivid metaphor will often convey an idea more forcefully than a lengthy, abstract explanation." "Build up your descriptions from details that make readers see." "A good narrative has a focus or point to it that is not obscured by irrelevant details (remember what we learned about focus in the last unit?)"

What is wrong with practical pointers and helpful hints? As I have suggested, pre-teaching the problems of writing causes students to adopt the strategy of error-avoidance, the intention clearly being to keep them from making mistakes. The learner is put in the situation of trying to understand and keep in mind all this advice when he should be thinking about the needs of the subject. The textbook writer is in the position of having to predict the mistakes that some mythical average student might make. The result is that, in true bureaucratic fashion, the text generates a secondary set of problems beyond those that an individual learner might truly have to deal with in the assignment itself. That is, he has to dope out first of all what the advice means at a time when it can't mean very much. Often he makes mistakes because he misconstrues the advice. In trying to stick to what he was told, he is in fact working on two tasks at once—the fulfillment of the advice and the fulfillment of the assignment. Since not all learners are prone to the same mistakes, some of the pointers are a waster of time for him personally; he would not have erred in those particular ways. The exhortations and injunctions often inhibit thought, but most critically of all, they prevent both the learner and his responders from knowing what he would have done without this pre-teaching. It is essential to find this out. The learner has to know his own mind, what it natively produces, so that he can see what he personally needs to correct for. Students who fulfill the advice well have passed the test in following directions but have missed the chance to learn the most important thing of all—what their blind spots are. After all, allowing for the audience, catching interest in the first sentence or paragraph, guiding the reader with punctuation, making transitions, varying the style, using metaphors, giving narrative a point—these are commonsense things. What interests me is why a student fails to do these things in the first place. The fact is, I believe, that writing mistakes are not made in ignorance of commonsense requirements; they are made for other reasons that advice cannot prevent. Usually, the student *thinks* he has made a logical transition or a narrative point, which means, again, he is deceived by his egocentricity. What he needs is not rules but awareness. Or if he omits stylistic variation, metaphor, and detail, he does so for a variety of reasons the teacher has to understand before he can be of use. Scanty reading background, an undeveloped eye or ear, a lingering immaturity about not elaborating are learning problems that exhortation cannot solve. Particular instances of failing to do what one thinks one is doing, and of failing to use the full resources of language, should be brought to light, the consequences revealed, the reasons explored, the need for remedies felt, and the possibilities of solution discovered. Unsolicited advice is unheeded advice, and, like time-clock feeding, imposes the breast before there is hunger.

A second class of material found in textbooks is expository. Here we have the definitions and explanations of rhetoric, grammar, logic, and semantics. In other words, information about language and how it is used. Part of the game played here is, to borrow the title of a Henry Read poem, the naming of parts. The assumption seems to be the primitive one that naming things is mastering them. It goes with the attempt to convert internal processes into an external subject. By pedagogical slight of hand, an output activity is transformed into something to be read about. The various ways of constructing sentences, paragraphs, and compositions are logically classified and arrayed. The student can then be put to work on writing as if it were any other substantive content: he can memorize the nomenclature and classifications, answer questions on them, take tests, and on some fitting occasion, "apply" this knowledge. The explanations tell him what it is he is doing when he strings utterances—not he of course but some capitalized He, for this is the realm of general description and theory. The material may be up to date—the new linguistics and the new rhetoric—but the method couldn't be older: "There are three kinds of sentences—simple, complex, and compound." "Articles, demonstratives, and genitives make up the regular determiners." "An inductive paragraph goes from particulars to the main statement, and a deductive paragraph begins with the main statement and descends to particulars." "Ideas may be presented in any of several patterns: they may be repeated, contrasted, piled up in a series, balanced symmetrically, and so on." "The elements of fiction are plot, character, setting, and theme." "People use the same words, but don't mean the same things by them."

Such generalities, like advice, induce in the students a strategy of avoiding errors, of trying to do what the book says instead of doing justice to the subject. Whereas advice tells you what you should do with language, exposition tells you what people do do; it codifies the regularities of practice. The message is essentially the same—apply these rules and you will be all right. Good teaching, rather, helps the individual see what he in particular is doing with language and, by means of this awareness, see what he in particular might be doing. There is no evidence that pre-teaching general facts and theories about how people use language will help a student learn to write.

The teaching of grammar as an aid to composition is a special and notorious case in point—special because huge numbers of textbooks on grammar and linguistics are sold and used on the utterly unfounded assumption that studying the regularities of general practice will improve writing. Massive research has failed to support this assumption. In *Research in Written Composition*, published in 1963 by the National Council of Teachers of English, Braddock, Lloyd-Jones, and Schoer have said, on page 37:

In view of the widespread agreement of research studies based upon many types of students and teachers, the conclusion can be stated in strong and unqualified terms: the teaching of formal grammar has a negligible or, because it usually displaces some instruction and practice in actual composition, even a harmful effect on the improvement of writing.

It may be true that a lot of this research is, by the highest methodological standards, not very good. But the fact remains that no one has ever been able to prove the assumption. It is also true that the body of research reviewed in that book did not include studies on transformational grammar, which is only now being put to the test in this respect. But the *quality* of the grammar, whether it is prescriptive or descriptive, makes no difference. Speaking in the summer 1965 issue of the *Harvard Educational Review*, Peter Rosenbaum, himself a transformational linguist, dealt with the possibility that teaching transformational grammar might improve performance in the literate skills. He asks us to consider an analogy from physical education:

To teach a potential quarterback the mechanics of the forward pass is to teach him how this type of event works. It is not to teach him how to make it work. The Newtonian theory itself gives us no reason to believe that instruction in the mechanics of the forward pass will affect the quarterback's becoming a good passer one way or the other. Similarly, to study and practice the constructs of a transformational grammar may result in an understanding of how the student's language works, but not necessarily in an understanding of how to make it work.

The two main things teachers have hoped to accomplish by teaching grammatical constructs are greater conformity of the student's language to the usages of standard English (using "good grammar") and greater variety of the student's construction so that he will avail himself of the full linguistic repertory offered by English. Now, in addition to accepting research evidence on composition such as was surveyed by Braddock and others, most linguists I know of would also maintain that conforming to the usages of standard English comes about by conversing with people who use standard English and by reading writers who write in it. To hope, by means of grammatical formulations, to shortcut through the deep, cumulative learning that comes from speaking or reading is to indulge in wishful dreaming. These formulations cannot seriously compete with the profound conditioning of speech habits acquired in the learner's native environment. As for expanding one's linguistic repertory, that certainly must be done by *producing* sentences oneself. Input indeed is needed: the learner must hear and read a lot of sentence constructions that would not initially come to his mind. But he needs to try out the forms he takes in. The time spent studying *about* language should be spent conversing, reading, and writing.

Since the most natural assumption should be that one learns to write by writing, the burden of proof is on those who advocate an indirect method, by which I mean presenting codifications about language in the hopes that students will apply them. The case against grammar holds also against theories of rhetoric and composition, of which there are many good ones today. The fine formulations of Francis Christensen about a generative rhetoric, for example, or of Kenneth Pike's tagmemics disciples, are very valuable contributions to the understanding of sentence and paragraph development. Teachers should study these, for, like grammatical formulations, they may help the teachers understand what their students are doing or not doing in their writing. But to teach such formulations, through either exposition or exercises, would hinder more than help. The indirect method has been tried for generations and found drastically wanting. That is one reason why the teaching of writing is a disaster area today.

A third class of materials comprising textbooks is exercises. Sometimes the student is asked to read some dummy sentences and paragraphs and to do something with them. For example: "Underline the one of the following words that best describes the tone of the sentence below." "Rewrite the sentence that appears below so that one of the ideas is subordinated to the other." "Change the order of the sentences in the following paragraph so that the main point and the secondary points are better presented." "Read this paragraph and underline the one of the sentences following it that would serve as the best topic sentence." "Make a single sentence out of the following." Or the student may be asked to make up sentences or paragraphs of his own: "Write a sentence describing some object or action, using modifier clusters as in the examples." "Write a descriptive paragraph following a space order (or a time order)."

Exercises are obviously part and parcel of the approach characterized by advice and exposition. They are merely another way of pre-teaching writing problems in advance of authentic composition. A point raised and explained in the text is simply cast into the form of directions so that the student will apply the point directly. The philosophy here is a curious blend of hard-headed logical analysis and folklorish softheadedness. That is, the teaching of "basics" is construed in this way. Basics are components, particles—words, sentences, and paragraphs. The learner should manipulate each of these writing units separately in a situation controlling for one problem at a time. He works his way from little particle to big particle until he arrives at whole compositions resembling those done in the outside world. The single-unit, single-problem focus derives from linguistic and rhetoric analysis done in universities, not from perceptions about learning. The folklorish part is represented in the old saw about having to crawl before you can walk. But crawling is an authentic form of locomotion in its right, not merely a component or subskill of walking. For the learner, basics are not the small-focus technical things but broad things like meaning and motivation, purpose and point, which are precisely what are missing from exercises. An exercise, by my definition, is any piece of writing practiced only in schools—that is, an assignment which stipulates arbitrary limits that leave the writer with no real relationships between him and a subject and an audience. I would not ask a student to write anything other than an authentic discourse, because the learning process proceeds from intent and content down to the contemplation of technical points, not the other way.

When decomposition precedes composition, furthermore, many unintended and harmful things occur that seem to go on unnoticed because we are fastened on the logic of the subject instead of the psychologic of the learner. Scientists have long been aware that when you isolate out a component for focused observation, you are changing it. Live tissue under a microscope is not live tissue in the body. A sentence or paragraph stripped of its organic context, raised several powers, and presented in the special context of analysis and advice represents serious tampering with the compositional process, the consequences of which are not well recognized.

First of all, when it is the stipulation of the text or the teacher and not the natural limit of an utterance, a sentence or a paragraph is too small a focus for learning. How can you teach style, rhetoric, logic and organization in a unit stripped of those authentic relationships to subject and audience that *govern* the decisions about word choice, sentence structure, paragraph structure, and total continuity? Judgment and decision-making are the heart of composition. With exercises the learner has no basis for choosing one word or sentence structure over another, and rhetoric becomes an irony once again. It is a crime to make students think that words, sentences, paragraphs, are "building blocks" like bricks that have independent existence and can be learned and manipulated separately pending the occasion when something is to be constructed out of them.

Second, a student doing a paragraph exercise, say, knows the problem concerns paragraph structure, whereas in authentic discourse the real problem always is this, that *we don't know what it is we don't know.* A student may do all of the exercises correctly and still write very badly because he is used to having problems plucked out of the subjective morass and served to him externally on a platter, and has consequently developed little in the way of awareness and judgment. For example, he *can't* decide where to break into paragraphs because he must write only one paragraph.

Third, students adopt a strategy for beating the game of exercises: they take a simplistic approach, avoid thinking subtly or complexly, and say only what can lend itself readily to the purpose of the exercise. To make the paragraph come out right, they write things they know are stupid and boring.

Fourth, the poetic justice in this strategy is that the exercises themselves ignore the motivational and learning needs of the student. The result is just the opposite intended: the learner dissociates the technical issues in the exercise from honest discourse. The learner becomes alienated, not only by this but by the hidden message of exercises, which says, "We are not disinterested in what you have to say; we just want a certain form." His defense is to do the exercise by the book in an ironically obedient fashion to show them for just what they are. You bore me and I'll bore you. This dissociation in the minds of students between school stuff and writing for real is one of the deep and widespread symptoms that has made English teaching ripe for reform.

The last three kinds of materials are not bad in themselves but suffer from being embedded in the paraphernalia I have been polemicizing about. For this reason I will deal with them briefly. The first is the presentation of samples of good writing to serve as models. As I have said, learning to write entails a lot of reading, but when passages from the old pros are surrounded by rhetorical analysis and pesky questions about how Saroyan got his effects, a disservice is done to both reading and writing. How would you as an adolescent react to a message such as this: "See how Steinbeck uses details; now you go do that too." And there is no evidence that analyzing how some famous writer admirably dispatched a problem will help a student recognize and solve his writing problems. From my own experience and that of teachers I have researched with, I would say, rather, that models don't help writing and merely intimidate some students by implying a kind of competition in which they are bound to lose. The assumption is still that advance diagnosis and prescription facilitate learning. The same reading selections could be helpful, however, if merely interwoven with the writing assignments as part of the regular reading program but without trying to score points from them. Learners, like the professional writers themselves, incorporate anyway the structures of what they read; what they need is more time to read and write authentically. The service publishers could do is put out more straight anthologies of whole reading selections grouped according to the various kinds of writing but unsurrounded by questions and analysis. The student should write in the forms he reads while he is reading them. There can be a lot of discussion of these selections, but the points of departure for discussion should be student response to the reading.

Another kind of textbook material—writing stimulants—is closely related to models because sometimes these prompters are also reading selections. Or they may merely be the textwriter's own prose as he tried to set up ideas or talk up topics, two intentions that are better realized in class conversation. Sometimes the stimulants are photo-graphs—possibly a good idea, but the pictures are always too small in the textbook. Whatever the kind of stimulant, the wiser course is to let it arise out of the daily drama of the student's life in and out of school, including his regular reading. In this way the stimulants are automatically geared to what the students know and care about. To present stimulants in a book is to run an unnecessary risk of irrelevance and canned writing.

At last we come to the assignment directions themselves. They of course are justified, but for them who needs a book? Even the windiest text writer could not get a textbook out of assignment directions alone. It is better anyway for the teacher to give the assignment because he can adapt it to his particular class—cast it in a way that they will understand, relate it to their other work, and so on.

Let me summarize now my concerns about presenting materials to students as a way to teach writing. They install in the classroom a mistaken and unwarranted method of learning. They take time, money, and energy that should be spent on authentic writing, read-ing, and speaking. They get between the teacher and his students, making it difficult for the teacher to understand what they need, and to play a role that would give them the full benefit of group process. They add secondary problems of their own making. They sometimes promote actual mislearning. They kill spontaneity and the sense of adventure for both teacher and students. They make writing appear strange and technical so that students dissociate it from familiar language behavior that should support it. Their dullness and arbi-trariness alienate students from writing. Because they predict and pre-package, they are bound to be inappropriate for some school populations, partly irrelevant to individual students, and ill-timed for all.

I believe the teacher should be given a lot of help for the very difficult job of teaching writing. A lot of what is in textbooks should be in books for teachers, and is in fact partly there to educate them, not the students. The real problem, as I think many educators would admit, is that too many teachers cannot do without textbooks because they were never taught in schools of education to teach without them. Textbooks constitute a kind of inservice training in teaching methods and in linguistic and rhetorical analysis that they never received before. Thus the trial-and-error approach would be considered too difficult for most teachers; they wouldn't have the background, perception, and agility to make it work. The extreme of this belief is that teacher-proof materials are necessary to compensate for teachers inadequacy. If this is so, then let's be frank and solve the problem by renovating teacher training and by publishing more books for teachers on the job, not by putting materials in the hands of students. If it is acknowledged that textbooks do not exist because they embody the best learning process but because teachers are dependent on them, then we would expect them to dwindle away as the education of teachers improves. But I don't see that texts are a mere stop-gap measure. There is every indication that they will become more powerful, not less. The investments of everyone are too great. I don't mean just the publishers, who are merely supplying a demand; I mean that we are all caught in a self-perpetuating cycle that revolves among education schools, classrooms, school administrations, and publishers. The teaching of writing will not improve until the cycle is broken. It is not up to the publishers to break it; they will put out whatever teachers call for. Although a number of teachers do teach writing without texts, it is too much to expect a revolution to start in classrooms without a lot of change in school administration and schools of education, which is where the cycle can be broken.

If I have strayed here into essentially non-educational considerations, it is because I believe the only justification for textbooks in writing is an essentially non-educational one. My main purpose has been to propose that writing be taught naturalistically, by writing, and that the only texts be the student productions themselves. I regret that I have had to speak so long against something, but it is not enough to propose; a way must be cleared. I see tremendous evidence against the pre-teaching approach, embodied in textbooks, and no evidence for it. The great advances in language theory, on the one hand, and in programming techniques on the other, are unfortunately reinforcing that approach. The prospect that frightens me is that we educators are learning to do better and better some things that should not be done at all. We are rapidly perfecting error. Which is to say that I think we should heed better the feedback we get about the consequences of our teaching actions.

THE PROBLEM
OF DEFINING A
MATURE STYLE

Francis Christensen

The topic assigned me for this paper was "Grammar and Rhetoric
—Putting the Two Together," and I proposed to deal with two
questions—*whether* they can be brought together and *how* they can
be brought together. But reflection on these questions, together with
some recent reading, made me face up again to another question.
Grammar and rhetoric are complementary, but their procedures and
goals are quite different. Grammar maps out the possible; rhetoric
narrows down the possible to the desirable or effective. In the area
of style or, more narrowly, of syntax as style, our province in this
paper, the key problem for rhetoric is to know what is desirable or
effective. In matters of style, how do we as teachers know what to
say *yes* to and what to say *no* to? Unless, as some appear to contend,
we are merely to turn on the spigot and watch the water flow without attempting to direct the flow, where do we direct it? How do
we avoid mere subjective impressionism or, worse, mere caprice and
whim.

No one can teach composition, or evaluate the compositions of the
students he teaches, without acting upon some assumptions about
style. These assumptions are rarely consciously formulated; they
manifest themselves in the hit and miss comments we make on
student papers and, for most teachers, they are derived ultimately
from the handbooks. For decades, the handbooks have been derived
from one another. Their chapters on the sentence are mainly negative, rules for salvaging misbegotten sentences. Where they are
positive, they are couched in terms of simple, compound, and complex sentences or of loose, balanced, and periodic sentences. When
one weighs the magnitude of the tasks of the schools in teaching

From the *English Journal* (April, 1968), pp. 572–9. Reprinted with per-
mission of the National Council of Teachers of English and Francis Christensen.
Francis Christensen teaches in the Department of English at Northern Illinois
University of DeKalb, Illinois.

writing against this trivial kit of tools for doing it, one wonders about our right to call ourselves a profession.

Judging by what we say, we seem to consider it the goal of the schools to develop a "mature" style. I would amend this to say a mature style in the idiom of our own day. The nub of the problem is the meaning we are to give to the term *a mature style*. Without a clear understanding of the syntactic features of a mature style and some semblance of a consensus among ourselves, we can do nothing to advance our students' progress toward it.

And let us not forget that, if we succeed in our teaching, the features we have settled upon will mark the style of the generations we teach. What we teach and the way we teach it, do have an effect, and the effect can be bad as readily as good. For example, in the essay on sentence openers in my *Notes Toward A New Rhetoric* (Harper & Row, 1967), I compared the advice given teachers in an article in *College English* with the practice of professional writers. The effect of the advice would be to subvert any sense for style the student might have and to enjoin a contorted academic prose, what I called pretzel prose. Such prose must be called bad prose if we take our standards from professional writers.

With this much on the contrast between grammar and rhetoric and the importance of the choices that must be made by rhetoric, I turn to the problem of defining a mature style—of describing, that is, the syntactic features and the frequency and position of such features as appear in what we would be willing to call mature writing. I will undertake it in two stages. First, I will summarize two reports of research into the syntactic features of the writing of school children, reports that are being taken as affording "the appropriate criteria for describing growth of syntactic fluency" (Mellon, p. 29) or, in other words, as defining the "parameters of normal growth" (Mellon, p. 27). Both are research studies financed by the U. S. Office of Education. One is by Kellogg W. Hunt, *Sentence Structures Used by Superior Students in Grades Four and Twelve, and by Superior Adults* (Cooperative Research Project No. 5–0313), the other by John C. Mellon, *Transformational Sentence Combining: A Method for Enhancing the Development of Syntactic Fluency in English Composition* (Cooperative Research Project No. 5–8418). A critical analysis of these studies will set the stage for my own, far different, appraisal of what constitutes syntactic maturity or fluency, an appraisal that has far different implications for curriculum making.

Hunt first took the measure of the traditional measures of "maturity" and then used them to measure the "glacially slow" progress of school children from Grade 4 to Grade 12 and finally compared the level of their attainment with that of what we called "superior adults," these being writers of articles in *The Atlantic* and *Harper's*.

He found sentence length, one of the traditional measures, highly unreliable because any sequence of independent clauses can be punctuated, deliberately or unwittingly, so as to make the sentences long or short. (One of the least able of the fourth-graders wrote sentences longer than those of any of the adults.) He replaced the sentence by the T-unit, defined as the "minimal terminable units":

"terminable" because it is grammatically allowable to terminate them, like sentences, with a capital letter at one end and a period or other terminal mark at the other; and "minimal" in the sense that they are the shortest units into which a passage can be thus segmented without leaving fragments as a residue (pp. 8–9).

Thus each main or independent clause, together with its subordinate elements, is a T-unit; a compound sentence such as this has two T-units.

For the children whose writing he studied, at Grades 4, 8, and 12, the *length* of the T-unit proved the "most valid measure of maturity" (p. 9). That is, year by year, though at an almost infinitesimal rate, the T-units of what the children wrote grew longer.

There are two ways, the report indicates, of attaining this greater length—by increasing the number of subordinate clauses associated with the main clause or by lengthening the clauses (both main and subordinate) that constitute the T-unit. The second of these gives *clause length* as a measure, and this proved the second most valid measure (p. 10). The children's clauses grew longer by more adding and embedding. The other way increases the *ratio* of subordinate clauses to main clauses or to the total number of clauses, and this ratio proved the third most reliable measure (p. 10). The children used more and more subordinate clauses.

But the three kinds of subordinate clauses are not of equal value as measures. Only adjectival clauses vary chronologically in such a way as to provide a measure of development. Noun, or nominal, clauses vary with the subject or topic. Movable adverbial clauses show no pattern, varying with neither subject nor age. Thus the ratio of adjective clauses is a better measure than the ratio of subordinate clauses. And the fact that twelfth-graders have reached the adult level in frequency of adjective clauses suggests further that the added length of T-units written by skilled adults comes from the added *length* of the clauses.

The final stage of Hunt's study was to determine what constructions account for the added length of the clauses. The answer is (1) nominals such as noun clauses and phrases in place of nouns and pronouns and (2) modifiers embedded before and after nouns to lengthen the noun phrases. Further analysis of the noun phrases give depth of embedding as a further measure of complexity.

The growth of Hunt's subjects toward syntactic maturity as measured by his measures was not such as to give us teachers of English any cause for elation. It was so slow as to be scarcely measurable, and is to be attributed, probably, less to the pupil's instruction than to "the cognitive growth that results in his making fuller use of permitted grammatical operations" (Mellon, p. 23). And at the twelfth grade it was still far short of the performance of skilled adults.

One important question for teachers is whether the rate can be enhanced. An answer of sorts has just been given by John C. Mellon in the study referred to, *Transformational Sentence Combining.* . . .

I cite this study because it accepts the diagnosis of syntactic maturity that I have just described. Mellon says,

> Clearly, Hunt has shown that the hallmark of mature syntactic fluency is the ability to "say more," on average, with every statement. Increased use of relative transforms means in effect that the student more often makes secondary statements, either fully formed or elliptical, about the nouns in his main sentences. Greater use of nominalized sentences means that he more often predicates upon sentences, as it were, than upon simple nouns. . . . Generally speaking, then, the above embedding transforms, together with measures of depth of embedding, cluster size, and unique nominal patterns, constitute the appropriate criteria for describing growth of syntactic fluency (Mellon, p. 29).

Other of Mellon's statements place the emphasis on the same syntactic elements:

Treatments for promoting growth on the part of secondary school students may therefore be designed in the knowledge that these children have long since acquired, and that they normally use, the full roster of kernel sentence types and transformation rules.

It follows, then, that growth of syntactic fluency can result only from increased use of sentence-embedding transformations (p. 26).

But in general, it is the nominal and relative transforms whose consistently greater frequencies per T-unit characterize growth of syntactic fluency (pp. 27–28).

Describing growth is one thing, producing it is another. Mellon's experiment was to include, in the work of a seventh-grade class in transformational grammar, exercises in combining short sentences into sentences that would be long and whose clauses would be long by virtue of nominalizing and relative embedding. He supplied a main clause and a number of input sentences together with simple transformational rules for combining them. The result was "complex" sentences, averaging over thirty words, that say much in little. His guess was that this kind of exercise in the grammar class would show up as more "mature" sentences in the composition class taken by the same pupils though the two classes were entirely unrelated. His hope was that the rate of growth measured by Hunt's measures would be doubled. It *was* doubled, but the difference was not one noticed by the teachers who read, College Board fashion, the pre-post compositions. These readers rated the compositions of the control group higher.

This fact, the lower overall rating of the work of the students whose syntactic fluency had been enhanced, brings me to my critique of these developmental studies.

Producing the kind of growth stipulated by these studies may be possible, but is the kind of growth stipulated the kind of growth we want? Has the fourth-grader really grown toward maturity in style if after four years he measures up to the present eighth-grader or after eight years up to the present twelfth-grader[1]—or even doubles that rate? *Maybe the kids are headed in the wrong direction.* Maybe the lines of their growth, projected upward, would never meet the

---

[1] "Enhanced growth of syntactic fluency, however, merely means that children of a certain age . . . would produce writing whose structural parameters had theretofore been associated with the normal productions of children some years older" (p. 38).

lines projected downward from the writing of skilled adults. Maybe, unless the direction is changed, unless the twig is bent, they will never write like *skilled* adults, but write, like most adults, the lumpy, soggy, pedestrian prose that we justly deride as jargon or gobbledegook.

The very hallmark of jargon is the long noun phrase—the long noun phrase as subject and the long noun phrase as complement, the two coupled by a minimal verb. One of the hardest things to learn in learning to write well is how to keep the noun phrases short. The skillful writer is the writer who has learned how to keep them short. On nearly every page of this paper I have had to resort to syntactic devices to keep them within bounds—devices, such as this appositive, that are practically unknown to our textbook writers. Northrop Frye might have written this sentence:

The curriculum is at best, however, a design to be interpreted by teacher with varying degrees of ability and insight for children with different equipment in intelligence and language background.

Instead, he wrote this one:

The curriculum is at best, however, a design to be interpreted by teachers, for students—by teachers with varying degrees of ability and insight, for children with differing equipment in intelligence and language background.

As a skillful writer he has found a device to avoid a long noun phrase of twenty-four words. Although his sentence is longer by four words, it is immeasurably clearer and more emphatic.

The long noun phrase is not only all too easy to write; it is hard to read. In his concluding chapter Professor Hunt offers some tentative findings on the "syntactic factors of readability" (p. 80). Of his five measures of syntactic maturity only one affects readability. That is clause length, and it affects it adversely. "As difficulty increases and readability decreases, it is clause length that increases" (p. 81). He concludes from this that, in teaching reading, "sentence attack skills [analogous to word attack skills] should focus on the structures which contribute to clause length . . ." and he identifies these as "the sentence-combining transformations, or the clause-consolidating processes" (p. 81).

I would draw an altogether different conclusion. I would say that we should not in our grammar and composition courses focus on tying syntactic knots that we must add courses in reading to untie. A mature style must say much in little, agreed, but a mature style must be easy to decode. The long clause is not the mark of a mature style but of an inept style—the easy writing that's curst hard reading. The real problem in writing is to reconcile these two seeming opposites—to pack much into little, but to pack it so that it can be readily unpacked. It can be done. A mature style is one that does it. It can be taught. But we can learn how to teach it only by learning how professional writers do it. We must set our sights, from the beginning, on the practice of professional writers. We will not learn from children the kind of syntactic fluency exemplified in the sentence by Northrop Frye.

I come now to what seems to me the radical flaw in these developmental studies. *They have lumped together two quite different classes of construction.*[2] The sentences of all but the most immature or inept writings are made long, in part, by a class of constructions far different in rhetorical effect from nominalizations and relative

[2] In a letter to me Professor Hunt recognizes this point: "I now think I can put my finger on the center of the confusion. It is this. You count as a clause something quite different from what I count as a clause, and count as a nominal something quite different from what I count as a nominal. So, when confronted by identical sentences, you say the clauses and nominals are short whereas I say the clauses and nominals are long." He illustrates the difference by analyzing one of my sentences: "The very hallmark of jargon is the long noun phrase—the long noun phrase as subject and the long noun phrase as complement, the two coupled by a minimal verb."

His grammatical analysis of the sentence is accurate: "The sentence has as complement a very long expression beginning with a single noun modified by another noun and by an adjective. Then that 4-word expression is developed by a long appositive containing the original expression twice repeated but each time presented with different modifiers. Finally these two expressions are brought together by the summarizing absolute." The difference is in the interpretation: "The whole thing is one nominal, one complement. . . . I would say that it has a mean clause length of 30 words. I suppose you would say it is a 10-word clause [i.e. has a 10-word base clause]. I would say it contains a very long nominal as complement to the minimal verb BE, a nominal 24 words long, but I suppose you would say the complement nominal is short, 4 words long."

Precisely, and I am arguing that from the standpoint of rhetoric there is a world of difference, as in Frye's, between the sentence as written and as it might have been written, with a complement nominal of 18 words: "The very hallmark of jargon is the long noun phrase as subject coupled by a minimal verb to the long noun phrase as complement."

embeddings. This class is the so-called sentence modifiers. Since this term is inaccurate (they modify one another as well as sentences), I will call them free modifiers, in contrast to bound modifiers. To be useful for rhetorical purposes and hence for curriculum planning, any study of the syntactic resources of the language must keep these two classes of modifiers apart.

Bound modifiers are word modifiers. They are close or limiting or restrictive modifiers. They are, in a sense, obligatory, and, being obligatory, they do not give the writer the freedom of choice that rhetoric demands. Free modifiers, on the other hand, are modifiers not of words but of constructions, from which they are set off by junctures or punctuation. Grammatically, they are loose or additive or nonessential or nonrestrictive. The constructions used are prepositional phrases; relative and subordinate clauses; noun, verb, adjective, and adverbial phrases or clusters; and, one of the most important, verbid clauses or absolutes.

These free modifiers give the options that rhetoric demands. They give the skilled writer the devices for keeping his clauses short. Variations in their kinds, positions, and frequency differentiate individual styles. Students can be taught to use them, and it is here that grammar and rhetoric can be brought together in a fruitful conjunction to bring about a mature style truly in the modern idiom.

To bring the discussion down to the concrete, I chose from the issues of *Harper's* I had at hand (January and February 1964) four of the essays used by Professor Hunt. I chose two by nonprofessional writers, both M.D.'s, Allan Barnes and Thomas S. Szasz, and two by well-known semiprofessional writers, David Boroff and Paul Goodman. And then from the current *Harper's* (August 1967) I chose two by professional writers—Willie Morris, introduced in this issue as the new editor-in-chief of *Harper's*, and David Halberstam, introduced as a new contributing editor. I regard Halberstam as the best writer of the six.

The table shows the count made on fifty T-units of each.

The T-units average 19.5 words, compared with Hunt's count of 20.3 for skilled adults. The variations from left to right seem to have no significance.

With the free modifiers, however, the variations are significant. The total number of words in the free modifiers varies regularly

Relative Length of (1) T-units, (2) Freed Modifiers, and (3) Base Clauses
(Based on 50 T-units)

	Non-professional		Semi-professional		Professional		
	Barnes 1/64	Szasz 2/64	Boroff 1/64	Goodman 1/64	Morris 8/67	Halberstam 8/67	Average
1. T-units—100% of total words							
Total words	967	832	944	911	1037	1155	
Average per T-unit	19.3	14.6	18.9	18.2	20.7	23.1	19.5
2. Free Modifiers—32% of total words							
Initial	129	94	51	107	70	76	
Medial	28	36	93	23	20	103	
Final	55	106	154	169	242	313	
Total words in free mod.	212	236	298	299	382	492	
Average words per T-unit	4.24	4.72	5.84	6.0	6.6	9.8	6.2
3. Base Clauses—68% of total words							
Words in T-units	967	832	944	911	1037	1155	
Words in free mod.	212	236	298	299	332	492	
Words in base clauses	755	596	646	612	705	663	
Average per base clause	15.1	11.9	12.9	12.2	14.1	13.3	13.3

from left to right from 212 to 492. In Barnes 22 per cent of the words are in free modifiers, in Halberstam over 42 per cent. A large percentage seems to be a mark of the skillful writer. The positions vary too, and significantly. Nonprofessional writers, remembering perhaps what they were taught in school, tend to put them up front; professional writers tend to use them at the end—to write, that is, what I have called cumulative sentences.

The length of the base clauses is significant too, but significant in another way. The base clause of a T-unit is what is left when the free modifiers are subtracted. This subtraction separates the two classes of constructions described above. The base clause may or may not have bound subordinate clauses; from this point of view grammatical form of the bound modifiers is irrelevant. The significance here is not in the variation in *length* of the base clauses but in the fact that *all these writers have managed to keep them short.* The average length is 13.3 words; and, mark this carefully, this is less than the length of the T-units of Professor Hunt's twelfth-graders, 14.4 words. And mark carefully the conclusion to be drawn from this—the difference lies in the free modifiers. The T-units are long but the base clauses are short—kept short in large part, as in the example from Northrop Frye, by the full use of free modifiers.

A paragraph from Halberstam's article, "Love, Life, and Selling Out in Poland," will help make it clear what free modifiers are and what they look like in context. In the initial position all words and constructions that stand before the noun phrase that is the subject are free modifiers regardless of punctuation; position alone marks them as free—e.g. *perhaps* and *for me* before *it* in two of the sentences. Every medial or final word or construction that is set off is a free modifier. Here the free modifiers have been put in italics. (The reader may wish to mark them with transparent watercolor markers, using a different color for initial, medial, and final elements; this will make the relative proportions evident at a glance.) In Roman type are the base clauses and the coordinators that join base clauses.

These countries were once the center of the storm, and *as the Curtain was coming down* their hotels were filled with correspondents, *pushing and crowding each other, playing what is known in the trade as journalistic boomerang (you take a rumor, throw it out, and by the end of the day it has touched so many other people that it comes back to you fresh and vital, passed on by people you haven't even spoken to).* The storm is now in Saigon, *where several hundred correspondents cover the story of whether that country will or won't go Communist.* Their editors are in a sense right, for there is little news from Eastern Europe—*some change, some restlessness, but little hint of revolution.* These are small countries; you can take all the political developments in the Polish Communist party in one year, and *perhaps* it will be one story. Yet *for me* it was an extraordinary time. My colleague David Binder, *who shared the lower half of the tier, the Balkans, with me,* agreed emphatically. *When the Times wanted to transfer him to Bonn, a bigger story and a bigger bureau,* he went reluctantly, *leaving what he had come to call "my people."* We shared, *I think,* the same feeling for being a reporter there, *of watching in a way being involved in the simple yet moving business of the daily struggle of these people with the state. Cast in the most unnatural circumstances,* they go on in the struggle relentlessly, *living lives with an infinite degree of moral complexity, daily honor, daily dishonor.*

In this paragraph of 260 words, the 13 T-units average 20 words in length, compared with 19.5 for the six-author sample. The 13 base clauses have altogether only 90 words, only 35 per cent of the total number of words, an average of only 7 words each. But to make up the average of 20 words these base clauses have an average of 13 words each in added free modifiers; of the total of 170 words in free modifiers, 31 are in the initial position and 14 in medial positions, leaving 125 in the final position. Thus about half of the words of this paragraph are final free modifiers.

By contrast, the ten sentences produced by Mellon's experiment average 30 words in length, compared with 19.5 for the six-author sample and 20 for Halberstam's paragraph. The free modifiers average only 2.8 words per sentence, compared with 6.2 for the six-author sample and 13 for Halberstam's paragraph. The base clauses average 27.2 words, over twice the length of the base clauses of the six-author sample and nearly four times the length of those of Halberstam's example. Such sentences are atypical, not to say abnormal. Only three of them have any free modifiers. The six free modifiers include one initial prepositional phrase, three nonrestrictive adjective clauses and two noun phrases used as nonrestrictive appositives. Only the last are significant markers of a mature style.

There is no reason, of course, why such exercises should not call for a full range of free modifiers. An adequate course in grammar will include all of them. But their *use* can best be taught in the rhetorical setting of the composition course, where the student must supply the content and where the very structure of the sentence can help to *generate* the content.

I do not pretend, of course, that the paragraph from Halberstam is typical or that the six-author sample is adequate, but I submit that they are representative of what will be found in the writing of skilled adults. And I submit that Mellon's experiment, as an interpretation and application of the developmental studies by Hunt, proves that these studies, *as interpreted and applied,* will set us off on the wrong track. They seem to me to repeat in technical terms the slogan of a few years back "Load the patterns," a slogan I criticized in my article "A Generative Rhetoric of the Sentence" (reprinted in *Notes Toward a New Rhetoric*).

I will conclude with a statement of what I believe will be found to mark a mature style in the idiom of our own day. Both Hunt and Mellon are aware of the need for better measures, and I offer two as hypotheses to be tested.

1. A mature style will have a relatively high frequency of free modifiers, especially in the final position. The frequency of free noun, verb, and adjective phrases and of verbid clauses will be high.
2. Such a style will have also a relatively high frequency of structures of coordination within the T-unit—what might be called intra-T-unit coordination. Inter-T-unit coordination, producing compound sentences, should be regarded as a feature of paragraph rather than sentence structure.

The very fact that these two classes of structures are not common in the writing of school children is proof in itself that they are marks of a mature style. If the research I am inviting proves that they are indeed reliable indexes, then future research will be needed to determine the points in a spiraling curriculum where they can be introduced and how they can best be taught.

GIVE YOUR STUDENTS
THE WRITER'S
FIVE EXPERIENCES

Donald M. Murray

The other day a young high school teacher asked me, "I've been assigned to a writing course this fall, what should I teach?"

"You don't teach anything," I answered. "You let the students write, you read what they've written with the class, and then you each try to help each of them say what he has to say."

It was good advice, the distillate of what is practiced in university writing workshops across the country. But it was unfair to give the young lady such a quick answer. The beginning English teacher—or the experienced English teacher who is inexperienced in teaching writing—needs more than such glib counsel, for we are all taught the virtues of lesson plans, syllabi and course outlines. We gripe about them, but still depend on them. I know that I certainly lean on a lesson plan, and the more inexperienced I am in teaching a course, the more heavily I lean.

As teachers we are taught to prepare lessons to bring to our students. We see ourselves as beasts of intellectual burden who haul fact, interpretation, commentary, analysis, and information into the classroom to dump it on the student.

This does not work in the writing course, because there is no great body of knowledge to lug into class. There are only a relatively few simple principles, constantly reborn out of the writer's experience—recurrent problems and recurrent solutions. And these principles of writing not only seem irrelevant to the student, they are indeed irrelevant until he discovers them for himself in solving his own writing problems.

Teaching writing has its peculiar difficulties. For example, you can

From *The Leaflet* (November, 1968), pp. 3–9.

Donald M. Murray is a writer who teaches English at the University of New Hampshire. This article was originally presented as part of the LaMancha Project.

rarely prepare a class and therefore you feel as if you come to the class naked. This, of course, is not the case. You bring all that you know to class so that it can be brought to bear, spontaneously, on the problems faced by individual writers on the page. The writing teacher must be prepared to diagnose the student writer's problems and to respond to them. The students must be forced to take the initiative in the writing course. The course is most successful when students discover their own problems, and when they discover their own solutions. You, the teacher, create a climate in which this process can take place and you succeed the most when you interfere—or teach—the least.

Writing is a skill, or an art, and, therefore, the composition course is a laboratory or workshop course. You can't learn to write by reading before the fact, by discussion before the fact, by critical analysis after the fact, or by lecture before or after the fact of writing. These are all valid teaching techniques, part of the writing teacher's arsenal. But the emphasis in the course must be on what the student is doing, for writing simply can not be taught theoretically, in the abstract. Writing must be experienced to be learned.

This teaching role in which the teacher responds instead of initiating does not threaten the status of the shop teacher, the art teacher, the music teacher, the science lab teacher or the football coach. But it does seem to frighten and threaten the English teacher who too often envisions himself as a modern Moses who brings the tablets, possibly xeroxed for class distribution, down from the mountain each day. The English teacher's model is usually, unfortunately, his college English professor, and therefore he feels guilty if he, the teacher, is not continually talking. I am an English professor, and I certainly do love to talk, but I am convinced that listening is an efficient educational procedure most of the time, at least in the writing course.

We also have an understandable tendency to over-organize our courses. Perhaps we want to impress our superiors, our colleagues, our students, or just to give ourselves a sense of security. We plan to teach diction in the third week in September, iambic pentameter in October, parallel construction in November, the essay in December, description in January, footnotes in February—everything neatly organized into some pattern which seems rational to the teacher in advance of the beginning of school. I am a great organizer, and my course outlines are a matter of enormous pride and satisfaction to me. I scatter them about me as if they were rose petals of purple ditto. When I began to teach, after years of being a full time writer, I didn't know what to teach or how to teach it, but I did know how to make outlines. Each year, however, my outlines have become less formal because I have traveled from school to school during the past few years and seen hundreds of lesson plans which are often impressive, usually contradictory, and almost always irrelevant to what the successful teacher is doing in class. In the writing course the course outline is a crutch which should be discarded as soon as the students begin to write. As they write and reveal their composition problems the students design their own course. That is the way it should be, and the professional teacher should be flexible enough to teach the course his particular students need this term, not the course he planned or hoped to teach.

But what is the teacher to do at the beginning of the term if the writing course starts not when the teacher talks but when the students write? The teacher spends his time creating an environment in which a student can work, and discipline under which he must work, and then the teacher enters into the course with his students by writing himself.

It is terrifying to reveal yourself to your pupils by trying to practice what you've been preaching, but once a teacher engages in the writing process with his students he will never be the same again. Writing teachers are fortunate to be able to share the excitement of learning with our students. We too can pass through the five experiences of the writer. We don't hide behind our desks but sit down with our students and write. Afterwards we sit beside them and accept their criticism while they accept ours. And then we all go back to rewrite.

In this process each writing course recreates itself. Each year is new, each class is new, for the process of writing can never be perfected. There is always a new challenge, a new discovery, and there is no satisfaction in teaching to be compared to the excitement of entering into the educational experience of your students, forever young, forever learning. You can share your students' intellectual explorations of the five basic experiences of the writer.

THE EXPERIENCE OF SEEING

The first experience of the writer which the student writer should share is the experience of seeing. The writer has to see to have something to say. Before anything else, the writing course is the practice of perception. The teacher may demonstrate what it means to see, using photographs, a tour of the school, and his own observations for demonstration. He may expand the perception to other senses, using records, odors, textures, to make the student aware of his own world. He may also read, or have the students read, excerpts from literature which show the writer's awareness of his world, as long as the teacher realizes that literature is only one way of viewing the world. It may be the best way for the teacher, but it may not be the most effective way for the average student.

At first the experience of seeing may only be expressed through lists of specifics—describe a person or a place, with 25, 100, or 250 specifics. Such exercises help the student feel the writer's awareness which produces the raw materials for his writing.

Eventually the student may move from description to analysis and to theoretical writing using the same technique of listing specifics, for the scholar or the scientist first collects his evidence or his data, and then, as it accumulates and begins to assume a pattern of its own, he begins to discover an evolving meaning. This process is similar to a photograph slowly appearing in developer. The writer begins to see the meaning through the specifics which he has collected. First, however, the student writer has to see, and the teacher's task is to create an atmosphere and an attitude which will encourage the student to see.

THE EXPERIENCE OF FORM

The second experience is the artist's fundamental experience of form. The writer experiences form as he feels the irrelevant becoming relevant, the random assuming pattern, the apparently pointless unrelated fact pointing toward meaning. The writer—the artist— brings order to disorder. Form may be a story, a letter, a scientific report, a paragraph, a novel, a scene, a list—anything which makes sense of the multiple impressions which our brain collects from both the library book and the conversation on the street corner.

The artist doesn't so much admire form as he hungers for it. He needs form to give him meaning. His business is to design ideas into thoughts, and the student writer must learn to organize his perceptions. He should be free to toy with his facts, since the writer may be most disciplined when he is most playful, teasing a meaning out of evidence which once seemed irrelevant or contradictory.

Once the student has built a form for himself which stands up to a critical reader he will never be quite the same again. Form is something you—and the reader—can hold on to, something that makes it possible for a reader to recognize your meaning. The student writer must make his own paragraph, poem, report, or story which has successful form. He must know the sense of completeness the writer feels when he has made something which was not there before, when he has experienced form.

THE EXPERIENCE OF PUBLICATION

Next, the student writer must suffer the exciting, terrifying experience of publication. The writer is the man revealed by the printing press. All others escape but the writer's words are examined coldly by an objective audience. We see how well he writes, and by seeing how he writes we see how he thinks. Indeed, we see what he is.

The printing press waits, and in the writing course its deadline should be irrevocable. Everything may be avoided except the moment of publication. The printing press may, of course, be a ditto machine, a real printing press, carbon paper, a bulletin board, a mimeograph, a xerox, an overhead projector, but there must come a time when the student writer has his own words wrenched from him so they appear naked before his own eye, apart from apologies and explanations, good intentions and sincere promises.

The writing course moves forward because the student faces the same discipline as the writer: the arbitrary deadline. It may be the end of the hour, the end of the day, the end of the week, but the student must face a frequent, inflexible deadline. Score is kept, and the student must deliver a draft or a revision. The subject, the form, the length may and should be his, but the deadline is the publisher's. There is an hour when the work, at last, must be passed in and the writer revealed. The teacher may vary the deadline or even change it in special cases, but the editor knows the professional will not deliver unless he faces a deadline and the copy is taken from him. Writing is never completed; the process of revision, reconsideration and editing goes on until the final deadline is met.

Then, when the deadline has passed and the writer is published, he is tested. Publication is the writer's big game, the concert hall recital, the opening night, the combat fire fight, and the writing student has to be bloodied if he is to learn. He has to suffer the awful revelation of what he has said compared to what he meant to say.

THE EXPERIENCE OF COMMUNICATION

The student should also, before the composition course is over, have the experience of communication. Few students have enjoyed good listeners at home or at school, and yet we all have the basic need for communication and understanding. We laugh at the trite complaint, "My wife doesn't understand me." But often in cliches lie truth. We all want to be understood, to communicate our dreams and our fears, our hopes and our apprehensions, our experiences and the implications we see in them.

Once the student has found an audience he will catch fire. He will be motivated to write once the basic satisfaction of communication has been given to him, and this is where the teacher plays his most important role. The teacher creates an environment in which the student finds an audience of his peers and in which the audience of his peers has been trained to respond constructively to a piece of writing in process.

The teacher, however, should be the class' most expert reader. He should perceive, through the confusion of the student's writing, the potential meaning. He is able to diagnose the student's fundamental problem and to prescribe possible solutions which the student may try. He is never, however, the final reader. He should always think of himself as a coach or a tutor or an adviser who is helping the student to speak to his own audience. The student writer will, and should, suspect the teacher's reaction. The student must discover he can communicate to his own audience.

THE EXPERIENCE OF FAILURE

Finally, the student must learn to live with the most important writer's experience of all: the experience of failure. We live in a success-oriented society, and it is hard for the student and the student's parents to understand that the writer always fails, but he uses failure in the process of writing. Failure is never pleasant, but too often it is essential. Sometimes the first draft may be the final draft, but usually the writer tries to say something, and fails, and through failure tries to say it better, and fails, but perhaps, eventually, he says it well enough. The writing course is an experimental course. It is a course in process, a course in practicing, a course in trying, a course in choice, a course in craft. Failure should not be accepted passively, but failure should never be defeat. The student should learn to exploit his failures as he rediscovers his subject, re-researches his information, redesigns his form, rewrites and edits every sentence.

What shall I teach this fall in my writing courses? As always, I approach the first day with a sense of inadequacy, a sense of apprehension, and a most exciting sense of anticipation. I do not know what I will teach, but I do know what my students will learn. Slowly, at first, the class will begin to hear some individual voices speak. And we will listen to these voices and try to help them become more effective, more confident.

My students will begin to learn how to write, not because of what I will tell them, but because of what they will experience. They will experience sight, they have something to say; they will experience form, and discover how to say it; they will experience publication, and become writers; they will experience communication and know they can reach at least one other human being; they will experience failure and begin to discover the craft of writing. They will, in just a few weeks, pass through the five experiences of the writer and begin to teach themselves to write.

THIS IS WHAT
CAME OUT

Alex McLeod

. . . I became interested, school full of girls, can't be bad, could be some good material there. It was hinted that there might be a visit, so get your hair done and send us some pictures or even better actual samples. A girl in our class—ex grammar—says that at this place she went to, all that was talked about was boys, don't get none of that trouble at a mixed, from either sex.

Well after thinking about it I couldn't determine what I was going to write about, so there I was, at home, Beatles blasting out songs in my ear, pencil in hand thinking about what I was going to write.

So I wrote, with interruptions to listen and turn the records over and brief interruptions to play along with the records on my guitar. This is what came out, about nothing in particular, unlike some things that you will read, its just an account of writing this writing.

—15 year old boy

Most teachers want to make their pupils aware of one another's work. Many of us go to some trouble to see that the best things they write are read to the class, or displayed on the walls, or published in a magazine. But nearly all the things we ask them to write are done for a teacher reader, or perhaps for the teacher and the class; some school magazines are written for the school and the staff, but it is very rarely that we find writing done in school for the writer's friends and equals. If we do find it, we might think it irrelevant— those carefully prepared lists of the achievements of heroes of sport

From *English in Education* (Autumn, 1969), pp. 87, 88, 90, 92, 94, 96, 98, 100, 102, 104, 106, 108, 110, 112, 114, 116, 118, 120.

This article arises from work carried out by the Writing Research Unit at the University of London Institute of Education, which has undertaken an investigation into the written language of pupils in secondary schools, aged 11 to 18. The project is directed by James Britton and financed by the Schools Council.

Acknowledgement is made to colleagues in the Writing Research Team: Nancy Martin, Dennis Griffiths, Bernard Newsome, Harold Rosen and especially to James Britton.

or pop; or subversive—a clandestine sixth form magazine, for instance, such as was produced in a school where I once taught, and sold off the premises.

The work described in this article arose from the setting up of a situation in which a hundred and fifty fourth form boys and girls in five schools were given a chance to write whatever they wanted to say to each other, without having to consider their teachers at all. It is a small part of a five year project in which we are looking at some of the writing of these pupils—and another hundred and fifty who are three years younger—in all subjects, as they progress through their secondary schools. In addition, once a term we are able to give them a set task, one which all the pupils in all five classes are asked to do. In February 1968 they were asked to prepare a folder of work to be sent to a class of pupils of the same age in one of the other schools. No restriction was placed on what they wrote; it was done by asking each class to appoint a secretary, who was given a large envelope to collect everything that was written, and this was sealed and sent off without being read by the teacher. The teachers, although excluded so unceremoniously, were interested in the idea and helped to work out the scheme. Then they introduced the idea to their classes, and set the whole thing in motion. It was agreed that they might ask the pupils to think in terms of: 'Who we are, what we do, and what we want' but this was intended only as a starting point. They were told that they could take up the suggestion in any way they liked, and that they might bear in mind what they would like to read from another group of children of the same age.

The folders were duly posted off to the secretaries and everything in them was read out or passed round the class. They were then sent on to the Writing Research Unit.

HOW THE CLASSES TOOK UP THE OFFER

Two of the classes are in mixed comprehensive schools, one is in a mixed grammar school and the other two are in direct grant schools, one for boys and one for girls.

One class was not enthusiastic at first:

I don't mind telling you I didn't like the idea of it at first and I just couldn't be bothered.

but after a few days a number of them, particularly the girls, began to see some exciting possibilities and became fully involved. In fact, the longest piece in the whole collection was done by a girl in this class, and the girl quoted above ended on a rather different note:

I'll give you my address in case anybody's interested (her address follows) I hope I'll see some of you at the ice rink on Monday. I'll dare say you'll know me because I'll be like Linda, only worse. Bye.

The second class set to work willingly and appointed a boy to co-ordinate their contributions; however he was soon deposed and replaced by a girl, who arranged the pieces in order and wrote an overview. This is part of it:

But really our class gets on well, its good tempered, and very happy working together.

That's the advantage of a mixed school, boys and girls working together seriously. We grow up through adolescence together, and learn to find out about each other.

A complication arose because this class had been told that they would be sending their folder to a class of girls. When most of them had completed their contributions it was discovered that this was a mistake and they were to send it to boys. Much of what had been written was scrapped, and this chance error affected nearly everything finally included. The implications of the change of audience from girls to boys are considered later in this article.

The third class immediately embarked on a discussion about what they, as a class, should do. The suggestions put forward seem to have become a kind of consensus, because almost all the contributions of this class have a superficial similarity of plan. Many of them headed their work *Profile of* 4A. The teacher, having introduced the idea, took hardly any part in this discussion though she would, if asked, have discouraged the idea that a common strategy was desirable.

In the fourth class there was very little discussion. They just decided what to do and got on with it. Their work shows very great variety, and it is hard to imagine, from reading what they wrote, that anyone in this class was to any extent influenced by anyone else. The fifth class is accustomed to working in groups. When they were told about the project they immediately formed themselves into their normal friendship groups and set about deciding what to do. Much of what they wrote could only have been produced by a working group; in nearly all of it one can detect some of the effect of group planning.

THE WRITER'S SENSE OF AUDIENCE

Woah South Londoners! Strangely enough being able to write to you whatever I want is a bit difficult since at the moment I'm in rather unproductive mood. Nevertheless I think I feel strong enough to tell you all about ME (who is fascinating) . . . I am also an exhibitionist, and I have a rather exaggerated view of myself. Nevertheless I think I'm interesting, clever, witty, good-looking, charitable, honest, tolerant, kind and nice to know.

Boy

The writer of this piece seems to be fairly sure about what sort of person it will be read by.

In the course of this research project we have started from the hypothesis that one of the factors which exert a very great influence on the nature and quality of secondary school pupils' writing—and this is probably true in some measure of younger children and of adults too—is the writer's sense, while he is writing, of his reader. We believe that the writer forms an internal notion, sometimes more and sometimes less consciously, of a particular reader, or of a reader of a particular kind, and that in his writing he expresses a relationship with his reader in respect of a topic. We have called this the writer's sense of audience. We divide the audiences first into four main categories:

a. *The Self.* Though writing purely for oneself is rare, the self as a first stage audience has a powerful influence in some other categories.
b. *The Teacher.*

c. *A Wider Known Audience.*
d. *An Unknown Audience.*

Most writing done in school is, naturally, for the teacher, and we distinguish four teacher categories,[1] i.e. differing roles in which the teacher is seen.

Child (or adolescent) to trusted adult
Pupil to teacher, general, an ongoing dialogue
Pupil to teacher, special relationship
Pupil to examiner

Our overall results suggest that a very large amount of the work normally done in school comes into either the 'teacher, general' or the 'teacher examiner' category.

The pupil whose writing is addressed to a wider known audience may be taking up the position of an expert addressing laymen, or at least people who have no knowledge of this particular topic, or he may be writing for his peer group—his friends and acquaintances. He may also, especially if group methods of class organization are being used, write as a member of a working group; this group audience may or may not include the teacher, but if it does, it will not be on quite the same basis as in the teacher audience categories.

Finally, a writer may be writing for an unknown audience—his readers, or his public. This doesn't mean that the audience relationship has disappeared. The writer has internalized the idea of the like-minded reader, or of those he seeks to interest in what he has to say. He will have an idea of what sort of people he is writing for, although he doesn't know who they are.

[1] A rigorous description of the distinctions to be made between these four teacher categories would require a disproportionate amount of space in this article. The 'trusted adult' relationship will be described more fully where something rather like it occurs in the analysis of what these children wrote. Teacher audience writing is, expectedly, almost non-existent in this collection; what little there is probably got there because the habit of writing for the teacher was, for a few children, too strong to be discarded at will. Here is an example:
  Monday is derived from Monandaeg, Old English for moon's day. In ancient times the goddess of the moon was called Diana. Woods were sacred to her because she was supposed to hunt in them at night by moonlight.

Before the investigation described in this article was begun, we had examined a large selection of children's writing, in all school subjects, from pupils throughout the whole secondary age range, in 58 schools. We had found a small amount of writing which we put into these wider audience categories—*expert to laymen, child (or adolescent) to peer group, group member to working group,* and *writer to his readers, or public.*

One of our reasons for asking our research classes to send work to one another was to find out what sense of audience would be found in such writing, and, we hoped, to get more written in these wider audience categories. The audience we set up for them was an unknown one, in the sense that none of the writers had ever met anyone in the other classes, but it was one whose age and status as pupils was known, and whose interests could probably be guessed.

FROM KNOWN TO UNKNOWN

We were not disappointed. Almost all the writers moved right away from the teacher audience and set out to establish an informal relationship with their peers in the other schools. Most of them succeeded, and the various strategies they employed are examined here.

Some thought that by writing in a way that would interest their own friends, they would be sure to catch the attention of their contemporaries in the other schools. One group, in fact, wrote mainly for each other, but they knew what they were up to. In one class, nine girls, all close friends, set themselves a number of rather intimate and daring questions. They were passed round, and each girl wrote an answer to each question. Everything they wrote, because of the way they had arranged it, was written in the first place for the rest of the group, and only through them for the pupils in the other class. This had the effect of excluding anything that they were unwilling to show their friends. They saw the task we gave them as an opportunity to have some fun, but they wanted to have fun in a way they could be proud of; they were not putting themselves on public display without careful consideration of what was worth displaying.

The following are some of the questions, with in each case one of the nine answers, each one from a different girl.

How many times have you cried this year, and why?

Yes, I cry. I suppose it must have been about three or four times this year! Mostly during sad films, but once 'cos some certain person didn't speak to me, and I was furious! Yes well! I usually go into my bedroom when I'm going to cry, and throw things all around the room because I'm furious, then burst into floods of tears on the bed.

What would you do if you discovered you had fleas?

I would shave my hair off and have lots and lots of wigs. Fleas don't like hair which is not what they have been having a nibble at before! I would be quite upset to lose my hair, but not unduly because I would know I was losing my fleas too.

Do you write a diary, if so why, and what do you write?

I keep a diary and mine is also completely and utterly unprintable, C——— is the only person who's ever had even a very small part of it. (At least I sincerely hope she is!) Some days I don't even mention what I have done during the day, although that's mainly only on weekdays, because nothing of interest has happened. I only write things that have happened if they are especially unusual. Apart from that I write my opinions of things, people etc. (and what would happen if they ever read them I dread to think) and, well . . . all sorts of other rubbish! I think I'd better leave it at that.

At first sight, these pieces appear to be nothing more than fairly simple answers to light-hearted questions, with more emphasis on gaiety and good humour than on honesty and accuracy. Taken individually, they are just communicating a little bit of unimportant information, but read all together the collection has a different function, and the girls were probably aware of this, even though it may not have been put into words or fully understood. This more complex function is to give an impressionistic sample of what they are like out of school, or possibly, how they want their friends to think of them. The collection is like a poem in just one way—the total effect is very much more than the sum of its parts, and the parts are related to the whole in some rather subtle ways. The emphasis is much more on expressing themselves than on communicating trivial information, but this expressiveness is highly selective and fairly disciplined, directed, as it is, to the group's image of itself.

There are traces, in some of the other pieces, of writing for one's own friends—the in-group joke would seem to be an indication of this—but most of the boys and girls took up the opportunity we gave them in the way we intended it and attempted to write for the unknown peer group. Many must have clearly imagined their readers as people exactly like themselves and their friends, and so took a fairly intimate relationship for granted. Some of these, like the nine girls quoted above, were careful to avoid writing anything they would not like their friends to read. This piece by a boy, makes sharp comments on some of his class, but they seem to be comments he would make to them too. Having noted with approval that most of the teachers have realised that they are growing up, he continued:

Now we are treated as young adults then we were treated as kids. Mind you most of us were at that age. Also we have grown one year older and somewhat wiser. Still we have got the "holdbacks" who have not matured along with the rest of us they are still as babyish as ever. Of course we have all the different kinds that go to make up a form, the exhibitionists, the showoffs, the sexy (I like them), the "think themselves sexy but aren't", the loudmouthed, the bigheaded, the quiet, the mini skirts, the tall, the short they're all with us.

Others soon realized that there could be no comeback, and they could make comments about their friends, or their teachers, in perfect safety. Another boy in the same class wrote:

We have a Scottish twit who hasn't done it yet so that shows what he's like.

We have a slavedriver for P.E. called ————. He flogs us to death, but you can't help liking him.

Some of the people in this form are pretty stupid because they support crap teams like Fulham, Chelsea and Liverpool instead of the great, almighty Wolves.

I am completely unprejudiced and I like the hippies (The True hippies. It's what you think, not what you wear). John Peel for king. We've got quite a few scrubbers in the form, but there are some nice girls as well.

He is one of many who, by their comments on their friends, tell their readers a great deal about themselves.

The pieces just quoted are examples of a strategy that was adopted by many, the modified letter, though the degree of intimacy of these 'letters' varies enormously. Several, especially girls, took up, in their letters, the kind of position they probably would with other teenagers they had just met—showing a determination to be above all, warm-hearted and friendly.[2]

In one class, they were probably helped towards this very relaxed and friendly relationship by the misunderstanding, mentioned earlier, about which school their folder was being sent to. Their annoyance enabled them to be more expressive and personal, and to convey more of themselves, than they could otherwise have done. Certainly those who seem most upset about it are the most expressive.

What the hell can a girl write to a boy about, there's not very much but even though it might be boring I'll tell you about myself. Not the usual thing about colour, eye colour etc, but about what I think. I think for a start that this whole project has been completely mucked up. We were meant to be writing to girls but we're not so it's a lot better for us girls because, well you're boys and there is a difference.

The sex of the audience, if known, was a strong influence. Four of the classes either knew that their readers would be of both sexes, or didn't know whether they were writing for boys, or girls, or both. The misunderstanding in this one class gave us strong evidence to show that, as one would expect, most boys and girls write very differently for members of their own sex from the way they write for the opposite sex. The only piece written by a boy for a girls'

[2] This apparently worked. A few weeks after the folders were sent off, we heard that some girls from one school and boys from another were meeting. Their schools are about thirty miles apart, so they met in the West End of London. Nearly a year later there was still a link between some members of these two classes.

class, that was allowed to go in the folder when they found it was
going to boys, was heavily crossed out with a ruler and coloured
pencil; the writer's name and address were obliterated, and he
added at the end: 'This was done under the impression of these
being girls'. Here is its last paragraph:

Well as I said I like girls (now you are saying but he didn't say he
likes girls, well you would be right on the "as I said" but not on the bit
"I like Girls") I tell you one thing of your over 38″ round the "bust"*
don't call on me (oh by the way my phone number is 01-........ if
you don't believe me look up .... in the London exchange
directory) you could say I like girls of about 34–24–36 well *I do*. The
only other things that I can think of are that I am obsessed with sex and
that I have green eyes, dark complexion (no I'm not a wog) and I have
black hair, if you are interested phone or write to me and I will gladly
reply.

                                                                Signed C.D.M.
p.s. don't forget your particulars.

The rest of the class, even though they were annoyed about having
to scrap what they had done, found the change of audience such a
strong determiner of what was suitable that they were prepared to
do it all again.

The letter approach could be made to serve many different kinds
of relationships. There is a fairly clear distinction we can make
between two ways of thinking about the task; on the one hand,
attempting to judge what the reader wants, and trying to provide it,
and, on the other, writing from one's own special interests and
concerns, on the assumption that they are likely also to interest one's
contemporaries. These two approaches are seldom entirely separate,
but it is useful to make the distinction, because they appear to have
provided some of our writers with different ways of moving towards
writing for a public audience. It will be remembered that in our
general statement of the audience categories, we suggest that in any
piece of writing, the *writer* expresses a *relationship* with the reader
in respect of a *topic*. It is the way in which the relationship set up,
and the topic selected, affect each other that we are concerned
with here.

---

* I could have used a better word to describe "bust".

Those who thought mostly in terms of the readers' probable interests often began with topics which they decided were of concern to all pupils-teachers, prefects, discipline and school organization; or of concern to all teenagers—sport, pop, clothes, sex, growing up, relationships with each other and with adults; a few moved on to areas of general concern, or things they thought should be of general concern, like war, drugs and politics. In terms of the audience categories, this is writing for an unknown audience, but it is still strongly influenced by the known peer group.

Here is a selection of extracts arranged according to topic.

SCHOOL

Everybody walks in the room and sits down the noise begins to rise. Four of the girls sitting in the corner yabbering. Mick sitting there calling everybody peasants. P——— chuckling and sitting sideways and R——— leaning back. G——— telling another horror story. Mrs. ——— walks to the front and says 'Right 4D' as always and then squats on the front desk as usual. She starts discussing today's work occasionally punctuated by a reprimand for example 'Now what do . . . so and so shut up!' Her temper can be very mercuric and one minute laughing and yelling. She is constantly brushing back her hair. At the end of the lesson she says that there will be detention for anyone forgetting the homework it never comes.

Boy.

In general, we use our masters to the utmost advantage, especially students or masters straight from training school. Such a master was Mr. ———. His frightened leniency and industrious effort to avoid obtaining an unsavoury reputation, together with his unfortunate mannerism which sounded like QHHHHHHHHH! produced disastrous results.

Boy.

'OH NO!' she shrieked, 'It's the language Lab.—anything but that. I hate it—"Instant headache" we call it. We have that Irish-French drawl going on and on all the time'. She always thought the bell at the end of this lesson to be the best of the week.

Girl.

One of our girls moved recently, and as she is in the GCE lists, the grammar school, which was local, took her in. The change from Comprehensive to Grammar almost killed her. She came home crying every night because she was so bored. One of her mates lets her live in during the week, and she goes home of a weekend. So now she is back at our school. One of our R.E. teachers is a well known folk singer. One used to play at Huddersfield with Denis Law. One's dog is on the telly. William, who is used in the Pal adverts. We have quite a bunch at our.school.

Boy.

TEENAGER INTERESTS

When Lulu had finished, the lights dimmed, then, all of a sudden the Empire Pool was filled with screaming teenagers. 10,000 teenagers to be exact.

The spotlights were on the stage and out came: Davy, Micky, Mike and Peter, all of them wearing red velvet suits. They looked smashing! They sang some of the songs from their L.P., then each of them sang by theirself.

Gradually one by one the girls were fainting, crying, going hysterical, and one actually jumped over the balcony. I nearly fainted while I was there, it was so hot, with everybody tramping you down to get a look at the fabulous Monkees. I must admit I tramped down a couple of girls myself.

Girl.

I have many hobbies my favourite being boys—French especially. When I leave school (I can't wait for that day) I want to be an actress, journalist and choreographer and also to write books and plays and film scripts and have a bash at dress designing as a sideline; I don't think I could bear a regular job! I'm an atheist, I love alcohol, especially 'Rum and Black' and 'Cinzano Bianco', also 'Vin Rouge' at lunch time.

Girl.

SUBJECT OF GENERAL CONCERN

On 31st October Rolling Stone Brian Jones was taken to Wormwood Scrubs to start a nine-month sentence for drug offences. He admitted to being in possession of a quantity of hemp and allowing his flat to be used in the smoking of hemp. As Brian Jones was taken to Wormwood Scrubs many teenage girls wept.

Girl.

The Vietcong trapped in their lair
And now the riot in Grosvenor Square
And bombing of Hanoi so people say
Is the bloodiest deed in the world today.
Thousands of G.I.'s killed a day
And in go more to pave the way
And still LBJ doesn't care
About the way they win the war.

Boy.

One boy wrote a series of imaginary letters from Mr. George Brown to The Prime Minister, and his replies, and ended with a clipping from *The Times* of Mr. Brown's real resignation letter. This is how it begins.

EXCHANGE OF LETTERS

Certain letters which have not been released to the public have recently come into my possession. I have great pleasure in disclosing their contents today, as they provide an interesting insight into the reasons for the recent resignation of a prominent Cabinet Minister.
'My dear Harold,
I have been thinking over our tussle in the House at 1 a.m., and my last resignation attempt at 5 a.m. I now realise that I was too hasty in resigning, and though I think that we must do something about the way in which important Government decisions can be taken without consulting me, I would like to reassure you of my complete confidence in your leadership and this Government.
As you have not yet accepted my last resignation, I hereby withdraw it.
Yours,
George'.
'Dear Mr. Brown . . .'

MOVING TOWARDS A PUBLIC AUDIENCE

This move from peer group to public audience is taken a stage further by some of those who wrote stories or poems. Many of these are built round ideas of special interest to the teenage reader, but they have also an appeal to a much wider audience; in fact many of them can be accepted on the same terms as writing by adults. This does not mean that the peer group readers would like them any less; they are in fact the contributions which are likely to have been enjoyed most of all by the readers. The writers of these pieces are often combining the two approaches to the audience—through their guesses at others' interests, and through their own special concerns.

Most of the stories are about boy/girl relationships and several of them are concerned with the sexual aspects of these relationships. All those who wanted to write openly about sex, and most of those who set out to explore sexual relationships in any depth, chose to do so in a fictional narrative. A few may have written these stories just to show how uninhibited they could be—we had, after all, invited them to write exactly what they wanted to write—but others seem to have chosen to write a story to enable themselves to handle a subject they were deeply involved in, but one they were unwilling or unable to deal with in discursive prose.

. . . it seemed now it had really happened to me. We were in the bed about half an hour and not a word had been spoken. He got up, pulled me with him and we stood by the window kissing, with our bare bodies against each other. He picked up his clothes and started to dress, he nodded to me beckoning me to get dressed. We were both dressed by now, he grabbed hold of me in his arms and said "I love you", his first real words he had said to me and they were beautiful. I whispered the same back and we walked arm in arm down the stairs. We didn't go back to the party, he started to walk me home. We reached my door, he kissed me and said, "Well it was nice knowing you".

Girl.

In that story, the peer group audience probably determined the subject matter, and the writer was probably hoping to shock and delight her readers. She gives a fairly clear indication of what she is up to in a note at the end:

If anyone would like to write to me giving comments on this, or as a friendly relationship, my address is on the first page. I would like somebody who is good for a laugh.

But others, having selected a similar subject, were much more concerned about shaping the material into a form which measured up to their own standards of good writing. Here is the end of another story.

Once again a respectful silence endured in the compartment and again a soft floating mustiness descended like a curtain in the theatre at the end of a performance.

Walking arm in arm down the wide corridor the boy and girl looked in all reality the young lovers. The train stopped, rumbling and creaking. Coming to a door they kissed and then after a pause they got out, hesitating.

Alex winced under the sharp sunlight. He turned to the girl. 'I love you' he said.

An awkward silence surrounded and trapped them in an iron shell for a moment. She blushed and . . .

'I've got to go'.

'I'll see you soon, won't I?'

'Yeah, sure. Look, my parents are over there, I really must go'.

'Yes, bye then'.

'Goodbye'.

The girl then goes off to meet her parents, and he his. On the way home in the car he muses.

'What the hell shall I do about her', he murmered.

'What, dear?'

'Nothing, mum, nothing'.

Softer and more cautiously he thought out loud.

'I mean, everything has changed, hasn't it? I can't just live like before. After all, I'm sixteen, I'm mature and, I'm in love. I can't just drop her', then doubting, 'can I- No I can't desert her now. I must tell dad, he is easier to talk to.'

Comforted and strengthened by the opiate of resolution he sat back and relaxed. His resolution calmed him and strengthened him for the ordeal ahead.

Turning, 'Who was that girl you were with?' his mother asked.

Like a tidal wave of doubt, one sentence struck down his defence and drowned it in a whirling eddy. His comfort was snatched from around him and he felt naked sitting there.

'O-oh just a girl friend'.

'Oh? What is her name?'

'It doesn't matter', he said, 'you would not know her'.

Boy.

Writing of this kind leads us to suggest that another audience factor, apart from the 'adolescent to peer group' and 'writer to his readers', is exerting an influence. This boy is doing what many adult writers do, that is, making *himself* the first stage audience for his story. What he is offering to his public audience is something he wants them to take seriously, and to respond to with as much sensitivity, and insight, and judgment as he has put into writing it.

A minority of those who wrote stories felt no need even to choose a theme that would appeal specially to readers of their own age. One girl, although she was working in a group that had chosen *Youth* as its theme and she wrote *Youth in the Future* in the corner of the first page, seems simply to have written the story she wanted to write. This is how it begins:

THE RIGHT TO DIE

The situation was not noticed until it became desperate. It was strange that a race so advanced should overlook something so simple—so elementary. But perhaps that was the reason. It is often the case that a highly civilised race cannot comprehend the fundamental facts of life.

It had all begun when the secret had been discovered. The secret that man had striven so long to discover. Everyone had been shocked and thrilled. Man's biggest fear was death and now he had even overcome that.

If the people had not been so advanced there would have been an uproar when it was made known that the Secret had been discovered. But everyone knew that his turn would come in the end if he was patient —besides, the Ultimate Computer forbade violence of any kind and there would be merry Hell to pay if there was a disturbance.

The serum which granted the miracle was almost worshipped—treated as a god—if religion had not died away and been forbidden many years before.

The serum was tried out first on grade 3C people. Their intelligence was high enough to warrant their preservation, but not high enough to be a terrible loss if the experiment failed. It didn't fail and soon half the population had been given the serum of Eternal Youth. They were unbelievably happy.

THE SELF AND THE UNKNOWN READER

For some of these boys and girls, the fact that the readers were unknown was a special stimulus. Just enough was known about them to make the writers feel confident in approaching them. Some have been mentioned who made it an opportunity to write gossipy, mildly scandalous comments on their friends and teachers; others took it as a chance to show off and a few as a chance to be malicious. As far as we can tell, there are only two pieces which would be likely to annoy the teachers, though one can't be sure because different teachers set up totally different expectations.

But there were a few examples in all five classes of something of quite a different kind. This was the tendency to write about themselves in a way they would be unlikely to write for even their close friends. The audience category 'child (or adolescent) to trusted adult' is widely but thinly spread in our samples of writing for teachers. The writer puts himself into a relationship with his reader in which anything and everything may be written about, with the absolute confidence that the reader is sympathetic and can be relied on. Some outstanding examples of this kind of writing are to be found in Herbert Kohl's *36 Children*.[3]

We have from time to time been surprised by finding writing similar to this 'trusted adult' type in examinations. It seems that some adolescents imagine and project a similar relationship with an unknown reader; the opportunity to write for a complete stranger sometimes removes some inhibitions and they write about the things that matter most, or their uncertainties and worries.

Here, in the middle of a piece cast in the form of a letter, a girl suddenly drops her role of bright, chatty, fun-loving teenager, to be self-critical in a candid, open manner. This might not have been thought significant but for the fact that several others in her class commented on her moodiness and fits of depression. She is, we think, touching on the aspect of herself that makes her feel insecure.

I love Paris. I love art and design too, I'm fairly good at it but I need a lot of developments in my style. I'm always described as the moody girl because I'm very temperamental. That is the most outstanding feature of my personality. If you want to know what I look like, I'm very small, a little well built, a bit spotty though everyone thinks I've got a good skin, my hair is permed curly, I've blue eyes which people say are nice. I sometimes put a lot of make-up on them. In general I'm fat and ugly.

[3] Herbert Kohl: *36 Children*. Gollancz, 1968. New American Library, 1967.

She is, in fact, nothing of the kind.

Writing like this occurs in parts of the contributions of several members of all five classes. But, for a few, personal problems provided the focus for the whole piece. Here is the start of one; also by a girl:

I always seem to be in trouble with someone. I don't think I've done anything wrong but someone or other is always on at me for some reason or other.

It's usually my parents. If there is something I particularly want to do, or somewhere I particularly want to go I always seem to be doing something disastrously wrong just beforehand and then my parents say: "Right, that's it. You can't do it", or 'you needn't think you're going now. If you can't do something for us, we can't do anything for you'.

They always seem to misinterpret my actions.

Her piece is about five times this length, but it is all about the same problem.

The following one just might be fiction, but we think it probably isn't entirely so. Even if it is, it seems unlikely that the writer would want his friends to read it. He didn't put his name on it. The names have been altered.

HOME

I suppose if I had not been so engrossed in my own activities during the summer I would have realized sooner that something was wrong at home.

(The next two pages tell how he overhears an argument between his older brother and his parents. The brother, Mike, is leaving home because his parents dislike his girl friend. She is pregnant. A.McL.)

'Michael', thundered my father who, although left out of the argument, knew how to deal with rudeness. 'Apologise to your mother'.

'I'm sorry', said Mike shortly. 'We're leaving now. I will let you know when we are getting married, and we'll visit you for Tim's sake'.

'It's a bit late to think of him now, what have you done with him in the past, you never had a game with him without him coming in in tears; that boy's a nervous wreck, thanks to you'.

'I'm not arguing any more, Carol and I are leaving now, I'll send you our address'. I ran upstairs, and climbed into bed.

As the front door opened, I heard Carol say 'Please both of you, don't condemn us both out of hand. I know how you feel, but I truly love Mike. I am pregnant, it's not Mike's, but we are going to tell the child he is its father. Please, if you hate us both so much, don't show it by sending us away forever for Tim's sake'. The front door shut.

I hid my face under the bedclothes and began to cry.

Writing like this for a stranger can never be the same as writing for a known and trusted friendly adult, but it does have a good deal in common with it. It may also be a stage in the development towards something else. There may well be a point when adolescent writers realize that revealing themselves—their inner experience as well as their external world—not only provides a way of coming to terms with their experience, but is also a ready way to interest other people, especially when the expressing of the experience is given shape and form. So we think that writing for a trusted adult may provide another route along which some young writers may move towards writing for the unknown reader, and the general public.

It was suggested earlier that the writer himself provides a first audience for much worth-while writing, though this is often subordinated to the demands associated with some other audiences. Sometimes, however, the writing task itself exerts an influence which tends to keep the self audience in the foreground, particularly when the writing is a tentative exploration of ideas which are of special interest to the writer, and may not concern others much. One girl wrote a personal diary covering the week in which her form's folder of work was being compiled. It takes up eight closely written quarto pages—she also wrote a story, a discursive piece about pop groups, and drew five pictures of her friends and teachers—and it probably began as a modified letter to the unknown peer group. But by the fifth day she seems to be using it more and more as a way of ordering her own experience, and appraising her own actions for her own benefit, and any audience except herself is of secondary importance.

Again the names have been changed.

Monday 18th March 1968

Managed to get to school on time. I really hate Mondays it's my worst day. Terry wasn't in school today so I never saw him at all. I didn't really care. I've been thinking (it hurt!) I wouldn't really mind if he went out with Anita again.

People tell me they really used to like each other a lot, been brought up together or something.

They said the only reason he packed her up's because she was moving soon. She's a trouble maker. I hate her all over, ugh!

Well Terry phoned up and said that he'd meet me tomorrow in school and make arrangements if we go anywhere in the night. I doubt if we will. He said outright 'Chris, I'm going round Doreen's to see Anita, alright? See you tomorrow then, tellah'.

I really couldn't blame him, he liked her better than me when he went out with her, now I'm not sure.

Although this girl may, in her absorption with her own concerns, have largely lost her focus on her audience, the class that read this diary found it specially interesting. So do we. It seems that a move towards writing for the self may result in a heightening of interest on the part of the reader; such writing will very often find its own audience.

One of our wider audience categories, 'expert to laymen', failed to appear in this collection of work. All we can say then, about this category, is that the impulse to inform the unknown readers, or to let them catch a glimpse of the writer's expertise in a particular field, was not an important stimulus for the boys and girls in these five classes.

In one class, and to a lesser extent in two of the others, there is an interesting incidental effect. In this one class they wrote a great deal about each other, so that when one has read the thirty pieces, one has a detailed, composite picture of the class as a whole and some of its individual members. One boy is mentioned by name in eleven contributions, and by implication and innuendo in most of the others. The effect is a little like *Humphrey Clinker;* the leading characters are seen from so many angles that one feels one knows them very well; but this cannot be illustrated by a brief quotation. Some of the recipients of the folders were interested in the possibilities of this sort of composite presentation.

OTHER VARIABLES

There are many factors not so far mentioned which will obviously have had considerable influence on what these five classes wrote, but about which we can only make rudimentary comments. Teachers, not only in the year in which the work was done, but throughout their education up to that time, will have contributed in countless way to their ideas, interests and general orientation, and, in particular, will have helped to set up notions about what sort of thing it is possible or desirable to write on a particular occasion. But it is certainly not possible to attribute anything they wrote to the influence of any particular teacher, though in a different kind of survey it must be enormously interesting to attempt to do so.

There is a very wide distribution of ability, social class, family background and parents' educational expectations for their children in the five schools. However, we are not at this stage able to say very much about the effect of these factors on the response of pupils to the kind of opportunity we offered them. We know there is much to be said, but it will have to be deferred to a later stage in this research programme.

THE EFFECT OF OFFERING A WIDER AUDIENCE

In this investigation we set out to obtain more work which might come within our wider audience categories. In the event, nearly everything that was done came into one or other of these categories, with 'adolescent to peer group' and 'writer to his readers, or public', covering more than ninety per cent of the total.[4]

It only remains to make a brief comment on the quality of the work done. This was not, of course, our main concern on this occasion, though an appraisal of progress is built in to the whole of our four-year programme in these schools. In none of these pieces, not even those done in pencil on scraps of paper, has the writer failed to consider his audience. The feeling one has with poor quality work done in the normal course of events in school, that the writer is merely meeting the demands imposed on him, is absent. One might say that some of these pupils misjudged their audience, and others failed to interest them, but we believe none failed to take

---

[4] In an earlier analysis of 536 scripts done in the course of normal English work in 58 schools, 1.1% were classified as 'pupil (or adolescent) to peer group', and 4% as 'writer to his readers, or public'.

notice of them. So even the least inspiring work in this collection never falls to the level of ordinariness one meets at times in normal school work.

At the other end of the scale, there is a substantial amount of writing in the folders of all five classes which was, in the first place, listened to or read with delight and admiration by the classes who received it, and later proved so fascinating to the research team that we have come back to it again and again when we wanted to find examples of original and unusual writing. In a few cases we have been able to establish with the class teachers that what the pupils wrote on this occasion was better than what they usually do. What we think is much more significant is that a large amount of it is substantially different from what they normally do, and this may be why a large number of them seem to have welcomed the opportunity it gave them, and why almost all of them seem to have enjoyed reading it.

We believe, too, that we have some evidence here to suggest that, when writing for the general public is thought to be something to be aimed at as part of an English course, this may be assisted by taking account of the two routes towards it that have been described—first through extending and developing the idea of the peer group audience to the point at which it merges into the wider unknown audience, and second, by nurturing and cherishing, whenever we find it, the occasional impulse to write for a single, sympathetic and trusted adult, because in such writing, as the writer grows more mature and learns to judge his own writing by his own standards, he can advance to the point when he is ready to offer something of himself to the world in general.

Several poems were written in these five classes. Only one has so far been quoted, and that is hardly representative. It is perhaps reasonable to end with a poem in which it is possible to observe both the processes mentioned in the paragraph above. This writer's topic has some peer group orientation, but the poem itself is clearly 'writer to his readers'. Would he be able to write like this if he had not, at some time, been able to express himself freely for some trusted, sympathetic adult reader?

WHEN WE WERE SIX

When I was six, and sitting
Bored with master, mind and teachings,
In the musty heat of summer 'fifty-nine;
The ancient refuge of all schoolboys
Came to light,
And in this way I left the room—
For private business of my own.

My visit, prolonged to its utmost
Alas, was finished, and on going out,
With all intent of being bored,
Met my hushing school-girl chum,
Who, although had
Held my sphere of admiration,
Had not been dubbed with words to such effect.
With furtiveness she took me by the hand,
Unwilling at first, for I knew not,
And for that matter cared the less,
For being led, in such a way, by her:
But for once,
Exception to the rule, I went with more delight and zeal,
To find the worst or best to be.

There we sat, the corridor our company
and there, a pleasured face of pride,
Uncanny to a reckless child,
Beamed out, and with a mother's care,
Revealed a 'plane;
A shining frame; and quickly with a pre-staged act,
Brought forth her dainty dish.
And there against the science rule,
Our time stood still; and where
The waitress girl resumed her form
And waited till I sipped the goodness of her wine;
And where good Cupid shot unique,
And for this once aimed true,
My heart waits;
And fears the day to come, where girl and plane
Lie hidden in the depths of memory;
And where, I doubt again, our genuine hearts
Would meet another time.

Or truly, if by now, the other heart has gone.

A WRITING LESSON

John Harvey

Situation: general. Harrow Way is a co-educational secondary modern school, which, at the time of writing, has been open for nearly two years. It began with a first year intake and is intended to build up a year at a time. The first and second years at present in the school are divided alphabetically into five groups for all lessons: there is no remedial group as such, though some children are extracted from English and Math lessons for teaching in small groups.

Situation: specific. The lesson I am going to describe was given in a single forty minute period with a second year group; there were twenty-eight children in the group at the time. While there is only one child in the group with a reading age of below nine, there are only three children of particularly high English ability.

Myths: one. With a mixed-ability group, one is unable to introduce material and work of a high enough level to stretch the most able children due to the need to cater specifically for those who are less able.

I am sure that the opposite of this is true. However well intentioned the 'D' and 'E' stream teacher may be, a combination of factors generally force him to the position where he selects 'easier' material for his groups than he does for his 'A' stream. The joy of a mixed-ability group is that all of the children are exposed to the most interesting and demanding material, and that in the mixed-ability situation they are able to benefit from and enjoy it. We do not aim our material at the slowest or at the average; we simply choose the most interesting material we can find.

Myths: two. It is neither possible nor desirable to 'class teach' a mixed-ability group.

There is a need for a great deal of small-group and individual work, just as there would seem to be in a streamed group. There are also occasions when the group as a whole seems to benefit from

From *English in Education* (Autumn, 1969), pp. 24–28.
John Harvey is the Head of English at the Harrow Way Secondary Modern School.

sharing and discussing an experience with the teacher. It is also possible to embark upon a writing lesson which is essentially teacher-directed.

The work outlined below is by no means representative of the normal way in which we would approach written work in the school; we hope there is no normal way. It is perhaps a useful variant, to be used sparingly. There would seem to be value in asking the children to think and write in an intense and compressed situation. (Since teaching this and similar lessons, I have read *Poetry in the Making*: Faber in which Ted Hughes lays great stress on this technique).

For the lesson to be in any way successful, three things seem necessary. The group must have had a good deal of previous experience of imaginative writing; they must be used to reading their writing aloud and listening to the work of others; they must be willing to be quiet during the periods of writing and listening.

The children have preparation books in which most written work is worked on in the initial stages. These were taken out and I wrote the words 'Red and White' on the blackboard. We had several weeks of snow and I asked them to write a few lines describing snow in a specific place: in a field, on the road, on the trees and so on. The writing could be either in poetry or prose form; most chose poetry. The group were told they had just a few minutes to do this, after which I would ask a number of them to read out loud what they had written. This was to be the 'White' of the title.

At this point, Ann, who is one of the most able children in the group, wrote:

> A flat stretch of white, downey feathers,
> Lying flat in a deserted field.

Straight in with a metaphor. Edward, who is of average ability, wrote:

The garden has a sparkling white dazzling snow, glistening in the morning sun soft, refreshing, tingling.

Russell, a boy somewhat below average, wrote the following— and here as elsewhere I have kept to the original spelling and punctuation.

Ice on a lake shiny slipery and smooth and impossible to walk on, the water under neath moving flowing.

We listened to perhaps half-a-dozen children reading their first pieces, after which I asked them to bring in the contrast, to add the red, to make the red blood. They could simply continue with their first piece of writing, or write a separate piece.
Ann:

> A bird falls dead,
> Bright red blood ouzes from a small hole
> In its chest.
> It merges with the whiteness of the snow
> Turning the snow to a bright pink.

Edward:

Now, a dead bird falls on the crisp snow dead from freezing. A fox comes, bites the scrawney article. Now nothing left but dark scarlet blood contrast against gleaming whiteness.

Russell:

Blood, red glowing and dull from the dead carcass of a rat oozing into the snow turning the snow pinkish and watery.

As throughout the lesson, I had moved round the room while the writing was in progress, helping with spelling but not with ideas. When we had listened to some of these pieces being read aloud, I passed round a duplicated sheet of extracts, which we read through together. The sheet was as follows

> The fox drags its wounded belly
> Over the snow, the crimson seeds
> Of blood burst with a mild explosion,
> Soft as excrement, bold as roses.

R.S. Thomas: January

> The eagle glides
> Noiselessly to his capture,

Digs his talons into his cousin;
He tumbles down
To the earth below.
The white snow turns pink
As the blood of the beast
Soaks into it.

Stephen Lewis: A Night in Scotland

. . . the blood of the slain lay caked with the snow which covered the ground and . . . when the snow melted, the blood flowed along the furrows and ditches for a distance of two to three miles.

From the Yorkshire Archaeological and Topographical Journal describing the Battle of Towton in 1461

. . . Recall the cold
Of Towton on Palm Sunday before dawn,
Wakefield, Tewkesbury: fastidious trumpets
Shrilling into the ruck; some trampled
Acres, parched, sodden or blanched by sleet,
Stuck with strange-postured dead. Recall the wind's
Flurrying, darkness over the human mire.

Geoffrey Hill: Funeral Music

Reddish ice tinged the reeds; dislodged, a few
Feathers drifted across; carrion birds
Strutted upon the armour of the dead.

Geoffrey Hill: Funeral Music

The second extract comes from a poem entered by one of the boys in another group for the previous year's poetry competition. I read the extracts to the group without discussion or explanation. They were then asked to write a longer, finished piece of poetry or prose with the title 'Red and White', which could be a continuation of their first pieces of work, or something different again. About 70% began work on a new piece, and most of these wrote about war, due, I suppose, to the impact of the Hill poem and the extract from the Yorkshire Journal. Interestingly, though, most of those who wrote about war set their writing in the present century. Even where an

entirely new idea was now worked upon, there are signs of a carry-
ing-through of words and phrases from the earlier pieces. They were
given between ten and fifteen minutes for this part of the work.

Ann retained the idea of 'feathers', the colour change from white
to pink. It is probably not one of her very best poems, though the
final image does much to save it.

> Blood soaked bodies lie crumpled,
> Strewn across the plateau,
> Their arms ripped from their bodies.
> White feathers of snow
> Filter through the trees
> Land slowly and silently
> Over the bodies.
> Drops of scarlet blood
> Drip into the snow.
> The snow changes
> From a bright red
> To a rainbow pink.
> Empty shells
> Fill with blood,
> A trophy of war.

In the final version which she wrote into her exercise book later in
the week, Ann changed the word 'bodies' in the first line to 'corpses',
and 'plateau' in the second to 'field'; the punctuation was a little
tidied and the final word given a capital 'W'.

Edward's poem retains the idea of freezing, but otherwise is a
completely different piece of writing. I found it by far the most
satisfying piece of work done by anyone in the group; the language
is accurate and evocative, the tone is individual and constant, the
idea portrayed at the end mature. I would think it is the finest poem
Edward has written since coming to the school.

> As you pass the stiff bodies,
> frozen in the snow, their eyes
> frozen open, looking, as if to say . . .
> Why?
> A rifle lying by its firer, still, useless.
> Frozen horror lingers in a thin mist, a wind drifts
> through the hollow battle field. A slight slow
> falling snow obscures the dead.
> A tank rumbles its passengers

to their doom. Red blood lying cold in the snow.
Look around. Grey overcoats on red bodies.
Peace, horrible death-smelling peace, now that
the wind has stopped.
All of this terrible feud, blood, death, destruction.
All that is written in the papers is
GERMANS DEFEATED IN RUSSIA.

By chance, Edward was the first to read his completed work aloud and I can remember the chill of excitement as he read it.

Russell's piece of prose had also moved from nature to war.

Death the soldiers were led to their death like pigs to the slaughter. They were the (unreadable) the forlorn (unreadable) left behind to their death so others could escape, courageous bold and brave, not afraid of death but waiting for it, then, Charge, with bayonets fixed they charged they charged their last charge they were cut down by a hail of bullets, but kept going until they were wiped out now they were dead every man was dead the earth was stained with their blood then it snowed slowly silently. It snowed beauring those brave men and the snow in memorial turned red.

Now Russell would almost certainly have had help with some of the spellings here—bayonet, courageous, slaughter—and more assistance was, obviously forthcoming, from teacher, friend or dictionary, before the final version reached his exercise book.

Death the soldiers were led to there death like pigs to the slaughter. They were the rearguard the forlorn hope. Left behind to die, so others could fight again. Courageous bold and brave, not afraid of death but waiting for it then, charge, with bayonets fixed they charged, they were cut down by a hail of bullets, but kept going! Until they were wiped out. Now they were dead every man was dead the earth was stained with their blood then it snowed, slowley, silentley, gently, and it was the last time they would ever charge. I bearied those brave men all of them lost. The snow turned pinky red in memorial.

He has not just corrected errors of accuracy, in the course of doing which he has made further mistakes, he has obviously thought about the writing as a whole and has tried to reshape it to achieve the right impact.

I would judge the results of the lesson as pleasing and worthwhile. The method seems to have much to commend it, with groups
of mixed-ability or otherwise, though I should not like to see it used
too often. It does provide a group with the opportunity to share a
creative experience of a fairly intense nature and to achieve a
definite end within a short period of time.

SOME CONSIDERATIONS
WHEN MARKING

Leslie Stratta

INTRODUCTION

For many teachers of English, especially young and inexperienced teachers, the marking of written work can be a problem. There are several, but different, reasons for this. Teachers are sceptical about the value of marking, especially its ability to improve written competence; they are uncertain what to look for, and consequently are uncertain about criteria; some are unhappy about marking 'creative' writing, arguing that by doing so violence is done to the pupils' 'creativity'. Because there is this uncertainty, it might be profitable to explore the subject in an article of this kind, considering some of the attitudes, values and standards teachers of English might bring to their pupils' written work, in the hope that some of their uncertainties can be resolved. The article will, therefore, confine itself to the day to day on-going writing of the classroom rather than writing for examination purposes,[1] and it will be slanted more towards secondary than primary writing, although it is hoped that some of the exploration will also be of benefit to teachers in the top end of the primary school.

THE WRITING EXPERIENCE

Before considering marking in any detail, it might be profitable to consider first, albeit briefly, some aspects of the writing experience

From *English in Education* (Autumn, 1969), pp. 45–56. Reprinted with permission of the publisher and the author.

Leslie Stratta is a Lecturer in Education at The University of Birmingham, England.

[1] Britton, J. N., Martin, N. C. and Rosen, H., *Multiple Marking of English Composition*, The Schools Council Examinations Bulletin No. 12 (H.M.S.O. 1966). This is one of the most recent discussions of marking English Composition for examination purposes.

itself, in the hope that these will throw into sharper perspective the role of marking.

Vigotsky, discussing writing in *Thought & Language*, suggests that 'the development of writing does not repeat the developmental history of speaking. Written speech is a separate linguistic function, differing from oral speech in both structure and mode of functioning. Even its minimal development requires a high level of abstraction. It is speech in thought and image only, lacking the musical, expressive, intonational qualities of oral speech. In learning to write, the child must disengage himself from the sensory aspect of speech and replace words by images of words. Speech that is merely imagined and that requires symbolisation of the sound image in written signs (i.e. a second degree of symbolisation) naturally must be as much harder than oral speech for the child as algebra is harder than arithmetic. Our studies show that it is the abstract quality of written language that is the main stumbling block, not the underdevelopment of small muscles or any other mechanical obstacles.

Writing is also speech without an interlocutor, addressed to an absent or imaginary person or to no one in particular—a situation new and strange to the child. Our studies show that he has little motivation to learn writing when we begin to teach it. He feels no need for it and has only a vague idea of its usefulness. In conversation, every sentence is prompted by a motive. Desire or need lead to request, question to answer, bewilderment to explanation. The changing motives of the interlocutors determine at every moment the turn oral speech will take. It does not have to be consciously directed—the dynamic situation takes care of that. The motives for writing are more abstract, more intellectualised, further removed from immediate needs. In written speech, we are obliged to create the situation, to represent it to ourselves. This demands detachment from the actual situation'.[2]

If Vigotsky is correct in arguing that 'In learning to write, the child must disengage himself from the sensory aspect of speech and replace words by images of words', that 'writing is also speech without an interlocutor, addressed to an absent or imaginary person or to no one in particular' and that unlike speech 'The motives for writing are more abstract, more intellectualized, further removed

[2] Vigotsky, L. S., *Thought and Language* (M.I.T. & Wiley, 1962), pp. 98–9.

from immediate needs', then it is small wonder that many pupils find writing difficult to master. The problem is shown even more clearly in a further point made by Vigotsky when he argues that 'the physiological functions in which written speech is based have not begun to be developed in the proper sense when instruction in writing starts. It must build on barely emerging rudimentary processes'.[3] Although Vigotsky is talking about pupils at the infant and early junior stage, some of the points he is making have relevance for older pupils, for, as we all know, although many pupils manage eventually to overcome these difficulties and write with ease and confidence, many do not, and leave school only partially or barely literate. Part of the reason for this may be poor and haphazard teaching, but part may be that many pupils continue for quite some time to find it difficult to write to 'an absent or imaginary person or to no one in particular', and consequently continue to find it difficult 'to create the situation (and) to represent it to (themselves)'.

Before discussing further the implications of Vigotsky's argument, it might be profitable, at this juncture, to consider, again briefly, why it is important for pupils to write with competence. One obvious reason is that in a literate society people need to be literate, and writing is one aspect of literacy. However, another reason, not quite so obvious, is that in the act of writing we are encountering experience in a different manner from when we talk, which is the mode of language we operate in most of the time. Whereas talk is, on the whole, a spontaneous, public mode of language which we are continually using to organise, order, and make sense of the flux of experience we are encountering hourly in our lives, writing is a more reflective and private mode of language, when we have more time to think over our experiences and ideas and explore them anew, perhaps seeing them afresh and gaining new insights into them. Presumably, as teachers of English, we want to encourage a reflective attitude in our pupils, and a preparedness to explore anew. Writing would seem appropriate in developing these abilities.

THE CLASSROOM CONTEXT

If writing is a more reflective and private mode of language than talk in which to operate upon experience, and if Vigotsky is right

[3] Vigotsky, L. S., *Thought and Language* (M.I.T. & Wiley, 1962), p. 100.

when he says that 'it is the abstract quality of written language that is the main stumbling block', then the implications of both for the teacher of English are far reaching. It is obviously important that the English classroom must be a place where reflective work can go on, but equally important it must be a place where pupils, whether junior or secondary, are helped through the difficulties of operating in a mode of language more abstract than speech. And the difficulties may, at times, be as great for the pupil with good syntactical control who is trying to explore new or difficult experiences, as they are probably all the time for the pupil with poor syntactical control who is exploring more familiar experience. In order then to help pupils, especially those who have poor control of writing, to move with less difficulty to the more abstract activity of writing, it would seem sensible if initially some attempt were made to explore experience in more concrete terms, where pupils would be more likely to be at ease, and consquently succeed. One obvious starting point is through talk, another is drama. Through talk pupils begin to probe and explore their experiences in a very concrete manner. And by initially interchanging impressions and ideas in this concrete manner, they can begin to get at least a partial control over the subject eventually to be written about.

But for talk to be successful during this initial probing, there must be a climate of mutual respect between pupil and pupil, and pupil and teacher; the classroom must become a place in which it is natural to talk over things, to put forward very personal or tentative, even sometimes silly thoughts, without fear of ridicule or scorn. It must be a place where talking over ideas and exchanging impressions can take place in small groups, as well as in the larger class group. And it must be a place where, during these initial probings, the teacher sees his role changing as the situation demands. The delicacy and complexity of his role is hinted at in this passage from *Growth through English*. The 'teacher can help by noticing and reinforcing a potential change in the level or direction of the discussion, summing up an attitude perhaps, making an issue quite explicit, or calling for an instance when generalizing seems to have lost touch with reality'.[4]

It is in the context of this kind of classroom atmosphere, together with the awareness of the difficulties that pupils face when trying

---

[4] Dixon, J., *Growth through English* (N.A.T.E. Reading, 1967), pp. 34–5.

to write, that we teachers of English need to ask the question—
what then is the function of our marking?

SOME CRITERIA

Many of the important issues can probably be quickly, and
dramatically, raised by looking at the following piece of writing[5]
from a boy aged 16 years.

SAYING GOODBYE

Only an hour to ago befor I leves to cattes the train which will take me
to portmorth with a thurnded other fellows, Going to the same place. for
all your nown they mike be on the sane boat. I wounder whats its like in
the R.N. Mike be good, seeing atlacing all day. And new port each week.
half an hour to before the train. I wonder that mums thinkin I pett his
evy her eyes out right now. Shes all, right, she won be seeing men lie every
day and night. she got dads pensiver and the ransen bock. finteen mins
heft peter get redy for the startion's Come on mum where's dad, 'In the
car'. 'right'. We araidy at the startions the train just aggraidy. every
kissing their muns dads wives childs good bye. We good-bye mums
goodbye I write to you evert day and I see you every time I am, on leve.
Bye mun, bye dad bye they must be take it bad. her only son going to war
for the first time. Bye.

Howard.

Because there is a problem of deciphering, this ill-spelt, poorly
punctuated piece may, at first sight, cause irritation, difficulty, indifference and even hostility. However, if one takes the trouble to
get below its surface appearance and endeavours to read the piece
as the pupil might have wanted it to be read, the transformation
can be both dramatic and rewarding.

SAYING GOODBYE

Only an hour to go before I leave to catch the train, which will take
me to Portsmouth with a hundred other fellows going to the same place.
For all you know, they might be on the same boat. I wonder what it's like

---

[5] London Association for the Teaching of English, *Assessing Compositions*
(Blackie, 1965), p. 19. This pamphlet is a valuable discussion of the problems
of assessing composition.

in the R.N. It might be good seeing the Atlantic all day, and a new port each week.

Half an hour to go before the train. I wonder what mum's thinking. I bet she's crying her eyes out right now. She's all right. She won't be seeing men die every day and night. She's got dad's pension and the ration book.

Fifteen minutes left. Better get ready for the station.

'Come on mum, where's dad?'

'In the car'.

'Right'.

We're all ready at the station. The train is just ready. Every one is kissing their mums, dads, wives and children goodbye.

'Well goodbye mum. Goodbye. I'll write to you every day, and I'll see you every time I'm on leave. Bye mum. Bye dad. Bye'.

They must be taking it badly. Her only son going to the war for the first time.

'Bye'.

                                                                    Howard.

Once deciphered, we see immediately that the piece, at several levels, is very competent indeed. For example, there is a skilful suggestion of time passing, with the tempo increasing as the minutes ebb away; there is a sensitive awareness of the situation, shown exceptionally cleverly from one angle; the writer is able to move easily from the inner world of the young man's thoughts to the outer world of action and decision making.

By approaching pieces of writing of this kind then in a positive rather than negative frame of mind, we are more likely to discover where, and in what manner, the pupil has succeeded. And by taking the trouble to dig below the surface appearance, the teacher demonstrates that he is genuinely interested in what the pupil is trying to say. (Of course, to be able to do this, the teacher has to be a sensitive and practised reader).

Once one approaches marking in this way, however, looking first for achievement, the question of standards is immediately raised, for despite this pupil's sensitivity and skill, the fact still remains that his control is poor at the very important levels of syntax and spelling, both crucial aids to the reader. It is at moments like this that one is brought sharply up against the question—how is one to respond to the writing of one's pupil's? Could it not be argued by demonstrating to the pupil that one is genuinely interested in what he has to say, despite his obviously poor control of syntax and spelling, that this is tantamount to accepting slovenliness and sloppiness? If, of course, the teacher sees his role as assessor, marking each piece of writing against a fixed standard, this standard being concerned in the main with syntactical and spelling accuracy, then any response which is sympathetic to the writing despite these deficiencies could be construed in this way. If, however, the teacher believes that it is essential for his pupils to learn to handle the written mode of language flexibly, sensitively, exactly and fluently, so that the langauge used, across the spectrum of personal to impersonal styles, conveys the experience into words in as faithful a manner as each pupil is individually capable of at that moment; and if he wants his pupils to become increasingly aware of the possibilities of language, its subtleties, power and limitations, then he will know that response is more complex than being concerned mainly with syntax and spelling; just as each piece of writing is concerned with more than only this. Consequently, he will know that marking is a more complex activity than merely spotting syntactical and spelling errors. In recognising a pupil's strength the teacher is not automatically endorsing his present limitations, being sympathetic need not mean an acceptance of inferior work from a sentimental attitude to the pupil. A sympathetic approach will accept the pupil's present standard as a starting point, but will always desire to raise it in the best possible way. But how to raise it is, of course, what teachers of English, in the main, find very difficult.

SOME PRACTICE

If the teacher accepts each pupil's present standard as a starting point, it soon becomes obvious that these will differ between pupils even in the same class, let alone the same year. Consequently, responding and marking, if they are to be most helpful to each individual, will have to be concerned with individual needs, and must be thought of as means of helping each pupil in his personal growth to maturity. Howard's needs, for example, are very different from this 14 year old's, who says little but with greater control of syntax and spelling.

FACES

A person's face gives you your first impression of them, yet you must be careful of the long thin-lipped criminal's face which conceals a loving heart. Or equally careful of the jolly, round-faced murderer, whom you would not associate in any way with crime. Yet some are easier to decide about; the butler's quiet dignity, the porter's honest boredom, the schoolboy's happy smile during games, his bored look over the evening's prep. Quiet concentration is often evident in the face of someone reading.

Faces are to a certain extent a person's individual badge. They come in all shapes, sizes, and expressions. Long faces, round faces, craggy faces, thin lips, thick lips, blue eyes, grey eyes, moustaches, beards, clean-shaven faces, hooked noses, straight noses. Faces show many of the person's thoughts and reactions, through the eyes, but mainly through the shape of the mouth, or what it says. Faces can have many expressions, sad, happy, laughing, crying, contented, painted, smiling, surprised, shocked, angry. Indeed a face is what gives you your first impression of somebody.

Probably the most effective way of helping each pupil is to discuss his work with him individually. If, as has been suggested, the classroom is a place where things are talked over in an atmosphere of mutual trust and respect, then the talking over of individual work on completion will give the teacher the opportunity to show in some detail where the work succeeds and where it might be improved or reshaped. It also reaffirms the teacher's interest in his pupils as individuals. This, however, is perhaps a counsel of perfection at least for the secondary school teacher, for the classes of thirty or more pupils and perhaps only five or six periods of English per week, he cannot see each pupil individually after each piece of writing. He can, though, see some, perhaps four or five. And if he is systematic, he can perhaps see all his class individually two or three times per term, which is better than not at all. There is also something to be gained from talking over the work with individuals, or groups of pupils, while they are in the process of writing. By doing this, the teacher can advise and suggest in a manner which has immediate personal relevance, something not easily done if the work is taken away on completion. Similarly, correcting can be explained in an individual manner. Points of syntax, for example, have a better chance of being understood because of this individual attention. Again with classes of thirty or more, individual attention is difficult; but if the teacher works systematically with different pupils each time writing takes place, he can, with luck, see each pupil individually approximately once every three weeks or so.

Most marking, however, takes place away from the classroom on completion of the writing. And this can have its advantages, in that the teacher can consider coolly each piece of work free from the immediate pressures of the classroom situation. The suggestions which follow may be more appropriate for this kind of practice.

Marking for individual needs may frequently mean marking selectively. And this can take different forms. For example, were Howard's work to be marked comprehensively at the level of syntax and spelling, one could have the teacher write as much as the pupil, which would be ineffective for two reasons. Firstly, there would almost be far too many different kinds of corrections for him to understand and begin to come to terms with, and secondly, more importantly, he would almost certainly be demoralised. However, if one were to mark the syntax and spelling selectively, concentrating perhaps at the level of syntax on full stops for sentence endings and capital letters for sentence beginnings, and at the level of spelling on some of the most frequently used words, such as 'go' and 'before',[6] the pupil might have a better chance of understanding his weaknesses, which might subsequently result in his gaining a more sure control of the written mode.

Another form of selective marking, at the level of syntax or spelling, is to mark in some detail perhaps only the first or final side of a piece of written work. In marking only the first side, one is probably concentrating on the most controlled part of the work, and in marking only the final side, one is concentrating on probably the least controlled, when one's pupils may well have been flagging. Individual needs will determine where the teacher chooses to concentrate his attention.

Selective marking need not, of course be concentrated exclusively on syntax or spelling. One could, for example, inform the pupils beforehand that the piece of writing will be marked for ability to describe a person's external appearance realistically, or to organise the points in an argument, or for an exciting adventure, and so on.

---

[6] McNally, J. and Murray, W., *Key Words to Literacy* (Schoolmaster Publishing Co. Ltd., London, 1962). This publication has a useful list of the most frequently used words.

In this way, the pupil's attention can be focussed on an aspect of writing the teacher feels it important for him, at that moment, to try to gain more control of, without there being undue distraction from other aspects. As has already been argued, one is, of course, working towards mastery of many aspects, not least syntax and spelling, but for many pupils this is a slow and difficult task, which may be helped, at least in the early stages of their attempting something new, by being invited to concentrate only on this new aspect and being assured that the writing will be marked selectively.

One important consideration when marking is to recognise that writing is not an undifferentiated task, but that there are several different kinds of writing tasks, and many pupils will find not all of them easy to control. The kinds of linguistic resources and strategies that a person needs in order to handle these different writing tasks are as yet unknown, but what some teachers are slowly beginning to realise is that many pupils seem to find narrative easier to handle than argument, and it may be this sequence which pupils need to move through in order to gain a flexible and fluent control of different writing styles, from the personal to impersonal.[7] In the light of this, undifferentiated judgments on a pupil's ability to write must be seen as crude assessments indeed of his ability. As we mark, we must have some awareness of the different demands each writing task makes, and consequently mark accordingly. A breakdown in syntax need not necessarily be due to carelessness, but could equally be caused by the pupil attempting to grapple with a complex, or painful experience, which is just eluding him at that moment, either because he cannot quite control the style of language which the experience demands, or because he cannot quite focus up the experience sharply enough.

Yet another consideration the teacher must be aware of is his prejudices regarding subject matter, and pupils. To be objective is, of course, difficult, but the teacher, when marking, must be concerned not to let his prejudices cloud his judgment. A pupil he likes, writing about a subject he likes, is in grave danger of not being marked or advised for his needs, if the teacher is blind to his own prejudices.

[7] Britton, J. N., Martin, N. C. and Rosen, H., *Abilities to Write* (*New Education*, October, 1966).

I should like now to consider the comments one makes about the written work of pupils, and the giving of numerical marks for each piece. If, as I have tried to argue, responding and marking is a positive activity, aimed to help pupils gain better control of the written mode, and to help them in their personal growth to maturity, then the comments the teacher makes, both orally and written, are of vital importance. It is, therefore, essential that they are personally meaningful to the pupil, showing him where he personally has succeeded and where he personally needs to concentrate more attention. Thus, comments such as 'poor' or 'good' tell the pupil little or nothing, and suggest that the teacher is either uncertain about how to respond, or is unwilling to do so. To tell Howard, for example, that he must 'try harder with punctuation', or that his work is 'fair' would almost certainly be meaningless. It might be more profitable to comment that he has 'sensitively caught the young man's thoughts and skilfully suggested the passing of the final hour before departure'. Positive personal comment such as this can help him to accept more readily the further comments one would want to make on some aspect of the uncertain control of syntax.

With regard to numerical marking, it can be argued that if marking is for the pupil's benefit, it is essentially the teacher's remarks, and not numerical marks, which are important. Consequently there is no need to mark numerically and pupils begin to accept this. While I personally am sympathetic to this point of view, the fact remains that many teachers will not be convinced of this, arguing that pupils prefer to receive marks in addition to comment. This being the case, how then is one to mark Howard's piece? At the level of imaginative insight, and control of time passing, his work would score high, perhaps eight or nine out of ten; but at the level of syntax and spelling, his work is poor and would score low, perhaps only one or two out of ten. How does one resolve this conflict? If one averages out the two marks and gives five out of ten, this again would tell Howard nothing. It certainly would not tell him in what respects the writing has succeeded or failed. One partial resolution, and it is only a partial resolution, is to give two marks, one for technical control, the other for imaginative insight, good argument, or whatever it is that one has required of the pupils. At least, by dong this, one is telling the pupil something more meaningful about his work, than any crude global mark will tell, for he does realise, to some degree, where he has succeeded and where more effort needs to be concentrated.

At this juncture, it might be worth considering those pupils who are never really poor, but who never really produce exciting work. If marks are being given, does one continually give these pupils an average mark? If one is convinced that the pupil is trying, it would seem to me that a never varying average mark hardly encourages him. If marking is for personal needs, then it would seem to me that there is a pressing need, in order to encourage him, for the averagely competent pupil to be told every so often that his work is very good, whether or not it really is. Nothing can be more depressing than to try hard yet never have one's work enthused over.

PREVENTING ERRORS

So far, this article has been discussing the kinds of responses we, as teachers of English, might make to the work after it has been written. I should like now to consider what we might do, prior to receiving the finished work, in order to help pupils gain more sure control of the written mode, especially at the level of syntax and spelling.

An important consideration, frequently lost sight of in the secondary school especially, is that a pupil needs to be given sufficient time to write. If, as has been argued, writing is a more reflective, personal way of encountering experience than the more spontaneous public way of talk, and we think it essential that our pupils be encouraged to develop a more reflective attitude to experience than some, at least, have already, then they must be given time to reflect. The secondary school timetable, chopped up daily, as it is, into several small chunks, too often militates against this. Where possible writing ought to take place within a double rather than a single period, or if this is not convenient and writing is started during a single period, time should be allowed, either at home or in a subsequent period, for the work to be completed. The quality of the writing will almost certainly be that much poorer if pupils are constantly racing against the clock; and this will be especially so if they are encountering a new style, or exploring a new facet of experience, for the first time.

If pupils then are to be given time to reflect, they must also be encouraged to do so. Too often, with students in training at least, one sees interesting preparatory work have less effect, because pupils are not restrained from writing immediately about almost the first thing which appeals to them, or enters their heads. Had they been encouraged to make notes before writing, in order to try to sort out and crystallise their ideas more sharply, the quality of their work would, almost certainly, have been that much better. Obviously, with pupils struggling to gain a rudimentary control of writing, one would not, at first, insist on note making, for the prior aim with them is to facilitate ease and desire to write. But once a measure of control has been gained, it is important to encourage a more reflective attitude.

In addition, it is also important to encourage pupils to work more carefully and meticulously. Many errors of syntax and spelling, for example, are caused through carelessness, not ignorance, and can be eradicated, in time, when pupils are encouraged to check over their work carefully before handing it in. It is important, however, that they are systematically reminded to do this, for unless this is done with each piece of work, meticulous habits may never be formed, at least with some pupils. This is especially so with work done at home, for here there may be distractions which help to re-inforce, or even cause, careless attitudes. Consequently, work done at home will often need to be read through more carefully before it is handed in, and it would seem sensible, therefore, if the teacher himself collected it in the English lesson, but before doing so, allowed some minutes for it to be checked through.

Despite all that one does in helping pupils, there are some who seem always to find aspects of writing, especially syntax, difficult to control. It may be, as Vigotsky argues, that writing is 'speech in thought and image only, lacking the musical, expressive, in-tonational qualities of oral speech', and that for this reason these pupils are unable to hold written sentence rhythms and tunes in their heads. This problem can, at times, be overcome if the pupil is asked to read aloud his work, either to the teacher working with him individually, or on completion and prior to handing in. On reading aloud, many pupils seem to hear more clearly the sentence rhythms and tunes, and often discover the errors themselves.

HANDING BACK

Equally important as writing is the manner in which the written work is handed back for unless this is done thoughtfully and tactfully, the time spent on reading and commenting on the work can be largely time wasted. If all the pupil does, after his writing has been returned, is to glance cursorily at the comments, note a mark if one has been given, and finally confine the work to the limbo of his desk, to be taken out again only when called upon to write a further piece, then most of the teacher's effort will have been wasted. And as importantly, an opportunity will have been lost to extend each pupil's horizons, through discussing and savouring the work of the whole class. Time spent handing back writing can be time well invested, and if most is to be gained from this activity, it cannot be hurried.

Perhaps its most valuable aspect is that the pupils are considering language in operation, trying to understand more about words and experience. Also valuable is that in discussing their work they are being helped to build up both confidence in ability to control the written mode, and pride in achievement. But in order for this to happen, it is again essential that response starts positively. The following piece, written by a 13 year old, might be well worth discussing positively before one draws attention to its shortcomings.

A BUILDING SITE

The strong muscular men swing their mullets, sweat with the saw at the toughest wood, laying and cementing the bricks in their rows, and controlling the various machinery. The powerfull cranes move to and fro carrying their heavy loads from one place to another, the loaded lorries bring continuously the various materials required, and the sound of sturdy drills burying themselves deep into the stuborn gravel.

The sound of noisey hammering, of tractors, and drills echoes around the site as men set about their work. The foreman shouting his orders destinct and clear as he inspects the work, and men talking as they give each other an helping hand.

If one were to choose this piece to discuss with a class, one might focus on its rhythm, for this, I would suggest, is one of its strengths. The discussion might, for example, explore the muscularity of the rhythm, and ask what, if anything this adds to the experience, echoing, as it does, the muscularity and toughness of the men and their work. And if it were thought to be appropriate, one might, in addition, introduce another piece for consideration, perhaps from an adult writer, where rhythm again echoes sense. By looking at an example of writing from the pupil where the experience is probably more familiar, and juxtaposing it against one from an adult where the experience may be less familiar, one can extend individual experience.

Or one might choose to explore the interesting, if occasional, use of vocabulary such as 'sturdy drills' and 'stubborn gravel', by asking the class to consider in what way the meaning would alter, and whether this would be important, if the writer had written 'hard gravel' instead of 'stubborn gravel', and 'strong drills' instead of 'sturdy drills'.

Group discussion of this kind, sympathetically exploring how a pupil has tried to order experience and put it into words, can open new horizons into experience for the whole class, and, as importantly, illustrate something of the possibilities of choices in language, and how these modify experience.

In addition to discussion of this kind, one can discuss points of syntax with the class, especially those which might be creating difficulties. This might be done by writing on the board an example from the work, where perhaps the control has broken down, and then inviting the class to discuss how it might be improved. In this manner the pupils are examining an example of living language (as distinct from many 'exercises', the language of which is usually sterile and divorced from experience), where a pupil has tried to organize experience for a purpose. In addition, one is hoping that the pupils are beginning to understand why mistakes are being made.

If the comments written by the teacher at the end of a piece of work are to be read and understood, pupils will need time for this. An appropriate moment might be after a selection of their work has been discussed, and all of it returned. Pupils can then settle down to read the comments, ask for further elucidation where needed, and then perhaps write some corrections, for example reshaping a sentence or two where control has broken down, or where the meaning has faltered.

DISPLAYING WORK

For a pupil's written work to have its fullest impact, it needs to be read, not only by the teacher, but by other pupils in the school. Nothing can convince him more that his work has little or no significance, if after writing it, it is remorselessly confined to the darkness of his desk. If work then is to be read by a wide audience, it needs to be displayed in classroom, corridor or hall, where other pupils can see it, and subsequently talk about it. Interest will be quickened by these displays, not only in the writing itself, but also in presentation. Once it is recognised that writing which is to be displayed should be presented in a pleasing manner, aspects of writing, such as handwriting and general layout of the page, will be seen to play an important part both in inviting the reader to read, and helping him to do so. Discussion of layout of presentation can show clearly that neatness in writing has relevance, and can help to improve general standards of care. The importance of presentation can be taken further if pupils are invited to mount displays. Discussion of layout, considering, for example, juxtaposition of pictures, photographs, newspaper cuttings, and so on, can open awareness of the significance of aesthetic statements, in addition to written statements.

CONCLUSION

It might be appropriate to end an article of this kind by posing the question—are there some pieces of writing which are better not commented on, and some which perhaps defy, even transcend comment? The following short poem[8], written by a 14 year old girl in a Secondary Modern School, is perhaps in this last category. How do you respond to it, and how would you comment upon it?

[8] I am indebted to Mr. Michael Hughes for this poem, which was written by a pupil in a Sussex school.

HE DIED FOR HIS COUNTRY . . .

A letter came telling me
'He died for his country'
What will I say
When my fatherless child asks why and how?
'He died for his country'
The boy won't understand—
The suffering and pain he went through,
And me—the heartache and longing.